pp xvii & 82 contradict

CENTRAL AUTHORITY AND
LOCAL AUTONOMY IN THE
FORMATION OF
EARLY MODERN JAPAN

Central Authority and Local Autonomy in the Formation of Early Modern Japan

The Case of Kaga Domain

Philip C. Brown

Stanford University Press, Stanford, California 1993

Stanford University Press
Stanford, California
© 1993 by the Board of Trustees of the
Leland Stanford Junior University
Printed in the United States of America

CIP data are at the end of the book

The costs of publishing this book have been supported in part by an award from
the Hiromi Arisawa Memorial Fund (named in honor of the renowned economist
and the first chairman of the Board of the University of Tokyo Press) and
financed by the generosity of Japanese citizens and Japanese corporations
to recognize excellence in scholarship on Japan.

To my families, here and in Japan

Acknowledgments

In researching and writing this book, I have developed a very sharp appreciation of the extent to which any monograph is not simply one person's labor of love, but a collaborative effort in significant degree. In the long course of preparing this work, I may have incurred greater debts than most.

During my research in Japan I benefited immensely from Professor Takazawa Yūichi's guidance at Kanazawa University. His insistence that I work with manuscript documents and his patient instruction opened opportunities for critical perspectives on Japanese history that I would not have otherwise had. Then, and often since, Nakano Setsuko, also of Kanazawa University, has provided assistance, encouragement, and much valuable advice. While at Kanazawa University, I was also fortunate in having as companions in the graduate research room Fukuzawa Motokazu, Mise Kazuo, and Ōno Mitsuhiko. Kigoshi Ryūzō, an indefatigable student of Kaga villages, has generously shared data and critical perspectives with me.

Though most of my time was spent in Kanazawa, I also relied on the good offices of Andō Seiichi (now at Osaka Technical University) and Yasuzawa Shūichi (Historical Documents Section, Kokuritsu Bungaku Kenkyū Shiryōkan). In more recent years, I have been fortunate to work and consult with Aono Shunsui (Hiroshima University) and Matsushita Shirō (Kyushu University).

I owe a great deal to my principal teachers: H. P. French, Jr., who first introduced me to Japan; and Frank Miller, John Gates, the late Robert Hall, Jr., Richard H. Mitchell, Robert Hartwell, and F. Hilary Conroy, all of whom nurtured my interest through college and graduate schools. Professors Conroy and Miller were flexible enough to help me follow my own inclinations when others might have demurred. Marius Jansen and Martin Collcutt generously permitted me to attend their seminars on both regular and irregular bases.

Richard Smethurst was my kind and generous host at the University of Pittsburgh during my year as an Andrew Mellon Postdoctoral Fellow. He, Mae Smethurst, Keith Brown, Anne Jannetta, Seymour Drescher, and other members of the history and Asian studies faculty provided a refreshing and invigorating environment for me to make manuscript revisions.

Through the times that were difficult, members of the Washington and Southeast Regional Seminar on Japan and the Triangle East Asia Colloquium were a wonderful source of support. Their responsiveness to my work and ideas were important oases of intellectual stimulation and support. Of these people, the fellowship and assistance of several friends and colleagues has meant a very great deal to me: Margaret McKean, Kris and Kay Troost, Thomas Mesner, James White, Ellen Nollman, and Richard Rice. In addition, I would like to acknowledge the support of James Bartholomew and the participants in the Midwest Japanese Seminar.

A number of people kindly read this manuscript in whole or in part: William Hauser and Conrad Totman (both on more than one occasion); Evelyn Rawski; and colleagues at Ohio State University who share my interests in state formation and peasant society, Allan Wildman, Eve Levin, Randolph Roth, and Kenneth Andrien. Their observations, questions, and criticisms have done much to improve the organization, readability, and interpretations of this study.

In addition to these people and their institutions, library staff at several repositories have been especially helpful: Kanazawa City Library, Ishikawa Prefectural Library, Ishikawa Prefectural Historical Museum, Toyama University Library, and the East Asia section of the Library of Congress. Without their cooperation, many of the materials I have relied on would not have been available to me. In several instances cooperation went far beyond the call of normal duties. Once, when time was short and my camera broken, I was permitted to take 300-year-old documents out of a library to be photocopied.

Throughout my research and writing, I have received generous financial support from the American Philosophical Society, the Andrew Mellon Postdoctoral Fellowship program (University of Pittsburgh), a Fulbright-Hays Doctoral Dissertation Fellowship, the Institute of Pacific Studies, the Japan Foundation, the Japan Institute at Harvard University, the Japanese Ministry of Education (Mombusho), the Northeast Asia Council of the Association for Asian Studies, and the Social Science Research Council.

The College of Humanities, Ohio State University, has supported preparation of the final manuscript.

Sumiko Otsubo, my research assistant at Ohio State University, has efficiently and cheerfully assisted in checking notes, preparing the bibliography, and myriad other functions.

Some sections of this work appeared in substantially different form in my articles "The Mismeasure of Land" (1987) and "Practical Constraints on Early Tokugawa Land Taxation" (1988). I gratefully acknowledge the permission of *Monumenta Nipponica* and the *Journal of Japanese Studies* to reproduce parts of those works here. I also thank the Toyama University Library for graciously granting me permission to reproduce selected illustrations from "Kenchikata hissho," and the Wajima City History Office for kindly allowing me to use an illustration from *Wajima shi shi*. *Hokuriku Shigaku* has also granted permission to reproduce a map.

While I have benefited greatly from the assistance of others, I am sure that some errors of fact or interpretation remain. I am solely responsible for them. Despite their presence, I hope my supporters will feel that their efforts were worthwhile.

P. C. B.

Contents

Tables, Maps, and Figures		xiii
A Note to the Reader		xv
1	Introduction	1

PART ONE: *Controlling Land*

2	The Formation of Kaga Domain	39
3	Kaga Land Surveys	58
4	Land Tenure	89

PART TWO: *Controlling People*

5	Putting Down Roots	115
6	Early Rural Administration	133
7	Early Land Taxation	147

PART THREE: *Tightening Control*

8	Villager-Samurai Tensions	171
9	Reform, Innovation, and Centralization	192

10	Conclusion	219

Appendix A: Sources of Village Tax Data, 1582–1636 243
Appendix B: Glossary 250
Notes 255
Bibliography 287
Index 301

Tables, Maps, and Figures

Tables

1.	Early Land Survey Documents of Kaga and Noto, 1581–98	61
2.	Range of Official Yields in Six Localities, Late Sixteenth Century	81
3.	Private and Taikō Kenchi, 1583–98	84
4.	Hypothetical Allocation of Cultivation Rights to 22 Shareholding Families in 10 Kuji Groups Under the Warichi System	104
5.	Intervals Between Land Redistributions for Eight Villages, Late Seventeenth Century to Late Nineteenth Century	106
6.	Land Distribution in Fukuno and Kumabuchi Villages, 1582	109
7.	Exemption Rates in Notojima Villages, 1585	154
8.	Changes in Exemption Rates for 17 Noto Villages, 1583–91	155
9.	Wasteland as a Percentage of Assessed Value in Noto and Etchu Villages, 1583–92	155
10.	Land Taxes as a Percentage of Assessed Value in Noto and Etchu Villages, 1583–92	156
11.	Changes in Effective Tax Rates for 17 Noto Villages, 1583–91	157
12.	Patterns of Forgiveness of Late and Unpaid Taxes, 1582–92	161
13.	Average Unpaid Taxes and Tax Forgiveness, 1582–92	163
14.	Tax Rates for Eight Villages in the Pre-Inspection and Post-Inspection Eras	181
15.	Range of Variation in Land Tax Rates in Kamiyasuhara Village, 1643–53	200

Maps

1. The Traditional Provinces of Japan — xvii
2. The Kaga Area — 31
3. Major Military Divisions of the Kaga Area, Spring 1581 — 43
4. The Expansion of Maeda and Chō Domains in Kaga, Noto, and Etchu — 45
5. The Honda Family's Fiefs, 1614 — 122

Figures

1. A Typical Land Survey Report from Kaga — 64
2. A Kaga Domain Survey Map — 74
3. Crossed-Rope Survey Measurement — 93
4. The Structure of Rural Administration, 1581–1648 — 175
5. Assessed Tax Rates, 1582–1636 — 180
6. The Structure of Rural Administration in Noto, ca. 1633–51 — 201
7. The Structure of Rural Administration, ca. 1670 — 210
8. Interaction of the Nominal Authority and Capability of a State — 232

A Note to the Reader

Because the three principal national leaders of the day did not hold the same title, I have referred to them (and the later Tokugawa shoguns) collectively as hegemons throughout the book. As is customary, Japanese names are given in the Japanese order, with family name first and given name last. All years in the text have been converted to the modern calendar, but in quoted documents the original Japanese era name and year have been retained. In all cases in which dates are more detailed, they are given either in the form "Genna 6.6.3," which refers to the third day of the sixth lunar month of the sixth year of the Genna era, or in the form "1620.6.3," where the Western year replaces the era name and date.

For convenience I summarize the relationships among the various Japanese measures discussed below. Since weights and measures were not standardized during the period under discussion, it is impossible to provide precise modern equivalents. The figures given below are approximate. Some variants are noted in the text. Currency exchanges depended a great deal on the quality of the coins involved, and no modern approximations can be presented.

Linear

1 *sun* (a Japanese "inch")		
10 *sun*	=	1 *shaku*
6 *shaku*, 3 *sun* (a Japanese "foot")	=	1 *ken* (about 2.2 yards; 1.8 meters)

Area

1 sq. *ken*	=	1 *bu* (about 4 sq. yards; 3.5 sq. meters)
30 *bu*	=	1 *se*
10 *se*	=	1 *tan*
10 *tan*	=	1 *chō* (about 1 hectare or 2.5 acres)

Volume

1 *koku*	=	5 English bushels; 180 liters
1 *to*	=	.1 *koku*
1 *sho*	=	.01 *koku*
1 *gō*	=	.001 *koku*
1 *shaku*	=	.0001 *koku*
1 *kyōmasu*	=	1.9 quarts; 1.8 liters

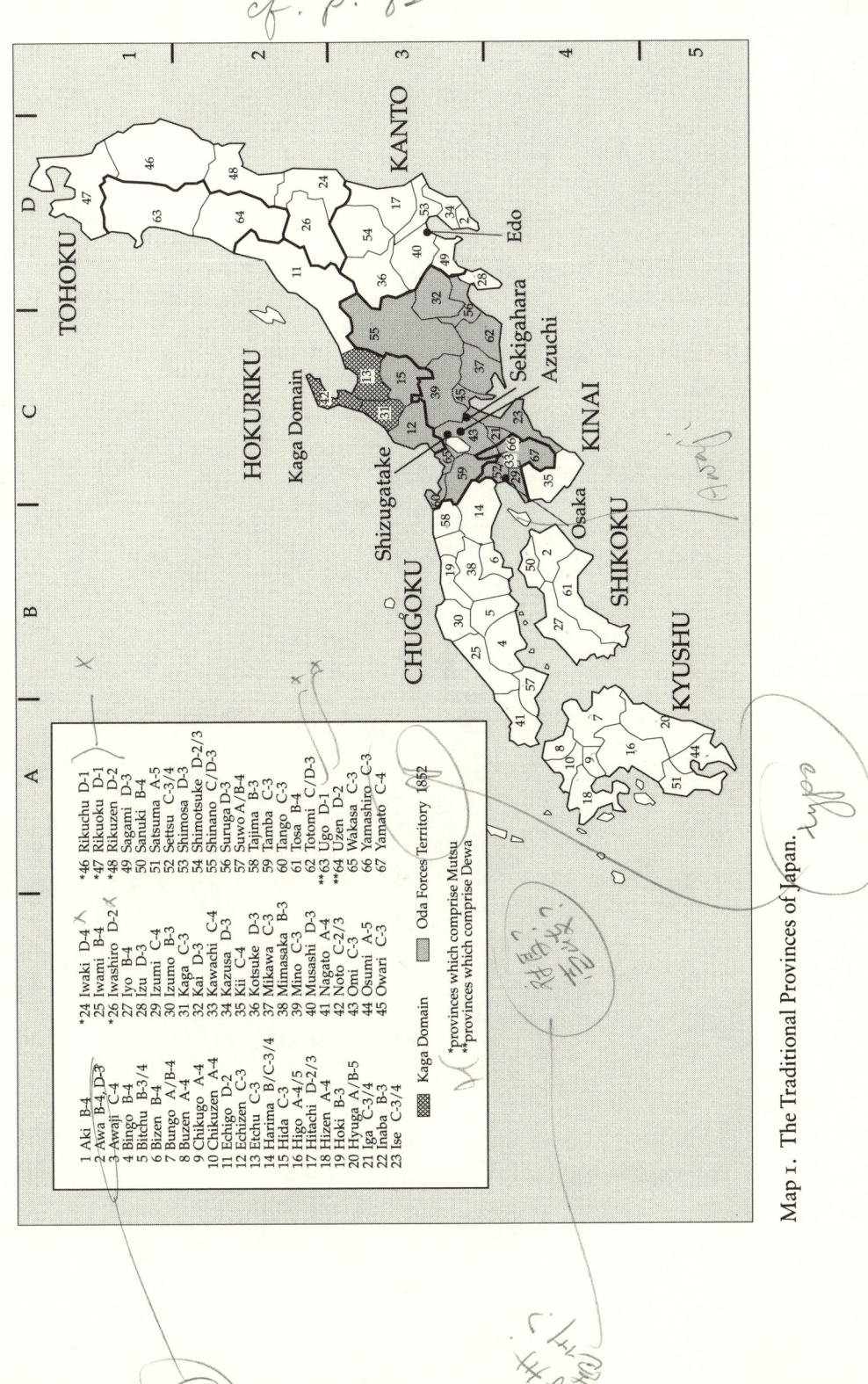

Map 1. The Traditional Provinces of Japan.

CENTRAL AUTHORITY AND
LOCAL AUTONOMY IN THE
FORMATION OF
EARLY MODERN JAPAN

Mine was the classic misadventure: I had wanted to master a source in order to confirm my youthful convictions, but it was finally the source that mastered me by imposing its own rhythms, its own chronology, and its own particular truth. My initial presuppositions had been stimulating, but they were now outmoded.

—Emmanuel Le Roy Ladurie

We must train ourselves to see *at once* both the minutest of minor details and the most grandiose of grand designs. We must search, with magnifying lenses, deep in the fabric of the social intertexture for the winding paths taken by each and every filament; but also step back to appreciate the art and meaning of the overall pattern of the social tapestry.

—Vivienne Shue

Chapter **1**

Introduction

The century following the outbreak of the Onin Wars in 1467 saw Japan's political order disintegrate into shambles. Up to that time the Ashikaga shoguns maintained a semblance of stability. The founder of the line, Ashikaga Takauji, had had the emperor appoint him Seiitaishōgun, "Great Barbarian-subduing Generalissimo," in the early fourteenth century, and to the extent that he and his successors exercised national authority, it was largely through the military organization of their own house, the Bakufu (literally, "tent government," an allusion to the shogun's command tent), in combination with the leaders of several large private military organizations. Like all shoguns, the Ashikaga derived legitimacy from imperial appointment. The emperor was the symbolic head of the political order. He exercised little real authority and typically bestowed the title of shogun when a military leader could demand it without fear of other generals seriously challenging him. Although military prowess brought the Ashikaga to power, their political and administrative influence was limited outside the family's private lands. They established the seeds of a small national bureaucracy and limited national taxation, but much of the shogun's preeminence was cultural. He depended greatly on the cooperation of the other military governors, who—at least collectively—were more powerful.[1]

The outbreak of widespread warfare brought even that semblance of central control crashing down. The Ashikaga family continued to pass the title of shogun from generation to generation until 1573, but it was a largely empty honor. In an environment in which civil wars raged for a century, no one could ensure the passage of revenues from imperial lands to the throne, and consequently, the emperor's prestige and economic foundation declined drastically as well. But though both offices were gutted of substance, the families that held them hung on; no one sought to usurp those positions or to replace them with new ones. The titles lay inert for some opportunist to resuscitate at a later date.

Local as well as national leaders faced a formidable challenge just to survive. This was the age of samurai. Warlords great and small fought in bloody clashes to expand territorial control. Intrigue and deceit were rampant. Neither rank, status, marriage ties, adoption, nor hostages could provide guarantees of stability in an age when lèse majesté, fratricide, and even patricide were well known. Lesser military figures, as well as prominent members of the military aristocracy, plotted against their superiors, allies, and relatives. The treachery of the age is reflected in the nicknames historians use: the age when "the low toppled the high" (*gekokujō*) and the age of Warring States (Sengoku Jidai).

The mid-sixteenth-century arrival of Europeans further complicated matters. The Europeans were potential allies and a source of revenues. Trade with the "redbeards" turned handsome profits, which could finance military ventures. Just as important, Europeans brought with them new weapons, hand-held firearms, the harquebuses. The Japanese soon made their own in quantity. Their widespread use disrupted the old forms of combat and encouraged a new approach to military organization and tactics. Though not nearly so accurate as the bow, harquebuses could be used by quickly trainable recruits. Their use was not restricted to an elite of professionally trained soldiers. This encouraged the formation of mass armies, the construction of large, more defensible castles on plains, and the negotiation of large-scale alliances. Militarily and politically, European contacts were beneficial to those lords who chose to capitalize on them. Furthermore, the firearms they introduced created and expanded the role for commoners in the armies of Japan, permitting increased social mobility.

If this was an age of considerable disorder, it was also an age of opportunity for many. Especially from the mid-sixteenth century, small men could carve a place in history for themselves. Takeda Shingen, the subject of Akira Kurosawa's epic film *Kagemusha*, was one of those who rose from humble beginnings to national prominence. So did the three men who came to lead the nationally hegemonic coalitions after 1570, Oda Nobunaga, Toyotomi Hideyoshi, and Tokugawa Ieyasu.

Opportunities were not restricted to those who would be king. Turmoil marked every level of society and dissolved social ties, liberating new forces to transform the basic character of society. In the regions around modern Osaka, townsmen reacted to the decline of effective political control by organizing themselves. They did so with such effectiveness that they were able to establish self-governing, autonomous city governments such as the Council of Elders (Egō Shu) in Sakai. In the regions surrounding major commercial centers, packhorse teamsters banded together to protect their interests and those of the communities from which they came. As with similar groups throughout the world, these *bashaku ikki*, with their inter-regional connections to the towns and villages along commercial routes, served as catalysts for local and regional political movements.

These developments in commercially mature areas of central Japan had rural counterparts elsewhere, and through them, local gentry wrested control of district affairs from the authorities in Kyoto.[2] The creative energies of the day did not necessarily take a violent turn. Largely self-governing villages (*sō*) became quite common. They developed their own mechanisms for resolving disputes and distributing the rights to scarce communal resources (common lands), distinct from the desires of an immediate overlord.

The competitiveness of the age fostered administrative creativity, too. To be sure, daimyo continued to rely heavily on marriage and kinship ties to supplement fief grants as a means of securing their retainers' loyalty.[3] But they also experimented quite freely, especially those whose territories had expanded beyond a size that permitted direct personal control. Domain laws were codified to legitimate daimyo rule.[4] New tax systems were developed. Many daimyo made repeated efforts to update the tax rolls through land investigations (*kenchi*). Some daimyo successfully curtailed the number and power of landed retainers.[5]

A daimyo's domain was a complex administrative unit. In one sense it was his personal possession, but he usually did not administer all of it directly. Some of the land was granted to retainers as fiefs. In the early sixteenth century these retainers had a very high degree of autonomy. For ordinary administrative purposes the daimyo was not allowed to enter a retainer's fief on his own. He did not administer justice there or have the right to inspect the land. He could (and often did) demand an accounting of its economic resources, but he could not, through his own agents, verify the accuracy of the reports he received. As mid-century passed, the larger daimyo began to break down this autonomy, gaining the right to enter fiefs for an increasing number of reasons and restricting the retainers' authority to administer their holdings.

As domains grew in size, even the part that the daimyo administered directly often became so large that personal, resident oversight (such as that associated with local seigneurial lords in early modern France) became impossible. One common alternative was to delegate tax assessment and collection to salaried underlings. Another was to make a contract with a village (so-called *hyakushō uke*), binding it as a corporate unit to deliver a set amount of produce and/or cash to the lord. Both profited from this arrangement. Villages (or at least their leaders) gained increased autonomy, and daimyo could extend their revenue base over areas in which they could not exercise direct day-to-day oversight. Nascent in the mid-sixteenth century, these trends accelerated as Japan moved into the seventeenth. By the early modern era the most prominent domains were so large that they often encompassed several counties (*kōri*) or whole provinces and required the development of depersonalized, semibureaucratic controls.

All these developments—larger domains, with larger armies, the gradual consolidation of daimyo authority, and the reduced need for samurai resident in villages—created pressures on landed retainers and rural samurai, especially the farmer-warrior who was not a professional soldier. As daimyo extended their own financial resources, they could afford to increase the size of their salaried army rather than rely on fiefs to reward their followers. More and more these men were housed in the daimyo's main headquarters, his castle town. At the same time, the growth of professional armies reduced the need to rely on farmer-warriors. Rural warriors often found themselves faced with the choice of becoming either full-time, professional soldiers or full-time farmers. In some instances local residents made the decision for them, forcing them out of the village and into the daimyo's castles. On other occasions the daimyo made the decision. In these circumstances, landed retainers, who now accounted for a smaller proportion of the daimyo's army, found it difficult to resist inroads on their traditional administrative prerogatives.

Among the daimyo who cobbled together effective systems of domain control, three dominated the late-sixteenth- and early-seventeenth-century political scene: Oda Nobunaga, Toyotomi Hideyoshi, and Tokugawa Ieyasu. They are collectively referred to as the Three Unifiers or the Three Heroes. Technically, the designation "Three Unifiers" is not correct because Oda Nobunaga (1534–82) never held a unified military command over Japan. But he was clearly moving in that direction at the time of his death.

Long viewed as a totally ruthless but highly effective military leader, Nobunaga began his career in Owari province. He succeeded in unifying half the province after his father's death in 1551, and in the next two decades he conquered the rest of Owari and the large neighboring province of Mino, to become one of the most powerful lords in central Japan. From that base, he assisted the last Ashikaga shogun to secure his position in 1568. Within three years he destroyed utterly the large temple complex at Hieizan in Kyoto, which had served as the headquarters for armed Buddhists who represented a major regional military force.[6] With much of central Japan secured and confident of his own power, he forced the shogun to flee Kyoto in 1573, never to return. At the time of his assassination by a disgruntled retainer named Akechi Mitsuhide, Nobunaga controlled all of central Japan and was the most powerful daimyo in the land, a status well symbolized by the magnificent castle he built at Azuchi, not far from Kyoto.

Among those who accompanied Oda Nobunaga on his ascent was the son of a farmer-warrior born in rural Owari, Toyotomi Hideyoshi (1536–98).[7] His status at birth was so low that he did not bear a surname. Hideyoshi only joined Nobunaga's band in 1558, but based on his battlefield successes, his lord granted him the large domains of the Asai family after its defeat in 1573. When Nobunaga was assassinated, Hideyoshi quickly avenged his fallen master and then set out to conquer all Japan. Hideyoshi was a superb general, but he also knew how to compromise. After Nobunaga's death, a good part of his success in creating a stable nationwide military organization can be traced to his willingness to bend and to be generous with former enemies. By 1590 he had defeated his last domestic opponents, the Gohōjō. His military control was sufficiently strong that he organized two large invasions of the continent, in 1592 and 1596, the first time in a millennia that a Japanese army had sought territory on the mainland.

At the time of Hideyoshi's death in 1598, his heir was a small child. Hideyoshi had provided for that eventuality by establishing a council of Five Elders to act as a collective regency after his death. But the Five Elders soon split into two factions, one led by Ishida Mitsunari, the other by Tokugawa Ieyasu. Matters came to a violent head on the battlefield at Sekigahara in Mino province in 1600. Ishida and his allies were vanquished, and the Tokugawa forces were now well on the way to establishing a new, peaceful political order.

Like Oda Nobunaga and Toyotomi Hideyoshi, Tokugawa Ieyasu (1542–1616) was born in central Japan.[8] He was the eldest son of the lord of Okazaki castle in Mikawa province and claimed distant descent from the imperial family. Known as the Old Badger, he could be aggressive, wily, and patient. He expanded his own domains, sometimes in league with Nobunaga and Hideyoshi, sometimes separately or even in opposition to them. By 1590 he had made his peace with Hideyoshi and participated in the destruction of the Gohōjō. When the conflict was over, Hideyoshi offered Ieyasu the newly conquered lands. Acceptance meant giving up his home territories, but Ieyasu ultimately paid that price. In a small swampy village in eastern Japan, he built his new headquarters. Called Edo, it became one of the largest cities in early modern Japan. Today it is known as Tokyo.

Tokugawa Ieyasu's position was not entirely secure after his triumph over Ishida. Toyotomi Hideyoshi's son remained alive, nurtured on the glories of an earlier day at his father's castle in Osaka. For a decade and a half after Sekigahara, the Toyotomi enclave offered a potential competitor to the Tokugawa's domination of Japan. Matters were ultimately resolved on the field of battle. In 1614 and 1615, in two campaigns at Osaka, the Toyotomi forces and their allies were defeated. Except for an uprising at Shimabara in 1637, this was the last military threat to Tokugawa supremacy until the mid-nineteenth century.

Oda Nobunaga, Toyotomi Hideyoshi, and Tokugawa Ieyasu controlled Japan more firmly than anyone had for centuries. Each man exploited old symbols to create an ideology to support the new order. The military chain of command was, of course, the first of these. Through it, daimyo were subject to traditional military service (*gun'yaku*), but that obligation became more rigorously tied to the value of each daimyo's domain under the new order.

Investiture remained one of the greatest tools hegemons had for rewarding or punishing daimyo. New, larger fiefs could be offered to those who were trusted; a reduction or outright confiscation was a clear possibility for unreliable lords. Transfers affected all classes of daimyo, regardless of whether they initially achieved daimyo status through their own efforts or as reward for their service to the hegemon. By 1600 the vast majority of all daimyo had faced the challenges of occupying a new territory. The Tokugawa continued this practice during the early seventeenth century. Transfers to new domains were so common that the lords of the day are sometimes referred to as "potted plant daimyo."

Even when daimyo gained a larger fief, they lost some of their autonomy in the transfer. By moving daimyo away from their traditional bases of authority, Oda Nobunaga, Toyotomi Hideyoshi, and the Tokugawa gained an increased measure of control over subordinate generals. Daimyo received their new lands as a gift from their overlord, not as something they earned by dint of their own conquests. This increased their sense of indebtedness and reinforced the bonds of obligation, if not principles of altruistic loyalty.

More important, transfers created a new degree of dependence on the overlord by weakening the daimyo's basis for independent action. They cut the traditional ties between a general and his home base. These customary links had a dual significance. First, they had given the daimyo a sense that he had a right to control that territory based on his own ability to defend it. The rights to the territory were autonomously generated. By accepting a new appointment, the source of the rights of possession shifted. They now came from the overlord's investiture, and (barring enemy conquest) their retention was in some measure dependent on his continued goodwill.

Second, ties between a daimyo and the local leaders of his home territory were strong enough to give him an autonomous base of financial and military support. When a daimyo moved into a new territory, he lost that base of support. Until pacified, the local population might even pose a serious threat to effective rule. (That rebellion was a real possibility is evidenced by uprisings in Higo in 1588 and in northern Japan in 1590.) In these circumstances, the daimyo was vulnerable in a way and to a degree that he had not been in his home province. If a difficult situation arose, he could not call on long-standing local allies to help. He was more dependent on the assistance of his overlord to deal with local opposition than he would have been in his home territory.

As in Europe, marriage was used to strengthen alliances. But in Japan adoptions were a significant means of cementing these ties as well. A finely woven net of marriages, adoptions, and concubinage linked the hegemons to the most important daimyo, and the major daimyo to one another. With the passage of time this net expanded to cover more and more daimyo. In addition to arranging specific marriages for political purposes, the hegemons oversaw and regulated even the marriages and adoptions of nonrelatives. The use of family members as hostages, widespread but unstructured under Oda Nobunaga, Toyotomi Hideyoshi, and the first Tokugawa shoguns, was being employed systematically by the mid-seventeenth century.

Each of the Great Heroes sought to restore the prestige of the imperial household and to use its aura to legitimate his own national preeminence. They made gifts to the emperor and encouraged their allies to do so as well. In this way, they transformed the fallen imperial lineage into a glittering symbol of a unified nation. All took court titles and engineered appointments to imperial offices for themselves. At a formal level they received their authority through these appointments. Part of this effort involved enhancing or fabricating genealogies to show ties to the imperial line. Yet each dealt with the emperor and imperial titles in a somewhat different way.[9] In all of this, only Tokugawa Ieyasu revived the office of shogun (1603), and only the Tokugawa's house government came to be referred to as the Bakufu.

The hegemons also capitalized on newer tools to create an ideology in support of their rule. The practice of codifying house laws, begun by some of the larger daimyo in the sixteenth century, expanded, with both daimyo and shogun participating. Another concept that originated earlier, "public authority," or *kōgi*, was widely exploited by sixteenth-century daimyo and hegemons alike. Each claimed to represent public authority, that which was exercised for the good of the land rather than for selfish ends.

A Bakufu legal code, the Laws of the Military Houses (*Buke sho hattō*), enumerated the major mechanisms of daimyo control. Issued in 1615 by Tokugawa Hidetada, Ieyasu's son and successor, the code provided a set of general moral guidelines and basic laws for daimyo and samurai. In addition to encouragements to study "the arts of peace and war," to be frugal, to comport themselves in accord with their status, to appoint capable officials and to avoid debauchery, daimyo were specifically enjoined from the kinds of activities that might challenge the Bakufu. That is, they were forbidden to marry, travel, or repair castles except as the shogun permitted. In addition, they were forbidden to hide fugitives. Each of these activities had the potential to provide a basis for anti-Bakufu alliances. If daimyo learned of any violations, they were to report them to the shogun.[10] A revised version of the Laws, issued in 1635, systematized the Bakufu's previously informal system of hostages and combined it with a requirement that daimyo spend alternate periods (usually a year) in Edo. When they were away from Edo, important family members were left behind as security. The entire system, called *sankin-kōtai*, required daimyo to expend a great deal of their income on travel and on maintaining two full households, one in the domain and one in Edo.[11]

Daimyo, too, pursued strategies to make landed retainers more dependent on them. Samurai were encouraged or ordered to live inside the daimyo's castle towns. Their judicial and administrative authority within their fiefs was increasingly restricted. Daimyo insisted on entering the fiefs to inspect them, limited the holders' access to natural resources and corvée labor, closely regulated the taxes retainers could assess, and sometimes simply rendered the fiefs a fiction by taking over all administrative responsibility. Many took the ultimate step of abolishing fiefs altogether. By the middle of the seventeenth century samurai generally were confined to castle towns and thoroughly dependent on the daimyo for their incomes.

Legal barriers between social classes grew. Class structures hardened, and the opportunities for crossing class lines declined. Townsmen generally could not own farmland, and the villagers' ability to move to other communities was restricted. Efforts were made to disarm the commoner population, most notably in Toyotomi Hideyoshi's 1588 Sword Collection Edict, ordering the confiscation of commoners' swords. Not only did this so-called sword hunt aim to ensure a compliant population; it also differentiated the samurai from the rest of society. Henceforth, samurai were to be professional warriors first and foremost. Only they were allowed to wear two swords and hold domain offices.

The systems of assessing land value (for the dual purpose of assessing taxes and allocating domains and fiefs) were transformed widely. Land came to be valued commonly in units of putative rice yield (the *koku*, roughly 4.96 English bushels)—the amount of grain land would supposedly have produced had it been planted to rice. Rice was the most valuable of the common grain crops, and in an age when the bulk of villagers' taxes was collected in kind—and largely rice—this made considerable sense.

Side by side with this transformation came a widespread reinvestigation of the area and value of village lands. Since many historians associate several historically important developments with land surveys, it is useful to look briefly at the procedures, at least as they are commonly understood.

Surveyors purportedly measured each individual field and assessed its quality. The land was generally divided into three quality grades for paddy and four for dry fields; superior, average, and inferior paddy; superior, average, inferior, and low-grade inferior dry field. Based on the quality of the land, each grade was assigned a yield expressed as an amount of rice per *tan* (about one-tenth hectare) and measured in koku. Superior dry field was considered the equivalent of average paddy, and each grade of land was rated two-tenths of a koku higher or lower than the next grade of land.[12] Though the assessed value of the grades varied from region to region, the principle of a two-tenths difference for each grade was standard.

As surveyors worked, each field's size and grade were recorded in a land register, along with the name of a villager, in most cases presumed to be the cultivator. The sum of these values and listings was the assessed value for the village and used as one basis for land taxation.

This period also saw the widespread conversion from the Sengoku era's (ca. 1480–1580) complex and often apparently arbitrary land tax system to a new system based on sampling yearly harvests. The new system, called the *kemi* or annual inspection system, is usually credited with helping to increase domain revenues.

All of this institutional development took place in the context of a national polity that reflected a balance of power among daimyo and hegemons. No national bureaucracy arose. No system of regular, nationwide taxation developed. Yet none of this stood in the way of stability. Hegemons possessed sufficient influence to manipulate the daimyo and maintain peace.

In addition to the efforts of the ruling class to alter Japan's governing institutions and society, peace itself had an important transforming effect. The economy grew rapidly once civil war ended. That alone created economic incentives for commoner and domain lord to make investments to increase their income. Daimyo and village alike extended irrigation systems and improved maintenance. They built water control projects. Transport routes were more secure, encouraging the flow of goods. Within the villages, the removal of warriors created new, more simple landholding arrangements. The new conditions of tenure stimulated increased agricultural production and, ultimately, the development of commercial rather than predominantly subsistence agriculture.[13] It was in this dynamic environment that domains became the building blocks of the early modern Japanese political order.

The Issues

The turmoil of the late sixteenth century and the birth of early modern Japan have transfixed a large number of scholars for the past half century, and particularly since the end of the Second World War. The developments of the period have provided the grist for some of the most interesting debates among Japanese historians and have stimulated an enormous volume of literature. All of these scholars stress the era's pivotal historical significance. Araki Moriaki speaks of a "feudal revolution" that led to the rise of serfdom in Japan.[14] The members of the Kōza ha group of prewar historians spoke of the establishment of "pure feudalism" during the period.[15] Fujita Gorō discovered a "feudal reaction" (*hōken handō*)—a hardening of rents in kind (*seisanbutsu chidai e no kōtei*) and the establishment of a feudal society based on a dependent peasantry (*reinōseiteki hōken shakai*).[16] The concept of a "feudal regeneration" (*hōken saihensei*), first employed by Hayakawa Jirō in the late 1930's, has continued to animate prominent postwar scholars such as Nakamura Kichiji, Kitajima Masamoto, and Wakita Osamu.[17]

Other historians view the period as giving birth to absolutism (*zettai shugi*) in Japan. During the 1960's proponents of the so-called Bakufu-Domain State theory (Bakuhan Kokka Ron) stressed the interconnectedness of major developments on the national level—for example, the interaction of the system for assessing daimyo military obligations to hegemons (*gun'yaku*), the establishment of land values based on putative rice yields (*kokudakasei*), and the invasions of Korea in the 1590's—in reinforcing and building a nationwide state authority.

Emphasis on conscious state-building has since led to the investigation of the late medieval concept of public authority (kōgi) as a foundation for the early modern state's legitimacy.* Prominent as a means of reinforcing the preeminence of the daimyo in the middle to late sixteenth century, kōgi was transformed by Nobunaga, Hideyoshi, and Tokugawa Ieyasu into a device to reinforce their national hegemonies.† In the West, John Whitney Hall writes of a "sixteenth-century revolution"; and Mary Elizabeth Berry sees the development of a new form of government for Japan, a federation.[18] Still other historians, in Japan as well as in the West, have seen in this era the development of unique feudal arrangements with a remarkably strong center, a "centralized" form of feudalism.

These schools of thought vary in the degree to which they see the transition to the early modern era as revolutionary, progressive, or reactionary, but their adherents all see the creation of a strong central authority as the hallmark of the era. They commonly describe the new polity as a "unification administration" (*tōitsu seiken*) or "unification power" (*tōitsu kenryoku*) to signify the political reunification of Japan after a century of civil wars. This reconstituted central authority is widely viewed as the source of the political, social, and economic transformations outlined above.

Before discussing the specific developments thought to have increased state authority, we should note that at one level nearly all historians acknowledge a substantial degree of autonomy for the daimyo: when the system is described in the abstract. A common descriptive term for the political system, *bakuhan taisei*, distinctly refers to the political structure (*taisei*) of the Bakufu and the *han* (domains) of the daimyo. It suggests

---

*Japanese scholars commonly do not define "state." For the purposes of this study, I accept a very broad definition: "The state is a geographically delimited segment of human society united by common obedience to a single sovereign" (Watkins, "State," p. 150). But readers should be aware that, by some social scientists' definitions, early modern Japan may not have been a state. Some would rule out forms of political organization like "feudal" linkages as real states and contrast them with states as a "modern" form of political organization. Others rule out democracies as states or characterize them as lacking a high degree of stateness. In addition to Watkins, see the related articles in the same source by Crick, Fried, Southall, and Sternberger. Nettl, "The State as a Conceptual Variable," is a standard starting point for more recent studies. See also Skocpol, "Bringing the State Back In."

† Somewhat paradoxically, these developments came at the same time that a number of medieval scholars challenged the assumptions of Kinsei (early modern) specialists that certain institutions and policies were typical or definitive of Kinsei Japan. The origins of some developments (e.g., land surveys, the collection of samurai in castle towns, and the separation of major social classes) have been pushed back in time. The retort of Kinsei historians is that the resemblances between Kinsei and earlier patterns is superficial, and that the Kinsei versions are qualitatively different. See Kobayashi, "Sengoku sōran," pp. 343–51.

that nearly equal prominence be accorded domain administrations and the Bakufu, with both formulating policies in complementary if not cooperative fashion.

A few scholars go even further and suggest greater local autonomy. The legal historian Ishii Ryōsuke argues that the early modern political system might better be referred to as the *han-son* or domain-village system.[19] George Sansom notes that the daimyo were obligated, under the 1635 provisions of the Laws of the Military Houses, to enforce the shogunal will: "In all matters the laws of Yedo must be observed and applied at all places in all provinces."[20] Nonetheless, he is cautious in evaluating the law's impact and concludes that it was unenforced, leaving daimyo to administer their domains autonomously. The political scientist James White, examining the state's monopolizing of the legitimate use of force, sees state capability as relatively weak until the Bakufu began actively intervening in the domains after the mid-Tokugawa period.[21]

Comparative history provides a second perspective that also tends to devalue the strength of the early modern Japanese state. For many Japanese historians, European nations have been the measuring stick by which to judge state growth in their country.[22] In the West the comparative approach has led to a shift in the terms of debate in recent years—from the discussion of early modern Japan as a "feudal" society to an assessment of its status as an absolutist state. The comparison was implicit in much earlier writing, as indicated by descriptive terms that sought to account for the apparently greater strength of the Tokugawa order (e.g., "centralized feudalism"). Berry made the comparison explicit. Employing an institutional and policy checklist of attributes of absolutist states, she judges the early modern Japanese state to have been weaker than its contemporary European counterparts because it lacked state mercantilism, a national public treasury and system of taxation, a national bureaucracy, and the like.[23]

Responding to Berry, White notes that these comparisons idealize state growth in Europe, assuming that there was only a single model of absolutism—that based on the history of the strongest states.[24] Because historians applied an inappropriately strict definition of absolutism, they mistakenly concluded that the early modern Japanese state fell short of European monarchies. In fact, White argues, a state need not be very strong to be comparable to many absolutist monarchies, which were often quite decentralized—an argument that again suggests the early modern Japanese state was weak.

Such cautious depictions of state authority fade to the background, however, when scholars consider the most dynamic era of state-building in

Japan, the late sixteenth and early seventeenth centuries. Sansom and White view Toyotomi Hideyoshi's nationwide land survey (the late-sixteenth-century Taikō kenchi) and related measures as nationally effective central initiatives.²⁵ Berry, Hall, and Araki all support the Japanese historians' traditional evaluation of Hideyoshi's land surveys: central government ordinances were enforceable, were implemented in fact, and were the source of, or greatly furthered, the generally acknowledged wide-ranging reforms in rural administration, land tenure and taxation, and class separation.* Although Ishii Ryōsuke seems to stress the importance of the villages, he devotes only a few paragraphs of his institutional history to them. His concern is with the Taikō kenchi, Hideyoshi's sword collection edict (the *katanagari* or "sword hunts"), and the legal separation of social classes—in short, with the power of the emergent central government.²⁶

This argument for effective central reform extends into the age of the Tokugawa shoguns (ca. 1600–1868). Scholars describe a central authority great enough to meddle in domain administration. Hall and Ishii, for example, see the Tokugawa shoguns' use of *azukeru*, "to hold in trust," as a conditional grant of authority to daimyo; continued rule of a domain depended on a daimyo's ability to administer it in line with Bakufu decrees. They contrast the term's implications with earlier vocabulary indicating the daimyo's unconditional proprietary, administrative, and judicial authority over domain lands.²⁷ Under the Tokugawa (as under Nobunaga and Hideyoshi), domains were subject to escheat and transfer. Shoguns commanded the means to force their standards on daimyo. While admitting that the exact conditions of investiture were vague, scholars who take this position argue, as does Hall, that "daimyo were accountable to the overlord's laws, to the expectation of . . . good administration." ²⁸ Even in Ishii's

---

*Asao Naohiro, "Sixteenth-century Unification," p. 78, notes that the power structure was formed top down, not based on a consensus of daimyo, developing *kōgi* into an absolute legal norm beyond proprietary land rights. Wakita, "Social and Economic Consequences of Unification," pp. 103, 121, 123, stresses the role of central initiative. Hall notes, "Not since the eighth century adoption of the Chinese institutions of imperial government had Japan been ruled under as comprehensive a system of laws and administrative procedures, and historians have been quick to expand on its significance" ("Introduction," pp. 12–13). See also Susser, "Toyotomi Regime," pp. 150–51, who contends that "the establishment of kinsei-type daimyo domains was predicated on the existence of an effective central authority with the right to issue orders to implement policies and the power to compel the daimyo's compliance." The presupposition of effective nationwide central authority, by no means tenable in many modern states, is particularly suspect in the case of societies lacking the mass-mobilizing power of modern communications—air and rail transportation, telephones, telegraphs, national news media, and the like. See Migdal, *Strong Societies*; White, "State Growth"; Berry, *Hideyoshi*, p. 118; Araki Moriaki, *Taikō kenchi to kokudaka sei*, pp. 149–52; Hall, "Hideyoshi's Domestic Policies," p. 213; and Hall, "Japan's Sixteenth-Century Revolution," p. 16.

relatively circumspect evaluation, the dominant image is of domains strung passively together like beads on the Bakufu's string.²⁹ The legal historian Mizubayashi Takashi, in a work specifically designed to incorporate the most recent scholarship on the era, goes even further. In his view article 13 of the Laws of the Military Houses defined daimyo as members of a bureaucratic hierarchy, not part of a master-retainer relationship.*

Literature on the formation of the early modern political system is heavily laced with the supposition of prodigious state authority. It widely presumes that there were no constitutional limits on the overlord's power to promulgate and enforce edicts. At the very least, such limitations have not been the subject of investigation or active debate.

The Grounds for the National Argument

Centrally issued policies are seen as crucial in four domestic areas.† They are thought to have legally separated Japanese society into four major classes: samurai, peasants, artisans, and merchants.‡ They created a new, uniform system of land taxation based on the annual inspection of crop yields and land valuation based on putative rice yields (*kokudaka*) and accurate land surveys. In the process, this new system of taxation gave cultivators secure tenure over the land they farmed. Finally, the central administration reformed local administration, placing the village unit at its heart. Let us look more closely at the grounds for this argument.

Hideyoshi's land surveys. Perhaps no single policy of the late sixteenth and early seventeenth centuries better illustrates the emphasis on the reach of the state into the domestic affairs of each domain than the Taikō kenchi, the land surveys of Toyotomi Hideyoshi. Many survey edicts and registers have survived. Scholars, analyzing them, see broader social, economic, and political implications in these surveys than in any other single policy instrument of the time—more than the separation of warrior and commoner,

---

*Mizubayashi, *Hōkensei*, p. 164. Kasaya, "Nihon Kinsei shakai," appears to be a lonely voice arguing that substantial elements of local autonomy were maintained despite the higher authorities' best efforts to exert their control.

†My analysis here is limited to domestic policies of hegemons and their impact on the domains; however, a similar assumption of substantial state capabilities underlies much of the discussion of Japanese foreign relations during this era. Those who stress the imposition of a national seclusion policy (*sakoku*) on Japan assumed that it was enforced from the center. Ronald P. Toby paints a much more nuanced picture in *State and Diplomacy*. Domain influence and initiative are particularly evident in Satsuma's dealings with the Ryuku Islands and Tsushima's trade with Korea. Without their independent actions, the ties to the continent that the Bakufu exploited might not have been created at all.

‡Three smaller classes also existed: the court nobility, the priesthood, and outcastes.

the urbanization of the samurai, the sword collection efforts, the creation of villages as formal, local administrative units, or the foundation of a new system of land taxation and daimyo/retainer control (the kokudaka system), to name only the most significant. Indeed, the land surveys are seen as performing an important role in advancing each of these developments.

Hideyoshi's land surveys are typically thought to have had five basic social and administrative consequences, namely, they provided land values on which to base fief allocation, extraordinary dues, and privileges for daimyo and landed retainers, finely adjusted to the social and political importance of the holder within the national or domain hierarchy; they installed a nationwide land tax system that greatly improved the ruler's knowledge of his land tax base and increased his revenues; they transformed the village into the basic formal unit of local administration, taxed as a collective unit by domain lords (there were no national taxes on villagers and townsmen; villagers divided the burden among themselves), with defined boundaries that clarified who shared responsibility for paying the community's taxes; they defined the status of villager (*hyakushō*), who now had official land ownership rights as well as obligations to cultivate the land and pay taxes; and they helped to separate the samurai and townsmen from commoners—those listed in survey rosters were not to be treated as warriors, and those not on the survey registers were ineligible to purchase rights to cultivate or manage arable land.

This view rests in large part on four important claims (for some authors, assumptions) about the distinctiveness of Hideyoshi's land survey process:

1. Unlike pre-Taikō kenchi surveys, which were simply estimates (*sashidashi*) presented to the daimyo by villages and retainers and were made according to diverse private standards, Hideyoshi's surveys were qualitatively different, based on actual measurements employing precise, nationally uniform methods and standards. In George Sansom's typical description (italics mine):

[Hideyoshi] decided on a land survey in *every* province, to be carried out under the *supervision of his own officials*. . . . This [survey] was to impose a *unified* system of land tenure and land tax *throughout the country* and Hideyoshi's officials proceeded to put such a system into operation. . . . He brought the agriculture of the *whole country* under his control.[30]

Or as Hall puts it, "By adopting a new unit of area measurement which differed from the one in use from Nara days, [Hideyoshi] literally forced the entire nation to reassess its land base."[31] Japanese historians like Kanai Madoka also stress the comprehensiveness of Hideyoshi's land surveys.[32]

Across widely different schools of historians, the national character of the Taikō kenchi and its instigation at the behest of Toyotomi Hideyoshi are taken as undisputed historical fact.³³

All basic survey procedures are assumed to have been standardized. Scholars disagree on when the process was complete, but the consensus is that a national system was in place by the mid-1590's. The length of the measuring rod for land surveys was set at six *shaku*, three *sun* (a little more than two yards). This formed the basic unit of length, the *ken*, on which area calculations were made. One square ken was a *bu*; 300 bu equaled a *tan*. The standard for volume measurement became the *kyōmasu* (about 1.9 U.S. quarts). These units of measurement became standard for official purposes, but, according to Kodama Kōta, were not necessarily those used by the populace. Though deviations from the national standard are occasionally noted, they are treated as insignificant exceptions.³⁴

2. Since surveys were precise, actual measures, they were suitable for determining who held rights to property. The cultivator's tie to the land was based on his listing in the survey register. Because many survey documents list a name by each field's dimensions, historians commonly agree that the survey conveyed some legal right to the land to that person.* Again, Sansom's explanation is representative:

The main purpose of Hideyoshi's land policy was achieved once he established the principle that the actual cultivator and no other was responsible for the tax on the yield of a specified area of land registered in his name. By this measure alone he . . . created a new peasant class with uniform rights and duties which they could not escape, and diminished, if he did not destroy, the independence of the rural gentry.³⁵

The exact nature of these rights is subject to dispute. Some scholars, including Araki Moriaki and Sasaki Junnosuke, have argued that these rights liberated hereditary servants and others from the confines of large patrilineal extended families, which (they say) dominated rural society up to that time.³⁶ They view this new autonomy as a direct result of Hideyoshi's desire to establish small independent nuclear family households as

---

*See, for example, Hall, "Japan's Sixteenth-Century Revolution," pp. 16–18. There are probably no more important documents for assessing landholding rights and obligations than survey registers. The only other major sources are the laws against the sale of land in the 17th century. In Western societies land surveys are associated almost exclusively with determining landholding rights, so we readily accept claims for the utility of survey registers (*kenchichō*) in analyzing social class structure within a village, patterns of landholding, and so forth. However, as explained below and in Brown, "Mismeasure of Land," there is substantial reason for a more critical assessment of Japan's early modern surveys.

the base of both agriculture and the land tax system: the surveys enforced a redistribution of land and bound cultivators to the land like serfs.

Other scholars do not subscribe to the redistribution view but do insist that the surveys conveyed the legal status of peasant to those listed in the registers. Wakita Osamu argues that land, through registration, became a form of private property. Kozo Yamamura, too, sees the surveys as making those listed into landowners, although they did not thereby become economically independent of extended family lineages.[37] In his view this set the stage for the long-term diversification and commercialization of rural economic activity.*

Thus, although there is substantial debate over the nature of the rights conveyed, there is general agreement that the peasants' legal status was established and protected by Hideyoshi. This extension of central authority into the day-to-day affairs of villagers stood in marked contrast to the practices of the Sengoku daimyo and the Ashikaga shogunate.

Recording names in the survey registers drew a clear class boundary. As it defined peasant status it simultaneously excluded the listed families from the samurai class. Conversely, samurai and townsmen were legally excluded from peasant status because they were not listed. They could not possess rights to the use of land. Previously, ties between lord and peasant were personal. The new arrangement broke these personal bonds, yet still tied agriculturists to a particular village. In legal principle, they were not free to migrate.

Marius Jansen presents a more modest interpretation, seeing surveys as accelerating the hardening of status lines but not completely effecting the separation of the classes.[38] As already noted, other ordinances are seen as contributing to this process, but survey registers constitute some of the earliest and most widespread evidence that the lines of class demarcation were drawn in practice.

3. The kokudaka system of taxing and valuing land in rice was comprehensive, measuring all the land the authorities set out to evaluate. No

---

*The current stress on the development of something akin to private landownership owes much to debates sparked by Araki Moriaki. In his 1959 work, *Bakuhan taisei shakai* (see especially pp. 57–63), Araki advanced the radical contention that Toyotomi Hideyoshi's extensive land surveys took land away from a class of small overlords (*sakuai hitei*) and established a direct link between the domain lord and the individual peasant cultivator and between the cultivator and the land he farmed. By virtue of listing a farmer's name next to a specified plot, the land became his.

Though many take exception to Araki's emphasis on the "revolutionary" impact of Hideyoshi's land surveys, scholars representing a broad spectrum of historical specialties and schools of thought accept the notion that the surveys granted villagers land rights akin to modern private ownership. The noted legal historian Ishii Shirō argues that Hideyoshi's sur-

doubt some hidden fields (*onden*) escaped the tax net, but that was too small a problem to have detracted from the overall success of the enterprise. Up to now certain proprietors within a domain had been protected from interference in their lands by the daimyo. Hideyoshi's surveys ended these rights (called *funyūken*). Landed retainer, temple, and shrine alike were surveyed without exception. Furthermore, where under earlier arrangements the land tax was not always levied on dry fields, only rice paddy land—including residential land as well as dry fields—had to be registered.[39]

4. As real, comprehensive measures, surveys formed a rational means of increasing the effectiveness of land taxation. Most scholars contend that the kokudaka system substantially increased the peasants' tax burden, consuming about two-thirds of their harvest.[40] In addition, with the *taka*, or assessed value of land, now based on its putative rice yield, taxes were collected exclusively in rice, rather than cash or other crops.[41] In the view of most scholars, this switch forced an increase in rice production in order to pay taxes. Unlike the previous (kandaka) tax system, which measured land value by the ideal amount of taxes the land produced, the new system used the putative yield of agricultural land to express its assessed value.* The

---

veys were not detailed enough to provide a basis for "title" to the land but believes that with the passage of time and the development of greater accuracy in procedures, the surveys did provide a basis for defining a peasant's claim to a piece of land. In addition to Ishii, *Nihon kokusei shi*, pp. 150–202, see Yamamura, "Pre-Industrial Landholding Patterns." Both scholars are highly critical of the Marxist-influenced mainstream of Japanese scholarship. There were limits to peasants' tenurial security, but in general these were the limits of modern property ownership. Sale of the land could be forced if the peasant defaulted on a mortgage or failed to pay his taxes. In this interpretation the peasant/farmer could not be told to farm different fields each year.

Provocative as this entire body of work is, it has not taken into consideration the *warichi* system of redistributing arable lands (see Chap. 4 for a fuller discussion). The terms of the debate over the Araki thesis by definition precluded consideration of a category of land "ownership" that, if discussed at all, is deemed exceptional (see, for example, Furushima, *Nihon hōken nōgyōshi*, pp. 130–33). Araki has since published his own thoughts on the warichi system in a 1983 article, "Ryūkyū ni okeru chiwari seido."

Theoretical income should be emphasized. Some deductions were made from the taka for irrigation expenses, shrine festival expenses, etc. (see Nagahara, with Yamamura, "Sengoku Daimyo," pp. 44–46). What has been described here is the standard model for the operation of the kokudaka system. Other models were to be found; many were variants of this basic system. The most distinctive was the *tantori* method, which set rates at a flat amount per *tan* of land based on the grade of land. The tax rate might have been changed occasionally but generally remained constant. In case of a severe crop failure, the loss was calculated by converting the shortfall to an amount of land lost from production. This amount was then subtracted from the total area of the village. If yields were 20% below normal, for example, 20% of the area of the village would be subtracted from its normally cultivated area. The tax rate remained constant. For standard descriptions of various tax mechanisms of the Tokugawa era, see Andō Hiroshi, *Tokugawa*, pp. 128–261; Ōishi Tsunetaka, *Jikata hanrei roku*, 1: 32–198, 2: 1–34; and Murakami and Arakawa, *Sanpō jikata taisei*, pp. 39–106.

nature of tax assessments also changed. Under the earlier system taxes due were set without specific reference to the yield of the land, whereas taxes were now recorded as a percentage of the assessed value and were periodically reassessed in light of crop yields. The tax rate commonly varied annually.[42]

In short, from the analytical perspective of most scholars, the qualities of national scope, standardized survey procedures, and precise, actual, comprehensive measurement signify a great difference between the land surveys of the Sengoku era and the Taikō kenchi. More important, the distinctive features of the new system are seen as reflecting a fundamental change in the nature of daimyo. Sengoku daimyo controlled their own domains independent of any national central authority. In contrast, the early modern daimyo were in many respects subject to the authority of Nobunaga, Hideyoshi, and eventually the Tokugawa Bakufu. Hegemonic authority extended farthest into the domains through the specification of land survey procedures and the timing of most surveys. The hegemon or shogun could send his officials directly into the daimyo domains and into each village to conduct surveys and through them, determine administrative boundaries and class lines. In effect, not only landed retainers, but daimyo, too, lost their funyūken.

Despite some mild caveats, Berry's arguments nicely illustrate these lines of demarcation between the Sengoku and early modern eras. She notes imperfections in the implementing of the tax system and concedes that a few daimyo may have conducted their own distinctive surveys, but she nonetheless concludes that these should not "conceal the extent of [Hideyoshi's] reach." It was a considerable one, in her view: "He oversaw the registration of much of the country's land; he demanded that Toyotomi deputies or daimyo officials, not local landholders, supervise that registration; he defined universal standards of measurement that were employed widely; he required the direct inspection of land and its yield."[43]

Class separation. Whether attributed to Oda Nobunaga, Toyotomi Hideyoshi, or the Tokugawa, central administrative fiat has typically been viewed as effecting a rigid, legally prescribed class separation (*hei-nō bunri*). Traditionally, Hideyoshi's contributions have been emphasized, specifically in his handing down of the sword collection (1588) and class separation edicts (1591).[44] The urbanization of samurai, whether at the encouragement of Hideyoshi or as a result of the Tokugawa's limiting the number of castles to one per province (1615), is also credited with creating a hard division between peasants and warriors.[45] As noted above, land surveys, too, purportedly played a significant role. People listed in survey registers were not allowed to possess swords (the symbol of warrior status), and when a daimyo was transferred, listed families were not permitted to transfer with him.[46] Furthermore, village residents were not allowed to move freely from their home villages.*

Recent writings suggest a more complicated process, and one that began much earlier than previously suggested. George Elison finds the origins of class separation in the policies of Oda Nobunaga.[47] Late medieval and Sengoku specialists see its beginnings in complex developments involving peasants pushing samurai off the land, as well as daimyo transferring landed retainers into concentrated fortifications and urban areas.[48] Local leagues (*ikki*) and "peasant contracts" (*hyakushō uke*) encouraged the separation of full-time warriors from rural communities. These historians also argue for the emergence of villages as increasingly autonomous administrative units at an earlier point.

Even before the dominance of the Three Heroes, changes in military technology and attempts to increase the stability of the retainer band encouraged the movement of samurai from rural to urban settings. Daimyo reduced the proportion of warriors holding fiefs and enlarged the ranks of salaried retainers. These measures increasingly marked warriors as full-time professionals who were not engaged in farm management or ownership. We would have difficulty explaining the growth of the effective military and administrative control that supported the Three Great Heroes without acknowledging the extent to which their efforts were predicated on the weakened links between peasant and landed retainer. Nonetheless, this process was not complete by 1580.

Despite this accumulating evidence—and the attempt of scholars like Sasaki Junnosuke and Hara Shōgo to show that the establishment of a class separation system in principle (under Hideyoshi) and its actual implementation proceeded on a different timetable[49]—most historians have yet to abandon the traditional emphasis on the orders of Hideyoshi and others in this matter. More than a few recent studies still insist on the radical transforming role of Hideyoshi's edicts.[50]

Land taxes. The reach of daimyo and hegemons is commonly portrayed

---

*Marriage to and adoption by residents of other villages were permitted. These changes and notice of the temporary relocation of villagers as servants were recorded in the registers of religious affiliation (in those regions where they were carefully kept). Although this allowed local authorities to keep track of residents and indicated their legal status as residents of their natal villages, the registers often became a legal fiction that failed to prevent real migration.

as increasing in the realm of land taxation. Scholars debate the degree to which increased control over land and people led to confiscatory taxes. Most Japanese historians, especially Marxists, argue that up through the early eighteenth century, land taxation left little or no "surplus labor" in the hands of villagers. To these scholars the early Tokugawa era represents the "first stage" of Tokugawa feudalism—which is to say, the stage characterized by confiscation of the peasantry's total surplus production.*

Dissenting voices are few. Takeyasu Shigeji and Hayami Akira argue that the early Tokugawa land tax system lacked the capacity to confiscate all of the villagers' surplus. Nonetheless, in their counterarguments they do not directly analyze land tax mechanisms and rates.[51] In addition, Miyakawa Mitsuru notes that after Hideyoshi's land surveys and the adoption of the inspection system of assessment, land tax rates in many areas fell from their late-sixteenth-century peaks.[52] Though he does not claim that this was the general trend, it allows him to recognize the need to keep an open mind on the question.

At the heart of these concerns lies the system of annual inspections (*kemi*). In principle the inspection process was straightforward. Tax assessors selected several fields in each village and took sample cuttings. Three or four samples of each grade of paddy were commonly taken. (Dry fields were not usually sampled.) The yields from the cuttings were averaged and multiplied by the basic domain tax rate, usually 40 percent or 50 percent of the average. The percentage taken as tax depended on official estimates of local production costs.[53] The average tax rice per *tan* was then converted to a percentage of the village's assessed value to calculate the village tax rate.†

---

*According to these scholars, it was only in the "second stage" of Tokugawa feudalism, characterized by less confiscatory land taxes, that peasants could begin to accumulate a surplus. Among students of the very early Kinsei era, Araki's work has been the key argument to which they have felt compelled to respond. The majority of recent studies of land tax systems attempt to expand on this interpretation. (See Araki, *Bakuhan taisei shakai*, pp. 117–52.) On the transition from the "first stage" to the "second stage," Ōishi Shinzaburō's study of the Kyōhō Reforms is most frequently cited (see his *Kyōhō kaikaku*, pp. 121–67; see also Sasaki, "Bakuhansei"; and Asao, "Bakuhan sei dai ichi dankai"). Although these authors disagree about how long the "first stage of Japanese feudalism" lasted, they agree that the early tax system effectively took virtually all the peasants' surplus. Many scholars have subsequently attempted to place a third type of assessment system, the *domen* system, into this two-stage format (see, for example, Tanaka Seiji, "Kinsei zenki"; and Nakaguchi, "Kinsei shoki sohō"). The domen system was introduced in some regions to adjust for increases in yields after the initial official productivity estimates (*todai, kokumori*). It was generally used over a short period and was often replaced later by the fixed tax rate system.

† In fact, there were several varieties of kemi. In some cases dry field crops were inspected. Reductions in fixed tax rates (*jōmen*) were also based on sample cuttings. The basic steps outlined here are consistent with these variations. Sasaki, *Daimyō*, p. 22, and Sasaki, *Bakuhan kenryoku*, pp. 101–10, present data from 17th-century Kaga domain budgets.

Several features of the inspection system encourage scholars to argue that it appropriated the villagers' agricultural surplus. First, inspections apparently provided detailed knowledge of rice yields. Based on that knowledge, officials could accurately calculate the proportion of crops to take as taxes. Second, annual inspections appear highly rational. In principle they permitted authorities to raise taxes to take advantage of increased yields or to lower them when yields fell. Inspections forced peasants to share any increased output with domain lords and landed retainers while simultaneously providing a prudent mechanism to alleviate the villagers' distress in bad times. Third, and perhaps most important, the model farm budgets on which land taxes were based contained no provision for peasants to retain any more of their income than that required for the continued operation of their farms. In theory villagers could not accumulate any profits from farming. Superimposed on assumptions of the thoroughness and completeness of land surveying, these features together mark the inspection system as confiscatory.[54]

Scholars frequently treat Hideyoshi and his seventeenth-century successors as the agents who established standard tax rates and the general principle of annual inspection of crop yields. Hideyoshi's "Wall Writings of Osaka Castle" (1595) declared a standard rate of two-thirds of the harvest to the lord, one-third to the peasants.[55] (This rate is often cited to bolster arguments that the tax burden grew much heavier in the late sixteenth century.) Under the Tokugawa, most scholars agree, the standard fell to 60-40 or 50-50.* But whatever the rate, an explicit standard suggests that daimyo were obligated to employ annual inspections to calculate each village's taxes. Additionally, to credit Hideyoshi with fully implanting rice-based taxation is to credit him also with making rice "near money," a major medium of exchange during the early modern era.[56]

The national restructuring of local administration. As the three preceding sections have made clear, the village is critical to understanding the transformations of the sixteenth and seventeenth centuries. Although late medieval villages increasingly took local administrative matters into their own hands, the common view is that villages did not harden into official administrative units within domains until the early modern era. Again, the Taikō kenchi are held to be pivotal in this development. The survey registers created an administrative unit for purposes of taxation. That secretarial

---

*Similarly, Bakufu shifts from annual inspections to fixed land tax rates are treated as setting a new, 18th-century pattern of assessment procedures. I refer here to the shift from the kemi system to the jōmen system, which presumably accompanied the Kyōhō Reforms.

act forced residents to cooperate in a key aspect of local administration. Villagers themselves had to determine who owed what amount of tax to daimyo or retainer. They also had to ensure the delivery of payments to tax collectors at the appropriate time. Surveys supposedly fixed village administrative boundaries for the first time. Japanese scholars generally view this development negatively. The new, arbitrary units are typically considered inflexible, violating more natural village configurations based on residents' cooperative economic and social interactions. For good or ill, these units are taken as a new focus of administrative interest and the foundation of a new rural order.

One finds the same stress on the role of central authority in most case studies. Local developments are either treated as reflecting national policies or, where potentially divergent data are acknowledged, their implications are minimized. Typical are three Western-language studies of Tosa, Satsuma, and Bizen, in which the focus is primarily on the organization of the upper levels of domain administration and the consolidation of control over the retainer band.[57] When discussing Hideyoshi's land surveys, these studies stress compliance with national orders. Hall, for example, notes that despite an early divergence from Hideyoshi's pattern of survey in Bizen province, its leaders fell into line after 1594.[58]

This emphasis is not limited to Western scholars. The historian Hara Shōgo, laying the groundwork for a rare attempt to integrate central and local developments, criticizes his predecessors for viewing the development of the state from a strictly national perspective. He argues that local events are viewed only through the national lens without exploring the interaction between national developments and the domain, thus ignoring, for example, the local dynamics involved in the formation of legally distinct classes.[59]

The late-sixteenth- and early-seventeenth-century hegemons clearly possessed new capabilities. No one can doubt the military control they exercised over daimyo: they commanded national armies strong enough to invade Korea twice in the 1590's and to put down the Shimabara rebellion (1637). Nor can their influence over key aspects of daimyo's personal lives be denied—hegemons had a large say in their marriages and adoptions, made them reside in the capital, and forced them to submit hostages.* Hegemons also exacted (irregularly) money and corvée duties from daimyo,

---

*Some may disagree with my making personalistic ties part of the creation of a state apparatus, preferring instead to focus on rational bureaucratic characteristics as the thrust of nonfeudalistic state development, but as Joel Migdal points out, and as students of Japan know well, personalistic ties play a very important role in many highly developed modern states.

primarily for military projects and the support of the imperial household. They could compel a substantial degree of compliance with their orders in each of these matters and, in principle, all their orders were enforceable by attainder.

Goals — Yet these powers were directed explicitly and overwhelmingly at two restricted spheres of activity: controlling the daimyo's personal behavior and securing the hegemons' own military position. Hideyoshi (from 1590) and the Tokugawa especially succeeded in preventing daimyo from forming alliances with each other or with foreign powers, and kept them under close scrutiny. But nowhere do we find any direct evidence of a daimyo's being compelled to follow centrally ordered practices in the internal administration of his domain or even to live up to a generalized standard of good administration.

An examination of the Bakufu's use of its powers of fief transfer and attainder, the most powerful administrative enforcement mechanism at its disposal, reinforces the impression that the shoguns were concerned more with the person of the daimyo and maintaining public order than with enforcing administrative law. Transfers were much more common than attainders. If they were employed as a punitive device, one would expect to see a very large number of reductions in fief size. Yet fully 49 percent of the 551 cases of peacetime transfer (1601 to 1760) reported by Fujino Tamotsu involved an increase in fief size; 45 percent involved no change in size, and only 6 percent some loss of land—very ambiguous evidence for punitive intent. Furthermore, transfers were directed predominantly at smaller daimyo.[60]

Fujino does not list the reasons for the transfers, but he does for the 235 cases where a fief was confiscated in peacetime during the same 160 years. These clearly show the restricted nature of the Bakufu's concerns. The vast majority of attainders (88 percent) involved succession issues, personal misconduct, "madness," lèse majesté, miscellaneous nonadministrative causes, or sections of the Laws of the Military Houses dealing with the daimyo's personal behavior and military security. Maladministration accounted for a mere 3 percent of the total (six cases), and even then, all the cases were associated with another reason—harsh rule or popular disturbances—which suggests that maintaining public order was the primary issue. Malfeasance in office and miscellaneous violations of the law are ambiguous categories in Fujino's listing, but even if all represented violations of Bakufu administrative directives to daimyo, they would account for only 9 percent, or 21, of the cases.[61] At most, then, 12 percent of the attainders can be tied to the administrative actions of daimyo within their domains; half that percentage is probably still a generous estimate.

The Strong State–Weak State Dichotomy

Beyond these two restricted fields of demonstrated hegemonic concern, there is much reason to debate the widespread emphasis on state policy as an agent of local change. This stress is unsatisfying from two points of view. First of all, it glosses over the evidence of widespread institutional variation and the implications of that underacknowledged historical fact. If the hegemons were resolved on subjecting daimyo to the laws of a central authority, we should find more local institutional uniformity than actually exists. Even if full uniformity was not achieved, we should see more consistent efforts on the part of the hegemons to enforce their laws than the preceding discussion indicates—for example, regular attempts to punish daimyo for maladministration when rural revolts (*hyakushō ikki*) broke out or there was a clear violation of central administrative ordinances. Defining the enforcement apparatus remains a significant problem. Berry, who argues strongly for Hideyoshi's role in fostering social change, also notes that he built no such mechanism. During his life and later, the hegemons' authority to confiscate fiefs and transfer daimyo suggests a basis to compel the implementation of central ordinances within domains; yet regardless of how useful that authority was for eliminating political rivals and managing the balance of power among daimyo, it is difficult to demonstrate that they employed it *systematically* to impose central rule.[62] Under the circumstances, developments within domains must be examined if we are to understand the social transformations that appear to accord with central edicts.

Second, the state-centered interpretation leaves little room for villagers as significant contributors to domain policy. Their image is overwhelmingly that of respondents to domain initiatives. Even those who stress the villages' selectivity in incorporating domain and Bakufu ordinances into their regulations and the traditional sources of local leaders' authority see the daimyo and shogun as defining the key elements of the governing institutions and policies that linked villages to higher authority. Others, looking for a popular voice, stress violent reactions. But in both cases, the possibility of a creative institutional contribution to the early modern order is neglected.[63]

In part these shortcomings result from a conceptual problem raised by White, that is, current studies frequently confound two different measures of the state's strength vis-à-vis society. The first is acceptance by major political actors of the idea of an overarching state organization and a willingness, however grudging, to cede powers to the state. I think of this characteristic as *nominal authority*. The second measure is a state's ability to carry out policies that realize the goals it sets for itself. This is a state's *capability*.[64] While related, these two attributes do not go hand in hand. A nominal authority to act does not, in itself, imply a capacity to do so or to do so effectively. A direct correlation cannot be assumed. A state can be ceded a broad range of nominal authority by society, or a narrow range. Similarly, its capacity to enact its programs over the resistance of society may be great or extremely limited.

Different combinations of nominal authority and capability can illuminate various configurations of state-society relationships, each of which recognizes the reciprocal influences of the two. These configurations supplement the more structural emphases in other typologies such as Max Weber's. They ignore the institutional forms of state (federal, feudal, tribal, rational-bureaucratic) and deal with state-society interactions regardless of state structure. Each configuration poses distinct opportunities and challenges.

In states with highly developed nominal authority and capability, leaders possess a recognized claim to operate in a broad range of activities. Furthermore, they set their own agendas with relative freedom and implement policies that will achieve their goals, even if subordinates in the state apparatus or outside it have their own, contradictory objectives. These are strong states.

At the opposite end are weak states, where the leaders' range of nominal authority is narrow and their capacity for action is highly restricted by political actors inside or outside the state structure. These states, or at least their leadership, may be struggling to survive.

Between these two poles (the most commonly used terms for describing state-society relations), the interpretations stressing Hideyoshi's land surveys, tax system, class separation efforts, and reorganization of rural administration tend toward the strong-state model. Yet comparisons with absolutist states tend to emphasize what Japan lacked, and therefore leave the impression that it conformed more closely to the weak-state model.

Three considerations suggest that looking for complex interactions of nominal authority and capability is a more helpful approach to analyzing state-society relations than this bipolar characterization. First, a broader view reminds us, in thinking about state growth, of the need to verify the impact of central ordinances on society. The relationship between society and state should be taken as problematic. We cannot assume the efficacy of central pronouncements. Even unchallenged proclamations do not imply an effective implementation of policy.

Second, sensitivity to a greater array of interactions between nominal authority and capability draws attention to the fact that the alternative to strong-state status is not just a weak state. There is a significant middle ground to be explored on its own terms. Awareness of this middle range helps to highlight not only what a given state configuration lacks, but also the attributes it possesses. Common sensibilities stress the importance of state capabilities. If a state lacks the ability to put policies into practice; it is perceived as weak, and its proclamations are seen as largely inconsequential. Where a state is unable to meet certain needs demanded by society, the disparity between nominal authority and capability may hold the potential for the government's overthrow. Yet in other circumstances, for example, in the course of early modern state-building, the growth of nominal authority may be useful even if it outstrips the government's actual capabilities. The potential for a positive evaluation of such states is substantial and should be taken seriously.

Finally, an awareness of the tension between nominal authority and capability helps move us away from a Eurocentric conceptualization of states. This involves a move away from a simple checklist of comparisons of Japan and the ideal of an absolutist state that emphasize the development of specific institutions such as a national bureaucracy, an autonomous judiciary, and related institutions. It separates the issue of an emerging rational-bureaucratic order from the successful creation of a strong and stable order that releases society's energies to increase wealth, support a larger population, support artistic and cultural development, and the like. In fact, Japanese political organization had elements of the Weberian rationalized state, but these were largely restricted to domain administration, not the emerging national state.[65] Early modern Japan lacked a national bureaucracy funded by nationwide tax revenues. Nonetheless, the national order as a whole was stable and capable of meeting the challenges it faced for more than two centuries.

To the extent that past research has confused the late-sixteenth- and early-seventeenth-century state's claims to authority with effective implementation, it has overvalued the ability of men like Oda Nobunaga, Toyotomi Hideyoshi, and Tokugawa Ieyasu to transform local political, social, and economic organizations. Emphasis on central political initiative is partly a consequence of early difficulties in researching this field. But the challenges inherent in researching and writing Japanese local history were reinforced by conceptual confusion. Both created difficulties for scholars who might otherwise have examined more critically the emphasis on the early modern state's capabilities.

More than 250 domains dotted seventeenth-century Japan. That fact alone has complicated the construction of a "typical" path of social, economic, and political development. Even where good documentary collections held the promise of illuminating new elements in this great transformation, it has taken much of the postwar era to identify and index the most important of them. Resources for those purposes went first to collections that directly addressed the role of prominent political leaders like Toyotomi Hideyoshi and institutions such as the Tokugawa Bakufu. The elitist emphasis represented an important and logical starting place, since the elite's activities and organizations tend to be the best and most conveniently documented. Studies based on this emphasis have contributed greatly to our understanding of early modern Japan.

Nonetheless, now that local documentary bases have become more accessible, the elite focus has become restrictive. The stress on central political initiative encouraged the development of models and concepts that fail to take account of the richness of early modern Japan's history. Two tendencies have developed. Historians have been reluctant to use the data from just one region to challenge the conclusions of the established view. Indeed, local history is often explored merely to illustrate those interpretations; Hall explicitly states that this was his intent in writing *Government and Local Power*.[66] Traditionalists, when they refer to the few acknowledged deviations from central ordinances at all, often characterize them as representing "backward" regions, undervaluing their potential interpretive import.[67] Though this description conceals the shadings of historians' work, I think that it properly characterizes a very common orientation.

To my mind, this use of local history to illustrate national trends has severe limitations. One risk is that it employs an *a priori* standard for selecting what is representative. The documents left by the political center predominantly shape the study, and with it, the findings. In the Japanese case, at least, the influences of local social, political, and economic forces in creating the early modern order may in consequence be understated. The absence of this local perspective has, I believe, left us with a fairly monochromatic explanation of change.

The perspective on change from below can provide a very different impression from the top-down view with which most of us are familiar. Questions about the prevailing emphasis on the growth of effective central political authority began as I looked for land registers as part of planned research on agricultural commercialization. The administrative systems I discovered did not conform to patterns that I had been led to expect. As I sought alternative evidence, I gradually "climbed the hill" (as a Japanese expression has it) and shifted to an examination of the relationship between state, domain, and village in the first century of the early modern era. What I found confirmed my early doubts. I then sought to assess the extent to which the process of institutional development (not necessarily the institutions' specific content) I found in one domain, Kaga, was representative.[68] This work further suggested the limits of central initiatives and the robust institutional creativity of both domain and village.

Throughout this study, I periodically draw attention to the range of institutional variation I found. This variation indicates that daimyo and village addressed the common tasks of domain formation through experimentation, and that they settled on a range of solutions. These variations, inadequately accounted for by an interpretive emphasis on centrally conceived programs, are evident in the most fundamental early modern institutions. They are especially evident in the case of land tax and tenure policies—the implementation of Hideyoshi's Taikō kenchi and its correlates, the establishment of early modern landholding rights, the kokudaka system, the separation of commoner and warrior, and the direct incorporation of villages into domain administrative structures.

Discovering the boundaries between domain and central authority requires the use of local histories to test generalizations about the extent of national social, political, and economic changes and the role of the political center as agent in promoting them. That same testing helps to assess how far the image of a stronger central authority was transformed into fact. I believe that this kind of research will show that there was more institutional color in early modern Japan than is commonly acknowledged.[69]

This effort requires immersion in local materials and their local contexts, rather than simply viewing them through a national lens. The standard vocabularies in which early modern specialists write are very often simply those of a single locality. It may be that the administrative unit from which the terms are drawn is large (e.g., the Tokugawa Bakufu), but that does not ipso facto make them a nationwide standard. Local terms, even when pronounced and written the same way, can have very different meanings. For example, the term *men*, which is commonly used to refer to land tax rates collected by the domain lord, had a very different, indeed opposite, meaning in late-sixteenth-century Kaga domain: it referred to an "exemption," the part of the crop that villagers were allowed to keep, not what they paid in taxes. Likewise, village and low-level administrative documents must be placed in their local institutional contexts rather than be subjected to a tyranny of interpretations derived from the study of Bakufu institutions.

The use of local history I am suggesting here does not claim many adherents among students of Japanese history. In Western languages, James L. McClain's study of Kanazawa, Kaga domain's major castle town and administrative headquarters, is a rare example of it. But though he effectively questions common assertions of the domain lords' complete control of castle town development, his focus is on the relatively few people who resided in large urban areas. The economic historian Matsushita Shirō and the institutional historian Hara Shōgo are among the few Japanese scholars to use case studies explicitly to test the implementation of central ordinances.[70]

Kaga as a Case Study

The domain of Kaga, in western central Japan, provides our context for a closer look at the epochal transformations of this era and for exploring the relationships between central administration, daimyo rule, and the village.

The geography of the region represents a cross section of much of Japan. Except for having one of Japan's rare sand-dune beaches, at Chirihama, there is little to distinguish the region from other sections of coastal Japan. Located between the Japan Sea and the Japan Alps, Kaga domain occupied the area that corresponds to modern Ishikawa and Toyama prefectures and the ancient provinces of Kaga, Noto, and Etchu (see Map 2). Narrow plains line most of the coast that forms the western border of the region, from the Kaga Plain north and west around the rocky, cliff-rimmed Noto Peninsula, past Noto Island and then north again along Toyama Gulf. Inland from the coast, travelers quickly ascend to a region of foothills. Soon after they find themselves on either the high plateau of the Noto Peninsula or moving into the higher, often snow-capped mountains—Tateyama, Gokayama, and Hakusan—extensions of the Japan Alps.

Throughout the region agriculture demands considerable effort. The upland soils are generally rocky and not especially fertile. Terracing is arduous, and even during the early modern era, parts of the Noto Peninsula were farmed as swidden rather than permanently cultivated.

The highlands contribute fertile sediment to lowland regions. Two relatively large plains dominate agricultural production. The largest, located in the old province of Etchu, is the Toyama Plain. Formed around four river systems, the Oyabe, the Shō, the Jintsu, and the Jōganji, the plain is composed of steep alluvial and diluvial fans. Cold mountain waters from the Japan Alps reduce crop yields in these areas.

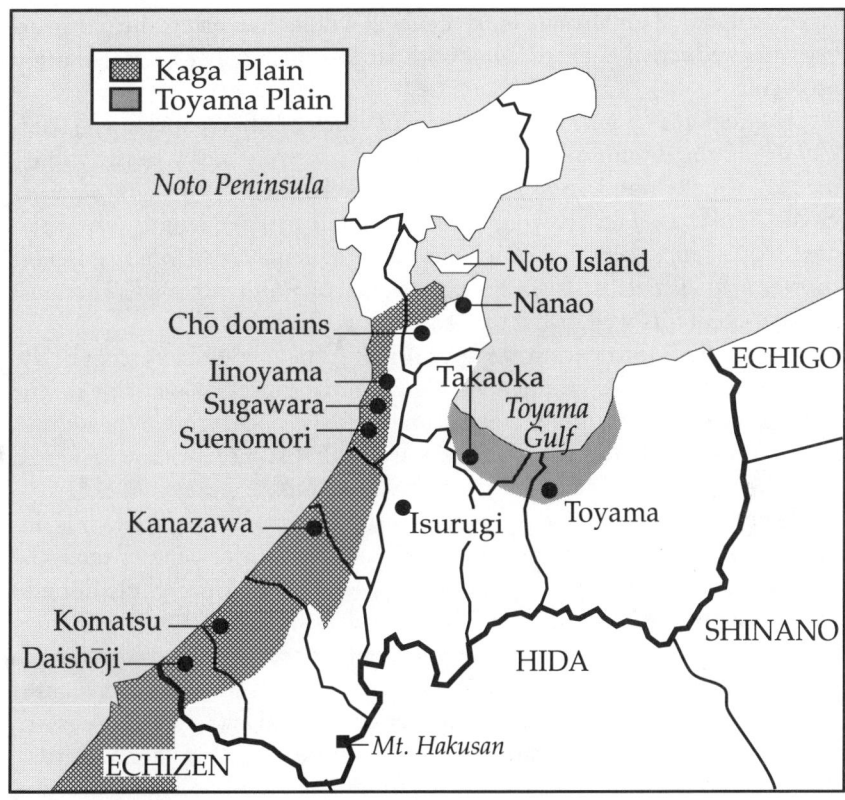

Map 2. The Kaga Area.

The elongated Kaga Plain, stretching along the coast from present-day Kaga City past Kanazawa and on to the Noto Peninsula beyond Hakui, is much narrower. Its most prominent features are a series of lagoons and marshlands. Drainage is poor in many places. Thanks to major investments of money and labor in extensive drain-and-fill reclamation projects, domain authorities, villagers, and the nationally prominent nineteenth-century merchant Zeniya Gohei progressively reduced these wetlands.

The steep descent from the highlands causes landslides and rapid sedimentation that once regularly clogged irrigation channels and raised river bottoms, causing floods where plain meets mountain. Even over short periods, soil deposition and flooding substantially shifted the course of rivers and made premodern farming along them a precarious pursuit. Today, maps reveal this heritage through place-names like Oshimizu, literally "Pushy Water." Yet even under these circumstances, there were always villagers, official planners, and entrepreneurs willing to convert the old riverbeds to productive fields through both large- and small-scale reclamation projects.

The region's climate, too, is typical of much of Japan. Spring and summer are hot and humid. Though snows are relatively heavy in the winter, they are usually not accompanied by extended periods of freezing weather in the lowlands. The growing season is about average length (200–220 days frost-free) except in the higher mountain inland areas, where it is a bit shorter (180 days frost-free). Precipitation is plentiful, among the greatest in Japan, and it is well distributed to support agriculture.

These conditions permit double-cropping, and about 40 percent of the arable today is double-cropped. Although statistics are not available for the Tokugawa era, agricultural treatises and village documents indicate that the practice was quite common, at least in the plains, by the eighteenth century. Rice was doubled with winter wheat, millet, or vegetables.

Population data for the seventeenth century are unavailable, so it is impossible to do more than suggest, using early-eighteenth-century data, the size of the urban population and the man-land ratio. Though the domain was not as fully urbanized as the Kanto (Edo) or the Kinai (Osaka) districts in the seventeenth century, probably something approaching 20 percent of the people lived in cities or towns. McClain estimates the late-seventeenth-century population of Kanazawa, the domain capital and chief castle town, at about 100,000, which made the city one of the largest in Japan. In 1721 the official population estimate for the three provinces of Kaga, Noto, and Etchu was 673,000. These two estimates alone suggest an urban population of 15 percent. But in addition to Kanazawa, there were other consequential cities and towns in the domain. Thomas Smith places the commoner population of Takaoka at 11,700 in 1714. Daishōji and Toyama, the castle towns of the two branch fiefs of Kaga domain, had populations roughly comparable to Takaoka's. And there were other towns, including Kaga, Mattō, Wajima, and Hakui, scattered throughout the domain. The heaviest concentrations of urban population were in the Kaga and Toyama plains. The villages that provided Kanazawa with labor or vegetables, oil, and other products were most affected by the demands of urban life; Noto had the lowest level of urban growth and economic diversification.[71]

Based on Bakufu estimates of the region's arable land area in 1721, each *tan* (0.245 acres) supported 6.6 people. This compares with a national average of 8.8 people per *tan*.[72] The figure for Kaga is probably artificially low, for the domain included only people aged fourteen (Japanese count) or older in its population estimates,* whereas many other parts of Japan included young children. (As in other parts of Japan, the domain excluded samurai from the count.) Nonetheless, this relatively high man-land ratio suggests that crop yields must have been very good, for domain farmers routinely supported a sizable urban population and the domain still exported large amounts of tax rice after the mid-seventeenth century.

Although the region is best known for rice production, its economic base was moderately diverse. Even before the formation of the domain, Kaga was known for its silk, which it regularly exported to Kyoto. Other items commonly produced in villages included paper, rice wine, and vegetables. Gold was mined at Hodatsu and several other locations. Salt manufacture was a major industry on the Noto shores. Coastal communities had well-developed fishing, and fine lacquer was produced at Wajima, on the Noto Peninsula, and at Yamanaka, not far from modern Komatsu City. A well-known pottery developed at Kutani, in the south of the domain, and Takaoka witnessed the rise of the metal-casting trade. Nonetheless, agriculture and its related enterprises formed the region's economic base.

Kaga domain was the largest in seventeenth-century Japan. The putative agricultural yield of the domain was 1,200,000 *koku*, or almost 6,000,000 (English) bushels.† By that fact alone it garnered a considerable measure of prestige. Furthermore, it earned a reputation as a leader in administration. A contemporary expression ranked Kaga first in politics, Tosa domain second ("Seiji wa ichi Kaga, ni Tosa").[73] It was a leader in administrative innovation and recognized as an efficiently run domain. These facts in themselves make Kaga worthy of study, but practical considerations add to its value as a laboratory in which to examine domain formation.

Rich collections of late-sixteenth- and seventeenth-century administrative and land tax documents permit a detailed analysis of the techniques that buttressed a stable domain administration in the face of both external and internal pressures. Domain officials compiled substantial compendia of ordinances for their own reference. Among other topics, these deal with tax assessment and collection methods, commoner labor and service obligations, restrictions on migration, village and district organization, appeals procedures for villagers, and land tenure practices.

Domain-wide statistical data remain only in very limited quantity.

---

*Japanese traditionally count a child as one year old at birth.
†Since the value of cash (gold, copper, silver) was computed relative to volumes of rice, I provide rice equivalents of these measures throughout. In any case there is no way at present to establish good modern monetary equivalents.

Serial population or economic data for this era are nonexistent. Most of the available documents are related to taxation. These documents, preserved in the homes of village and district headmen, include the results of land investigations and a sampling of yearly tax assessments, tax bills, and tax receipts. Since serial tax data are also missing, trends must be extrapolated from the limited cases for which individual annual land tax and land records remain. Finally, village officials also kept copies of village laws and descriptions of local practices. Despite lacunae, this documentary base is rich compared with the fragmentary material available on most other domains. Furthermore, since Kaga domain survived the entire early modern era, its documentary records allow us to track the complete transformation from a rough-and-ready military-political unit in 1581 to a stable civil administration in the mid-seventeenth century.

Kaga's territorial stability clearly accounts in part for the well-preserved documentation that made this study possible. It may also, in the eyes of some, mark this case as exceptional. This perspective would have some merit were Kaga a domain with long, hereditary roots in the region it dominated. But Kaga was in fact formed by outsiders, the Maeda family, who charged into Echizen, Kaga, and Etchu provinces as part of Oda Nobunaga's invading armies. As intruders, they faced the same fundamental problems as other daimyo who moved more often. In this sense the Maeda faced challenges typical of those confronting virtually all daimyo who survived into the Tokugawa era.[74]

Some Preliminary Observations

In the chapters that follow, I examine five key aspects of domain formation: (1) the process by which the daimyo commandeered fiefs of landed retainers (*kyūnin*) and removed them from the land; (2) the development of lower-level domain administration; (3) the growth of domain offices staffed by rural commoners; (4) the organization of land tenure; and (5) the maturing of the land tax system. Since these are the principal spheres in which scholars have seen the effective reach of an emerging central administration, any attempt to weigh the relative impact of central and local influences rests crucially on a close look at each development. We shall also look closely into the area in which rulers and villagers came into the most frequent (and sometimes violent) contact—the assessing and collecting of major taxes. Together, these analyses will go far in advancing our understanding of the process of class separation and the dynamics of domain-village interaction.

In general, the sources of domain policy can be separated into two basic clusters, external and internal. Kaga authorities undeniably took some steps in response to the orders of hegemons. But in some cases as they dutifully carried out those orders, their impact was broader than the center foresaw or wanted. Sometimes developments were the unintended by-products of policies designed to accomplish other goals. For example, the removal of early Maeda samurai from direct involvement in village affairs and agriculture may be seen as a result of the Maeda's transfer to Kaga (1581) rather than as a function of a centrally directed policy legally separating social classes. The political environment in which the domain grew, especially the need to fend off invaders, represents a second set of external influences. Yet as local security increased, the power of events in the broader Hokuriku region to shape domain growth declined. For example, decreasing villager participation in military activities is partially explicable by reference to the reduced threat of invasion of the domain. Overall, I find that outside the sphere of defense, external influences on domain policies were relatively unimportant.

The second cluster of factors, the domain's internal dynamics, conditioned most of the developments examined here. The dialogue between domain leaders on the one hand and landed retainers and lower samurai officials on the other was one of the two major creative forces. The friction between villagers and their overlords was the other. The interactions between these three sets of actors is especially evident in the processes that transformed rural administrative structures: the retainers' authority over their fiefs, the changing balance between commoner and samurai officials in the administrative structure, and the definition of land tenure.

In these interactions the rulers were not the only source of initiative; villagers, acting collectively, significantly influenced domain policies as well. In some cases, as when, like their counterparts throughout Japan before and after, they wrested concessions from their overlords, forcing reductions in land taxes or extended delays in payment, the changes were fleeting. But often and more importantly, their actions had an enduring effect on administrative policies and structures. Among other developments, they influenced the change to a little-known (in the West) but quite widespread system of land tenure called *warichi*, literally, "dividing the land." Under this system the village rather than individual households controlled access to plots of farmland. In other words, though landed retainers and domain authorities often took the lead in policy development, they did not act alone, much less in a vacuum. Commoner initiatives as well as reactions shaped policy initiatives and outcomes.

The relative strength of these initiatives was not simply a matter of villagers possessing greater absolute leverage than they are generally credited with. The inherent weakness of some standard domain techniques for extracting taxes and labor enhanced the villagers' bargaining position. Contrary to the assertions of many historians, I believe domain authorities did not possess sufficient knowledge of village agricultural conditions to tax at the levels to which they aspired. For one thing, some of the rationalization of rural administration was purchased at a substantial cost—the loss of the domain's ability to oversee closely and extract resources effectively from its rural subjects. For another, standard land survey methods, which historians have judged to be highly accurate, in fact were not. Consequently, domain tax administration was less effective than is commonly portrayed. In these local relations between ruler and commoner subject we see a trade-off of lower revenues for the promotion of internal stability and improved control of the retainer band.

In the sense that Kaga illustrates the dynamic interaction between center, domain, and village and shares with other domains an extended period of institutional experimentation, it is typical of early modern *han*. Its rulers' responses to common problems varied sufficiently from standard portrayals to highlight the fact that political leaders chose from a range of options in building stable institutional settlements. National hegemons, domain lords, and commoners formed mutually tolerable relationships within quite broad institutional parameters. Local forces greatly conditioned the specific institutional developments of any given domain. Identifying these pressures and suggesting the range of options available will, I hope, extend a part of the Sengoku era's image of tentative institutional experimentation into the early modern era.

PART ONE

Controlling Land

Chapter **2**

The Formation of Kaga Domain

The daimyo who came through the late-sixteenth-century civil wars to participate in the Pax Tokugawa traveled two different roads to a place in the new order. One path originated in the disparate, often small, warrior domains of the late fifteenth and early sixteenth centuries and led, for those with sufficient political astuteness, organizational ability, and luck, to celebrity as strong, independent leaders of large regional coalitions. Though some of these men managed to build broad, even nationally prominent alliances (e.g., Oda Nobunaga, Takeda Shingen, Uesugi Kenshin, and Tokugawa Ieyasu), more typical were families like the Date of northern Japan, the Shimazu of Satsuma, and the Mōri of Chōshū, who were defeated by one or more of these coalitions and were ultimately subsumed under the Tokugawa order.

The second route to daimyo status began in the lower ranks of a general who rose to national prominence. With the exception of those who rose under Ieyasu, the leaders whose fortunes were tied to one of the great generals still had to fend for themselves once their patron died.

The Maeda family followed this second path to fame and fortune. An overview of the process by which the domain was occupied and preserved reminds us that throughout the late sixteenth and early seventeenth centuries, the future of any general teetered precariously between glory and death, and that continued control of any territory by the same family could not be taken for granted. The domain's territorial development (distinct from its institutional evolution) can be divided into two stages, occupation and extension (1581–99) and preservation (1599–1636). Meeting the challenges of domain-building was primarily the task of the first daimyo,

Maeda Toshiie (r. 1581–99), with assistance from his eldest son, Maeda Toshinaga (r. 1599–1605). Preserving the family holdings was largely the responsibility of Toshinaga and his younger brother, Maeda Toshitsune (r. 1605–39), who remained a powerful force behind the daimyo who succeeded him.

The Opportunities of a Country at War

The basic pattern by which Kaga domain was formed was a common one—territorial acquisition by enfeoffment as well as by conquest. Leaders of the major military coalitions either made their generals lords of the domains they conquered or appointed them to rule in one region as a reward for military service in another. The newly acquired and often richer territory typically came at the cost of the general's giving up his traditional home territory. The Maeda were no exception.

What was far less common was the Maeda's enduring hold on so large a domain. It is for good reason that daimyo are often compared to potted plants, which could be picked up and moved to any part of Japan. Most of the other major daimyo, the Shimazu of Satsuma, the Mōri of Chōshū, the Uesugi and Date of northern Japan, even the Tokugawa, all coped with fief reductions or transfers, or both. Some, such as the Chōsokabe of Shikoku and the Gohōjō of the Kanto, were eliminated completely. From the epochal battle at Sekigahara in 1600 through 1700, there were 801 changes of domain leadership because of transfers, fief reductions, or attainders. Discounting those resulting from Sekigahara (181) and the Osaka campaigns (10), 610 of these changes took place in peacetime.[1] Since the number of daimyo at any given time was between 260 and 280, the turnover was quite high. It would be higher still if the last two decades of the sixteenth century were included. Under these circumstances, the process by which the Maeda retained control over Kaga under Oda Nobunaga, Toyotomi Hideyoshi, and the Tokugawa shoguns is of particular interest.

Maeda Toshiie (1538–99) was the archetypal warrior and leader of the sixteenth century, ascending from obscurity to national prominence while still a relatively young man. Born in Arako castle, in what is now the city of Nagoya, Toshiie entered an uneasy world, torn by the strife that marked the end of Japan's middle ages. His early years were dominated by his relationship to Oda Nobunaga. In Toshiie's youth, Nobunaga was just beginning the series of conquests and alliances that brought the greater part of central Japan under his control. By the time of his assassination in 1582, Nobunaga was arguably the preeminent military and political leader in Japan.

As with Toyotomi Hideyoshi, Toshiie's rise to prominence was intimately tied to the ascendancy of the Oda forces.

Toshiie was of modest origins. He was the fourth son of the lord of Arako, who held a rather small fief of about 2,000 kan, approximately the equivalent of an early-seventeenth-century fief of 5,000 koku.* In 1551 Toshiie entered the service of the family's more powerful neighbor and liege lord, Oda Nobunaga, and received a fief of 50 kan (about 125 koku). Five years later, in 1556, he proved himself in battle, fighting valiantly along with his lord against Nobunaga's own brother in a fray that cost him an eye. As a reward for his sacrifice and valor, he was granted a fief of 100 kan.

Toshiie's characteristic bravery was matched by a quick temper that at one point jeopardized his career. In 1559 he killed one of Nobunaga's companions, a tea master (*chabōzu*) named Jūami, for stealing the anchor pin on one of his swords. It was no small matter, for had he attempted to use the sword, the blade would have fallen off at the first thrust—a potentially lethal catastrophe. Jūami sought refuge from the irate Toshiie with another member of Nobunaga's band,† and Nobunaga refused to grant Toshiie permission to exact revenge. Toshiie, however, could not restrain himself and slew Jūami outside an armory under Nobunaga's very eyes. For this breach of his lord's orders, Toshiie was dismissed from service.

Toshiie regained Nobunaga's favor only after months of fighting on his behalf but not under his command—and completely unrewarded. After demonstrating such ardor and loyalty, he was readmitted to Nobunaga's service in 1561. He continued to serve Nobunaga well, and by 1568 he was endowed with a fief of 450 kan (about 1,125 koku). When his father died in 1569, Toshiie's valor and service were further acknowledged by Nobunaga: he inherited his father's domain of 5,000 koku and was made lord of Arako castle in preference to his older brother Toshihisa.

As Nobunaga's fortunes rose, so did Toshiie's. In 1575, at the battle of Nagashino, he was placed in charge of a front-line regiment of fusileers. The harquebus was the latest military technology of the day, and Nobunaga routinely kept these regiments under his direct control. Placing Toshiie in charge was a temporary battle exigency, but at a time when subordinate generals frequently changed sides in mid-battle, it also represented another sign of Nobunaga's trust and confidence in his loyalty.

---

*Domains were identified as large or small according to their value, not their physical size. In the 16th century this was commonly measured by the cash (*kandaka*) or rice (*hyō*) value of the taxes the land produced. The Arako fief of 2,000 kan in theory would have produced taxes valued at 2,000 kan of gold.

†Sassa Narimasa (d. 1588), a later Maeda nemesis.

Though the adversary in this case was a major daimyo, Takeda Katsuyori, Nobunaga's ambitions were threatened not so much by other daimyo as by the armies of the Ikkō sect of Buddhism. Headquartered in Kyoto, the sect's leaders had sought (with varying degrees of success) to coordinate the attempts of its adherents to keep autonomous control over their own districts. By the mid-1570's the Ikkō's main military forces were concentrated in the Hokuriku district, especially the provinces of Echizen and Kaga.² It was to the defeat of these forces that Nobunaga now turned his attention.

Toshiie, along with Shibata Katsuie and other Nobunaga retainers, played an important role in the conquest of these Ikkō-held regions. Toshiie's battlefield success against the Ikkō forces in Echizen province (modern-day Fukui prefecture) was rewarded handsomely. He was given a vastly larger fief—of 33,000 koku—at Fuchū (near modern Takefu city), carved out of the territory he had helped to conquer.³

This fief represented Toshiie's first acquisition of territory outside the Arako region. But this was no transfer in the "potted plant daimyo" style, at least as that phrase is commonly understood. The image conveys a sense of a complete break with past holdings. That was not the case here, or later, during the initial Maeda entrance into the Noto Peninsula. Only after his initial arrival in Noto did Toshiie lose control of his old domains at Arako.

Nobunaga's strategy of rewarding his generals in this fashion was really quite subtle, much more sensitive to the potential reactions of his followers than his heavy-handed reputation suggests. Lord and retainer were equally well served. First, of course, this approach rewarded military accomplishment. In addition, it placed (relatively) trustworthy allies in charge of conquered lands. Nobunaga provided a strong incentive for men like Toshiie to take a new assignment—a greatly increased fief. While this incentive has often been remarked upon, the decision to grant the new fiefs in addition to lands already held eliminated any trepidations Toshiie and other generals might have had about improving their fortunes at the cost of a complete break with their traditional holdings. Finally, by granting new lands in this manner, Nobunaga accomplished his aims without allowing his subordinates to build large, contiguous domains that might serve as bases for potential opposition: the daimyo could not be at two places at the same time, and governing fragmented territories was a difficult and more tenuous game than controlling contiguous lands.

At the time Toshiie entered Fuchū and later, when he was transferred to Noto, political and military power in the Hokuriku was fragmented and unstable. Both local leaders and those representing Oda Nobunaga's

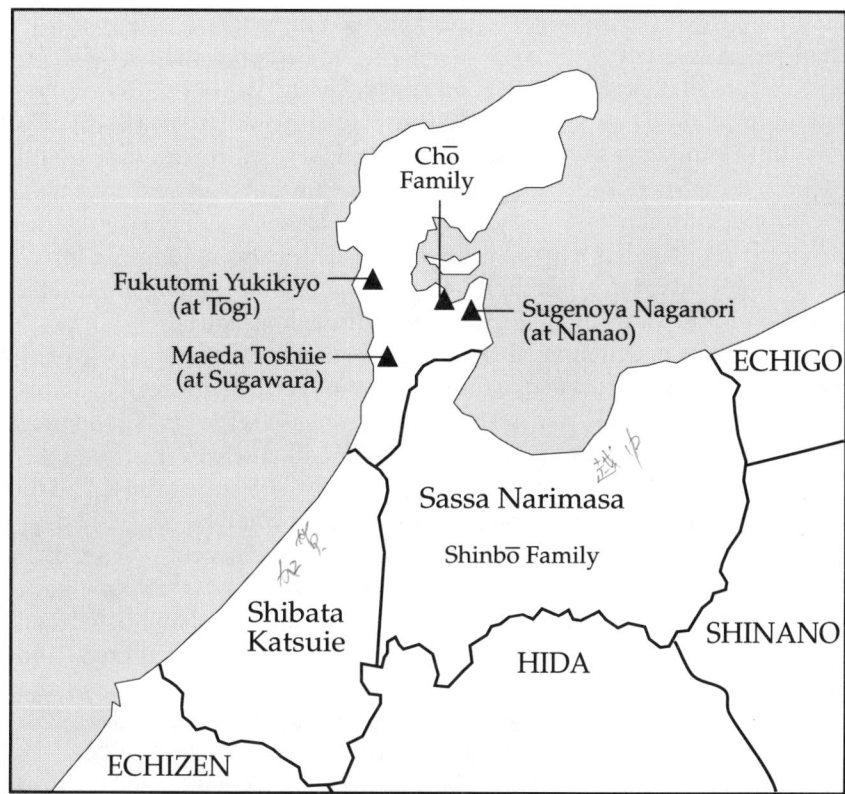

Map 3. Major Military Divisions of the Kaga Area, Spring 1581.

emerging coalition actively competed for dominance. The major military divisions of the region in the spring of 1581 are shown in Map 3.

In the early spring of 1581, Nobunaga simultaneously granted fiefs in Noto to Toshiie and two other retainers, Sugenoya Naganori and Fukutomi Yukikiyo. He had previously granted half of Kashima county (kōri) in Noto to the Chō family, powerful local notables since the middle ages. At somewhat greater distance, the men beside whom Toshiie fought in the battles to crush the Ikkō forces remained influential in the area: the province of Kaga was under Shibata Katsuie, and Sassa Narimasa was named overlord of Etchu in 1581.

While Nobunaga was alive, these men were all nominal allies, linked by their vertical ties to him. But those ties were tenuous at best, as suggested by Nobunaga's supplement to the Regulations for the Province of Echizen, which commanded that Toshiie and two other commanders, Sassa Narimasa and Fuwa Mitsuharu, "act as Shibata's overseers. . . . Hence you shall report without duplicity on the good and bad points of his conduct, and Shibata shall report on the good and bad points of yours."[4] Sugenoya, Fukutomi, Chō Tsuratatsu, and Toshiie shared a similar spy-on-thy-ally relationship in early 1581. Nobunaga's death severed the tie that bound them to a common cause and opened the way for full competition among the former brothers-in-arms. Consequently, Toshiie's ability to preserve his domain, much less expand it, now depended on his holding his forces at the ready, keeping a watchful eye on his neighbors and paying careful attention to the shifts in military alliances throughout Japan.

There were potential indigenous threats as well. Local military leaders were still not fully reconciled to the new, outside rulers of the region. Some, like the Nukui family, had recently allied themselves with Nobunaga's powerful archenemy, Uesugi Kagekatsu. The military power of the Ikkō sect and its local allies was waning; but they were still strong enough to be disruptive, especially when links to outside forces could be established.

Even as Toshiie received his new fief in Noto, his possession of it was threatened, and his military mettle tested. In early 1581, Nobunaga ordered Toshiie, Shibata, and Sassa and his local allies, the Shinbō, to bring their forces to Kyoto. Seizing this opportunity, Uesugi invaded Etchu and sparked an uprising in the mountains of Kaga (spring 1582).[5] Sassa and the Shinbō, soon followed by Shibata and Toshiie, were ordered back to defend their lands. Uesugi's army was thrown back, defeated at Uozu (in Etchu) in early summer 1582, and forced to retreat.[6] When Nobunaga died in the midst of this campaign, Toshiie broke off his pursuit and returned home, fearing a revolt of former enemies in his domain.[7]

Territorial Expansion

When Toshiie first entered Noto, there was little to foretell that he would make his domain the largest in all Japan. The unstable environment certainly militated against such an enterprise. Yet the very turbulence and fragmentation of power in Kaga-Noto-Etchu contributed to the Maeda's eventual success as lords of Kaga han. The various earlier assaults of Uesugi and Shibata had largely destroyed the Ikkō sect's main military base. Once the last Ikkō uprising was suppressed in the spring of 1582, only small, generally isolated pockets of resistance remained. On the Noto Peninsula, Toshiie was clearly primus inter pares—a position he could preserve so long as he remained sensitive to the potential for resistance within his domain.

Despite local and national instability, all but two counties in the con-

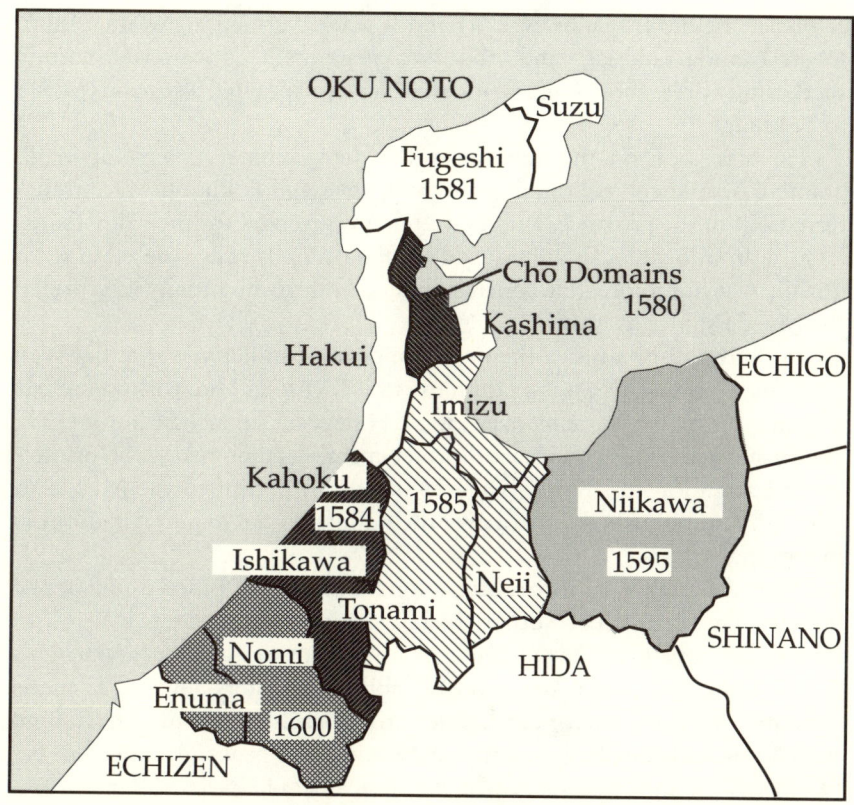

Map 4. The Expansion of Maeda and Chō Domains in Kaga, Noto, and Etchu.

tiguous provinces of Kaga, Noto, and Etchu were brought under Maeda control within 14 years. By 1600 those counties were in Maeda hands as well. Through a combination of military prowess, political astuteness, and favorable local conditions, the Maeda built and preserved a prominent position for themselves in early modern Japan.

In light of the rapid growth of the domain and the volatile situation Toshiie initially encountered in Noto, one would expect that the Maeda added land primarily through direct conquest. But this was not the case. The most significant territorial acquisitions came through awards from the hegemons of Japan.

On arrival in Noto, Toshiie established his headquarters at Inoyama in Hakui county. His camp was an old temple compound, but its water supply proved inadequate. Consequently he moved to Sugawara (Map 4), site of a former medieval manor (*shōen*) and a major shrine, Sugawara Tenjin, where Kunida Yukinaga and other local warriors headquartered. Toshiie successfully drew these samurai into his band and granted a stipend (*fuchi*) to Yukinaga.[8]

He was soon on the move again. In late summer 1581, Nobunaga granted Toshiie control of all Noto. Sugenoya and Fukutomi were transferred out of the province, and their domains given to Toshiie. Chō Tsuratatsu, a prominent local samurai and Nobunaga's ally, was ordered to serve Toshiie was not a foregone conclusion, and Hideyoshi initially interpreted the Maeda stance as hostile.

In the Kaga-Noto area the most important conflict was that between After Nobunaga's assassination in 1582, Toyotomi Hideyoshi set about building his own hegemony over Japan. Hideyoshi's penchant for seeking compromise with his potential or former enemies, combined with Toshiie's careful attention to shifting balances of power, permitted the Maeda to maintain undiminished control over their domains and to play a major role in national affairs.

The realignment of forces after Nobunaga's death pitted a number of his retainers against each other. Toshiie capitalized on these rivalries. In this, he had one great advantage: to help cement ties among Nobunaga's forces, Hideyoshi had taken two of Toshiie's daughters, Gō and Kiku, as concubines.[†] Those early personal ties proved useful in the months following Nobunaga's death, easing the negotiation of a peaceful settlement between Toshiie and Hideyoshi.[9] The rapproachment between Hideyoshi and Toshiie was not a foregone conclusion, and Hideyoshi initially interpreted the Maeda stance as hostile.

In the Kaga-Noto area the most important conflict was that between Toyotomi Hideyoshi and Shibata Katsuie. Their major confrontation came at the battle of Shizugatake, in 1583. The Maeda forces, arrayed outside the

---

*At this time the title was reserved for those in the service of a high official or warrior. A daimyo might himself be a yoriki, as Toshiie once was to Shibata Katsuie. Since half of Kashima county was bestowed on the Chō by Oda Nobunaga, independent of any relationship to Maeda Toshiie, the Chō lords, although Maeda retainers and aides, were able to maintain a substantial degree of independence. The Chō fief was the last retainer fief to come under full direct han administration. This was accomplished only after a major disruption in 1667. The fief was actually taken over by the han in 1671. Conditions were unsettled for some time after, and the principal han reform, the Kaisaku hō, which had been enacted in other parts of the domain between 1651 and 1656, was not fully implemented there until 1679. See Shimode, *Ishikawa*, pp. 129, 131–32, for a general outline of these events. Itō Tasaburō takes the Chō as typical of enfeoffed retainers ("Kinsei shoki daimyō ryō"), but they were exceptional in the degree and duration of their autonomous administration of their lands. Even the fact that they had a fief in one contiguous holding was unusual.

†Kiku was an illegitimate child.

actual battlefield, did not join with either side. But they were attacked by Hideyoshi's armies anyway, and pushed from their positions. Just as it appeared that the Maeda would counterattack, they suddenly and completely withdrew. Although they retreated to Fuchū, Hideyoshi's forces remained in hot pursuit, and many of the Maeda fighting men lost their lives, including several key retainers. Toshiie sent his fusileers out among Hideyoshi's advancing troops to harass them while he prepared his defenses, but ultimately no climactic battle materialized.

Hideyoshi offered a negotiated settlement, one that was quite generous. Perhaps Hideyoshi understood Toshiie's refusal to commit himself to either side. Toshiie certainly cannot be said to have acted decisively. Indeed, his apparent attempt to steer a middle course was typical of many of Nobunaga's retainers in the months following his assassination. There were, of course, good reasons to hesitate. Like a number of Nobunaga's generals, Toshiie had followed the custom of the time and sent family members as hostages to both the Toyotomi and the Shibata forces. Those hostages, held in warrant against any treachery and duplicity, were no doubt a consideration. Past connections between the two men, symbolized by Hideyoshi's ties to two Maeda daughters, may also have influenced his decision. Whatever the reason for Hideyoshi's unwillingness to fight it out with the Maeda, he met with Toshiie in 1584 and confirmed his possession of Noto. Later that year, Hideyoshi granted Toshiie northern Kaga (Ishikawa and Kahoku counties).*

Toshiie once again transferred headquarters. He occupied Ōyama Gobo, the former center of the Kaga Ikkō sect. Henceforth, the town was known as Kanazawa. Here Toshiie built his castle between the Sai and Asano rivers. Overlooking the Kaga Plain, naturally protected by the two rivers, Kanazawa was, from Hideyoshi's standpoint, an ideally located fortress for his new ally, protecting Echizen and the central provinces from northern invaders like the Uesugi. The new castle became the permanent administrative center of the domain.¹⁰

No sooner had these events relieved the pressure on Toshiie to the south than he found himself confronting a threat from a different quarter, Etchu. Sassa Narimasa had continued to pacify his domains, successfully subduing the remnants of the local Ikkō forces and developing a cooperative relationship with them.¹¹ Although Sassa had sent troops to aid Hideyoshi

---

*Iwasawa, *Maeda Toshiie*, pp. 92–103. According to Iwasawa, this "reward" indicated that Hideyoshi had made a deal with Toshiie before the battle of Shizugatake. But then why would he have attacked the Maeda? Since Toshiie had once had ties to Shibata, Hideyoshi may have wanted to ensure his removal from the battlefield.

at Shizugatake just a few months earlier, he now allied himself with Tokugawa Ieyasu (who was still a threat to Hideyoshi). Sharing a border with Toshiie (by this time firmly in Hideyoshi's camp) was bound to lead to a confrontation.[12]

Early in the fall of 1584, Sassa ordered the Shinbō troops to invade Noto.[13] Within the month Sassa's main forces invaded, too. By mid-October he was poised to engage Toshiie's forces at Suenomori castle, in Hakui county. The fortification was surrounded and placed under siege. Sassa's first sallies took a heavy toll on the defenders, and part of the castle fell to his forces and was burned to the ground.

Toshiie acted quickly on receiving news of the strike against Suenomori, collecting forces at two other local castles, Tsubata and Mattō. The day after Sassa's assault, these forces launched a counterattack. Although Toshiie's troops numbered only 2,500, he successfully moved on Sassa from the rear. When the dust settled, more than 2,000 soldiers had perished, but Sassa had been repulsed and sent packing back to Toyama.[14]

As Toshiie's army took the offensive and pressed Sassa the following year, Uesugi forces, now under Uesugi Kagekatsu, once again invaded Etchu and forced Sassa to fight on two fronts.[15] As a result of these battles, Sassa Narimasa's holdings in Etchu were considerably reduced. When he finally concluded a peace agreement with Hideyoshi, all he had left were Niikawa county and his castle at Toyama. By 1585 Ieyasu's ally had been rendered ineffective. For Toshiie and the Maeda, Narimasa's fall meant a much greater degree of security.

Suenomori was the last battle to take place within Maeda territory. A serendipitous combination of their own military skill and nationwide developments worked to the Maeda's advantage. They had had to hold their domain in the midst of full wartime conditions for only four years. To be sure, their military activities were not over: Maeda troops assisted in Hideyoshi's national campaigns to subdue the Tohoku, Kanto, Shikoku, and Kyushu daimyo over the next decade; they supported Hideyoshi's Korean expeditions; and in 1599 Maeda forces attacked southern Kaga in preparation for the battle at Sekigahara. But for all practical purposes, the Hokuriku region was now pacified. It had witnessed the penultimate competition among its local daimyo, freeing the Maeda to devote greater energies to the creation of a stable administration.

By this time Maeda Toshinaga, Toshiie's eldest son, had risen to some prominence in his own right. He, too, served Nobunaga, and with Toshiie, Shibata, and others, invaded and pacified Echizen. Toshinaga had married Hōsen'in, Nobunaga's daughter, in 1581. This union cemented ties between the two families and represented an expression of confidence in both Toshiie and Toshinaga.

Shortly after Toshiie transferred to Noto in 1581, Toshinaga took possession of his father's fief at Fuchū as well as the old family holdings around Arako. Once again Nobunaga's strategy of transfer subtly met the needs of his daimyo as well as his own. The family's retention of control in the old domain must have eased Toshiie's mind as he moved into Noto. At least the transition to the new domain did not represent an abrupt and complete change in fiefs. Toshinaga was en route to Fuchū soon after his wedding when Akechi Mitsuhide's treachery destroyed the unity of the Oda forces and cast doubt on the future of all Nobunaga's generals.

The extent of the disruption caused by Nobunaga's assassination, even within the ranks of one daimyo's organization, is well illustrated by the challenge Toshinaga next faced. When news of the assassination reached him, he sent two trusted emissaries to take Hōsen'in to the Maeda's home base, Arako castle, while he made his way to Fuchū. As he sought to respond to the confusion following Nobunaga's death, many of his soldiers deserted him, concerned about a possible attack by Akechi's forces.[16]

Toshinaga survived this embarrassment and continued to be treated with respect. In 1583, after the confrontation at Shizugatake, his fief in Fuchū was exchanged for a larger one, of 40,000 koku, in Kaga province. Toshinaga occupied the castle at Mattō. Two years later, after the Maeda's pacification of Etchū, Hideyoshi awarded Toshinaga three of the counties formerly held by Sassa Narimasa: Imizu, Tonami, and Neii. Toshinaga moved to the fortress at Moriyama, where he remained until moving to Toyama castle in 1597. At this time the domain at Mattō nominally reverted to Hideyoshi, but a Maeda retainer, Teranishi Hidenori, was named to administer it.* When Sassa Narimasa was ordered to Higo province in 1587, Niikawa county, too, was "temporarily" placed under Maeda jurisdiction. (In 1613 the Bakufu confirmed in writing that Niikawa was henceforth a permanent part of the Maeda domains.)†

In 1598 Toshiie retired in favor of Toshinaga. The territorial expansion of the domain was largely completed: it embraced the bulk of Kaga and all of Noto, land that had been acquired by appointment, and most of Etchū, land added by direct conquest. Only two counties in southern Kaga remained to be incorporated by Toshinaga.

---

*Teranishi was formally appointed *daikan*, or intendant (Heki, *Kanō dokushi nempyō*, p. 270).

†This confirmed what was apparently an oral promise by Hideyoshi that the Maeda would retain possession of Niikawa (*IKS*, 2: 200–201).

Had substantial territorial acquisition been all Toshiie had accomplished, he would have had a good deal of which to be proud. In fact, he had achieved much more. The size of his domain and his martial skills made him one of the most influential men in Japan. In addition, his valiant and reliable support of Hideyoshi made him a trusted ally. He became a prominent actor in Hideyoshi's emergent hegemony. He was entrusted with guarding the imperial capital, Kyoto, while Hideyoshi took the main body of his forces south to subdue Kyushu in 1585. Respect for Toshiie's skill and position culminated in his appointment as one of the Five Elders charged with protecting the five-year-old Toyotomi heir immediately after Hideyoshi's death. Another, less formal indication of Hideyoshi's feelings for Toshiie came in a comment he made about his adopted daughter, one of Toshiie's children, that "were she a man, I would make her Kampaku [Regent]."[17] Toshiie's closeness to Hideyoshi and his preeminence among the daimyo are pointedly represented in the loyalty oath Hideyoshi elicited from his most prominent generals following the Higo Rebellion of 1588. Like most of the 29 signatories, Toshiie took the Toyotomi surname and signed the document as Toyotomi Toshiie. More important, he was one of the first six, the most prominent signatories, and one of the only three among the six (along with Tokugawa Ieyasu and Ukita Hideie) who were not Oda or Toyotomi relatives.[18]

Preserving the Domain

If the general's tent and sword capture the spirit of the first stage of domain formation, the negotiating table might best characterize the second. After Toshiie's death in 1599, Toshinaga replaced him as one of the Five Elders. Yet Toshinaga's role in national politics was not as significant as this appointment suggests. Difficulties at home prevented him from fully participating in the events that established Tokugawa Ieyasu's preeminence; his primary accomplishment thereafter was to defend and preserve Maeda control of the domain. That mission continued to be important during the reign of his successor, Toshitsune. The domain's location and military prominence, along with a generally low profile in national politics and artful negotiation at critical junctures, ensured expansion into southern Kaga and the preservation of the domain.

Challenge to the integrity of the domain surely came sooner than Toshinaga would have liked. Some months before his death in 1599, Toshiie successfully warded off an attempt by Ieyasu to engineer his transfer to Shikoku.[19] His passing precipitated another threat to Maeda rule.

In late 1599, as Ieyasu prepared for direct confrontation with Hideyoshi's heirs at the epochal battle at Sekigahara, rumors cast doubt on Toshinaga's loyalty to the Tokugawa house. Ieyasu issued orders to chastise Toshinaga, but intensive negotiations under the direction of the trusted Maeda retainer Yokoyama Nagachika culminated in a peaceful solution. Hoshun'in, Toshinaga's mother, was pledged as a hostage to Ieyasu, the first in what became a universal Tokugawa system of hostage-holding in 1634.[*] The agreement further specified that Ieyasu's granddaughter would marry Toshinaga's younger brother Toshitsune, who also became heir apparent to the Maeda house.[20] This new Tokugawa influence over Toshinaga and his successor clearly reduced the potential for Maeda opposition, but (as became clear a decade or so later) it did not guarantee Tokugawa confidence in Toshinaga or the Maeda.

The rumors may have tarnished the image of the Maeda and instilled a measure of humility in Toshinaga, but the incident could not obviate Ieyasu's need for active Maeda support. Toshinaga and another younger brother, Toshimasa, commanded a major military force and were potentially useful allies against Toyotomi partisans in the Hokuriku region. After Ieyasu's victory at Sekigahara, such considerations, as well as the Maeda's meritorious service even before that decisive battle, led to the last of their territorial acquisitions.

Some historians wonder about Toshinaga's being so richly rewarded by the Tokugawa when he did not even participate in the decisive battle at Sekigahara, but the Maeda were in fact involved in important related campaigns.[21] They were active in the aborted Aizu forays against the Uesugi in June, but more important, they defeated their southern neighbors. Both Yamaguchi Munenaga and Niwa Nagashige, the overlords of Enuma and Nomi counties, allied themselves with the anti-Tokugawa Western army. The Maeda's destruction of this army in August removed any threat to the Tokugawa from that quarter.

Ieyasu could not have been more pleased. He wrote to Hoshun'in in Edo, "Recently I learned of Toshinaga's exploits at [Daishōji] in Kaga. He is being very faithful to me. I am much pleased by this news. Moreover, once we have broken up the northland, I shall reward him with it."[22]

---

[*]Shimode, *Ishikawa*, p. 121. Hoshun'in was in Fushimi castle at the time of Toshiie's death and during Yokoyama's negotiation with Ieyasu. She returned to Kaga in the spring of 1600 before being dispatched to Edo in mid-year (Iwasawa, *Maeda Toshiie*, pp. 373–74). Though hostage-taking was common at this time, it had not developed into a means of ensuring a daimyo's family's exclusive loyalty to the Bakufu. Giving a hostage to the Tokugawa did not exclude the possibility of sending other family members to another important lord. Toshinaga's brother Toshimasa sent a hostage to Osaka, headquarters of the Tokugawa's rivals, even while his mother was in Edo.

All the same, when Ieyasu sent orders for the Maeda forces to advance south to join the Tokugawa Eastern army, there was significant hesitation in the Maeda ranks. Toshimasa failed to dispatch his troops to march with those of Toshinaga. When Toshinaga at last set out by himself, he arrived after the battle's outcome had been decided.*

Though Toshimasa's refusal to participate and Toshinaga's late arrival at Sekigahara must have disturbed Ieyasu, neither proved an obstacle to his ultimate success, and he had good reason to be generous. The Maeda, especially Toshinaga, had served well in preparatory campaigns, and they represented a formidable military force. With his recent victory over the Western army and the challenge of consolidating his success, Ieyasu was once again in a position to prefer the carrot to the stick. Toshinaga was rewarded with Nomi and Enuma counties. Even the unresponsive Toshimasa was dealt with in a manner calculated to earn Toshinaga's continued support or, at least, not alienate him. Though Toshimasa became a *rōnin* (masterless samurai), his fief in Noto, inherited from Toshiie, remained in the family, as part of Toshinaga's domain.

Strictly speaking, before this time it is incorrect to speak of "Kaga domain," because the Maeda's lands, like those of other great families such as the Shimazu of Satsuma, were divided into separate domains, each under the leadership of a prominent member of the family. From both the standpoint of relations with the hegemons and local administration, the domains were distinct. Military levies on each of the Maeda daimyo were calculated separately. As Toshimasa's actions indicate, each responded to the events of the day based on his own perceptions of self-interest; and each (as we shall see in following chapters) made his own decisions regarding local administration. Sekigahara changed all that. With the reallocation of fiefs, one overlord alone, Toshinaga, now controlled a single domain that spanned three provinces and was valued at 1,200,000 koku.

Five years later, in 1605, Toshinaga retired because of ill health and moved to Toyama castle. He left the domain in the hands of his twelve-year-old brother, Toshitsune. Toshitsune had been born in Kanazawa castle in 1593, but had been sent to Moriyama castle to be raised by Maeda Nagatane. When Niikawa county was finally transferred to the Maeda in 1595, it had been formally given to the child Toshitsune, not his father.† At the

---

*Scholars offer different reasons for Toshimasa's failure to follow Ieyasu's orders, but there is some difficulty with each of the major explanations. It seems likely that his actions were in some way linked to the fact that his wife, daughter of Gamō Ujisato, had recently been sent to Osaka to stand hostage to Ishida Mitsunari and his allies of the Western Army (KS, 2: 167, 170; Heki, [*Kaitei zōhō*] *Kanō*, p. 853).

†Toshinaga continued to be regarded with some suspicion in Edo. His mother was retained as a hostage. Honda Masashige was employed as an intermediary in the dispute with

conclusion of hostilities with Niwa Nagashige (before Sekigahara), young Toshitsune was sent to Komatsu as Niwa's hostage. The following month, when Niwa lost his fief, it was formally transferred to Toshitsune (Niwa became his castellan).

Toshitsune was bold but not foolhardy. He valiantly led his forces in the Osaka campaigns against the remnants of the Toyotomi house. But the time had passed when he could make his major mark as a military figure. There were no battles between Sekigahara and Osaka, and only one other during the remainder of the century (Shimabara, in 1637). The Tokugawa hegemony brought a long-standing peace to Japan. Consequently, Toshitsune's principal accomplishments lay in creating an administrative foundation for the domain.

His first important role—the one that concerns us at the moment—was as conservator of the Maeda holdings. A few years after his installation as daimyo, a series of events sensitized him to the link between the domain's fate and that of the Tokugawa house. In 1611, still a long way from his deathbed, Toshinaga issued a testament (*ikun*) in which he stressed the need for Toshitsune and all of the retainer band to be loyal to the Tokugawa house. This followed by only a month Ieyasu's extraction of a pledge of loyalty from 21 of the great daimyo, including Toshitsune.

If these reminders were not adequate to instill a consciousness in him of how intimately the fortunes of his own house were tied to the Tokugawa's, demands that Niikawa county be returned to the Bakufu provided concrete evidence of the kinds of pressures the Tokugawa could bring to bear on the domain. Over a number of months the Bakufu placed the Maeda under a combination of overt and covert pressures to return that part of their domains. Aided largely by the astute negotiations of Senior Councillor Honda Masashige, the Bakufu efforts were thwarted in 1614.[23]

The Maeda position was again seriously threatened in 1631. In that year Toshitsune ordered various repairs made to Kanazawa castle, purchased military equipment, and took other steps to improve the domain's martial capabilities. To Bakufu authorities it appeared that he was preparing to take advantage of Shogun Tokugawa Hidetada's illness to challenge the Tokugawa house openly. After debating whether or not to resist the anticipated Bakufu expedition to chastise Kaga, Toshitsune came down on the side of

---

the Bakufu. This took place only after some substantial internal debate. Similar tensions arose before the Osaka campaigns. (See Ōno Mitsuhiko, "Maeda Toshitsune.") Like Toshiie, the new daimyo's mentor, Maeda Nagatane, was from Owari province. If he was related to Toshiie by blood, it was probably no close relationship, since Nagatane, also called Taima, married one of Toshiie's daughters. Nagatane's family was one of the more important of the han's retainer houses (Heki, [*Kaitei zōhō*] *Kanō*, p. 855).

peace. Once again, a prominent retainer, Yokoyama Yasuharu, negotiated with Bakufu authorities. And once again, mediation proved successful. Instead of a Bakufu assault, betrothal to another Tokugawa daughter further bound the Maeda to the shogunate. Toshitsune's heir, Mitsutaka, was married to Shogun Iemitsu's adopted daughter, commencing a regular pattern of intermarriage with the Tokugawa.[24] Although the requirement to reside in Edo, the shogunal capital, was not formally a part of the settlement, the fact that Toshitsune henceforth spent most of his time there was almost certainly related to the resolution of this dispute.[25]

Toshitsune's policy of preserving what the Maeda already held rather than recklessly risking it through a confrontation with the Bakufu was the capstone of a policy that had guided both Toshiie and Toshinaga in their relations with Hideyoshi and Ieyasu. Through it, the Maeda retained their position as the largest daimyo. Only the Bakufu controlled more land. Yet the heated (sometimes bloody) debates that took place in the Maeda councils over the proper response to signs of Bakufu mistrust attest that even at this late date, and despite paper pledges to the contrary, daimyo (and their retainers) saw themselves as autonomous lords. They did not conceive of themselves as mere cogs in the shogunal administrative machinery. The sixteenth-century conception of the daimyo as the embodiment of public authority (kōgi) survived the Oda and Toyotomi efforts to encompass a national public authority; and daimyo still contested similar Tokugawa attempts to coopt that position three decades after Sekigahara.[26]

These debates were not the only sign of the Maeda's desire to prevent themselves from becoming completely subservient to the Bakufu. Toshitsune took one additional step designed to protect the domain from reduction or outright confiscation by the Tokugawa: in 1639 he retired.

Toshitsune had tried several times before to obtain official permission to retire.[27] From the time he was suspected of opposition to Hidetada, he had tried to remove himself as a potential irritant to the Tokugawa and replace himself with his eldest son, Mitsutaka, in whom the Bakufu authorities had more trust. Mitsutaka's ties, by blood and marriage, to the Tokugawa house alone might have served to relieve the Bakufu's anxieties—his mother was Hidetada's daughter, and he was married to Shogun Tokugawa Iemitsu's adopted daughter—but he had also shown consistent loyalty to the Tokugawa.[28] In retirement, and with his trusted son as han lord, Toshitsune may have also hoped to gain a degree of freedom from the close scrutiny to which the Bakufu subjected him.

But Toshitsune had more in mind than merely maneuvering Mitsutaka into position to relieve the personal pressure on him and on the Maeda as a whole. As a condition of his retirement, he wanted to establish two relatively large branch fiefs under separate Maeda lineages. This request, which figured prominently among his many petitions for permission to retire, was designed to protect the Maeda line.[29] With two lines of the family formally recognized by the Bakufu and established in separate domains, each large enough to make its male members credible candidates for daimyo of the main fief, the domain would gain a measure of protection against the lack of an appropriate heir (someone who was clearly incompetent) or any heir at all. Toshitsune must have been well aware that of 106 attainders between 1601 and 1639, the most common cause—about one-third (35)—was interrupted succession.[30]

Under the provisions of the Laws of the Military Houses, the question of who was a suitable heir to daimyo status was a political decision arbitrated by the Bakufu. In principle the shogun could take any action he wished, but to have discontinued a daimyo line without apparent reason when there was a suitable heir would have alienated many daimyo. To that extent, even the Bakufu had to pay some attention to political realities.

Since there was little likelihood that every line of the Maeda family would lack a truly suitable heir, the strategy of establishing large branch fiefs gave the Maeda an inexpensive measure of protection against the confiscation of their domain. This tactic was employed by the Bakufu itself, through the designation of three branch houses, the *gosanke*, and by many other daimyo throughout Japan to preserve their lineage.[31] Such precedents encouraged Toshitsune to take the same action, to the same end.*

Toshitsune was finally granted his wish in the spring of 1639. At the age of forty-seven, he resigned, reserving lands of 225,000 koku centered on Komatsu to sustain himself in his retirement. He granted a fief of 70,000 koku, Daishōji han, mostly in Enuma county in Kaga, to his third son, Toshiharu; a 100,000-koku fief, Toyama, largely in Neii and Niikawa counties, to his second son, Toshitsugu; and the remainder of the domain to his eldest son, Mitsutaka.

The creation of two large branch fiefs also secured some military advantage. Although the Bakufu had issued orders in 1615 that each province should maintain only one castle, the Maeda kept at least six castles in operation through 1638.[32] In positioning his new fiefs, Toshitsune sagely

---

*Ironically, the Maeda never had to recruit an heir from these branch fiefs. On the other hand, the main branch of the family supplied successors for one of the large branch fiefs, Daishōji han, on five occasions after its formation, and for the other, Toyama han, on one occasion. At four other times Daishōji han provided heirs to Toyama han and Nanokaichi han, the small domain (about 10,000 koku) ruled by the line of Maeda Toshitaka, fifth son of Toshiie. (Wakabayashi, *Kinsei komonjo saihō*, p. 97.)

blocked the traditional routes of access to northern Kaga and the Noto Peninsula.*

There was only one significant change in Kaga domain's territorial configuration afterward, and this was aimed at facilitating the administration of the branch domains. In 1660 Toyama han exchanged 20,000 koku of land in Nomi county for villages in Niikawa, making all of its territory contiguous. To the same end, Daishōji exchanged its 4,300 koku in Etchu for the remainder of Enuma and six villages in Nomi.†

Conclusion

The Maeda, under Toshiie, Toshinaga, and Toshitsune, accomplished what few other daimyo could. Between 1581 and 1640, an era of great insecurity, they built the largest domain outside the Tokugawa house lands. That they were able to preserve this vast property they owed to their astute exercise of military skill and political wits.

Political and military power in Kaga, Noto, and Etchu was splintered at the time of Toshiie's arrival. Fragmented authority substantially reduced the potential for concerted local opposition to Maeda rule. Toshiie and Toshinaga successfully dealt with hostile neighbors through a combination of military strength and adroit political maneuvering. The Maeda and their allies defeated Uesugi, Sassa, Yamaguchi, and Niwa. Toshiie maintained a studied neutrality while Hideyoshi removed Shibata Katsuie.

The Maeda negotiated a successful relationship with each of the day's leading generals, Oda Nobunaga, Toyotomi Hideyoshi, and Tokugawa Ieyasu. They preserved their fief during the reigns of Hideyoshi and the first Tokugawa shoguns, when most daimyo houses typically forfeited at least part of their domains or were transferred to new locations.

Political astuteness saved the domain from possible confiscation or reduction on several occasions. Foremost in this effort was the Maeda's policy of seeking to explain their position to the Bakufu and resolve dis-

---

*The castle at Toyama was maintained throughout the Edo period. In 1639 the significance of Daishōji castle was apparently reduced. Whether or not it deserved to be called a castle and its surrounding area a castle town, as some contemporaries did, is debatable. There is no doubt that a military encampment remained there. (Heki, [*Kaitei zōhō*] *Kanō*, p. 523; *Kaga shi shi*, 720–23.)

† There were changes in the relatively small scattered holdings of the Bakufu and other daimyo within Kaga, Noto, and Etchu in later years, but these were not significant. The only loss of territory was when 18 villages in the Hakusan region became Bakufu territory (*tenryō*) in 1664 after all attempts to settle a boundary dispute between the Kaga and Fukui domains failed. Thereafter the territorial integrity of the domain was successfully maintained well into the 19th century, until after the Meiji Restoration.

putes in a peaceful fashion rather than challenging Tokugawa military power. The creation of branch fiefs ensured that the domain would not be lost for lack of a suitable heir and helped the Maeda maintain additional fortifications. Within domain councils the Maeda kept open the option of outright opposition, suggesting that they and other daimyo still saw themselves as autonomous lords.

While dealing with these problems, the Maeda also responded to other, nonmilitary issues. Ultimately, preserving the domain depended as much on the successful management of its people and resources as it did on the astute management of relations with the major military figures of the day. The institutions for ruling a domain in wartime proved ill-suited to the demands of local administration in the dawning era of peace. New means were required to secure a tranquil domain and to create an adequate financial base for its administration. Such institutions developed gradually through trial, error, and much experimentation. It is to a consideration of this process that we now turn our attention.

Chapter 3

Kaga Land Surveys

More than any other policy, the Taikō kenchi is treated as though the emerging state actually possessed the authority to intrude into the domestic affairs of each domain. Surveys were implemented in Hideyoshi's own domains beginning in 1583, and he presumably conducted them nationwide thereafter. At the highest level, they represent the dawn of a new kind of national authority, one that stemmed from a single figure who held powers so great that he could bend even the most entrenched and hostile daimyo to his will in the administration of their domains. On this interpretation, Hideyoshi was far more than a leader primus inter pares; it celebrates a man who possessed truly national administrative authority.

There is some confirmation of this picture. Survey documents in many parts of Japan do show some similarity, evidence for many that they reflect nationally standardized procedures. And indeed many of these documents are very impressive on their face: they contain much detail, the measurements appear to be precise, and the assessments seem to be based on differences in soil fertility. These characteristics add to the impression that they were compiled in compliance with Hideyoshi's specific orders and resulted from actual investigations by his designated surveyors.

The broad geographic and social impact ascribed to surveys makes a discussion of their use in Kaga a logical preface to an examination of the domain's institutional growth and its sources. The domain's survey methods developed for the most part in the first period of institutional evolution, 1581–1600. Only minor refinements took place during the second period, 1600–1626, the years in which the most systematic survey efforts were made.

Kaga's Earliest Land Surveys

Assessing the impact of land surveys is largely a technical question. If surveys can be found adequate to the tasks scholars have assigned them, and if they were implemented in accord with central directives, the case for an effective national authority would be strengthened, as would the case for rapid social, political, and economic change at the behest of Japan's late-sixteenth- and early-seventeenth-century hegemons. If not, we have evidence of more decentralized foci of change and a relatively gradual shift in policies that were more in tune with local conditions.*

Kaga's Earliest Land Surveys

Considering how important land surveys were in determining the tax base, measuring fiefs granted to retainers, and establishing han control over villages, it is surprising that scholars have only recently devoted substantial energies to the study of Kaga han's early land surveys.[1] This neglect is even more surprising given the emphasis scholars place on their social and political significance in the development of characteristically early modern institutions.

The common assessment is that Kaga's land surveys were conducted in accord with Toyotomi Hideyoshi's Taikō kenchi.[2] Less commonly stressed is the evidence that land surveys were undertaken by an emissary of Oda Nobunaga in 1581 or 1582.[3] In either case, the predictable conclusion is that the Kaga land surveys fit the "classic" Taikō kenchi pattern: they recorded the size of each field in a village, based on actual measurements by the domain officials; grade of the field, based on a thorough investigation of its yields; the field's official assessed value, based on its size and grade; and the name of the landholder.[4]

As James McClain puts it in his study of Kanazawa, Kaga han's castle town:

The Maeda daimyo acted to prevent the enfeoffed retainers from putting down permanent roots in the countryside. The opening move was a set of cadastral sur-

---

*The various terms used in the documents describing the amount of land in a village and arriving at its assessed value—*kenchichō, mizuchō, nawauchichō, kanchō*—clearly cannot be narrowly understood as indicating a detailed measurement by domain officials. Likewise the term *kenchi* had a broad meaning, not a narrow and technical one. It referred to a variety of different processes used to determine land area and value. That fact, as we shall see, has important implications for our understanding of the role of "surveys" in Kaga domain and their relationship to national survey edicts. It is with some misgiving, then, that I continue to refer to "land survey" or "survey documents" in the pages that follow. I use these terms as synonyms for land investigations. By using "survey," I do not wish to imply the use of the kind of procedures commonly associated with the Taikō kenchi or any similar survey.

veys. . . . As elsewhere, the cadastral surveys in Kaga domain represented the daimyo's claim to ultimate proprietary authority within the domain and demonstrated his right to intervene in the affairs of his vassal's fiefs. Beyond this, the surveys also created status distinctions between the peasants, who were listed on the survey documents, and the *bushi*, who were carried on the Maeda's roster of fief holders and stipendiaries—a distinction that was reinforced by the sword hunts of the 1580s and 1590s.[5]

Despite the broad acceptance of such propositions, they break down when the Maeda land surveys are examined in the context of Kaga han's institutional development. It is to that task that we now turn.

Since Etchu was under the jurisdiction of Maeda Toshinaga, not Toshiie, throughout most of the domain's first period of institutional development, and since it continued to be treated (at least in the area of our concern) in a distinctive fashion, it is best discussed separately from Kaga and Noto. Nonetheless, both regions had this in common: the evidence for the implementing of nationally standardized land surveys is very weak during the first years of their rule and nonexistent thereafter. Even within one domain the standardization of procedures was not accomplished. In addition, the domain lords did not make use of actual measurements, and the methods employed were incapable of serving some of the purposes commonly associated with land surveys (e.g., the assignment of tenure to individual households and identification of which villagers held legal status as full village members).

Kaga and Noto

Table 1 lists nine early land survey documents for the provinces of Kaga and Noto by date and location.[6] These are the documents that are mustered as proof that central political authority effectively reached into the domain's domestic administrative affairs. But the evidence is severely weakened by three considerations.

First, three of the villages, Haneda, Nagata, and Hayashi, were not part of the Maeda domains at the time. These were not Maeda surveys.

Second, two of the other villages, Mijiro and Notobe Kami, were in the domain of the Chō family. Although the Chō were vassals of the Maeda, their fief predated Toshiie's entry into Noto, and they maintained an unusually high degree of administrative autonomy. That they were the only retainers to have surveyed their own lands independently is one indication of that autonomy.[7] Consequently, the Chō land surveys cannot be considered representative.

Third, three of the four remaining surveys were conducted in 1582,

TABLE I
Early Land Survey Documents of Kaga and Noto, 1581–98

Date	Village and county	Province	Remarks
1581.7.25	Haneda, Nomi	Kaga	Pre-Maeda
1582.3.25	Kokubu, Kashima	Noto	
1582.8.8	Fukuno, Hakui	Noto	
1582.11.20	Kumabuchi, Kashima	Noto	
1583.9.22	Okinami, Fugeshi	Noto	
1591.9.21	Nagata, Nomi	Kaga	Pre-Maeda
1592.9.11	Mijiro, Kashima	Noto	Chō domain
1592.10.1	Notobe Kami, Kashima	Noto	Chō domain
1598.7	Hayashi, Enuma	Kaga	Pre-Maeda

SOURCES: *Kokufu son shi*, pp. 347–48; Oda Kichinojō, *Kaga-han*, pp. 219–21, 224–25; *KHNK*, 1: 387–467; Kigoshi, "Maeda," p. 21 n. 1.

which is too early for an inference of a centrally directed operation. In fact, Hideyoshi was just beginning to survey his own domains by 1583 and had not yet ordered surveys outside his home base. Furthermore, Toshiie did not achieve his rapprochement with Hideyoshi until early spring 1583. Consequently, the only survey that could possibly be related to orders from Hideyoshi is the one conducted in Okinami in 1583. Since the Maeda had already made their own surveys by then, the Okinami survey more likely followed an existing local survey pattern than a new procedure attributable to Hideyoshi's influence.

From the outset, then, the evidence for central initiative in the Kaga surveys is weak. It is still more problematical because the survey documents differ in important ways from the usual format of Taikō kenchi records. Moreover, the Maeda could not have used these surveys to advance the purposes to which Taikō kenchi land registers are said to have been put. Let us examine the Maeda's documents more closely.

The three surveys that can clearly be taken as representative of the earliest Maeda efforts—for Kokubu, Fukuno, and Kumabuchi villages—are not all of a type, suggesting that the Maeda were experimenting with different means of investigating land and determining the tax value of villages. In the Kokubu case, the officials prepared two different records.[8] The first lists the size and grade of each field (but not its type); the second lists the total holdings of each cultivator by land type, the estimated yield for his dry fields, and the estimated yield for the total village area. The yields for dry fields vary a bit from holder to holder but are generally about 1.1 to 1.2 bales (*hyō*) of rice per *tan*. (At this time a bale would have held about 1.5 bushels.) The average official yield for the whole village was about three bales per *tan*. Although field quality was rated (superior, average, inferior, low-grade inferior), there is no indication of a corresponding official yield (*todai, kokumori*) for each grade.

Unlike the Kokubu survey, the Fukuno and Kumabuchi village documents contain no indication of land quality, nor do they estimate a total village yield. Since one of the survey magistrates (*kenchi bugyō*) for Kumabuchi also participated in the Kokubu village survey, this difference is especially interesting. The inconsistency suggests that authorities had not yet determined a specific model for conducting surveys or reporting results.

These surveys were rough and ready, recording rather imprecise measurements. Indeed, they are much like what Japanese scholars call *sashidashi*, that is, survey results reported to the domain by the village. This imprecision is evident in all three documents.

For a start, there is an obvious and gross rounding of the figures in two of the documents. All the entries involving bu in the Kumabuchi and Fukuno surveys are expressed in units of five or ten (15 bu, 20 bu, 25 bu, etc.). Though five bu is not a large area (just under 0.025 acre), in most later documents finer measurements were the rule, not the exception.*

The Kokubu survey cannot be faulted on this count, for it does give odd numbers of bu. In this regard, it is as detailed as the Taikō kenchi registers that are generally considered to be actual measurements.[9] However, this document, like the others, does use rough units of measure for areas that were greater than several bu but smaller than a *tan*. Entries are expressed in units called *dai, han*, and *shō* (literally "large," "half," and "small"), or, respectively, about two-thirds, one-half, and one-third of a *tan*. Local scholars consider the use of such units an indication of estimation and a sign that the documents were not based on actual measurement.[10]

At best, then, these kenchi can be considered approximations of how much arable and residential land the three villages contained. We do not know what steps the surveyors took, if any at all, to gather or verify the data. Indeed, it is probable that the survey magistrates merely drew the documents up from data submitted by village or district representatives.[11]

Though the earliest documents record the names of villagers, they are clearly exceptional. Most extant survey records do not contain this level of detail. They also do not list measurements and land grades for individual

---

*This is true also for later documents in areas of Japan more closely approximating the standard form of Taikō kenchi reporting. Even assuming a precise measurement was made, and the figures were then rounded off, the distortions would have been great. The practice in this era was simply to drop uneven amounts, resulting in a substantial understatement of the area measured. See Brown, "Mismeasure of Land," pp. 134–35.

plots of land. In fact, later evidence indicates that the domain was not at all interested in dealing directly with individual villagers or parcels of land.

The typical survey document for Kaga han notifies the village as a whole of its official assessed area or productive value. The style is simple and straightforward. The 1586 document (*uchiwatashijō*) for Kumabuchi village, for example, reads in total: "Land Survey of Kumabuchi Village in Onomi District, Kashima County. Amount: 8 *chō*, 7 *tan*, 110 *bu*; paddy, dry field, residential lands, all inclusive. Within this area, 6 *tan*, 20 *bu*, is wasteland. Based on a survey of the daimyo's fields as above, this land is conveyed to the villagers as stated. Tenshō 14.4.10. Hashizume Shōemon, Mitamura Sanai, Watanabe Hikozaemon, Tatsukawa Tōnai. To the villagers of Kumabuchi Village in Onomi District."[12] As we see, the document merely states where the village was; how much land there was and what share of that was unproductive; when the document was issued; and who the survey magistrates were. (For another example, see Fig. 1.)

Based on these documents, the argument that the domain was at this point following a central directive to make field-by-field measures and record the names of cultivators in the registers is untenable. There is no concern here to confirm or establish the cultivator of the land as the legally responsible taxpayer or to define a legal class position for any families. These documents provide no evidence that the domain authorities saw the early surveys as a device to list villagers and distinguish them from warriors and townsmen. The surveyors' concern was simply to establish a tax base for each village.

The Kumabuchi document is the one instance in which we can compare the results of a later survey with an earlier, more detailed register. From a look at the survey of the village in 1582, it is clear that the estimates for that year formed the basis for calculating the village's new (1586) assessed value: the 1586 total of 8 chō, 7 *tan*, 110 bu, is only five bu greater than the 1582 total. Plainly, despite strong evidence that the 1582 document was a rough estimate of the size of the village's taxable lands, domain surveyors did not conduct an actual measurement of Kumabuchi village in 1586 but relied on the earlier estimate. And they continued to rely on estimates. (The fact that typical survey documents make no effort to determine precisely who was responsible for each plot of land raises the question of why villagers' names appear in the earliest reports. Apparently the listing of the size of individual landholder or cultivator fields was simply a convenient way to label each field. This helped ensure that all fields were included in a reasonably comprehensive estimate of the village tax base.)

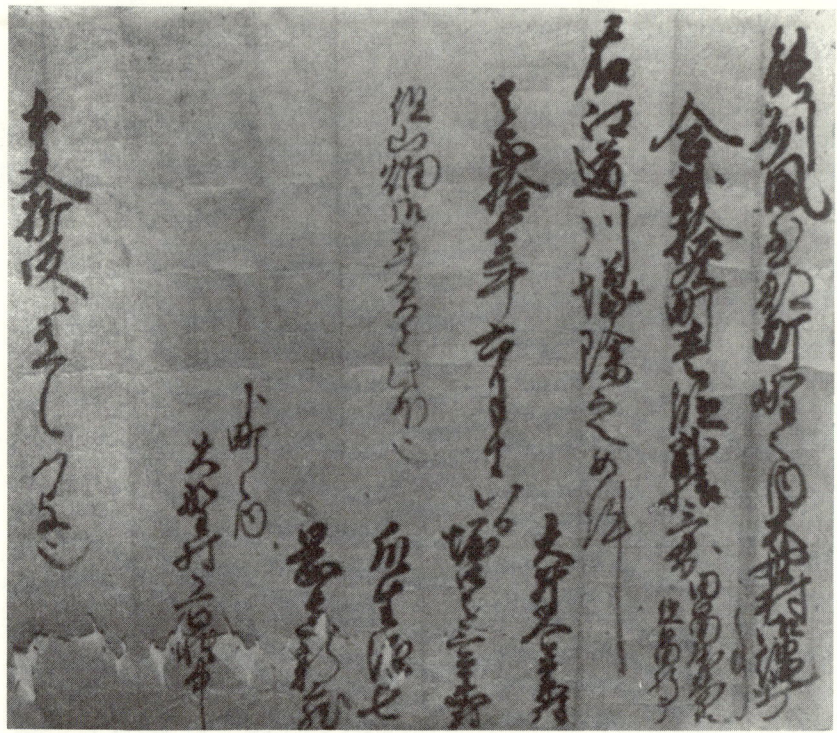

Fig. 1. A typical land survey report from Kaga. Note that this constitutes the entire report. Unlike the field-by-field ledger book one associates with surveys, this document simply reads: "Survey Report of Noto Province, Fugeshi County, Ōno Village in Machino (district): Total 29 *chō*, 1 *tan*, 23 *bu* paddy, dry fields, and residential land combined (however, dry field area adjusted by *ori*). The preceding is reported exclusive of irrigation streams, roads, rivers, and tumuli. Tenshō 17.6.18. However, the annual tax on mountain dry fields is assessed separately." It carries the signatures of four surveyors and is directed to the villagers (*hyakushō*). Source: *WSS*, 2, "Shashin" p. 10, no. 22.

The documents discussed so far come from the very earliest surveys and represent the Maeda's attempt to assert authority in their new domains by establishing the tax base of their holdings. Throughout the early years of their occupation of Kaga and Noto, they repeatedly conducted investigations to this end. Their efforts were particularly intensive, though not demonstrably comprehensive, in 1582–83, 1586, and 1589; a similar effort may have been made in 1591. The surveys of 1586 and 1589 were probably more complete than those of 1582–83.[13]

Carrying out land surveys at this point in the domain's history represented a substantial challenge. The potential for local opposition was, of course, a constant threat. But perhaps more important, the military demands on Toshiie were a source of disruption. For example, he probably intended to make a complete domain-wide investigation in 1582 but had to interrupt the process to concentrate on battles in Etchu and Omi.[14] In any case, major battles certainly impaired investigations in two ways. First, men who might have conducted surveys were shifted to military or other administrative duties. Second, domestic administration had to function smoothly enough to prevent popular disturbances that might interrupt the revenue flow and, in the extreme, force Toshiie to fight simultaneously on the domestic front, too.

With these considerations in mind, Toshiie's absences from the domain prompted a conservative use of surveys. Returning from Omi early in 1583, he suspended surveying while he was out of the domain. Toshiie ordered that only lands lost from cultivation be surveyed, and that they were to be investigated promptly. Toshiie indicated that when he returned again, he would renew investigations throughout the domain.[15]

What is noteworthy about Toshiie's actions is that they occurred despite the fact that surveys were estimates and probably based largely on reports from the villages. His caution indicates that *any* reporting of land values generated tensions between the new administration and its subjects. The conflict was inherent in the relationship between the administration and those taxed, and not a function of new, more precise techniques based on actual measurement.*

Etchu

The 1586 and 1589 surveys can be considered "domain-wide" only in the sense that they covered Toshiie's holdings in Kaga and Noto. Several sources report that there was a domain-wide survey in 1591, but documentation is very limited—too sparse to verify that on-site investigations were

---

*The argument for the rigor of the Taikō kenchi often offers up the threat of peasant opposition as proof of their accuracy and thoroughness. I would argue that any improvement in reporting, even if not especially comprehensive or precise, has the potential of generating opposition. Opposition may even be more likely if methods are not precise and consistent, thereby introducing a strong element of arbitrariness into the procedure. The fact of arbitrary and inaccurate official estimates of land area often led villagers throughout Japan to remeasure their villages and use their own calculations to assign land rights and taxpaying responsibilities. See, for example, the cases of Echigo and Hiroshima domain in Aono, *Nihon kinsei warichisei shi*.

conducted on a broad scale.[16] There is no indication that a survey occurred in Etchu at these times, either.

There are a very few survey documents for villages in Maeda Toshinaga's domains in Etchu. His early surveys appear even more sporadic than those of his father. They also reflect a somewhat different type of investigative process than Toshiie's.[17] Toshinaga initiated independent efforts to establish his authority in Etchu and to define his tax base.

Toshinaga, too, had not yet standardized survey procedures. Extant documents show much variation in content and format. None suggest that his practices were modeled in any way on Hideyoshi's. Some of the documents, such as this one, for Yanohō village, in 1585, are very much like the Kumabuchi report: "Paddy, dry field, and residential land together total 9 *chō*, 9 *tan* small, 48 *bu*. The above conveyed fields are correctly measured as stated, exclusive of irrigation streams, roads, and tumuli. Tenshō 13.9.12. Morikawa Zen'uemon; Hashizume Shōzaemon; Saitō Kyūemon. To the villagers of Yanohō Village in Himi County."[18] The only difference between the two documents is the specifying of the parts of the village that were excluded from taxation. (This is the first example of a practice that became common in later surveys throughout the domain.) As with many of the surveys in Kaga and Noto, the use of the relatively coarse measuring unit "*tan* small" suggests that the stated area was not based on an actual measurement.[19]

Other records depart from the Kaga-Noto style. A 1585 report for Kurabone village lists dry fields separately from paddy and residential lands,[20] implying two rates of assessed value or some other special consideration given to different types of fields. Documents from six years later show a further departure from typical Kaga and Noto surveys; they indicate yield estimates as well as area specifications. It is especially interesting that yields per *tan* are not uniform, as they are in the post-1583 Kaga and Noto records. A 1591 survey for Higashi Ebisaka includes an estimated yield of 2 bales (*hyō*), 1 *to*, 3 *shō*.* A document for Horita village for the following year not only includes a yield estimate but breaks the land into two classifications, superior and inferior.[21] The yield for superior fields was 5 bales, 8 *shō*, that for inferior fields 3 bales, 2 *shō*. Both documents indicate that the yield estimate was based on an actual measurement ("*shōzuke*"). The documents were issued in the ninth lunar month (October–November by the modern calendar), well into the harvest season, so it is possible the yields were based on harvest samples.

*"Kamisaka-ke monjo," *Etchū Shidan* 28 (March 1964): 53. One *to* is a tenth of a koku; one shō is a hundredth.

Assuming this was the case, the data confront us with a puzzle. The disparity between the yield estimates of the two villages is extremely large, large enough to suggest that measuring units had not yet been standardized. If a bale comprised five *to* in both cases, as it did in Kaga and Noto at this time, the yield for Higashi Ebisaka would have been 1.13 koku per *tan*; inferior land in Horita would have produced 1.52 *koku*, and superior fields 2.58 koku. The latter figure is far too high to be reasonable if it was based on either of the two measuring boxes commonly employed at the time, the *kyōmasu* and the *tonoko masu*; yields of that magnitude were not reached until the eighteenth or nineteenth century. Furthermore, it is unlikely that one village's inferior land would produce so much more than the overall yield in a nearby village in the same plain. If, however, the figure for Horita was based on the three-*to* bale used in the very early surveys of Noto, the yields would be reasonable and more comparable to the Higashi Ebisaka yield.* In any event, the variation in stated yields suggests a lack of standardized measures, even within a single domain.

The *Tenshōki* (Records of the Tenshō Era) and the *Uchiyama kyūki* (Ancient Records of Mount Uchi), two roughly contemporary compilations, report that a survey of Etchu was made in 1595, and that the province had a total assessed value of 380,300 koku.²² This was the year in which Niikawa county was transferred from Sassa Narimasa to the Maeda. Since the only documents supporting this report come from Niikawa county, it appears that the new lords simply investigated the area they had acquired and added the findings to existing records for the other three Etchu counties.†

The 1595 Etchu survey, like the early Maeda surveys in general, was probably not based on actual measurements. All four of the extant Niikawa documents bear the same date and were signed by the same four magistrates.²³ It was impossible to survey four villages with a total assessed value of 750 koku or more in a single day. That these surveys were based on estimates is further implied by the general failure to specify any area of land smaller than one *tan*. Units of measure as small as one bu were used in only one instance.‡

---

* One additional point concerning these yields: none of them, whether based on a five-*to* bale or a three-*to* bale, is close to the final official yield estimate of 1.5 koku per *tan* (360 bu) established in the early-17th-century surveys of Etchu. Only at that time, years after the implementing of the Taikō's survey policies, were procedures standardized.

† A tally sheet of the putative yield and taxes for 14 villages in the Himi area was compiled exactly one month before the Niikawa survey documents were issued (see *Himi shi shi*, pp. 1176–77). This document may have been part of a recalculation of the putative yield for all of Etchu.

‡ Akigashima village (*TKSS*, pp. 392–93). To be sure, these documents could have simply

68   CONTROLLING LAND

Viewed as a whole, the early Etchu documents show no evidence of the use of procedures akin to those employed in the Taikō kenchi. They do not record the size of individual fields or villagers' names. Procedures before 1596 were unsystematic; the format and content of the documents varied considerably. Units of measure were not standardized. Survey practices appear to have been based on local custom or, before the Keichō survey, (1604–6), even the practices of individual survey teams. Through this time, evidence of central authority in the surveys is nonexistent.

The Early-Seventeenth-Century Surveys

The procedures for investigating land were systematized during the first decades of the seventeenth century. In basic outline, the procedures employed in Etchu during the survey of 1604–6 and in Kaga and Noto in 1616 and 1620 set the pattern for all later surveys. However, this pattern in no way fits the one that historians take as standard. There was still no sign of direct central influence on the domain's methods or the intent of the surveys. Despite some refinements in presentation, the documents of the period bore a strong resemblance to the earlier ones. They do not, for example, list individual villagers and fields. There are also further indications that no actual measurements were taken.*

The Keichō Survey (1604–6) of Etchu

The Keichō survey marks the first verifiable general survey of the four counties of Etchu. (As noted, no documents have been discovered to confirm that the whole of Etchu was surveyed in 1595, as reported in the *Tenshōki* and the *Uchiyama kyūki*.) It also marks the last one. Consequently, changes introduced in Kaga and Noto during the Genna surveys of 1616 and 1620 (notably the 300-bu *tan*) were never implemented in Etchu. Etchu maintained its own practices until the abolition of domains after the Meiji Restoration. The units of measurement for arable land and yields were never fully standardized within the whole of Kaga domain.

---

been put in final form and signed on the same day. In the absence of more information on how and when the "survey" was conducted, the most we can make of the fact that the documents bear the same date and seals is that it tends to reinforce the other evidence that surveyors did not make actual measurements.

*The "atypicality" of these documents places scholars who still hold that standard styles of land surveys were the norm in Kaga in an awkward position. They must argue that these simple survey registers were based on standard procedures but the documents for the general surveys of the 17th century on which they were based have not survived. See Hara, *Kaga-han*, p. 91.

The Keichō survey was well organized. Niikawa county was investigated in 1604 by four teams of four men each. The groups that evaluated the other counties in the succeeding years varied in size from three to six members, but each county was examined by more than one team.[24] Their findings became the basis for later surveys where we find changes in a village's assessed value often framed as being "in addition to the assessed value [*taka*] of the tenth year [of Keichō]."[25] In other words, subsequent changes in village assessments were made explicitly as additions to or subtractions from the values recorded in the Keichō surveys.

At least 20 originals and copies of the survey documents from this general survey remain. Most are from Tonami county; the rest are from Himi.[26] Their format is not uniform. Some provide computations of arable land area, as well as the assessed value of the villages; others merely provide the assessed value. Tax rates are given for some villages but not others. The latter all appear to be villages held by landed retainers, where domain officials had no role in determining tax rates.

The Keichō survey marks several important changes in assessment practices in Etchu. Hereafter, with the possible exception of embryonic reclamation projects, documents recorded only the assessed value of a village; area measurements were no longer recorded. The use of distinct entries for various grades of land, seen rarely in earlier documents, was discontinued completely, not to be revived until the Meiji land surveys and land tax reform.[27] The assessed value of a village, excluding reclamation projects in progress, was reported in a single total. Furthermore, this total was no longer expressed in bales of rice (*hyō*), but for the first time in koku.*

The Keichō survey also confirmed the size of the *tan* used in survey measurements and the official yield estimate (*todai, kokumori*). The *tan* was set at 360 bu. The assessed value of the villages was computed by multiplying its taxable area and the flat official yield of 1.5 koku per *tan*. This formula, too, remained constant throughout the Tokugawa period.

Finally, the imposing of a flat yield rate was new. In some of the earliest documents, rates varied with the quality of the land, and in no cases did these correspond to the 1.5-koku standard ultimately employed. By 1598 parts of Etchu had converted to the rate used in Kaga and Noto—three

---

*The 1613.7.25 survey of Hinata village again uses bales and also provides both area and assessed value (*Himi shi shi*, pp. 1184–85). In both these matters it departs from procedures established in the Keichō survey. Despite such rare variations, the Keichō survey procedures seem to be standard. The concern to collect taxes wholly in rice became evident only as the domain sold more and more rice on the national market. Rice exports increased substantially after the Osaka campaigns, and it is in this period that officials strengthened tax collections in rice. We will return to this point in Chap. 8.

bales (of five *to* each) per *tan*, the equivalent of 1.5 koku per *tan*.²⁸ The Keichō survey spread the rate to the whole of the province. All later surveys of wasteland and reclamation projects also used this rate.*

These surveys, like those of the Tenshō era, were almost certainly not based on actual measurements by domain officials. For one thing, many survey documents were signed on the same day by the same survey crew. This is true of the records for Sono, Kurabone, and Man'o villages (dated 1605.12.1), and for five villages in Tonami (1605.12.4). One set of officials also surveyed both Kurakawa and Nakamura villages, and the documents appear to bear the same date. Since it took at least a week to measure a village, the magistrates in these cases clearly could not have made a complete survey themselves.†

For another thing, the survey teams could not possibly have covered all the villages in a county in just one year. Take Niikawa county, for example. That county, as we saw, was surveyed in one year by four teams of four men each. How many villages this involved is unknown, but we do know that Niikawa contained 837 villages in 1731,²⁹ and that some number of new villages were created by an administrative redefinition of boundaries and major land reclamation projects during the seventeenth century.

Assuming the number of villages had grown by 25–30 percent since 1604,³⁰ the surveyors would have had to measure 600 villages, or 150 for each team. Making the very optimistic assumption that it took only five days to measure a village, each crew would have had to work nonstop for 750 days, over two years. They could not possibly have taken actual measurements within the one-year period in which the investigation reportedly took place.

Moreover, it is unlikely that such a lengthy and intensive effort, which would surely have disrupted planting, weeding, and harvesting, and probably damaged crops as well, could have been conducted without sparking widespread complaints, if not outright opposition. Yet no evidence of complaints exists. Under the circumstances, the only reasonable conclusion is

---

*Kaga and Noto had converted to a five-*to* bale when the authorities began issuing land tax receipts in 1588 (Kigoshi, "Maeda," p. 25; Takazawa, "Tenshō-ki nengu san'yōjo," p. 723). The appearance of this rate in Etchu in 1598 is likely linked to Maeda Toshinaga's appointment as daimyo. The three surveys cited above were made a few months later (Heki, *Kanō dokushi nempyō*, p. 289).

† *Himi shi shi*, pp. 1181–82. One of the "surveyors" of Sono, Kurabone, and Man'o was in Osaka! (*Fukuoka chō shi*, pp. 1050, 1143, 1231–22.) A week is a very optimistic estimate of the time needed to complete a survey. Wakabayashi, *Kaga-han no nōchi sokuryō*, pp. 44–56, transcribes the diary of a survey magistrate assigned to Uchihisumi village in 1799. The magistrate was preceded by a village group chief (*tomura*), who made appropriate preparations for the official inspection. Even so, the magistrate spent eight days in the village. It is reasonable to conclude that the early Maeda surveys, for which we have no evidence of advance preparation, took somewhat longer, perhaps 10 days or more.

that domain surveys were based on estimates, not actual measurements of each village by independent domain surveyors.

The Genna Surveys (1616, 1620) of Kaga and Noto

The Genna 2 survey (1616) was conducted in Nomi, Ishikawa, and Kahoku counties of Kaga, and the Maeda lands in all four of the Noto counties; the Genna 6 (1620) survey was conducted in the Noto counties alone.[31] Enuma county in southern Kaga province may not have been surveyed on either occasion.*

Before embarking on the first of these investigations, the han promulgated its first formal regulations on land survey policy. Issued in the summer of 1616, the edict's major provisions may be summarized as follows:[32]

1. Henceforth, one tan was to consist of 300 bu, not 360.

2. Rivers, irrigation streams, and roads were to be excluded from measurement.

3. Recently reclaimed land was to be included in the total village assessment and treated the same as long-cultivated fields (*honden*). Any previous full or partial tax exemption on such fields no longer obtained; they were to be taxed at the full rate levied by the domain or landed retainer.

4. Lands not cultivated for a long time were also to be surveyed and recorded.

5. The surveyors' expenses in the field, except for the cost of their firewood and horse feed, were the domain's obligation, not the villagers'. Villagers offering gifts and surveyors who accepted them were to be punished.

6. The surveyors were to make estimates of the crop yields (presumably by test sampling, *bugari*) and if the yields were not properly reflected in the current tax rates, the tax rates were to be revised.

7. The survey crews were also to investigate and adjust the miscellaneous taxes of each village.

This was standardization of sorts—but only of policy, not of methods. Indeed, two striking aspects of the Genna regulations are the lack of any prescribed techniques for measuring land and recording data, and the failure to mention any purpose other than assessing the potential of villages to pay taxes. The regulations reveal no interest in the landholdings of individuals, no intent to define who was a villager and who was not, no effort

---

*At least there is no indication of such a survey in secondary sources, nor have survey documents from this period come to my attention. Although pre-Maeda documents are not extant, the fact that the todai for Enuma and Nomi counties was set at 1.7 koku per *tan*, rather than the Maeda's standard 1.5 koku, suggests that earlier surveys were used to assess the value of the villages within their borders.

to evaluate the relative value of individual fields, no interest in defining grades of land based on distinctive yield (*kokumori*), or any other broad purpose of the sort widely attributed to land surveys.

To learn more about the methods of valuation and the degree to which they were standardized, we must turn to the survey documents themselves. The Genna documents, like most of those discussed already, are simply written. No area measurements appear at all. The only information given is the total assessed value of the village, expressed in koku; the assessed value of specially exempted lands such as domain warehouses and facilities, temples, and tax-free land for certain commoner officials; the amount of permanent wasteland; and, in some cases, the village tax rate. (As was apparently true in Etchu, the tax rate was recorded only for lands directly taxed by the daimyo.[33])

In format, they resemble the Etchu surveys, and as in those surveys, they mark the transition to measuring assessed value in koku. Also as in the Etchu surveys, the documents for several villages were signed on the same day by the same officials. In Kashima county, for example, one crew signed four surveys on 1616.10.26.[34] In the same county, on 1620.12.28, one team signed five surveys, and another signed six.[35] Similar phenomena are evident in varying degrees in Hakui, Fugeshi, and Suzu counties. Calculating the time required to complete an actual measurement of the villages in one county, as we did for Niikawa county, yields similar results for most of the counties in Kaga and Noto. In the case of the 1616 survey, the likelihood that domain officials made actual measurements is further reduced by the fact that the surveyors started after the promulgation of the regulations in the summer of 1616.

Two additional considerations reinforce the impression that Kaga's land surveys differed substantially from the standard Taikō kenchi models. One of these, the system of communal land tenure called warichi, will be examined more fully in a later chapter. For present purposes it is sufficient to note that under this system, records of who farmed what piece of land were managed by the village, and that no one had a right to farm the same piece of land in perpetuity. Though a family generally retained its status as full-fledged cultivators in the village, the cultivation rights for a given piece of land were reallocated periodically by the village acting under its own authority. The very existence of this system indicates that the domain itself had no interest in determining who cultivated a particular plot.*

---

*The first explicit sign of domain interest in regulating landholding was the prohibition of land sales in 1615, just before the Genna surveys of Kaga and Noto. Even this regulation did not set rules for determining ownership or land use rights.

Kaga Land Surveys

The other confirming evidence is found in later, detailed descriptions of the domain's survey procedures. There are no seventeenth-century prescriptions for making measurements. The first description of measuring techniques appears in a manual called "Kenchikata Hisho," written in the late eighteenth century.[36] Unlike the standard *jūji nawa* method, in which surveyors used crossed ropes (hence the name; the crossed ropes looked like the Chinese character for "ten," pronounced "jū" in Japanese) to measure the length and breadth of individual fields, the procedures detailed here ignored individual fields and measured entire villages.[37] (This broad approach was well known in other parts of Japan, although it was more commonly used, at least in Bakufu territories, to measure large sections of a community rather than the entire village.) Domain survey maps like the one shown in Figure 2 and the documents on which the final survey reports were based clearly indicate that the Kaga surveyors took absolutely no interest in individual landholdings or the registration of individual village families with land use rights. Indeed, only irrigation streams, roads, and the like above a minimum size were measured separately and subtracted from the total taxable village area, so that small footpaths and water courses, though unfarmable, were included in the taxable total.

There is good reason to suppose that when Kaga surveyors did any measuring at all, they followed these procedures. For one thing, although "Kenchikata Hisho" mentions some alternative methods (e.g., how to measure circles), they were dismissed as over-fastidious. There is no evidence in that work or in any of the other detailed handbooks of local administration I examined of a major shift away from past practices.

Furthermore several of the procedures employed when "Kenchikata Hisho" was written were also used in late-sixteenth- and early-seventeenth-century Kaga. For example, all land was formally valued at 1.5 koku (in the earliest surveys, three bales) or 1.7 koku (in the case of Nomi and Enuma counties) per *tan*.[38] Adjustments for lower quality land were extremely limited, restricted to certain categories of dry fields. There was no recognized variation in the quality of paddy.

Even many categories of dry field were treated as paddy, at least by the mid-seventeenth century and probably earlier. The 1659 survey regulations ordered that "dry fields planted in paper mulberry, mulberry, tea, hemp, ramie, greens with edible leaves and stalks, and daikon are to be measured as paddy."[39] Only dry fields exclusively producing wheat, coarse grains, red beans, soybeans, other beans, and rapeseed were to be treated as lower quality land.

For dry fields subject to an adjustment, too, the practice remained un-

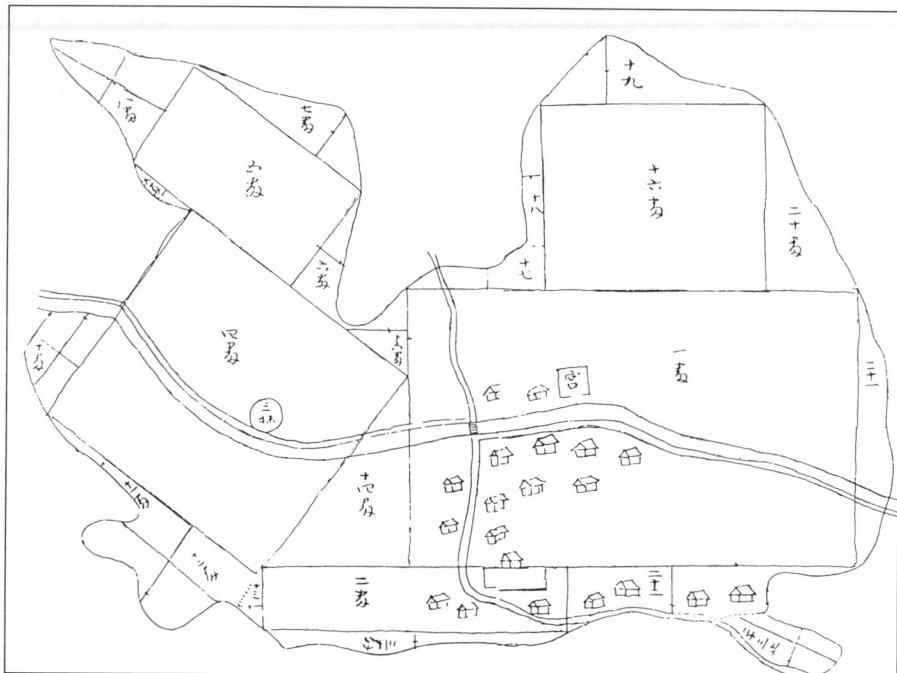

Fig. 2. A Kaga domain survey map. Note the typical division of the village into large sections for measurement. Redrawn from "Kenchikata Hisho," a late-eighteenth-century manuscript in the Ume no Yon section, Kawai monjo Collection, Toyama University Library, Toyama.

changed throughout the Tokugawa era: the formal value (putative yield) per *tan* was not altered; the adjustment was made by manipulating the field's measured area. This method was called *hatake ori*. Earliest written indications of the practice appear in 1589, but it was probably used earlier.[40] *Hatake ori* proportionately adjusted the area of dry fields to the value and yield of rice paddy. For example, if a dry field was thought to be half as productive as paddy, its area would be reduced by half. That half was then added into the village total, to be multiplied by the official per-*tan* yield. This procedure was clearly better suited to the wide-area surveys described in "Kenchikata Hisho" than to field-by-field measurements, which would have required more calculations. What is more, its consistent use from the domain's formative years through the nineteenth century suggests a continuity of other survey procedures.

The deliberate efforts to simplify the survey process in the early years are consonant with the widespread use of the methods described in "Kenchikata Hisho"; they permitted the measurement of very large segments of each village. They further reinforce the impression that Kaga surveys were not based on the standard model.

Kaga in National Perspective

The Maeda's investigations of land value between 1582 and 1620 reveal a substantial amount of experimentation before procedures were standardized. Nonetheless, they fulfilled three important functions of conventional land surveys:

1. They served to calculate the value of the domain as a whole. The domain authorities dutifully reported their figures to the central political authorities (in koku) as a basis for the assessment of extraordinary levies.

2. They served to allocate fiefs to major landed retainers and to calculate their contributions to the domain's military endeavors.

3. They served to record the value of the land against which taxes would be levied and to clarify village boundaries where they affected taxable land.

By all accounts, these investigations were fairly comprehensive. There is no indication that any lands were exempted from study. Though hidden fields may have been a problem within villages, no retainer's land, temple land, or shrine land was exempted.

But there are also significant differences between Kaga's land surveys and the standard model. Substantial evidence indicates that actual measurements were not made. We can speculate that actual measures were employed in spot-checking reports of village value, but there is no evidence to confirm this. The domain showed no interest in tying individual families to specific plots of land. Domain authorities did all they could to simplify the evaluation of land grades, ranking all but a few categories of dry field at 1.5 koku per *tan*. Even then, the koku measure itself was for many years a mere convention, employed in formally stating domain value; it did not become the standard unit of land value for local administrative purposes until the seventeenth century. Furthermore, when the "national" 300-bu standard was adopted, only Kaga and Noto ultimately took it up; Etchu went its own way through the entire early modern era.

These variations did not come from ignorance of Hideyoshi's wishes. Maeda Toshiie served as one of Hideyoshi's survey magistrates in Dewa, in 1590.[41] Consequently, they have some important implications for understanding early modern Japanese history at both the local and the national level.

First, Kaga clearly made no attempt to follow a nationally standardized model. Nor is there any evidence that Hideyoshi or the Bakufu tried to encourage the domain to follow the Taikō kenchi or the Tokugawa house procedures. Even if we were to assume that there was such an effort, we must conclude that, in Kaga domain at least, it failed miserably. The central authorities lacked the will, and probably the means, to enforce such a policy. Any attempt to enforce this kind of administrative order nationwide through the use of attainder would have represented an attack on all daimyo simultaneously. This would have entailed great political risk for marginal gains in resources.*

A second conclusion is that the kinds of surveys conducted in Kaga, even when they were actual measures (as a number of them, especially in later years, were), could not have served many of the purposes that scholars have supposed. The absence of any widespread records linking individual households with specific pieces of land indicates that domain surveys were not aimed at establishing land tenure, reallocating lands by forcing the breakup of extended family estates, or defining the members of a peasant class distinct from the samurai and townsmen classes. This fact encourages a reconsideration of how such policies were articulated, who participated in defining tenure rights, and where the initiative for defining them originated. It also suggests a need to reassess the sources of class separation.

Third, Kaga's survey procedures call into question the nature of the land tax system they were meant to support. Orthodox images stress the precision of surveys and their use of actual measurements in arguing for a more rigorous assessment of land taxes. At least in Kaga domain, actual measurements generally were not made in either the early or the province-wide attempts to evaluate the land tax base. Nonetheless, domain authorities recognized that land investigations were potentially disruptive of public order. From this perspective, we may ask whether the land tax system was *systematically* more exact and rigorous than under earlier forms of surveys. The answer to this question comes below in a discussion of the rate of taxation, but we can already conclude, from the minimal allowance made for different grades of land alone, that the system had significant arbitrary elements.

Persistent Procedural Variations and Limited Standardization Efforts

These considerations not only suggest a need to reevaluate the history of Kaga domain; they open similar possibilities on the national level.

*The political calculus might have been different if hegemons had derived a large share of their income from a regular national tax.

Although a comprehensive evaluation is beyond the compass of this study, let us consider certain evidence from other parts of Japan bearing on some of these issues.

Though some historians acknowledge that there were variations in survey methods, no one suggests they were significant enough to argue against the effectiveness of Hideyoshi's efforts to impose a uniform national standard. Berry, for example, notes that the problem of implementing national standards of measure and the kokudaka system was not fully overcome during Hideyoshi's rule, especially in the domains of independent (*tozama*) lords, but still concludes that "the *kenchi* also served the purposes of Hideyoshi's edicts by providing the daimyo with fairly accurate assessments of domain land, *computed according to universal standards* [emphasis added]."[42]

Assuming for the moment that Berry, Araki, and others are right in concluding that even in the domains of former enemies, Hideyoshi's efforts succeeded, the fact that a number of tozama lords acted autonomously is highly significant. In determining the capabilities of a state, its capacity to carry out its own agenda, precisely this category of local leaders provides the crucial test of state strength. These are the men who might seriously challenge the central authority when their own inclinations differ from those of their superiors. The state can be seen as effective only to the degree that it can consistently gain or compel the cooperation of such locally powerful men. To the extent that any of these local leaders can ignore the state's ordinances, adopting only those that suit their own purposes or tailoring them to their own ends, the state must be deemed ineffective.

In this context, Hideyoshi's ability to limit variations in the name or size of measuring units is a quick but significant indicator of the capability of his state. By definition, without a high degree of uniformity, there can be no claim to effective implementation of a universal standard. More important, if the central authority could not compel the use of uniform standards—value (putative rice yields or cash assessments), length, volume—standards that in themselves did not challenge the local balance of power between daimyo and domain residents, it could hardly coerce the daimyo into carrying out other, more socially disruptive policies often associated with the Taikō kenchi, namely, the restructuring of family holdings, the definition of land use rights, and the separation of warrior from agriculturalist.

Variations in measures of length were common and sustained throughout the early modern era. Standard length under Hideyoshi was, in principle, set at 6 shaku, 3 *sun*; for the Tokugawa lands, it was 6 shaku, 1 *sun*. Yet throughout the seventeenth century and beyond, well after the "standardization" of measures occurred, surveyors in many provinces used measuring rods that were as much as 2 percent to 8 percent off the mark, from 6 shaku long to 6 shaku, 6 *sun*. In one case, the measuring rod was a mere 4 shaku, 8 *sun*, fully a third less than the "standard" length.⁴³

Equally revealing of the limits of Hideyoshi's state was the variation in the units used to calculate official land values. Conventional interpretations stress the Taikō kenchi's introduction of the koku as a new, uniform standard of assessed value and measure of volume for grain payments of land taxes. Yet there is reason to suspect both the significance and the breadth of such a change, reason enough indeed to question whether it was even the specific intent of Hideyoshi or later rulers to create a uniform system of assessment based on the koku and of tax collection based on rice.

The kandaka system of cash assessments, generally regarded as the predecessor of kokudaka assessments, was not dominant outside the Kanto-Tokaido region. In Kyushu, Shikoku, Chugoku, and at least parts of Hokuriku, taxes had commonly been assessed in rice as well as cash. The Kinai had used rice exclusively. The units of measure were often bales (hyō), but the koku was used in some instances. The much-stressed transition from a cash-based to a crop-based system of assessment was not a radical departure for much of Japan. Consequently, the shift to the koku as a measure of land values would have been a minor change for these regions.⁴⁴

The widespread use of rice assessments after the Taikō kenchi, combined with the insistence on Hideyoshi's intent to impose this form of payment, leads us to expect virtually complete compliance. But this is not the case.⁴⁵ The kandaka system prevailed in at least part of the Bakufu domains through the mid-seventeenth century (again, note the inability to standardize even within a single political jurisdiction); and it was used in one form or another in the Date family's domains of northern Japan throughout the early modern period.⁴⁶

All these examples come from the domains of daimyo who had made their own reputation independent of Oda Nobunaga and Toyotomi Hideyoshi, but Matsumoto domain, which adhered to the kandaka assessments until at least 1613, is a different case altogether.⁴⁷ The daimyo, Ishikawa Kazumasa, left Ieyasu in 1585 to join Hideyoshi's ranks. Hideyoshi gave him Matsumoto domain (in Shinano) five years later. If the current lists of Hideyoshi's surveys in Shinano are correct, his officials had four chances to correct this seeming deviation through resurveys (1590, 1591, 1595, and 1598).⁴⁸ No "corrections" were ever made. Similarly, the Sanada (also in Shinano) and their successors in Ueda han continued to use cash assessments (*kanmon*) after Hideyoshi's survey, and throughout the Tokugawa era.[49]

Equally interesting is an inconsistency in Hideyoshi's orders to his survey magistrates. Hideyoshi ordered that his own survey of Aizu (1590) register lands by their cash value, kandaka, not according to the "new" standard. These instructions apparently were applied not only to Aizu but to all of Mutsu province. It is true that later reports to central authorities, as well as fief investitures, from many parts of this region stated domain values in koku, but that is not to say the measure was used in local administration.[50] That Hideyoshi ordered the use of kandaka in this very recently subjugated territory and did not insist on the conversion to koku indicates a lack of commitment to a uniform national standard.*

This example raises the broader question of how deep the change really was. In a number of instances, the reporting of domain value in koku had no impact on the measure used in the day-to-day administration of land taxes. Kaga, in reports to the central authorities in 1598, used kokudaka to state both the assessed value of the domain and the value of taxes collected.[51] But the kokudaka system was not employed in Etchu until the Keichō investigations and in Kaga and Noto until the Genna surveys, both carried out well after Hideyoshi's death. In assessing the value of land or the taxes due, bales of rice (hyō) were the principal units of measure, a practice that predated the Taikō kenchi. The value of villages near Edo under two *hatamoto* (direct shogunal retainers) was listed in Bakufu documents of the 1640's in kokudaka; but their taxes, even at this late date, were computed on the basis of a variant of the kandaka system.[52] Moreover, there were districts in which neither koku nor kandaka were used on the local level. Satsuma, for example, used *makidaka* (the amount of seed required to plant a given area of land) as a measure of land value. *Karidaka* (the number of sheaves of grain harvested from a given unit of land) was employed in Dewa.[53] Just as in Kaga han, the two systems existed side by side, each employed for discrete purposes.

Survey measurement procedures also varied substantially. Despite Yamamura's assertion that there were only "minor variations in the methods," procedures were never nationally standardized, not even under the Tokugawa shogunate.[54] We have already seen this in Kaga's surveys, but the variations extended well beyond Kaga's borders.

One common image of the transformation wrought in the late sixteenth

---

*This example stands in marked contrast to the case of Satsuma, which is commonly used to demonstrate Hideyoshi's ability to impose his survey standards even in a recently defeated enemy's land.

century is well illustrated by Berry's observation that "in Hideyoshi's period the *sashidashi kenchi* undertaken by local proprietors came to an end.... The paperwork kenchi was a thing of the past."[55] In fact, there are major exceptions to this statement. For example, Matsumoto han surveys were based on reports by villagers until at least 1613. Similarly, although the Satsuma surveys are often treated as examples of former enemies dutifully submitting to Hideyoshi's will, the investigations of Satsuma, Osumi, and Hyūga provinces, undertaken in close association with Hideyoshi's agents, were also sashidashi. The same applies to those of the Date domains. The surveys of much of Tohoku were also apparently sashidashi.[56]

Even where there were on-site inspections, they did not always involve measurements or conform to the standard model. We have already discussed one common variant, the measurement of very large areas that ignored individual fields. The *ikenchi* represented an even more radical variant. In this case no measurement was made at all; the surveyor merely made a visual estimate. In addition, villagers often conducted surveys for their own purposes, in a number of instances clearly avoiding field-by-field measures as the primary basis for the survey.[57] The use of each of these survey types in Bakufu territories, the administrative divisions most likely to conform to "standard" practices, suggests that there was no attempt at full standardization even without the pressure of conducting massive province-wide surveys in very short periods of time. Each type of survey could provide useful data for village and domain valuations without any need for standard survey practices or actual measures by Hideyoshi's representatives or even by domain authorities. In sum, the word "kenchi" referred to a variety of processes and did not have a narrow technical meaning.

In theory, assessments were pegged to expected yields, but it is unclear how those estimates were calculated. Some historians claim that yield figures were based on crop samples, and others that nonagricultural economic activities were considered, too.[58] Still others believe that assessed values bore little relationship to realistic yields. Whatever the case, regional variations in this realm are widely if not universally recognized.

Similarly, yields were in theory matched to soil fertility, but here too there was much variation (see Table 2). Variation was manifested in two ways: (1) the number of different grades of land recognized and (2) the range of values assigned to fields of similar quality. For example, we noted that Kaga domain imputed a uniform yield to all grades of paddy in each county (1.5 or 1.7 koku per *tan*) and made only limited adjustments for dry fields. Among other domains in the Kaga-Noto-Etchu region, the small scattered Noto domain of Hijikata Kazuhiko, a Bakufu retainer, divided

TABLE 2
Range of Official Yields in Six Localities, Late Sixteenth Century

Domain	Paddy		Dry	
	high	low	high	low
Kaga	1.5	1.5	1.5	?
Hijikata	1.6	1.2	0.6	0.18
Hachioji	1.05	0.41	?	?
Yonezawa	1.5	1.1	1.0	0.5
Dewa	3.2	1.6	?	?
Tosa	1.0	1.0	1.0	1.0

SOURCES: Oda Kichinojō, *Ishikawa ken*, p. 320; Yasuzawa, *Kinsei sonraku keisei*, pp. 26–33; *Hansei seiritsu*, p. 493; Kashiwakura, "Tokugawa," pp. 1018–19; Iinuma, *Kokudakasei*, pp. 107–8, 151.

paddy into three grades valued at 1.2, 1.4, and 1.6 koku per *tan*, and three grades of dry field valued at 0.6, 0.4, and 0.18 koku.[59] These and other disparities occurred in a region with economic conditions similar to those of the Maeda domains.

The inconsistency across the country was even greater. Thirteen villages in the vicinity of modern Hachioji, west of Tokyo, classified both paddy and dry field in four grades; the average assessed value for paddy ranged from a low of 0.41 koku per *tan* to a high of 1.05.[60] The range for Yonezawa han's paddy in the early seventeenth century was 1.1 to 1.5 koku; its dry fields were valued at 1.0, 0.75, and 0.5 koku.[61] Superior paddy in many areas was rated at 2.0 koku or more per *tan* in the late sixteenth century. In Echizen, Kai, Yamato, and other areas, Tokugawa-era assessed values ran as high as 3.0 koku.[62] In the far northern mountain villages of Murayama county, in Dewa, where soil fertility should have been low, mid-seventeenth-century superior paddy was rated between 1.6 and 3.2 koku per *tan*. In fact, superior paddy in most villages was valued at 2.7 koku or higher, an extraordinary yield for this period in Japanese history, even in the most productive regions of the country.[63]

The Chōsokabe survey, conducted between 1587 and 1590 (two years after the family's defeat by Hideyoshi), ranked all land at 1.0 koku per *tan*.[64] No distinction in soil fertility was made at this or any later time. The survey continued to form the basis for Tosa assessments even after the Yama'uchi took over the domain under the Tokugawa.

In certain cases authorities may have taken into account the value of a village's nonagricultural products in setting the yield figures. But that hardly explains why a region like Dewa, which was economically less diversified and less commercialized than many other regions, had such an extremely high valuation. Regardless of their origin, valuations unquestionably do not reflect "a thorough and rigorous reassessment of the yield of all paddies in virtually all provinces."[65]

One might argue that uniform survey methods and standards could only be achieved with repeated efforts. Certainly, it would be too much to expect an overnight transformation in the principles of land surveying. Yet there is little evidence that Hideyoshi made any concerted attempt to survey recalcitrant or incompletely transformed domains. In one significant case—Kaga domain's three provinces—he never attempted to conduct surveys himself, and so could not oversee a full conversion to universal standards. In addition, many of the provinces he purportedly surveyed were not resurveyed at all by his agents.

Several scholars have attempted to compile a record of the change to Taikō kenchi. The *Kadokawa Nihonshi jiten*, a 1976 historical dictionary, incorporates data from all major attempts to identify where and when land surveys were carried out. The editors distinguish between surveys seemingly deriving from an autonomous tradition and those thought to have been made at Hideyoshi's orders or by his standards. The latter category includes such cases as Aizu, whose surveys deviated from standards even though conducted under Hideyoshi's orders, as well as cases like Kaga, Noto, and Etchu, which reported domain values to Hideyoshi but used their own measurement procedures and standards. I have made only a very limited attempt to verify the existence of cases similar to Kaga domain. Other cases noted above as not involving actual measurements, and therefore not qualifying as part of the Taikō kenchi as the term is commonly understood, are also counted by the *Jiten* as complying: Shinano, Satsuma, Hyuga, Osumi, Mutsu (including Aizu). The inclusion of these provinces cautions us that statistics computed from this source overstate the degree to which Hideyoshi's orders were followed.[66]

Excluding all eight of these provinces, which clearly did not employ actual measurements, Hideyoshi surveyed only 33 of the traditional 65 provinces of Japan, or about half, between 1583 and 1598. (In contrast to Berry's estimate that he surveyed 20–30 provinces, this base figure is generous.) Furthermore, when we look for evidence of extended efforts to implement uniform standards through resurveys, we find that just 21 provinces were ever investigated more than once under Hideyoshi's orders; and that only 14 of the 21 resurveys took place between 1594, the year commonly taken as marking the standardization of Hideyoshi's survey principles, and his death.* At best, fewer than half the provinces Hideyoshi surveyed were ever

---

*Takayanagi and Takeuchi, *Nihonshi jiten*, pp. 1129–30; Berry, *Hideyoshi*, p. 112. The *Jiten* editors collapse the provinces of Iwaki, Iwashiro, Rikuzen, Rikuchu, and Rikuoku

resurveyed to effect his fully developed methods—rather modest evidence of repeated efforts at standardization.

These calculations assume that none of the surveys or resurveys was undertaken at the initiative of the province's daimyo, and that all surveys of a province in consecutive years were distinct efforts (a very unlikely prospect), not one continuing process. It is worth noting (1) that these computations represent a "best case" for the direct impact of the Taikō kenchi, and (2) that although Hideyoshi purportedly surveyed Shinano four times, he was unable (unconcerned?) to replace kandaka with kokudaka measures of land value—clear evidence against any consistent effort at standardization. In short, this "best case" reading indicates that Hideyoshi made a very incomplete effort not only in attempting to survey all Japan but also in trying to standardize survey procedures in the parts he ostensibly covered.

In addition, these data clarify the great extent to which surveys were privately instituted by daimyo—in 36 provinces, about 55 percent of the country, between 1583 and 1598. If we extend the period of our analysis somewhat, three more provinces were privately surveyed in 1582, another three in 1581, and two more in 1580. Most of these provinces were surveyed more than once, even without Hideyoshi's direct involvement and often before their daimyo allied with him. During the same time period, generals independently initiated surveys in 30 provinces (45 percent of all) that Hideyoshi had not yet surveyed; in contrast, Hideyoshi inaugurated investigations in only 25 provinces not yet surveyed independently by daimyo (a figure that shrinks by seven if we consider evidence back to 1580). The degree of autonomous initiative is also indicated by comparing how many provinces the daimyo and Hideyoshi surveyed each year. As Table 3 shows, private surveys equal or outnumber Hideyoshi's in every year but two. Before Hideyoshi's final campaign against the Gohōjō, the time when survival and pacification were his main preoccupations, private surveys were conducted in 63 instances as opposed to his 49. Many of these took place wholly outside of his sphere of influence.

There are some who hold that autonomous daimyo "tended to conform to Hideyoshi's own guidelines," and imply that his techniques represented a significant improvement over theirs.[67] In my view, this record of independent surveying, combined with the fact that many of the practices involved predated Hideyoshi's use of them, indicates that daimyo were as motivated as he to explore new, more effective survey techniques entirely on their own initiative, without any prodding by Hideyoshi.[68]

(Mutsu) into Mutsu province, and Uzen and Ugo into Dewa province. Sado, Oki, Totomi, and Iki have been treated as separate provinces in the province total.

TABLE 3
Private and Taikō Kenchi, 1583–98

Year	Hideyoshi's surveys	Private surveys	Year	Hideyoshi's surveys	Private surveys
1583	3	6	1591	10	12
1584	6	5	1592	4	5
1585	6	5	1593	2	4
1586	4	5	1594	5	10
1587	6	7	1595	9	9
1588	5	6	1596	3	7
1589	7	14	1597	2	4
1590	12	15	1598	4	5

SOURCE: *Kadokawa Nihon shi jiten*, p. 1130.
NOTE: Surveys in Etchu, Hyuga, Kaga, Mutsu, Noto, Osumi, Satsuma, Shinano, and Tosa have all been treated as private surveys. Surveys of Kaga, Noto, and Etchu listed in the *Jiten* that I have not been able to verify have been eliminated from the count.

The widespread practice of differentiating land grades in the late sixteenth century further supports this picture. It cannot be said to have had its origins in a centrally dictated survey policy, since land was graded in the surveys conducted by Oda Nobunaga and in some of those conducted under the kandaka system of cash assessments.[69]

The question of who initiated changes in survey practices and under what stimulus remains open. Not only was the adoption of the kokudaka system incomplete; even where the change was made, it required more time than is customarily acknowledged. A whole array of different standards and methods continued to be used for estimates of domain value in the late sixteenth century. Old data were sometimes converted to putative yields. In other instances the adoption of putative yields to value domains came first, and their use in local surveys and tax assessment occurred only some time later. Certainly this record is too meager to permit any claim that Hideyoshi established universal standards of measure or land value, too incomplete to support a claim that he standardized survey procedures, and too inadequate as a basis for the claim that somewhat earlier or contemporary independent surveys were markedly less precise than his.[70]

Motives for Diverse Practices

Though in theory domains based assessed values on soil fertility, the variation across regions was so great that other considerations must have guided the rate-setting process. It is not hard to single out political objectives as a major influence.

In a sense, a domain's judgment of its worth was a negotiated contract between Hideyoshi (later, the Tokugawa Bakufu) and its daimyo. The value put on a *tan* of land and the size of the *tan* itself reflected, among other things, the place the daimyo sought in the national hierarchy of lords and in his relationship with the hegemon or Shogun. It is sometimes claimed, for example, that tozama daimyo such as the Yama'uchi set their land values low to avoid having to contribute money to meet the emergency expenses of the hegemon or Shogun.[71] But this was not universally true for tozama lords. Kaga domain's assessed value was exceptionally high. By deliberate decision, the domain increased its apparent wealth.

The high assessed value of Dewa reflected a different political concern. That overvaluation was the result of a Bakufu tax agent's (*daikan*) attempt to maintain the fiction of an earlier assessed value in a district that had experienced a steep drop in cultivated land. In this case the image of continuity was preserved at the cost of a proportionate cut in tax rates to offset the artificially high valuation.[72]

The Dewa example well illustrates the aspect of the land tax system that permitted land values to be so dramatically manipulated. Ultimately, neither the assessed value nor the tax rate, *by itself*, was meaningful. The effect of one on villagers' tax burden cannot be known in the absence of the other. Consequently, villagers might accept high estimates of land value if the accompanying tax rate kept total taxes within a tolerable range.

These facts suggest that the transition to kokudaka, even at the relatively superficial level of domain value, was less related to the nationwide implementation of uniform land survey procedures than to the negotiation of the relations between a given domain and the hegemon or Shogun. Shōken Hyōzaemon, a *hatamoto* and would-be daimyo, shortened his measuring rod to 4 shaku, 8 *sun*, thereby increasing the value of his domain enough to qualify. Similar manipulations occurred throughout the Tokugawa era, at the least in Nambu, Tsugaru, Mito, and Daishōji domains.[73] Conversely, domain lords like the Chōsokabe could conceal some of their actual resources by undervaluing their lands.

Clearly, much more than simple economics was involved in all this. For in principle, anyway, extraordinary exactions were based on domain value. Had economic motives been paramount, every daimyo would have sought to lower the value of his domain to reduce that burden. This is demonstrably not the case, and in the absence of regular national taxation, some daimyo unquestionably viewed the added cost as an acceptable price to pay for some social benefit.

What did they buy for this increase in their own obligations to their overlord? The Dewa daikan's actions reflect samurai society's enormous concern for the public appearance of wealth, prosperity, and effective administration. Increased status was certainly another benefit. Promotion to daimyo rank carried with it not only increased social standing but closer proximity to powerful people. For some daimyo, loyalty to a hegemon could be demonstrated through a willingness to bear increased economic and military burdens. A large daimyo like Maeda Toshiie not only benefited from that perception, but also bolstered his own image as a powerful lord, someone whose needs and opinions coalition leaders and hegemons had to consider in formulating policy and political strategy, someone who might be sought out as a pivotal ally. Regardless of the motivations that underlay a particular domain lord's actions, the kokudaka system allowed daimyo room to maneuver for the status they wanted relative to others and in the eyes of the hegemon.* On the other side, local and varied though the contractual arrangements were, the system created an explicit standard by which hegemons could compute extraordinary levies on daimyo for major construction projects, the support of the imperial household, and military purposes.

In stressing the bilateral nature of the kokudaka system, I do not mean to imply that both parties negotiated from relatively equal positions or that each daimyo was completely free to set his own standard of value.[74] In a number of instances Hideyoshi may have enforced his policies quite effectively. His ability to do so depended on several considerations. The relative power of the parties at any given time conditioned the ultimate measure of domain value; other demands on their energies influenced both their position and their absolute military strength. Much as Hideyoshi may have desired high valuations, especially from recently defeated or newly allied daimyo, the cost of pressing for them could compromise more important objectives.† Hideyoshi accepted a low valuation of Chōsokabe domains in 1587 when he was still trying to subjugate Kyushu. Conversely, he forced Satsuma domain to accept a (nominally) high valuation seven years later, after he had subdued the last of his opponents, the Gohōjō, and had no other major domestic distractions.[75]

Differences in the timing of the transition to the kokudaka system, in

---

*The manipulating of the system for social-climbing purposes suggests that this expression of value carried a momentum of its own. The more that kokudaka became the standard for classifying daimyo wealth and determining obligations to the hegemon or Bakufu, the more likely a lord was to adopt, at least in his relations with other lords, the same standard. Its adoption clarified his position relative to other daimyo.

†Besides the direct incentive of exacting as much as he could from a domain lord, by setting a high valuation Hideyoshi could place additional financial burdens on former enemies and make it more difficult for them to build up a military force great enough to threaten him.

the formulas for assessing value, and in the measuring units used all suggest that assessed values were first and foremost the product of a political dialogue between the daimyo and Hideyoshi. They were not the end result of a device, unilaterally designed by Hideyoshi and systematically imposed throughout the land.[76] The kokudaka system was a key point of articulation between daimyo and their overlords, but it was a double-edged device, subject to manipulation by the daimyo as well as the hegemons.

Hideyoshi's state, in sum, was not what it is held out to be. His public proclamations were grandiose and marked by bombastic rhetoric, but his capacity to compel change was restricted.[77] Though the language of his orders was imperious, and their intent spelled out in detail, he could not overcome the contrary inclinations of many of his subordinate or allied daimyo. He managed to survey only a bare majority of Japan's traditional provinces, and even then, his principles were often thwarted. Old practices remained, new practices were manipulated, and though Hideyoshi clearly commanded more authority than his predecessors, that authority was not great enough to transform domain administration and local society. Kaga's deviation from standard practices was by no means unique.

However much Hideyoshi may have wished to encourage the adoption of a specific method of computing domain value, accomplishing that was, as a practical matter, a secondary concern. As long as daimyo presented a generally acceptable figure, the potential cost of enforcing the ideal standards and actual measurements greatly outweighed the marginal benefits central authorities might have gained. The risks of provoking open daimyo opposition were much too great. These were not limited to outright rebellion. The image of hegemonic authority was also endangered. To create a public issue over enforcement, even if ultimately successful, could seriously undermine the image of a hegemon's unchallenged authority, a tool useful in encouraging compliance even where his will could not be enforced in any final, objective sense.[78] The failure of Hideyoshi's Tokugawa successors to push ahead with the standardization of survey procedures and national surveys indicates that, like him, they were fully cognizant of the marginal gains to be made through such a mass effort.

The imperfect implementation of surveys encourages a reevaluation of the genesis of such great social transformations as the separating of warriors from commoners and the redefining of land tenure. If simple measuring units could not be standardized, more difficult problems like these could not have been solved by central fiat. After all, they have resisted easy solution by modern governments with much stronger state apparatuses than Hideyoshi or the Bakufu commanded. Again, this does not mean that central edicts were without influence, and in some instances Hideyoshi may have forced compliance. But on the whole, important policy decisions were made at the level of the domain and the village, not by the nascent state. The issue of agency is far more open, complex, and subject to subtle influences than we have held it to be.

With this analysis as a backdrop, the following chapters explore the development of the new social and political order in Kaga domain. Clearly its surveys were inadequate to the social tasks with which such investigations have commonly been identified. Yet in Kaga, too, classes were separated, land tenure issues were resolved, and retainers were removed from the land. Events there illustrate both the typical demands that confronted daimyo, samurai, and villager and the local forces that shaped the relationships between village and domain.

Domain administrators faced four key issues: how to create stability within the domain; how to tie villages to domain administrative organs; how to keep samurai loyal and at the same time prevent them from abusing the commoners; and how to raise adequate funds to run the domain. Samurai retainers were preoccupied above all with ensuring a stable and adequate income. Villagers confronted the challenge of protecting themselves from the harsh exactions of the domain and its samurai and securing adequate food, clothing, shelter, and perhaps even a measure of prosperity. Ultimately, daimyo, samurai, and villager each played a role in resolving these trilateral tensions and creating an environment in which all classes had a securer niche than they had had during the turbulent sixteenth century.

Chapter **4**

Land Tenure

Conventional historiography stresses the role of hegemonic policies, especially those of Hideyoshi, in transforming the land tenure system and class relations of late-medieval–early-modern Japan. Through national policies Hideyoshi and the Tokugawa recast man-land relations on a national scale, granted villagers a new measure of tenurial security, whether described as "private" or "serf"-like, and freed them from samurai managerial oversight.

In this chapter I explore how rights over land were distributed between members of the samurai and villager classes in Kaga domain and evaluate how the late-sixteenth- and early-seventeenth-century transformation affected the distribution of these rights. In the process we will explore a form of samurai tenure that was dying out, the broad authority of a landed retainer over his property, as well as the more typically restricted rights of that class of samurai. We will also examine a form of tenure in rural communities that provided one of the foundations of villages as administrative organizations.

Of the whole range of issues—social, political, and economic—that are linked to land rights, I will focus primarily on the question of who determined them and the extent to which they were nationally uniform. I will not attempt to explore the development of class divisions within the village or relationships between landlords and tenants, two prominent themes in Japanese writings on land tenure. Those are large issues that deserve fuller treatment on some other occasion.

Two concepts are central to an evaluation of land tenure. One is usufruct. To what extent does someone with rights in land control the use to which the land is put? Does he have to share the power to determine land-use with others? The other is disposability. What restrictions are there on the ability of an owner to transfer his rights to another? Can he dispose of his land as he wants, or does he have to defer to the wishes of others? When we think of modern property rights, we think of owners having maximum freedom to determine both how the land will be used and how to transmit ownership to other parties.

In terms of these two concepts, samurai tenurial arrangements shifted during the Sengoku-Kinsei transformation. In part this change resulted from a redefining of social classes. In general those who remained on the land lost any claim to samurai status. These families held maximum latitude in their rights to use and dispose of their land as they saw fit. They assumed the rights and obligations of *hyakushō*, a term connoting full membership in the village community. Those who retained samurai status, however, even in domains like Satsuma, where rusticated samurai remained a prominent feature of local society, lost many of their property rights.*

Samurai control over land generally was quite limited during the early modern era. Again, if we think of disposability and usufruct as the key elements of tenure, then samurai did not have tenure. As a rule landed retainers, direct shogunal retainers (hatamoto), and daimyo, as well as the Shogun for most practical purposes, possessed rights to the income from land, but not the rights of transferability, disposability, or free use.

The hegemon and later the Bakufu did retain a high degree of control over the disposition of both their own lands and those of the daimyo. They could and did transfer daimyo or hatamoto, and augment, reduce, or confiscate their domains. But even in transferring lands, the rights being transferred were limited and partook more of public, administrative rights and perquisites than private landownership rights. Though the Shogun, hatamoto, and daimyo could make law, administer justice, and levy taxes and the corvée on their holdings, and though landed retainers derived income and sometimes corvée services from their fiefs, they generally could not actively manage the use of their lands. They could not decide on their own what crops to plant, when to plant them, or how to cultivate the land. Within the samurai class, access to the other samurai perquisites was carefully controlled by one's immediate superior, the hegemon, daimyo, or hatamoto. With the exception of shogunal control over Bakufu lands, samurai rights over land were not freely disposable. There was no mar-

---

*Satsuma samurai who served in the rural areas were systematically rotated from the countryside to the cities and back. They did not return to the same rural location.

ket for these rights in which they could be bought or sold; they could not be used as security on loans (although the tax revenues from them were); and they could not be subdivided at will, or, in principle, freely willed to successors.

The removal of samurai from the land and the creation of these conditions throughout Japan are inarguable. So, too, is the samurai's loss of a semblance of ownership rights over the land. To the extent that this arrangement marked a new restriction of their rights over land, it might arguably be termed a "revolution" in land tenure.

The same word, "revolution," has also been applied to the changing relationship of rural residents to their land. In this area I believe both the mechanism that guided the transformation and the result require reevaluation. There are a number of problems with the common emphasis on the villagers' near-private landholding rights.

Even if one assumes that Hideyoshi consciously pursued a policy of establishing autonomous nuclear agricultural households, significant questions arise about the policy's effectiveness. One concerns the import of listing a villager's name in land survey registers. This practice, more than any other, is held up as evidence that cultivators were confirmed in their right to farm specific pieces of land, and that the surveys thereby defined them as full-fledged members of the village. However, as the historian Hayami Akira has pointed out, contemporary records listing households for the purpose of establishing labor dues (*buyaku*) often name many fewer households than the survey registers. This suggests that the survey registers did not legally define autonomous households or clearly define a family's relationship to the land; what was a family unit for one purpose was not a family unit for another.[1] The domain authorities did not use one type of record as a check on the other. In this area of administration consistency was not the hobgoblin of policy-makers. Even if the two kinds of records were a mirror image in some domains, that was not true throughout the land. The extent to which survey registers specified tenure rights needs to be determined domain by domain, and perhaps even by period.

Another question arises when one looks at developments in the late nineteenth century. Assuming that private landownership was effectively established by the early seventeenth century, what need was there for the early Meiji tax reformers to stress resurveying to this end? Data from old records should have simply been transferable to certificates issued by the new government. In fact there was much confusion in many regions over who was to be listed as a property's owner. Regardless of Hideyoshi's intent, he clearly did not succeed in establishing a system of private landownership strong or durable enough to obviate the need for new legal principles of private property in the nineteenth century.

Simply put, land-man relations in the villages were more complex than students of the late sixteenth and early seventeenth centuries generally acknowledge. They were too complex to have been the result of a centrally directed policy. Furthermore, the standard survey techniques that are seen as capable of defining individual landholding in villages were much too imperfect and incomplete for the task. Even the daimyo could not arbitrarily define the villagers' rights to land. In the final analysis, primary responsibility for defining land tenure lay at the village, not the domain or national level.

Consequently, the claim for a revolution—a centrally directed, rapid shift—in village land tenure is very questionable. In Kaga domain, village society showed significant elements of continuity in the sixteenth and seventeenth centuries. When rustic samurai remained in the villages, they did not generally lose their lands. They remained as large landholders and locally influential members of the community.

As a preface to the discussion of developments in Kaga, let us look further at two general subjects—the inability of surveys to define individual villagers' land rights and the corporate land tenure system commonly known as warichi, literally, "dividing the land."

The Weaknesses of the Surveys as Tools for Determining Land Tenure

Kaga's measuring techniques, however adequate for establishing a reasonable estimate of the amount of land to tax, were entirely inadequate for defining land tenure rights, since they made no pretense of measuring individual fields. But the standard techniques were not much better. The measurements recorded in survey registers are marred by substantial inaccuracies that severely limit their ability to define the boundaries of a family's land rights. These inaccuracies are of three basic sorts. First, the data were not based on measurements between actual field boundaries; they were simple vertical and horizontal measurements that attempted to approximate a field's area (Fig. 3). Second, the figures in the registers are not the original calculations but adjusted data. Standard rounding practices of the day systematically introduced a downward bias to the final, recorded measurements; the size of demonstrably unproductive fields (because of poor soil, extensive shade, and other conditions) was reduced; and other adjustments were made based on the surveyors' perceptions of overstrict measurements (up to 20 percent of the measured area). Since survey

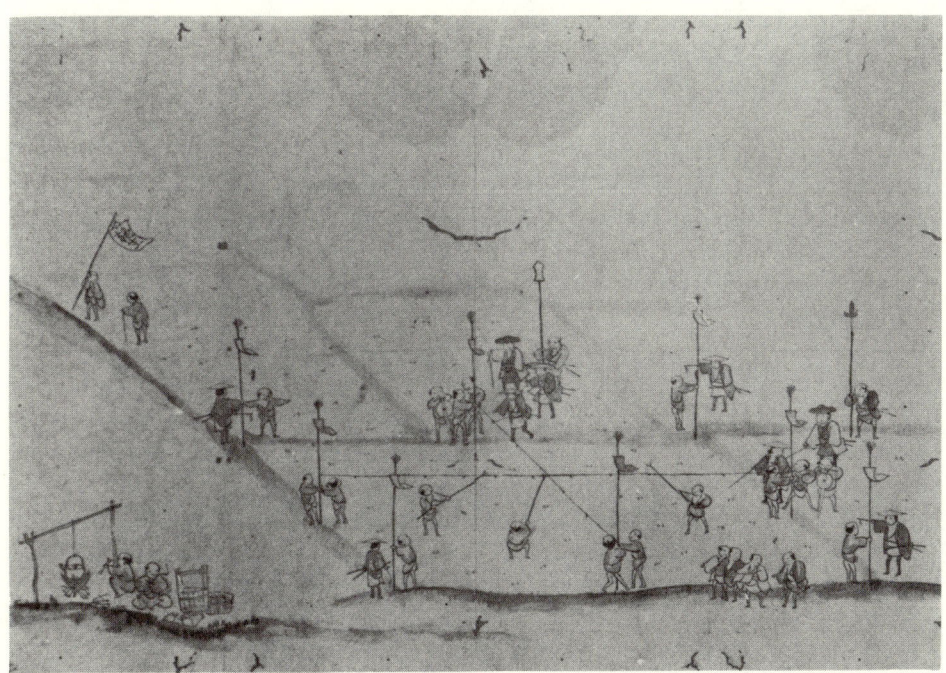

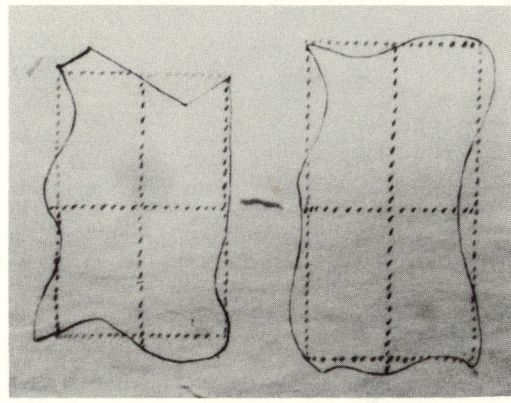

Fig. 3. Crossed-rope survey measurement. Top: An artist's record of the 1840–42 survey of Mito. Note the use of poles to keep the measuring lines from sagging. Left: Rather than measuring from actual boundaries, the crossed-rope technique measured rectangles that approximated the size of irregularly shaped fields. Although taken from a late-eighteenth-century Kaga survey manual, "Kenchikata Hisho," illustrations like these can be found in survey manuals issued throughout the early modern era.

registers do not record the details of such adjustments, it is impossible to manipulate the final data to arrive at even moderately accurate field dimensions. Finally, technological factors introduced inaccuracies. Particularly problematical was the use of hemp ropes, which varied in length as they got wet or dried out.[2]

In sum, none of the measurements were useful in determining boundaries. At best the registers located fields within rather large sections (*aza*) of a village. Within each section there were numerous plots of land.

No attempt was made to mark the boundaries of individual fields, either by erecting physical markers or noting latitude and longitude in survey registers.[3] Neither the emerging central administration nor the domain authorities regularly kept plat maps showing each field and to whom it belonged. Without these or similar devices, no outside authority could effectively guarantee rights to specific plots of land. Samurai officials were totally dependent on villagers for determining which piece of land belonged to whom.*

These deficiencies raise significant questions about the intent of Toyotomi Hideyoshi, the Tokugawa Shoguns, the daimyo, and the hatamoto. Could they have seriously expected to control landholding arrangements within villages using such primitive tools, especially in the absence of direct oversight by outside officials? I think not.

Given the methodological limitations of the surveys, there could be no other locus for the effective authority over land tenure than the members of the community itself. They typically arbitrated landholding rights within their own borders.† By default, if not by design, villagers alone possessed the powers of oversight and sanction necessary to enforce a given system of land-man relationships. Domain lords might attempt to systematize local practice, and hegemons might issue proclamations, but neither could ride roughshod over village decisions.

Warichi

Nothing better illustrates the power of local communities over land rights than early modern land redistribution practices. Although different localities employed a variety of names for these practices, I subsume all under the term "warichi" in the discussion that follows. In villages that practiced redistribution, a villager's access to given pieces of land was controlled by all the villagers possessing superior rights to land acting as a corporate unit. (A caveat. By using the phrase "corporate unit" and similar terms below, I do not wish to imply that a "natural" harmony—or in James Scott's phrase, a "moral economy"—existed in these villages. First, one

---

*This is one reason why villagers could so readily circumvent widespread seventeenth-century attempts to restrict the sale of land.

† Satsuma may constitute an exception to this generalization. Domain ordinances allocated access to land proportionally based on family composition (the *kadowari* or "gate-dividing" system). Since Satsuma stationed samurai in a large number of rural castles, it had the necessary manpower to enforce this system of land allocation.

segment of the village population was excluded from participation—those people without land use rights. Furthermore, as some of the following material on warichi in Kaga indicates, there were sometimes sharp divisions within a village over whether and how to conduct a redistribution. Documents compiled by villagers detailing the procedures they employed mask the tensions and disputes that had to be resolved throughout the process. The issues that warichi addressed needed to be dealt with in non-warichi villages, too, but their residents chose different approaches. Why these different choices were made and how internal disputes over procedures were resolved cannot be answered here. The descriptions that follow pertain to the outcomes and are not intended to imply harmonious village community bonds or interaction.)

The warichi system was aimed at redistributing land use rights, not wealth. Each holder of land rights exploited the same proportion of a village's arable land after a reallocation as before. The proportion of good, average, and poor quality land managed by each was also the same before and after. A holder was not forced to give up anything toward equalizing the distribution of wealth within the village.

The basic function of Tokugawa redistribution practices has been explained largely in the context of the early modern land tax system. The development of the warichi system was in part a reaction to the interaction between the administrative demands of tax assessment and the destructive forces of nature.[4] In contrast to modern systems of real estate taxation, domain governments (never the central authorities) collected land taxes from villages as corporate entities, not from individual villagers. The village by itself determined how much each taxpaying member owed. If one of them could not pay his share, the others had to make up the shortfall. The taxpayers thus had a shared interest in seeing that each family shouldered its responsibility. This interest was the source of much pressure on individual families from their relatives and neighbors. A family that was unable to pay its share of the land tax was encouraged to raise the money by mortgaging its property, selling its possessions or land, or selling its family labor (sometimes permanently). Such pressures could, in the extreme, force the sale of daughters into prostitution.

Warichi was one common means of ensuring that each taxpayer paid what he ought to pay and no more. It provided a flexible way for the village to allocate taxpaying and related responsibilities without tying members to a specific plot of land. In most cases redistribution equalized the average quality of land held by each taxpaying family in order to ensure some fairness in the payment of land taxes. The tax-allocation process was simplified, too. If all taxpayers managed fields of the same average quality, the village could simply assess each in proportion to the amount of land he controlled. Since different villagers within the same community were often subject to different tax rates from different overlords (retainers and domain), the warichi system also provided a means of averaging the tax rate for the entire village.

Land redistribution also spread the risks of a family's exposure to natural disasters. When land was lost from cultivation because of landslides or changes in riverbeds, for example, village lands were commonly reallocated so that the loss was shared by all the taxpaying villagers. In this very limited sense, there was a redistribution of wealth. Each participant suffered some loss, but no taxpayer was forced to leave agriculture as a result of the disaster alone. Unless very large portions of the village were lost, all taxpayers would have had land in other parts of the village that could still be harvested. All members continued to share the responsibility for paying land taxes and contributing labor to communal projects.

Not only did this system maximize the potential for survival of each full-fledged village member, it also maximized the pool of families that had a vested interest in the upkeep of the irrigation and flood-control systems on which they all depended and in the maintenance of village commons. The preservation of a family's economic interest in these endeavors ensured its willingness to contribute labor to them. In the parts of Japan where water-control facilities were routinely damaged by heavy rains, snow and ice, or other climatic or geographic conditions, the demand for cooperative labor could be regular, time-consuming, and intensive.

The warichi system represents a combination of the two other types of land use rights usually described by scholars of early modern Japan—those of common land (*iriaichi*) and near-private ownership. In the sense that the village taxpayers as a corporate unit determined who held rights to a specific plot and for how long, land subject to redistribution partakes of the character of common land. But warichi also embodied the kind of transferable rights associated with private ownership. Perhaps the closest modern analogue (imperfect as it is) is the joint stock company. Like the shares in a stock corporation, plots were treated as private property, with rights of disposability vested in the owner, but they did not represent the ownership of specific corporate assets. The participants in the warichi system inherited, bought, sold, mortgaged, and subdivided their cultivation rights, whether surreptitiously or legally, just as villagers did in those parts of Japan that did not employ the system. In effect they were buying and selling shares in a village-sponsored agricultural corporation or partnership, not titles to specific pieces of land.

Land redistribution of one sort or another was a widespread phenomenon. It was practiced in at least 23 of the 65 traditional provinces: Echigo, Echizen, Owari, Kaga, Noto, Etchu, Tosa, Ise, Tsushima, Hizen, Iyo, Iki, Iwaki, Hyuga, Satsuma, Mutsu, Hitachi, Tango, Yamato, Bungo, Chikuzen, Bizen, and Mino. (It was also practiced in Okinawa and the Ryukyu Islands.)[5] A more telling measure of its national significance is the assessed value of the land involved. In several domains redistribution was mandated by official fiat, and these alone accounted for 23 percent of Japan's total assessed value of 24,554,000 koku of rice in 1645.[6] Some of the largest domains fell in this group, notably Kaga (with branch fiefs, 1,200,000 koku), Satsuma (770,000 koku), and Tosa (490,000 koku). On top of this, there were a number of regions where redistribution was a very common practice even though it was not mandatory. In 11 of Echigo's 12 counties, the practice was close to universal. Adding in the bulk of Echigo's assessed value of approximately 1,143,000 koku brings the total proportion of Japan's assessed value affected by redistribution up to almost 27 percent, and even the addition of Echigo makes no pretext of comprehensiveness.

The stimulus for this development came from different sources. As already noted, some domain administrations attempted to enforce periodic redistribution throughout their realms. In other cases the decision to resort to redistribution was made within the villages. That this was by no means a rare phenomenon is evident in the fact that land redistribution was the rule in Echigo province, even though it was not the official policy of domain or Bakufu administrators.[7] Finally, redistribution might be employed in only a part of a village. In these instances the system commonly was a device for families involved in a cooperative reclamation project to allocate access to fields as they were opened, developed, and stabilized.

Discussions of land tenure routinely ignore the implications of warichi. For example the fact that there was widespread deviation from standard conceptions of tenure arrangements even in regions where we find field-by-field survey registers and despite proclamations by Hideyoshi suggests that land rights approximated private ownership. Such evidence further indicates that neither Shogun nor daimyo freely dictated to villagers the nature of land rights (much less the distribution of landed wealth, as some would have it).[8] In most instances, even in many of the domains that ultimately mandated redistribution, the impulse originated within local communities.

They, not the hegemons or daimyo, determined landholding policies.

The practice of redistribution raises a variety of interesting questions with which we cannot deal here (e.g., questions of origin, variations in procedures, and the impact on incentives for cultivators to improve their output). An investigation of these questions and others must be postponed to another occasion.* My discussion here is limited largely to developments in Kaga domain. More specifically, I focus on the questions of who controlled access to land use rights in the domain and how villagers, at least acting collectively, made contributions to the institutional foundations of domain administration.

Samurai Land Tenure in Kaga

From the outset the enfeoffed warriors who accompanied Toshiie and Toshinaga into Kaga, Noto, and Etchu were settled on the land in such a way as to deprive them of managerial control over the holdings from which they drew income. From this perspective the process of class separation was given significant impetus by the act of daimyo transfer itself. Toshiie settled immigrant retainers in a number of daimyo-controlled castles and not on their fiefs. Their benefices were not tied to specific locations. Though given the right to assess annual land taxes and exact corvée from specific villages, they were never locally resident and did not manage the lands within their nominal jurisdiction. Through these measures the Maeda took complete charge of defining land rights for this set of samurai.

The local samurai-gentry can be divided into two groups, those who had formed alliances with one or other of the Maeda's competitors, the Ikkō sect, Sassa Narimasa, or Shibata Katsuie, and those who lined up with the newcomers. Most of the families in the first group that did not flee the Maeda forces remained on the land. Early land registers and the genealogies of rural district administrators (called *fuchibyakushō*, and later, *tomura*) indicate that these families retained control over their lands and often earned special considerations from the Maeda. These samurai continued to oversee their lands as before, with full management and disposability rights. But opportunities for military service gradually declined, and

---

*It is worth repeating that land redistribution practices varied from region to region throughout Japan. In a given village the practice might be applied only to seedbeds or to mountain fields, not to all of the arable land. Significant variations also existed in the period between rotations. In some instances a natural disaster would trigger a redistribution. In others land was regularly redistributed at intervals of from three to 20 years. I discuss the influence of warichi on Meiji to early Shōwa landholding rights and tenancy practices in Niigata prefecture in "Feudal Remnants and Tenant Power."

in the end they lost almost all of their samurai attributes. They became simply villagers. The tenures of these families were largely uninfluenced by the Maeda.

As for the local warriors who went over to the Maeda they were absorbed into their new overlord's samurai band and generally enjoyed rights to assess corvée and land taxes on the same basis as the longstanding retainers. These families had initially established their own tenures by dint of their military skill. Though they maintained some of their traditional rights during the early years of Maeda rule, the daimyo ultimately gained complete control over these matters.

Within this second group of native samurai-gentry there was one exception, the Chō family. A brief examination of the position of the Chō and their landed retainers discloses the nature of medieval local overlordship when it survived the birth of early modern Japan. It also reveals a bureaucratization and depersonalization of retainer fiefs that parallels the bureaucratization and depersonalization of the domain's administrative organization.

Residents of the Noto Peninsula since the thirteenth century, the Chō had their ups and downs over the centuries. Their fortunes reached a nadir just before their alliance with Oda Nobunaga. Many of the Chō forces lost their lives when the family was expelled from its home base in the battle for Nanao castle. But when the Maeda occupied Noto as part of Nobunaga's victorious armies, Chō Tsuratatsu was ordered to serve the Maeda as *yoriki*, and the ancestral lands were restored. In 1582 Maeda Toshiie added to the Chō's holdings, granting them some of the territory of the recently defeated Tempyōji partisans of the Ikkō sect. This cemented a relationship between the two families that lasted long after Nobunaga's assassination.

Toshiie's benefice was not predicated on a sacrifice of Chō autonomy. More than the other seven retainers who held fiefs larger than 10,000 koku, the Chō maintained a surprising degree of administrative independence. Though this was by no means true private landownership (the Chō's managerial authority and rights of disposability were highly restricted), their rights of possession did allow them and their retainers to exercise enough control over the use of land and the resident population to preserve some of its elements.[9]

The Chō established their own administrative organization, which paralleled that of Kaga domain. Like the Maeda administration, the Chō's took on a bureaucratized and public character more than a private one. At the top of the administrative pyramid the Chō Elders (*karō*) managed administration and set policy. They supervised a treasurer (*san'yō bugyō*) to whom a county magistrate (*kōri bugyō*) reported. The collection of land taxes on Chō land was supervised by officials called *daikan*, who were also subordinate to the treasurer.

There was one daikan for each of three districts: the Eastern district, consisting of 17 villages; the Western district, consisting of 16 villages; and the Heartland (Oku) district, consisting of 22 villages. The daikan oversaw tax assessment, tax collection, the evaluation of wasteland, and related activities on the lands belonging to the Chō themselves. They also performed these functions on some of the Chō retainers' lands, but this occurred only in an unusual instance or in villages in which the retainers had only a small amount of taxable land.*

Commoner district chiefs (*tomura*) collected the household and horse tax (*muneuma yakugin*) and carried out other duties under the direction of the county magistrate. They also assisted the daikan in tax assessment and collection, organized corvée labor, kept track of reclamation projects, assessed all the major miscellaneous taxes and dues, and supervised the village headmen (*mura kimoiri*).

The Chō retained the medieval "right of nonentry" (funyūken), meaning that Maeda officials could not enter their lands.[10] When the rest of the Maeda holdings were surveyed, even in the early to middle seventeenth century, the Chō holdings were exempt. Instead, the Chō conducted their own surveys on a different model, one that more closely approximated classic descriptions of the Taikō kenchi.†

The Chō also used their own tax mechanisms. Retainer fiefs were valued by the taxes they purportedly yielded, rather than by their assessed value as in the other Maeda lands. Indeed, one of the purposes of the late-sixteenth-century Chō surveys was to set a uniform tax of 60 percent of assessed value, a rate that would henceforth be used in assigning fiefs. That figure, which became the official standard for both directly controlled Chō lands (*kurairichi*) and retainer lands (*chigyō*) in the 1620's, represented a kind of "fixed" assessment based on a flat village rate, rather than annual retainer or Chō assessments on parts of a village. Though retainers con-

---

*As in the Maeda case, a retainer could share villages with the domain or other retainers. Indeed, it was rare for a retainer to possess an entire village. Typically a large retainer's lands were scattered among two or three villages. A small retainer's lands might well be confined to a single village. (Kigoshi, "Kan'ei-ki Chōke ryō Kashima hangun," pp. 31–32; Itō, "Kinsei shoki daimyō ryō," pp. 22–23, 27–28; *KHNK*, 1: 48.) The Chō and their chief retainers also possessed residences in Kanazawa.

† Nonetheless, these surveys reflected the same political purposes as the Maeda's. For example, the 1592 survey implemented an arbitrary 45% increase in assessed valuation (Kigoshi, "Kan'ei-ki Chōke ryō Kashima hangun," p. 20).

tinued to set somewhat different rates from the "official" one, they do not appear to have varied a great deal from the 60 percent level.[11]

In addition to the land tax, the Chō levied several lesser taxes on their subjects: the aforementioned household/horse tax, ordinary labor dues (*hirabu*), miscellaneous nonagricultural assessments (*komononari*), and miscellaneous local (county, district, and village) expenses (*shō nyūmai*). Though the other subjects of Kaga domain paid these taxes, too, the distinctive feature in the Chō case was that these taxes were all administered by a retainer lineage, and not by the domain. Other retainers conscripted labor from villagers early in the Maeda occupation of Kaga, but they lost these rights by the very early seventeenth century. Only the Chō and their retainers continued to assess corvée and collect these taxes through mid-century.

The Chō retainers had a considerable degree of autonomy in their own right. For example, they could collect certain taxes from the villagers under their control that other villagers had to pay to the Chō, including their own version of the house and horse tax.[12] And although these men could not buy and sell their lands, they exercised full managerial control over them. Their samurai servants (*genin*) lived in the villages, and some villagers were tied directly to individual retainers. As an immediate presence in the villages, the retainers were in a position to play an active role in the management of agriculture. New lands were opened, and old ones cultivated, under their direction. In these respects the Chō retainers exercised usufruct over their fiefs and maintained a degree of "ownership" rare among early modern enfeoffed samurai.

Villager Land Tenure in Kaga

Although corporate landholding under the warichi system was not officially mandated in the early years of Kaga domain, and was almost certainly not the only form of villager land tenure, it is the only form we can readily identify. Out of necessity, then, we will confine ourselves to the operation of that system. (Corporate landholding, let us note, meant village control of access to individual plots; the village played no direct role in the management of cultivation. Each villager decided for himself which crops to plant, when to plant them, and all the other details of day-to-day management. He did of course have to defer to the collectivity in his access to irrigation water and, in some cases, to the green manure and other products of the commons.)

Redistributive practices in Kaga appear in domain records as early as the beginning of the seventeenth century. But if formal documentation was part of the process at all, local officials did not preserve the earliest written records associated with warichi. They had little reason to do so. Decades after a redistribution, when precedents had been incorporated in more recent records or superseded by modifications, the question of who had managed what specific lands lost its relevance. Consequently, we only know of the origins and basic principles of redistribution through somewhat later evidence. Some questions, such as the length of the interval between reallocations, can be judged only by looking at middle and late Tokugawa data.

The warichi system of Kaga domain represents the furthest possible extension of corporate control over arable land. In principle all kinds of village land were subject to redistribution. Although mechanisms were developed that protected the residential land of villagers who possessed fully disposable cultivation rights (*takamochi hyakushō*), land redistribution might indeed mean that a tenant would be forced to change his residence.[13] This potential clearly indicates the full extent to which corporate control could be exercised over matters that scholars have generally treated as "private."

During the period under study, warichi was almost exclusively a concern of the *takamochi hyakushō*. These villagers originated the system and retained almost total control over it, though from 1642 down to the late Tokugawa, domain officials intermittently attempted to systematize some of the practices for the sake of uniformity and fairness. (Ultimately, in the nineteenth century, domain policy-makers did establish uniform maximum intervals between reallocations.) In this regard Kaga offers us an opportunity to examine the ways in which domain administrators built on a village-initiated practice in constructing their policies and institutions.*

Since villagers themselves originated warichi, there was substantial variety in the specific procedures employed to reallocate land.† There were differences not only between villages but also within a village over time. In some cases, all the village's good, average, and poor land was proportionately allocated to each shareholder. This format ultimately dominated warichi procedures during the mid-seventeenth century and after. In other cases, such as those from Noto's Nafune district, original fields (*honden*) were divided quite equally among villagers as well as proportionally by

---

*In building on village redistribution practices, Kaga authorities were not at all unique. Several other domains took over village-based redistribution practices for their own ends. See Aono, *Nihon kinsei warichisei shi*, on this point.

† There was not even a fixed interval for reallocating land until the domain set a maximum of 20 years in 1838 (Oda Kichinojō, *Kaga-han*, p. 491).

land characteristics. These villagers held equal amounts of each category of land.

Even when domain authorities first sought to employ the warichi system for their own purposes, they refused to specify in any detail the procedures the villagers were to follow. The 1642 ordinance that first gave active encouragement to warichi and ordered it into domain-wide use did not specify what the standards of measurement were to be, which classes of villager were to be included, which lands were to be exempted, or any other procedural matters.[14] These matters were left to the villagers to decide for themselves, and the villagers would continue to be the arbiters of most warichi procedures throughout the early modern era.

The first step villagers took after deciding to conduct a redistribution, then, was to meet and discuss the exact procedures to follow. Once they settled on these, the "rules" were spelled out in a formal document (a village *sadamegaki*), and all participants agreed to abide by the conditions therein. This final formal agreement varied in length and detail, with greater detail becoming common later in the Tokugawa era. The following procedures were central to most redistributions in Kaga domain.

Villagers first determined which lands were to be redistributed and which were not. Lands subject to reallocation were called lottery lands (*kujichi*); those exempted were called *hikichi* (withdrawn lands).* In effect kujichi was a residual category that included all lands not specifically exempted from redistribution. Since exemptions were quite limited, the overwhelming majority of taxable land was subject to redistribution.

The domain established a uniform general exemption for productive land in 1671, but this ordinance was probably built on earlier village practices. The domain simply standardized the exemption, setting a limit on the amount of land of whatever type that could be "withdrawn." Up to a total of six *tan* for each 100 koku of assessed village value could be excluded.[15] Since 100 koku represented a minimum of 66 *tan* of land (about 22 acres), only a small share of village land was protected from redistribution, at most 10 percent of a village's arable and residential land. Nonetheless, it was enough to encompass most residential compounds, seedbeds, and other lands that required very heavy investments of capital and labor.†

---

*A third category had crept into use by the 19th century—*sōchi*, especially "thin" paddy that was jointly owned by the village and whose income was dedicated to the village budget ("Denchiwari," in Heki, [*Kaitei zōhō*] *Kanō*, p. 603).

†If someone had more residential land than his share of the legal exemption allowed, the surplus could be treated as constituting part of his share of arable land. In the case of the warichi conducted in Awabara village, Hakui county, in 1794, such lands would have been treated as coming from a shareholder's allotment of average paddy (*Sadamegaki* in *Hakui shi shi*, p. 665).

TABLE 4
Hypothetical Allocation of Cultivation Rights to 22 Shareholding Families in 10 Kuji Groups Under the Warichi System

Family	Share	Kuji group	Family	Share	Kuji group
1	1.25	A, B	12	.50	H
2	1.00	C	13	.50	I
3	.50	D	14	.25	I
4	.50	D	15	.25	I
5	.50	E	16	.25	J
6	.50	E	17	.25	J
7	.50	F	18	.25	J
8	.50	F	19	.25	J
9	.50	G	20	.25	B
10	.50	G	21	.25	B
11	.50	H	22	.25	B

NOTE: In this arrangement, all but Family 2 would participate in a second drawing for their part-shares: Family 1 with Families 20–22 in kuji B; Family 3 with Family 4 in kuji D; etc.

In addition to this small amount of residential and arable land, allowance was made for unproductive lands. Roads, footpaths, and shrines, for example, were exempted. The small amount of land located in the perpetual shadow of houses, road trees, or other large objects was also exempted from redistribution because it was considered unproductive.

Before the land was measured and evaluated, the village shareholders were divided into lottery groups called *kuji*. There were commonly 10 to 12 kuji, each of which drew for one share of each category of land.[16] Every participant belonged to at least one lottery group. If someone held rights to a sufficiently large amount of land, he might by himself constitute a kuji or participate in more than one. More often, several people formed a kuji. One of them, usually the largest holder, would serve as the group's official representative (*kujioya*) during the redistribution process. After the lottery established which kuji got which lands, a secondary lottery would be held among a kuji's several members to allocate the lands within the share.

Table 4 shows one arrangement by which 22 shareholders might be deployed to draw for their village's 10 shares of each category of land. In this arrangement Families 1 and 2, with a full share each, constitute their own kuji groups (A and C). Since Family 1 holds an additional quarter-share, it is also part of a second group (kuji B) and would draw a second time, along with Families 20–22, for a specific section of the land that group B drew in the initial lottery. Five groups would have been jointly managed by two families (D–H); one was shared by three families (I); and two were divided among four families (B, J).

Once the principles for defining the exemptions were settled and the kuji established, the village conducted its own land survey. The survey was more detailed than the domain's, making finer distinctions in quality in classifying the land. The purpose of the survey was twofold. Most obviously, it measured all redistributable land and assessed its fertility. But it also took topographic characteristics into consideration, in effect trying to assess a plot's vulnerability to natural disasters and fluctuations in climate. Surveying required a bare minimum of 15 to 20 people,* and the redistribution process as a whole involved a substantial cost to participants in terms of time, often four to six weeks. Any cash expenditures for the survey were borne solely by them.

After the land was measured and its productivity evaluated, all redistributable land was divided into sections (*wari*). Each wari contained land of comparable characteristics and quality. But the wari were not necessarily of the same size; a wari for one class of land might be larger than the wari for another. Villagers could and often did change these wari with each redistribution.† The wari were then divided into equal sections, one for each kuji, and each section was assigned a number, which was inscribed on a lottery stick. The share representatives (kujioya) then drew sticks for each section of each wari until all were assigned to the various kuji. As noted, when a kuji consisted of two or more shareholders, they held a second drawing to allocate the lands their representative had drawn among themselves.[17] Consequently, each field group (wari) would be divided at least once and more commonly, twice. This whole process could entail redrawing individual field boundaries.

The efficiency of the warichi system in protecting shareholders from a loss of land through natural disasters depended on what stimulated the redistribution. By and large, in the period with which we are concerned, the Kaga authorities did not encourage regular redistribution. Except for the mid-seventeenth century, the impetus generally came from the villagers themselves. But there were no clear stipulations on how often this was to be done. Warichi were implemented irregularly at the villages' discretion.

---

*By the 19th century 15 different specialists were officially involved in making the actual survey. Two commoner survey specialists, the head surveyor (*bunchinin*) and the measurer (*saotorinin*), received a salary from the village. In addition to district and village officials, and in addition to the survey specialists, a substantial number of people drawn from the middle and lower ranks of the villagers stretched measuring lines and placed survey markers. (Tochinai, *Kyū Kaga-han*, pp. 117–20.)

† The wari that Shinbo village designed for the 1812 land redistribution ranged from 45 bu to 540 bu in size. In two later redistributions the villagers restructured the wari in such a way as to limit these size differences. By 1867 only three were smaller than 270 bu, and only one was larger than 400 bu (*Hakui shi shi*, p. 675).

TABLE 5
*Intervals Between Land Redistributions for Eight Villages,
Late Seventeenth Century to Late Nineteenth Century*

Village	Time period	Number of redistributions	Interval (years)		
			Average	Longest	Shortest
Kitajima	1672–1865	9	24	43	12
Chōkeiji	1785–1871	6	17	20	15
Hongo	1666–1857	10	21	37	11
Shinbo	1722–1867	7	24	29	19
Tsubouchi	1733–1857	7	21	23	20
Myōga	1729–1871	7	24	40	20
Takasude	1772–1853	7	14	19	8
Jūnen'aki	1734–1859	4	42	83	20

SOURCES: Tochinai, *Kyū Kaga-han*, pp. 106–8; *Hakui shi shi, Kinsei hen*: 663; *Tonami chō shi*, p. 371.

In general some form of natural disaster appears to have been the stimulus for building village consensus on the need to conduct a redistribution.[18] A substantial loss of land was an indisputable event to be dealt with through redistribution, while more subtle shifts in the productivity of the land or small losses might be subject to some disputation.[19]

Though in theory nothing prevented redistributions in consecutive years if the villagers who desired a change could obtain a consensus in favor of it, practical constraints (the cost in time and money) militated against frequent warichi. In any event the interval between redistributions varied substantially. As illustrated by the records from eight villages in different parts of the domain (Table 5), the range was from as little as eight years to as much as 83 years. The shortest average interval was one occurrence every 14 years, the longest one every 42 years. Most redistributions were conducted every 20 years or so.[20]

Yet as the table shows, even within a village, the variation could be great. The residents of Jūnen'aki, for example, redistributed their land four times between 1734 and 1859, at intervals as short as 20 years and as long as 83. In nearby Takasude village, with seven redistributions in the relatively short span of 81 years, the shortest interval was eight years, the longest 19.[21] The recurrent redistributions in Takasude were the result of frequent flooding.[22] This wide variation in intervals reinforces the impression that warichi were triggered by an act of nature, and that in Kaga domain at least, the process functioned more as a device to spread the costs of natural disasters than as a way to ensure against tax inequities growing out of small changes in soil fertility. To the extent that the system was adapted to local circumstances, it was a more cost-effective form of insurance for shareholders than regularly scheduled distributions.

For many years the origin of warichi in Kaga domain was dated to 1642 and attributed to the domain policy-makers who enacted a package of reforms at that time.[23] This judgment was based on a mid-nineteenth-century document that described these reforms.[24] But though contemporary documents verify the domain's active encouragement of redistribution at that time, this is an area in which we have concrete evidence of the positive contributions that villagers, acting cooperatively, made to domain administration.

For one thing, we have evidence of the existence of redistributional practices as early as 1606. In the course of settling a village dispute in 1651, domain records specifically advised, "Regarding the repartition [*goban wari*] to be conducted this spring in Ota village in Tonami county, matters must now be settled quickly in accordance with the ordinance [*sadamegaki*] that resulted from disputes among peasants in 1606."[25] The reference to 1606 is early enough in itself to refute the old explanation of warichi's origin in Kaga. But if the principles recorded in this ordinance were sufficiently sophisticated to provide a model for the resolution of a dispute 45 years later, we can reasonably infer that they were the product of some years of local experience, and that repartition originated even earlier.

Village shareholder and tax registers provide additional evidence that redistribution predated formal domain encouragement. Here the evidence is implicit but no less strong for all that. Only redistribution, surely, can account for the surprising equality of land use rights found in some early-seventeenth-century shareholders' lists. Villages in the Nafune district of Noto province, for example, show a uniformity even to the thousandths of a koku in land value in 1635.[26] Furthermore, in the vast majority of cases where there were inequalities, they can be identified as the result of very recent reclamations. Shareholder lists from Satomura in the same district indicate that this system of equal access to land was in operation in some places by 1617 at the latest.[27] Similarly, we find the families of Fukamiya village, with only a very few exceptions, paying the exact same amount of land tax in 1640.* Such a high degree of uniformity within these communities suggests that they used a form of warichi to ensure equal access to all but recently opened land.

There is other indirect evidence that does not deal specifically with re-

*WSS, 2: 117–18. Although as these examples indicate, the reallocation of wealth was sometimes an objective of redistribution, such instances were confined to the early 17th century. This feature was not retained in later procedures for land repartition.

distributive practices but is consonant with them. Most significant are the land survey procedures that were employed almost from the time of the Maeda's entry. The approach to surveying was compatible with warichi. As we have seen, surveyors (if actual measures were made at all) did not measure or assess the quality of individual fields but only dealt with large sections of a village; and if any differentiation in the quality of land was made at all, it was based on various parts of the village's land, much in the way that villagers themselves might treat their holdings during the redistribution process. The domain's initial attempts to survey villages field by field made little intuitive sense if redistributions were already in use, a consideration potentially related to the rapid switch to less detailed investigations.

Even if warichi was not already in use in 1581, the authorities' tendency to ignore most gradations in soil quality created incentives for taxpayers to employ a more detailed categorization of land as they developed a system of allocating the tax burden among themselves. The gradations employed in standard redistributions factored in the micro-climates within villages and allowed greater sensitivity to differences in soil fertility than domain procedures.

All evidence suggests that before the mid-seventeenth century the decision to repartition land rights lay entirely at the village level. Indeed, domain ordinances issued in 1631 specifically indicate that this was to be done only by the consensus of all villagers (*mura chū*).[28] Although domain officials may have become involved in the process during a disruptive dispute, there is no indication that they sought to make the practice part of domain policy at this time.

Nothing in the warichi system as such prohibited an owner from selling or transferring his land use rights. And in fact rights were routinely transferred from one party to another through inheritance, sale, or foreclosure on mortgaged rights, much as stockholders today trade their shares on a stock exchange or pledge them as security on a loan.[29]

The earliest domain surveys, those that list the names of individual villagers, demonstrate rural socioeconomic inequality and the continued strength of pre-Maeda elites, but they are ambiguous as evidence of landholding patterns or for documenting the use of redistribution. The Kagahan specialist Wakabayashi Kisaburō found not only a substantial variation in the amount of land held by the people listed in the registers, but also a very uneven distribution of different types of land among them.[30] Table 6 shows the distribution in the villages covered in the two earliest documents, Fukuno and Kumabuchi.

Land Tenure

TABLE 6
Land Distribution in Fukuno and Kumabuchi Villages, 1582

Type of land	Fukuno villagers (N = 33)	Kumabuchi villagers (N = 25)
All types	8	5
Paddy and residential	3	2
Paddy and dry fields	1	5
Paddy only	10	1
Dry fields only	0	2
Dry fields and residential	0	3
Residential only	11	7

SOURCE: *KHNK*, 1: 73, table 7.

Some residents possessed all categories of land, but in neither village did this class represent more than 25 percent of the people listed in the registers. Several of those with the greatest apparent access to land seemingly did not have residential compounds. This suggests that the uneven distribution of different types of land did not necessarily correspond closely to differences in wealth within the village.

The 1591 registers from Mizushiro village (Chō domain) likewise show extreme variation across families in both the size and the type of holding. For example, Negoya's paddy "holdings" of about 33 koku were divided into 19 different fields, whereas Heiemon's 50 koku of paddy were divided into only 13. Total paddy "holdings" ranged from a low of just over one koku to a high of more than 50; totals for all a family's land ranged from a low of 0.075 koku to almost 52 koku.[31]

If, as I indicated in the last chapter, this style of register did not presume an "ownership" relation between the registrants and the land, a number of registrants might not have held superior land rights but may simply have been household dependents of others who did hold such rights. Thus, though these documents suggest an inequality in land use rights, the disproportionate access of households to different types of land may only reflect shareholders' parceling out different types of land to dependents and cannot be taken as evidence that warichi did not operate at this time. That a number of those listed had no identifiable association with any residential land further suggests dependency.

The fact of unequal access to land is significant in itself, but Hara Shōgo has also correlated these registers with other documents to reveal what happened to local notables right after Toshiie's arrival. In several instances he was able to identify locally powerful figures, including Ikkō sect leaders, who remained in the villages. All retained a prominent position in the village. Despite the Ikkō sect's opposition to the Maeda at Sekidōsan, even its adherents were listed as large landholders in these early registers. We find no evidence here that land investigations were used to redistribute the land rights of the pre-Maeda local gentry.*

The old elites continued to command a disproportionate share of land and local influence in the era in which we know warichi operated. Later land registers and related documents compiled by village and district officials generally show widely diverse patterns of landholding. For example, in 1671 all but two of the 30 shareholders of Minamiyama village in Suzu county held rights to between six and nine koku each; the exceptions had rights to a bit more than five koku and to almost 18.[32] More diversity appears in the register (same year) for Hiroguri village in the same county. Nine villagers held rights to from eight to 10 koku each, four to from 20 to 29, five to from 11 to 19, and three to 30 or more; only one villager held less than eight koku, and he held about seven.[33] In Etchu, Ōta village showed an even wider range. In 1651 the smallest shareholder managed 35 koku, the largest 279; 64 percent of the villagers held rights to between 50 and 90 koku. Within three years (1654), however (perhaps reflecting the impact of the domain's great mid-century reforms, the Kaisaku hō), a trend toward somewhat smaller holdings was evident: 67 percent now held between 20 and 60 koku. The leveling trend continued over the next decade, and by 1666, 76 percent held rights to between 10 and 40 koku.[34] Yet even with this reduction in the size of the farm units, none of the villagers in these later registers came close to holding plots as small as the smallest in the 1591 registers. The only exceptions, two tiny shareholders in Hiroguri village, were outsiders who rented rights to a local holding. These rights were probably not their only access to land.[35]

The ability to transfer land rights did not take place within a complete administrative vacuum, but the ineffectiveness of domain efforts further reflects the difficult time the ruling classes had regulating village land tenure. In late 1615 (28 years before the Bakufu took the same step), domain policymakers prohibited the sale of shares.[36] But as in other parts of Japan, villagers found ways to circumvent this restriction; two common resorts were to adopt a son and to "loan out" the rights. Before the end of the century (1696), the policy proved such a failure that Kaga once again permitted the sale of land as long as all of a family's rights were not sold.† (This helped to maintain a maximum supply of local labor to farm tax-producing land.)

*Hara, *Kaga-han*, pp. 16–23. Hara argues that survey registers tied local samurai to land. However, as I show in the following chapter, the lines between these people, Maeda retainers, and commoners were still quite fluid.

† This pattern held true in other parts of Japan: where not repealed outright, the restrictions on land sales were severely modified.

The prohibition on the sale of land use rights appears to have been directly related to changes in the procedures for assessing and collecting labor dues. Beginning in 1603, the domain moved to assess labor dues in cash instead of conscripting labor directly. The basis for assessing dues (the number of qualifying families in a village) did not change, but since the tax now had to be raised in the marketplace, this directive began to complicate life for taxpayers. The prohibition in land rights sales appears to have been preparatory to the switch two years later (1617) to pinning cash labor dues to holding size. Stopping land sales made the whole process of assessing labor dues on this basis much easier, but it also provided a strong incentive for large holders to reduce the publicly listed size of their holdings and to list dependent households separately. The social and economic dependence of those households (with their various ceremonial and labor obligations to the main family) were not lost, only the tax obligations.

Even if shareholding did not represent private landownership, it was still the measure of a family's wealth and the basis of its land tax obligations. In addition, of course, the size of a family's holdings was an important element in determining its social standing and political authority within a village and district.

Conclusion

The developments in Kaga domain illustrate well the limitations of both daimyo and hegemonic authority in the realm of land systems. Though the hegemons and Shogun influenced the relationship between daimyo or hatamoto and the land, their ability to influence what went on in the villages was almost nil. Because their tools for influencing local practices (land surveys, in particular) lacked precision, uniformity, and adequate documentation, they were unsuited to the task of determining tenures or land use within the villages. With these poor tools, there could be no centrally directed domain or national revolution in commoner landholding patterns.

Even daimyo exercised limited influence in late-sixteenth- and early-seventeenth-century tenurial arrangements. They were best able to influence the relationship between landed retainers and the land. Landed retainers, at least in the period examined here, were very poorly positioned to define their own rights to the land. The Maeda kept immigrant retainers outside the villages from the start. The Chō (and perhaps a few others) were the rare exception; and even then the relationship of landed retainer to fief developed along the same lines as in daimyo domains. Ties with villagers became increasingly distant, mediated by subordinates and limited by Chō directives as samurai concentrated in castle towns.

Daimyo were least effective in shaping commoner land tenure. They did have some influence, but as the policy of restricting land sales or the sale of use rights well illustrates, if the policy did not accord with the villagers' interests, they circumvented it, and ultimately it failed.

Villagers were in the best position to define or modify land tenure. They alone possessed the capacity to implement a given system of man-land relationships. They alone had the day-to-day contact with the land that allowed them to detect illegal changes, enforce local custom, and adjust regulations as needed. Outsiders lacked an adequate documentary base to oversee these matters.

Villagers did not merely react to domain initiatives affecting land tenure. The warichi system provides a concrete example of their institutional creativity and ability to influence domain policies. Throughout the early seventeenth century, village shareholders maintained control over the specific procedures of land redistribution. The domain authorities adjudicated disputes that villagers could not resolve themselves, and they stipulated that villagers could redistribute land only when there was a consensus, but that was as far as their involvement went. To the extent that village-domain interactions seen in warichi is suggestive, land tenure policies in other areas of Japan developed through a dialogue between village and domain.

An examination of the warichi system in Kaga not only clarifies the locus of decision-making on matters of land tenure policy; it also documents a substantial divergence from standard descriptions of the nature of village land tenure. Many areas in which warichi predominated do not conform to the standard model of nearly modern private landownership rights. The warichi system in Kaga domain dramatically illustrates how tenuous the tie between a villager and the land he farmed could be. Any given piece of arable land could be taken from him at almost any time and transferred to another villager based on the consensus of his fellow shareholders.

Corporate control or "ownership" impinged on "private" landownership, and types of tenure varied from region to region. An exploration of the full implications of this variation must await additional research. Nonetheless, the material presented here suggests the need for caution in assessing the role of central and domain authority in manipulating tenure arrangements to effect specific social and economic changes within villages.

PART TWO

Controlling People

Chapter 5

Putting Down Roots

The challenges the Maeda faced in occupying and extending their domain were typical of those faced by all "potted plant" daimyo ordered into new territories by Oda Nobunaga and Toyotomi Hideyoshi. Other daimyo may have been moved more often or suffered more complete and sudden breaks with their traditionally held lands, but the basic problems posed by transfers were universal. Conscious decisions had to be made about which retainers to take to the new domain and how to allocate fiefs in the new territory. Transfer presented daimyo opportunities to reconfigure to their own advantage the rights granted to fiefholders. Daimyo had to develop some strategy for establishing initial contacts with their new subjects. One additional concern was to determine who among the local samurai and rural leaders should be incorporated into the new governing structure, and in what capacity.

In each daimyo's resolution of these issues lie the origins of the varying degrees of class separation seen throughout Japan, the different pace and completeness of the urbanization of the samurai, and the diverse mechanisms employed to bring the people under control. The very fact of this diversity indicates that daimyo selected from many possible solutions only those that best suited their particular situation.

A brief discussion of several elements of rural administration illustrates the point. Standard interpretations, based largely on developments in the Kanto and the Kinai, describe a complete break between social classes and the ultimate evisceration of the retainers' administrative rights in their fiefs. Bizen province under the Ikeda seems typical of this pattern, as do many of the centrally located Bakufu domains. In contrast, Satsuma kept samurai on the land, intimately involved in rural administration. Samurai rotated periodically between urban and rural locations. Other domains lie in between these extremes. Tosa, under the Yama'uchi, first pulled samurai off the land, and then, under the land reclamation policies of Nonaka Kenzan, encouraged samurai to return to rural life as agricultural entrepreneurs. Retainers' rights in fiefs were never fully lost in Sendai.[1] In Kaga, though samurai were pulled off the land entirely, the commoner officials who were central to rural administration, the district administrators, took on samurai-like attributes; and despite the accepted view of villages as the administrative foundation of domains, Kaga's district administrators certainly overshadowed village headmen in their importance—especially early in the era.

The determination of administrative structures and the selection of local officials were made in a volatile context. A principal dilemma for "potted plant" daimyo was finding a way to control potentially rebellious subjects without alienating local talent essential for effective administration. The very real explosiveness of this situation is well illustrated by the Higo Rebellion (1588) and the outbreaks accompanying the subjugation of northern Japan (1590). In both instances newly enfeoffed daimyo tried to run roughshod over local warrior-gentry (*kokujin*). The result was widespread violence that threatened to disrupt Hideyoshi's dominance of all Japan.

The Maeda shared these challenges with other daimyo. The fact that Kaga was dominated by the Ikkō ikki for so long is commonly thought to mean that the Maeda faced an exceptional challenge in establishing a stable administration. The Ikkō adherents bore the Oda forces particular enmity, labeling them "Enemies of the Law." It was a view that the transregional leaders of the sect clearly took seriously, as evidenced by various Ikkō-instigated disturbances very early in the Maeda rule. But the absence of large-scale conflict even then suggests that local adherents were more concerned with protecting themselves from outside overlords than with ideology. Compared with the Higo and Tohoku situations, the Kaga Ikkō ikki was unusual in its longevity, but not in the basic concept that it embodied.[2]

Toshiie's initial solutions to the challenges of relocation focused on two goals: keeping the retainers he brought with him at some distance from the local population; and coopting local leaders in such a way as to fragment any ties between them and minimize the potential for resistance. The steps taken in pursuit of these goals set the domain on a path of reliance on district officials for local administration, a growing separation of warrior and villager, and an increasing centralization of domain administration in daimyo hands.

Landed Retainers, Old and New

We begin with an examination of the treatment of the retainer band. For the purposes of examining the settling-in process, the retainer band can be divided into two segments. The first comprises those who came with Toshiie and Toshinaga from Echizen and Owari, the second the local population who participated in military activities. The second group can be further divided into the families that had connections with the Ikkō ikki and those who, like the Chō, operated independently of it. In the latter instances Toshiie had to decide whether or not to incorporate any of these independent elements into his retainer band (kashindan), how to buy their cooperation if they were not made formal members of the domain's military organization and how to deal with those who might resist. Regardless of origin, he had to determine how to reward retainers for their service. In most instances this meant deciding under what conditions to grant them fiefs and of what size.

When Toshiie entered Noto, he was ordered to take along all of his retainers and their families. By then, two groups of retainers had formed: the Arako group (Arako *shū*), composed of vassals and blood relatives who had allied with Toshiie before he received a fief in Echizen (23 men); and the Fuchū group (Fuchū shū; about 80 retainers), composed of men who had joined him when he took over his first Echizen fief.

Toshiie quickly rewarded the most capable of these men as the new domain expanded. For example, Okajima Kazuyoshi, who held a 150-koku fief in Fuchū, received increases of some 5,800 koku in the first four years of the Maeda occupation alone. His fief totaled almost 12,000 koku by 1600. With these increases in fief came major administrative and military appointments. By the turn of the century, Okajima had twice been appointed castellan at major local fortifications. In 1615 he was appointed castellan of Takaoka castle, site of Toshinaga's retirement.[3]

Despite the order to take all his retainers with him within months of his transfer to Noto, Toshiie sent a few of his Echizen retainers off to serve Toshinaga in Fuchū. This had two distinct consequences. First, Toshinaga gained staff who were familiar with the area. The knowledge was useful both in administration and in defense of the new domain. Second, these retainers provided a link between Toshiie and Toshinaga that facilitated coordinated planning and, more important, ensured Toshiie's continued influence in the Fuchū domain. These men may have served Toshinaga, but they never lost their honored position as Toshiie's retainers. Yamazaki Naganori, for example, soon returned to Toshiie's service and by 1599 held a fief of some 15,000 *koku*.[4]

Full study of what occurred in Fuchū after the Maeda left lies outside the scope of our study, but the fact that Toshiie was ordered to take all his military followers with him is highly significant: it represents one set of circumstances that contributed to the separation of warrior and villager. The cases of men like Yamazaki notwithstanding, transfer from Fuchū meant that Toshiie made a decision on who was a warrior, and hence a member of his retainer band, and who was not. Long before Hideyoshi's class-separation and sword-collection edicts, the transfer of daimyo *by itself* forced a classification of subjects into those whose responsibilities were principally military and those whose responsibilities were principally non-military. The lines between classes were not hard and fast. Local men who were primarily farmers might support armies or even take up arms if battles developed in their areas. Nonetheless, the process of marking a division between warrior and commoner had begun.

Many of the middle- and lower-ranking retainers who were transferred to Noto and Kaga saw their families discontinued in the new domain. Even among the more powerful families there were casualties of shifting domain politics, and as we would expect during these turbulent times, battlefields also claimed a number of men before they had heirs prepared to take their places.[5] Despite these losses, the retainers of the Arako and Fuchū shū provided the upper ranks of the new domain's military organization.[6] Their families retained their preeminence throughout the early seventeenth century.[7]

Many locally powerful military figures survived the fighting prior to Toshiie's arrival. Those who chose to remain in the province had three basic options. They could passively submit to the new rulers and try to protect their fortunes by maintaining a low profile, concentrating on managing their farms. Or they could seek a position within the new order, often as local administrators. In practice, choosing this course meant leading an essentially civilian life, although a man might be called to serve in combat against invaders or ordered to provide labor and supplies for such military purposes as castle-building. Finally, local warriors could join the Maeda retainer bands. In this instance they would function primarily, if not exclusively, as warriors and not as landlord-farm managers.

Still, the last was not much of an option for most. The opportunities for local warriors to join the landed ranks of the Maeda retainer band were limited, and this fact, too, had an important impact on the isolation of samurai and villager. Most landed retainers were men who came with the Maeda from outside the Kaga-Noto-Etchu region. Of 147 retainer houses active in the early seventeenth century, only eight were from Etchu, two from Kaga, and one from Noto, which is to say, better than 92 percent of the families were from outside the region.[8] Indeed, a 1616 roster of the very prominent Honda family's retainers shows that only 7.3 percent of the 124 mounted soldiers were from Kaga, Noto, and Etchu, suggesting that local men did not even fill the secondary ranks of Maeda vassals.[9]

Over the long run, even those absorbed into the Maeda ranks fared very poorly. In general their power and income were reduced, not augmented by association with the new overlord.[10] The story of the Kikuchi family is illustrative. A former vassal of Sassa Narimasa, Kikuchi Takekatsu, lord of Ao castle in Himi, surrendered to the Maeda once the battle for Etchu was lost. He was allowed to keep his domain of about 10,000 koku but retired in favor of his son Izu. When Izu died in 1596, the family's holdings were reduced to 1,500 koku. The Toma family of Notojima fared even worse. They had held lands valued at more than 43 bales of rice under the Hatakeyama. At that time one of the Toma's responsibilities was to levy and collect the tax on oysters for their lord. Even though they continued to perform this duty for Toshiie after his arrival, they lost their landholdings.[11] Others shared the Kikuchi and Toma fate, and still more local warriors simply became members of the new administration, without ties of fief to the land and passing from one administrative assignment to another.[12] In sum, large fiefholders with pre-Maeda roots in Kaga, Noto, and Etchu, those with the best chance to create an autonomous local base of support, were weakened and restricted early on.*

If pre-Maeda local samurai were absorbed into the Maeda ranks in any substantial number, it must have been at the very lowest levels of the retainer band. Their fiefs would have been under 100 koku if, indeed, they had any fief at all. The Honda example suggests that though there may have been a slightly higher proportion of native sons among the subretainers, the percentage was still very low. Many of these low-level local samurai probably received a stipend rather than a fief, and thus had no contact with the villagers at all unless they were appointed tax agents.[13]

We have already encountered the only clear exception to this pattern. The Chō family occupied a special position in the retainer band. Though ordered to serve Toshiie when he took over in Noto, the Chō maintained

---

*In the 20 years following the reduction of the Kikuchi fief, several other important samurai families saw their fiefs discontinued (Urata, "Shoki Maeda-ke kashindan," pp. 17–19).

their direct link to Oda Nobunaga. And when Oda died, Toshiie re-granted them the land they held, thereby cementing a mutually beneficial defensive tie during the uncertain period following Oda's death. Hideyoshi acknowledged Toshiie's grant and treated the Chō as military dependents of the Maeda.[14] Though the new grant placed the Chō in a subordinate relationship to Toshiie, as we have seen, the Chō retained an extraordinary degree of administrative autonomy (conducting their own land surveys, for example), and a more traditional kind of rule prevailed in their fief than in other parts of Kaga domain, one in which a continued local presence kept them closely tied to the villagers.*

The Fiefs

The Maeda followed the prevalent custom of granting fiefs (*kyūchi*) only to their chief retainers. Though figures for the early period of domain development are not available, the proportion of the domain's land granted in fief was substantial, at least during the second decade of the seventeenth century. As the domain grew, the band of landed retainers expanded. In 1612, 590 landed retainers possessed about 235,000 koku of fief lands. Just after the Osaka campaigns, in 1616, 995 retainers held fiefs totaling 896,250 koku. A decade later (1627) there were 1,333 retainers with lands valued at about 940,450 *koku*. This amounted to more than 70 percent of Kaga's total assessed value.[15]

The sharp increase in the number of landed retainers and the proportion of lands held in fief cuts against the grain of the traditional view that more and more domain land came under direct daimyo control from the late Sengoku era to the late seventeenth century. The increase appears to have stemmed from the need to reward retainers for service in the two Osaka campaigns. However, there may have been an added consideration. If my calculation of land tax trends for the late sixteenth and early seventeenth centuries are correct, the daimyo's mechanism for land taxation began to fall apart. By shifting more of the responsibility for assessing and collecting taxes to retainers who benefited directly from the collections (as opposed to daikan, who were simply the daimyo's bureaucrats and lacked incentives to perform their duties efficiently), the Maeda may have hoped to improve the collection rate and rid themselves of some of the administrative responsibility for tax assessment. (Whatever the motivation, the shift of authority

---

*It was largely due to their close ties to the land that the Chō family and its retainers were able to resist the full centralization of domain authority in the mid-17th century.

was only temporary; by mid-century retainer fiefs were mere legal fictions and tightly controlled by the domain.)

Scholars debate just how much autonomy landed retainers had in the domain's early years.[16] Conclusions depend very much on what measure is employed. Perhaps the problem can be minimized if we consider the extent or limits of kyūnin authority from two distinct perspectives. The scope of activities within which they could act represents one criterion. Were they able to exercise judicial rights? What village resources were open to them? Which taxes could they assess and collect? A second criterion concerns the latitude with which they could act within the permitted range of authority. Within each category of action, how much decision-making power did they have? How much were they restrained by daimyo ordinances or custom?

If one conceives of mid-sixteenth century retainers as having unlimited authority (much like a small daimyo), then the great majority of early Maeda retainers operated within a relatively restricted environment. The daimyo reserved for himself full control of all domain forest resources; the right to bamboo, river, and other miscellaneous taxes; and complete judicial authority over commoners.[17] At the same time, within the retainers' two areas of competence—assessing and collecting land taxes and conscripting rural labor—they had a high degree of autonomy, at least early in Maeda rule. Indeed, villager complaints about the retainers' capriciousness in assessing land taxes and conscripting labor formed the basis for conflict between kyūnin and domain authorities over the next several decades.

Even though the Maeda granted only limited rights to fiefs and took steps to constrain the powerful local military figures, Toshiie and his sons were not content to stop with these measures. From the inception of their rule the Maeda, alert to the possibility that landed retainers might build on ties to the local population to establish a threatening power base, relied on a variety of measures to discourage close relationships between the two:

1. The initial grants of land to retainers were merely general statements of the grantholder's right to tax a specific amount of land within a large area, usually a district or county.[18] Even though this grant was followed by a document allocating the fief among specific villages, these were not named in the primary grant, so that a retainer would have had difficulty pressing his claims over any particular village. This method of fief allocation reinforced the landed retainers' sense of dependence on the daimyo.

2. The retainer's control was further weakened by the manner in which his lands were distributed. Generally a grant scattered his holdings among a number of different villages and often among different counties. Consider

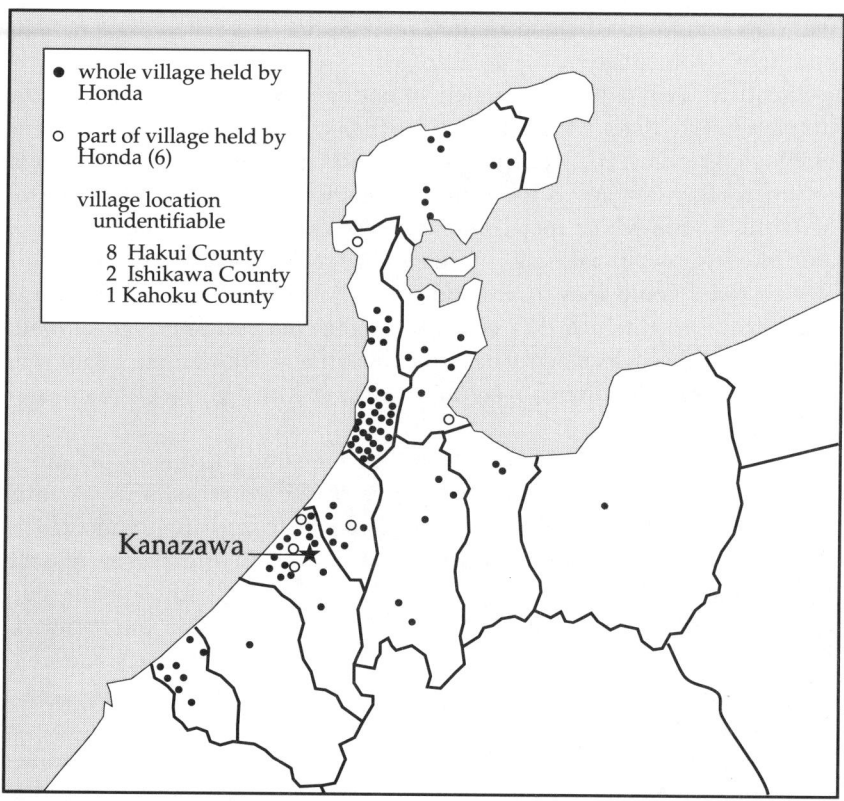

Map 5. The Honda Family's Fiefs, 1614. Redrawn from Urata, "Shoki Maeda-ke," p. 20.

the Honda family's domains in 1614, as shown in Map 5. Although most of the Honda's lands were concentrated in Ishikawa, Kahoku, and Hakui counties, some of the villages under their control lay in the farthest reaches of the domain, from Enuma county to Fugeshi county, and from Ishikawa county to Niikawa county. The villages close to Kanazawa may have been easy to reach for the purpose of inspecting crops regularly and setting tax rates, but several were not only far away from Kanazawa; they were far removed from other parts of the Honda domains. To tax these villages effectively required substantial efforts, and it would have been virtually impossible to maintain sufficient contact with them to form an independent power base. Although this fief is a relatively late example, some of the first fief registers attest to the very early use of this means of daimyo control.[19]

As a general rule, large fiefholders were more likely to be granted rights over entire villages; medium- and smallholders were more likely to possess only parts of villages.[20] Again, the Honda family holdings are typical. As Map 5 indicates, in only six cases did this powerful family share rights to villages with others. When villages were split this way, they were frequently partitioned among three or more retainers. Two villages in Ishikawa and Kahoku counties were split among seven retainers in 1599.[21] Yanase village in Tonami county was held jointly by 13 retainers.[22] In addition, many of these joint holders also shared their villages with the han.[23] The administration of fiefs, already encumbered by dispersal, was complicated where other shareholders set different tax rates in the same village. Argumentative residents used the lower rates of one retainer to bargain down another. Furthermore, other retainer tax agents could observe one's activities and this, too, discouraged close contacts.

3. The frequent redistribution of fiefs further disrupted retainer-villager relationships. Major redistributions took place in 1601 and 1627.* But even when there was no wholesale redistribution, fiefs were routinely shifted. In 1598, Fuwa Hikozo held five villages in Ishikawa county and three in Kahoku county. The following year he had six villages in Ishikawa and six in Kahoku—all different from the previous year.[24] All or part of the fiefs of three retainers in Noto were confiscated in 1615.[25] This same kind of redistribution or confiscation is evident on a larger scale in the 45 Tonami county villages under district chief Matauemon's jurisdiction in 1629–31. About half of them experienced some change in the kyūnin who drew taxes from their land.[26] Fief transfers of this sort reinforced the daimyo's control over the kyūnin and weakened their relationship with the villages. Both effects minimized the possibility of retainers creating an autonomous base from which to oppose the daimyo.

4. The concentrating of landed retainers in Kanazawa or local castle towns was another effective means of control. With rare exceptions retainers did not live on rural estates, and by 1600 the estates of the surviving pre-Maeda retainers had all but disappeared. Kyūnin whose fiefs were widely scattered through the domain could hardly live in or near all the villages they taxed even if they were posted to rural castles and fortifications. By one estimate, there were 54 rural fortifications during the early years of the domain.[27] Since this figure includes not only the largest castles (at

---

*Two other major redistributions took place before the middle of the 17th century, in 1639 and 1641 (Araya, "Kaga-han," p. 76; *WSS, Tsūshi hen*, p. 201; *IKS*, 3: 18). The fief exchanges of 1639 were tied to the creation of the branch han of Toyama and Daishōji; these were slightly adjusted in 1641.

Daishōji, Kanazawa, Komatsu, and Toyama), but also temporary fortifications constructed during the pacification of Etchu, it overstates the number of fortifications that housed landed retainers. Even so, the total is small enough to indicate that most landed retainers could not have lived sufficiently close to their lands to be anything but absentee landlords. Over time, as fortifications were consolidated, even the limited proximity afforded by these facilities declined.

In addition to these policies, many retainer families either died out because of military losses or were wiped out for political and economic reasons. Though no data have been compiled on the cessation of family lines before 1596, over the next 20 years an average of one fiefholding family a year disappeared. These retainers possessed sizable fiefs, averaging 4,500 koku each. Though the number of disappearances fluctuated from year to year over the next two decades, the size of the average fief lost fell to less than 1,000 koku. The families most affected, predictably, were those with large fiefs. Under Toshiie, 16 retainers had fiefs greater than 10,000 koku. By Toshitsune's reign the number had fallen to two. Over the same period those possessing fiefs between 4,000 and 9,999 koku fell from 24 to seven. In the five decades following 1596, the lands reallocated from discontinued families alone amounted to 123,000 koku.[28] The actual impact of the dying out of families was greater than this figure indicates since, in a number of instances, documents simply note a family's demise without indicating the size of its fief. The rapid increase in the number of fiefholders after the Maeda established themselves suggests that large fiefs were replaced by smaller ones in a conscious effort to prevent any individual retainer from amassing real power.

In sum, over the whole period from the founding of the domain to the mid-seventeenth century, domain policies created barriers to close contact between the landed retainers and the general population. This substantially restricted the retainers' effective administration of land taxation and corveé labor. Ultimately, it created frustration for all concerned.

The Fuchibyakushō

To this point we have discussed the fate of immigrant retainers and those local inhabitants who joined the Maeda ranks as enfeoffed retainers. We now turn to the families who stayed on the land, giving up the warrior component of their pre-Maeda life. These families constitute one of the most interesting classes of actors in the early annals of the domain, for in their collective biographies lies much of the story of class separation. The group of men local historians call *fuchibyakushō* provide considerable insight into this process. Neither clearly warrior nor clearly commoner, they became the pivotal link in local affairs, as district administrators. I leave a discussion of the fuchibyakushō's functions to Chapter 6; here I wish to examine their background and ambiguous social status, and the ways in which they made themselves useful to their new masters.

The Japanese term *fuchibyakushō* (literally, "stipended peasants") refers to people who were paid by the domain for the services they rendered. When applied to the very early years of the domain, the term is a misnomer, for these men were not peasants, at least not in the ordinary sense of the word. In important respects they resembled samurai more than peasants. Indeed, a number of them were associated with the armies of the Ikkō sect and other pre-Maeda military bands. Though later classified as rural commoners, in this period they are better thought of as local warriors in transit to commoner status.

Historians of Kaga domain tend also to limit the term to officials appointed in Noto. They do not acknowledge a similarity between local men who received a stipend and those who received some other form of compensation from the domain. But I believe that the wide variation in stipend size (from a high of 140 bales of rice to a low of three) suggests some fuchibyakushō were closer to samurai masters than farmer subordinates and argues for a flexible definition of this category of administration. Furthermore, if such appointments were confined to Noto, we must explain why that was. Given the existence of local officials who seem very close to the fuchibyakushō in all respects except the formal granting of a rice stipend and the need for the domain administrators to establish some link to local inhabitants, it seems unreasonable to adhere to a narrow definition of these functionaries.[29]

Fuchibyakushō came from the group of local farmer-warriors called *kokujin*, "provincial people." The services they performed for Toshiie extended into the military arena but were not limited to them. Their local ties to the land are evident from the fact that their stipends came from the tax proceeds of particular villages, typically from the one that served as their home base.

Most were descended from prominent families who had resided in the area for some time. Often they claimed important warriors as ancestors. Though claims of centuries-old samurai origins are suspect, a number of the fuchibyakushō were certainly active as low-level samurai at the time of the Maeda occupation. The family of Tomosada of Jin'e village, for example, served local military leaders such as the Yūsa and the Chō prior to the

Maeda arrival. In return Tomosada had received a partial tax exemption.[30] The family of Saneyori, Uwado village, came to the region from Echigo. During Sassa's invasion of Noto, Saneyori was involved in the defense of Nanao castle, along with the Hatakeyama, Chō, and Yūsa.[31] Though other fuchibyakushō—like Tarōemon (Nakagawa village), Shinbei (Tuschihashi village), and Yōichi (Nakashima village)—were apparently not fighting men before the Maeda arrival, they provided horses, supplies, and information to the new daimyo's forces.[32]

Toshiie's contacts with these families fit a broad pattern of overtures to locally influential people and institutions. This approach, evident from the earliest stages of his occupation of Noto, can be seen in the very large number of temples and shrines to which he made land grants.[33] These grants were nominally for the maintenance of religious buildings and priests, but one aim was certainly to win over the Ikkō sect adherents whom Oda Nobunaga had so recently defeated. The sect's strong military organization might have been broken, but its local leaders still had enough influence to persuade many followers to cooperate with their former enemies.

Although influencing Ikkō sect leaders may have loomed large in the policy-makers' minds, other prominent temples and shrines also received official support. Such actions helped to broaden the institutional base for Toshiie's fledgling rule and clearly were directed first at institutions that could exercise the most influence.[34] These actions simultaneously paved the way for integrating those institutions into the domain's control structure.

However necessary or helpful overtures to temples and shrines may have been, they were not adequate for the real goal: establishing functional administrative links to the local population. For this purpose Toshiie sought to enlist the support of locally influential men. His grants gave substance to a broad promise he issued when he arrived. In a call for assistance to his fledgling administration, he pledged to reward service to the domain in the form of either rice from the current harvest (i.e., a remission of taxes or stipend) or a permanent fief (*chigyō*). This effort to reach out was closely associated with anti-Maeda disturbances at the Tempyō Shrine at Sekidōsan in the summer of 1582. The first of these grants were issued only a month after that uprising was quelled, in reward for assistance in that endeavor.[35]

Toshiie's call for assistance fit nicely with the desires of ambitious local gentry. The men who became fuchibyakushō were as eager to curry favor with their new lord as he was to have their cooperation. Through pro-Maeda actions they hoped not only to earn the promised rewards but also to protect their existing perquisites. They were not disappointed.

Tabatabei of Sōgō village provides the clearest example of a man who managed to preserve his privileges this way. After the Maeda occupation of Noto, Sassa Narimasa gathered his forces for an assault on the Maeda stronghold at Suenomori. Tabatabei, learning of the pending attack, notified the castellan at Suenomori and officials in Kanazawa. In reward for his timely military intelligence, Tabatabei was confirmed in his possession of the mountain lands in Noto that had originally been conferred on him by the Miyake, local military leaders in Noto.[36]

Although most of the fuchibyakushō possessed a samurai pedigree of sorts, it was not their military contributions but their functions in local affairs that made them useful in the long run. Toshiie sent Hikosuke of Awagura village, for example, throughout Noto to assist in the setting and collection of taxes. In return Hikosuke got a stipend of 50 bales of rice annually.[37] Not a few of the men had held formal positions in civil or religious administration before the Maeda occupation. Yukinaga, a kokujin and the head of the Kita Shrine at Sugawara, had collected taxes from surrounding villages for the support of the shrine. Toshiie allowed him to continue his duties and gave him a stipend rather than replacing him.[38] Gembei of Goshō village was closely affiliated with the Ikkō sect. He continued to work for the new lords even without financial reward.[39] Like Gembei, a large proportion of these men probably had some connection with the Ikkō ikki, but extant genealogies rarely reveal the nature or degree of their involvement with the sect's formal organization.[40]

The specific contributions of each of the fuchibyakushō are not always recorded in the genealogies; but all of them actively assisted the newly arrived daimyo in the occupation and defense of his domain. They provided information, acted as guides, and assisted in the investigation of taxable land. Although genealogies may exaggerate the role of certain individuals, there can be little doubt that in general the fuchibyakushō earned the trust of the Maeda by their actions and continued to earn their stipends as local administrators. They served as a crucial link between the new daimyo, his officials, and the local population.

Though Toshiie's initial call for support made a distinction between two forms of reward, one paid like a salary from current domain revenues, the other granted as a fief, the ways in which those rewards were distributed suggests that no firm social or occupational distinction was intended initially. In practice the tax exemptions or stipends were as hereditary as the fiefs. Toshiie's purpose was to attract assistance from local gentry, not to create clear socioeconomic class distinctions.

The experience of two families who ultimately settled into this class

of civilian rural administrators nicely illustrates the lack of a sharp distinction between the form of reward dispensed and the recipient's social status. When Kamijima Yagorō, an enfeoffed retainer of Toshiie's, died in 1583, Toshiie recognized his son Yaroku as his successor. But Yaroku declined to follow in his father's footsteps and chose to become a fuchibyakushō instead. Conversely, the son of the fuchibyakushō Hirosuke was later enfeoffed as a landed retainer.[41] In both instances succeeding generations crossed what later became a line separating warrior from commoner. At this time the family of origin did not prevent the receipt of either type of reward. Nor did the receipt of one kind of award preclude the receipt of the other kind at a later date.

In the first two decades of the Maeda occupation in short, the distinction between grant types was one in name only. The type of reward received did not yet mark a hard and fast separation of warrior from rural commoner.[42] These locally influential people who linked the emergent domain administration and the rural population participated in both worlds.

The fact that not all local leaders used by the Maeda received a fuchi further complicates any attempt to link type of reward to status. Jirōbei (Kurami village) met Toshiie at Wajima and was appointed a tax collection agent. He was given a residential compound (*yashiki*) that may have been tax exempt, but not a stipend or a fief.[43] Like Gembei of Goshō village, the ancestors of Shōsuke (Imahama village) supposedly worked without stipend as *kimoiri-gashira* (chief headman) and *kumigashira* (head of a group of villages) in Imizu county during the late Tenshō period (1581–92).[44] Though by the records these men did not receive a fief or stipend for their services, everyone who worked for the regime was probably compensated somehow. That there is a measure of caprice in the reward structure reinforces the impression that compensation was unsystematized and did not yet reflect clear class-based distinctions.

The men whom local historians specifically refer to as fuchibyakushō were concentrated in the Noto area, but there are examples of local notables in other areas who received grants from Toshiie in return for similar services. Genjirō of Yoshino village (Ishikawa county) was originally associated with the Ikkō military organization. He came to Kaga from Echizen, where he had been a masterless samurai. Toshiie made use of him and gave him seven chō of land. His family remained on the land as commoners. Genjirō was not unique.* Since he and others like him fulfilled adminis-

---

*Tabatabei, mentioned previously, is another example; Jirōzaemon and Rokurōzaemon, discussed below, also fall into this category. See *Tonami shi shi*, p. 385; and *KHNK*, 1: 525.

trative functions and were later considered to be full-fledged villagers, it seems appropriate to see them as the equivalent of fuchibyakushō.⁴⁵ Thus, although in a narrow sense the fuchibyakushō system was confined to Noto, it represents the Maeda's overall approach to establishing a local administrative foundation.

Toshiie continued to extend his local contacts for several years after his arrival, and Toshinaga followed a related strategy in his domains. He granted a stipend of ten bales of rice to Jirōzaemon (Noga village) in 1594. The genealogy of Kambei's family (Fukutome village) indicates that their ancestor Rokurōzaemon was appointed a district official in 1594. A similar claim is made in the Watanabe genealogy.⁴⁶

To this point, I have stressed the role of fuchibyakushō as a local link for the Maeda, but these appointments served another purpose. In Kaga the Ikkō ikki and other local military bands bequeathed to the daimyo a number of leaders who were potential troublemakers. Accordingly, a key problem for the Maeda (and for all generals pacifying newly conquered lands) was finding a way to neutralize these potential opponents. In effect the strategy of granting stipends to fuchibyakushō did exactly this. It gave at least some of the earlier local leaders a stake in the new daimyo's success. Their status was strengthened and protected by official recognition from the daimyo. They received economic benefits from the domain. There is little likelihood that the fuchibyakushō would have found opposition to the Maeda attractive under the circumstances. The beauty of the system was that it accomplished the regime's goals without threatening the local leaders who were not directly coopted.

In addition, by appointing fuchibyakushō, the Maeda broke the previous equality that had existed among the village leaders under the ikki rule. Once some were given an interest in supporting the new rulers, the potential for unified local opposition and revolt was weakened. At the same time, the leaders who did not receive a stipend may well have been reluctant to revolt against their former comrades and place them in jeopardy by their actions. This was not simply a matter of fraternal feeling. The link to the daimyo could serve friends of the fuchibyakushō, too.

Although the system disrupted the old social patterns, it allowed the daimyo to deal with his new subjects without having to establish sustained, direct contact with each village. This helped to isolate traditional Maeda retainers from their new subjects. The Maeda's use of fuchibyakushō at once kept their retainers more dependent on them and minimized the potential for direct confrontations with villagers and their leaders. The domain administrators' relationship to villages was largely limited to the tax system, and they found an economical way to tap local administrative talent and knowledge for their own purposes. Fuchibyakushō could handle a variety of tasks without an extensive involvement of nonresident middle- and senior-level retainers.

This system had advantages for local gentry, too. It left much of the detail of district and village administration to their discretion. To this extent the strategy appealed to the desire of local leaders to protect their own interests. There was no outside force hell-bent on redistributing land or tampering with the prerogatives they had built up over the years.

The fuchibyakushō system may have been a sophisticated and useful way to put down roots in a new domain, but it leaves a puzzle for historians who want to identify the origins of class separation. The similarity between grants of land (*kyūchi*) and stipends, the obvious samurai background of most fuchibyakushō, the easy movement between that emerging status and the status of retainer, all suggest that there was no sharp division between commoner and warrior in the early decades of the domain. Though the samurai who came with the Maeda never settled on the land—in itself one point of departure on the road to separation—there is no clear break that tells us when fuchibyakushō lost their warrior roles and when it became impossible for retainers to return to the land. The form of Kaga land surveys further complicates matters. Since the surveyors made no effort to list individuals' names in the registers, we have no clue, not even an ambiguous one, to who was a villager in the eyes of the domain authorities. Nowhere is there a record of any specific order on the subject, nor did domain authorities act on the separation edicts issued by Hideyoshi.*

But if we have no clear dates for the separation of classes, it is possible to point to developments critical to confirming the commoner status of fuchibyakushō and the urbanized warrior status of retainers.

Most fuchibyakushō came from the local warrior class, men who fought largely to defend their home base, rather than to extend their territory. As long as there were battles nearby, they were useful to the daimyo either in their own right or as part of a local coalition. But they were never, as a group, well integrated into the daimyo's regular military organization. Consequently, they were not called on regularly to take up military duties outside their home province.

As the battles of the late sixteenth century moved farther and farther

---

*Sword hunt results were reported for one county in southern Kaga in 1588, but this territory was not yet under Maeda control. Within the domain senior villagers (*osabyakushō*) were brought to Kanazawa to sign a pledge, but apparently no large-scale confiscations of weapons took place. See Hara, *Kaga-han*, p. 40; KHNK, 1: 41, 98; and KHS, p. 376.

from the Hokuriku, fuchibyakushō lost their utility as soldiers and their opportunity to serve as such. The battle at Suenomori (1585) was the last campaign within the Maeda domains. None would again be fought nearby until the brief campaign in southern Kaga, preparatory to Sekigahara. Although the children of fuchibyakushō served in the households of retainers, and a few had the opportunity for military service, they were an exception. In practice, if not in legal principle, the fuchibyakushō and their families had become commoners by the late 1580's.*

On the other side of the coin, local peace gradually contributed to the consolidation of samurai in a few large fortifications. By 1599 major retainers had been assigned residences in the castle at Kanazawa, and from that point on, their focus for their families' professional obligations became the castle town, not the rural fortifications to which the adult men were posted.[47]

At the turn of the century, both trends had done much to reduce contact between warrior and villager. To retainers, villagers were a source of revenue and labor. Except when fuchibyakushō children served in the households of landed retainers, there was no consistent contact between the two groups. Practically speaking, local and national peace meant that brave young commoners had no opportunity to come to the attention of battlefield generals and to join the ranks of enfeoffed retainers or their salaried counterparts. The line between warrior and commoner was being drawn in practice simply as a result of changes in the proximity of military conflict. Individuals still crossed the status lines or existed in the interstices between the two social groups, but this was increasingly less common.

Conclusion

In putting down roots in their new domain, the Maeda behaved pretty much as one would expect under the circumstances. They placed their trust first and foremost in the retainers who came with them to the new domains. These men were a known quantity. Toshiie had worked with them over the years and had a sense of who was capable and trustworthy. (In an age of treachery the latter was no mean consideration.) These men were granted fiefs and positions of greatest responsibility.

Conversely, local samurai and gentry were granted limited opportu-

---

*The fuchibyakushō's role in local military conflicts remained in the minds of domain administrators; witness the order immediately before Sekigahara that they present themselves as hostages during the crisis, just as landed retainers had to provide hostages. (This was also an obligation of their successors, the tomura, during the Osaka campaigns.)

nities under their new lord. Certainly they were useful in promoting the defense of the domain and providing effective access to local resources, but they were not to be trusted with critical military responsibilities. Even those who were admitted to the ranks of the Maeda retainer band were phased out as it became practical to do so.

Only in the realm of local liaison did the Maeda employ influential indigenous people on a long-term basis. Because of their standing, they could make significant contributions to the new administration. They knew local conditions better than the interlopers, they had performed similar duties before the arrival of the Maeda, and their assistance could be purchased cheaply. Gaining their cooperation helped to break up old gentry alliances as well. The rural elite who filled these positions were as eager to use the new daimyo to advance their own interests as he was to use them. This symbiotic relationship functioned well for both, and it, or something like it, was probably also characteristic of other parts of Japan.[48]

The origins of class separation in Kaga lay in the early bifurcation of the local warrior-gentry's tasks, not in the orders of a central authority. To the extent that central authority played a role, it was indirect, an outcome of the decision to transfer Toshiie into Noto. As outsiders, already marked by their foreign origins, Maeda retainers were not allowed to create close ties to the villagers in their fiefs. Inhabitants who could have participated in local military campaigns early in the 1580's found their services irrelevant as the major campaigns in which the Maeda participated moved away from the domain. At the same time, the Maeda offered very limited opportunities for local samurai to join the ranks of their retainer band.

How many other domains followed this path to a substantial and practical, if not legal, separation of classes is unclear. Certainly the ubiquitous transfer of daimyo during the late sixteenth and early seventeenth centuries encouraged an increased distance between warrior and villagers throughout Japan. But how far transfers carried the process must in part have been a function of time and the proximity of conflict. The earlier and the more frequent the transfers in a region, the greater the opportunity for the process to work its logic. The greater a region's freedom from major conflicts, the better the daimyo's opportunity to move toward consolidating his military forces in fewer and fewer fortifications. There was nothing deterministic about the impact of transfers on domains, and in some cases the role of central authority in class separation may have been more direct. All the same, a daimyo's need to put down roots in a new territory forced him to reconsider how much autonomy to give villages, landed retainers, and even domain officials. The challenge of a transfer provided a significant opportunity to reconstruct the relationships between warrior and villager.

Chapter 6

Early Rural Administration

At the same time that Toshiie and Toshinaga determined relationships between their existing retainers and the kokujin of their new territories, they set about creating an administrative apparatus. As military rulers, they began gingerly, establishing only the most spartan of administrative structures. With the advent of peace, first within the domain and later at the national level, the Maeda, like other daimyo, focused more attention on resolving conflicts and inefficiencies in local administration.

Early administrative contacts between the domain and villagers were mediated exclusively by tax agents of the daimyo (daikan), landed retainers' agents (gedai), and nonsamurai district representatives.* Contrary to common descriptions of local administration in the early modern era, reorganizing village administration and maintaining close contact with village leaders were not significant concerns for the domain.

Small Districts, the Foundation of Domain Administration

Most historians tell the story of developing local institutions in Japan from the standpoint of the village. They stress how rural communities pressed for increased autonomy in the late middle ages through both peace-

---

*The term "daikan" was rather loosely used in practice. In Maeda domains it was occasionally applied to the landed retainers' tax agents (see *Oshimizu chō shi*, pp. 174–75). It could also refer to officials who had county-wide functions (*Shimo Niikawa gun shikō*, 1: 737). In this chapter I follow the most common practice (see, among others, KHNK, 1: 84), reserving it exclusively for those low-level agents of the daimyo who circulated throughout the domain in the performance of their duties. Some writers have preferred to call these officials *uketori daikan* or *kumi daikan* (see Kigoshi, "Maeda," p. 29; and *Noto Wajima Kamikaji-ke monjo*, pp. 86–87).

ful and violent means. The principal tools they used were the tax contract (*hyakushō uke*) with the overlord and the ikki, or local military league. Villages pledged to deliver an agreed-on amount of taxes but had the right to allocate them as they chose among their residents. This community autonomy was jealously guarded by the ikki, which brought together kokujin and other influential families to prevent excessive taxation and other intrusions into local affairs by overlords. Most of these military groups endured only long enough to accomplish a specific task, but some, like the Buddhist Ikkō ikki, lasted many decades. Early modern daimyo built on villagers' growing experience with self-government embodied in these trends.

The widespread emphasis on village development derives from two sources. First, the weight scholars place on the structure of land surveys contributes to this interpretation. Villages were the basic units of surveys, and they were widely treated as the units of taxation. There are even those who argue that the creation of the village as an official administrative unit violated the "natural" village of the late medieval era. On this view, intracommunal cooperation in "natural villages" flowed spontaneously from the community's day-to-day social and economic links. In contrast, cooperation in the early modern village came from the demands of an overlord who treated the village largely as a legal individual for the purpose of tapping domain labor, natural resources, and agriculture. Second, the village model is largely drawn from the Bakufu territories of central Japan, where villages were indeed the basic unit of commoner administration.[1]

In fact, however, the principal locus of low-level administration varied from domain to domain and over time. In some cases the responsibility lay with low-level samurai officials, as in Satsuma, or was shared with rusticated samurai (Tosa). In other cases commoner officials who presided over groups of villages held the pivotal position. Kaga domain fell into this category.

From the earliest indications of local government in Kaga domain, the district, a group of villages, provided the critical link between rural subjects, domain officials, and representatives of landed retainers. Except for tax documents and land surveys, individual villages do not figure prominently in the early ordinances that affected rural residents. The structure of village officialdom was not specified by higher authorities, and it remained unelaborated for decades. Villages, as nascent administrative units, had much autonomy. In this sense village autonomy contributed significantly to the separation of warrior and commoner. At the least, the lack of domain involvement in villages is a sign of how little time daimyo had for the minute regulation of rural community affairs of any sort.

Fuchibyakushō Administration

As indicated previously, a principal issue for newly arrived "potted plant" daimyo was how to gain the support (or at least, the acquiescence) of local leaders whose talents and cooperation were essential to effective administration. To fail in this effort risked major local rebellions such as those in Higo and Tohoku.

Ikkō ikki remnants challenged the political and organizational skills of the Maeda, but all "potted plant" daimyo had to contend with the same sort of obstacle. Like other ikki in Japan, the Kaga Ikkō ikki was oriented first and foremost to withstanding encroachments by outside overlords. An earlier view of the Ikkō ikki treated it as broadly popular, democratic, and egalitarian. In this view, commoners cooperatively held the province (*hyakushō no mochitaru kuni*) and therefore were more likely to resist the imposing of a hierarchical warrior order. But recent scholarship emphasizes the similarities between locally active Ikkō leaders and the kokujin of other parts of Japan. The Kaga ikki organizations even resisted the attempts of the sect's headquarters, the Honganji in Kyoto and Osaka, to control it. Local adherents stressed their own political agenda and defied the Honganji's attempts to act like other sixteenth-century daimyo. As we saw in the investigation of the fuchibyakushō's origins, a gentry of kokujin-like families controlled pre-Maeda Kaga. In this sense the task the Maeda faced was typical of late-sixteenth-century daimyo. All faced the problem of how to incorporate or subjugate the lower levels of the preceding rulers' military organization.[2]

The Maeda solved the problem by co-opting the fuchibyakushō as district administrators. Their appointment marked the beginning of an organizational emphasis on district-level administration. District offices became the highest and most important level of rural administration held by commoners.

The district emphasis in Kaga administration was not new to local inhabitants. In the middle of the sixteenth century, official documents were commonly addressed only to the district, and not to an individual hamlet or village. Sometimes districts became so closely associated with each other that they were clumped under one name. This was the case with the three districts of the Oshimizu area near the modern-day city of Hakui, which became known as Oshimizu san ka (the three districts of Oshimizu).

Small groupings of households, "villages" or "hamlets," gradually gained a small measure of the individuality that earlier had been sacrificed to the district (*gō, shō, in, sō,* etc.). At least this was the case from the perspective of higher administrators. If a village within a district was mentioned, the district name preceded the village or hamlet name. Menden village was not simply Menden, but Oshimizu Menden.[3] Yet even in this context, the group or district was still dominant.

Each group focused on a shared, practical concern—common access to water, mountains, grasslands, and other resources that were of vital economic importance to each hamlet.[4] The amalgamating of groups into larger ones (as in the Oshimizu area) suggests that the original groups expanded their need for cooperation to such an extent that some important decisions had to be made regularly on an intergroup basis. Consultations and perhaps joint appeals to higher authorities became common enough for them to meld into a larger group.

This process was not predestined or unidirectional. Examples of the opposite tendency also exist. Kami Machino sō is a case in point. In the mid-sixteenth century, it was broken into two groups. This was probably due to changes in patterns of local cooperation and interests.[5]

The undifferentiated and informal administrative structure of these district organizations reflected their flexible and practical nature. How much administrative power district groups had in the sixteenth century is debated. Some local historians believe they were self-governing.[6] Others believe they had no administrative role.[7] There are indications that district groups served some limited official administrative function within the overall context of Ikkō ikki provincial administration. In addition to the practice of addressing documents to groups of hamlets, the names of some districts reflect their role as low-level administrative or military units. Kanazu sho in Etchu was also called "go-ban-han" (fifth unit, half) and "go-ban ichi-gumi" (fifth unit, first group).[8] The numbering of districts in this fashion suggests a formal role for district organization in the Ikkō ikki chain of command.

Whatever administrative functions the district organization had were insufficient to foster a formal administrative structure. We have no record of an appointed or elected official who headed each district. Administrative matters were handled by informal discussions among the hamlet leaders and influential residents (*otonabyakushō*).

Under ikki rule, the largest formal administrative divisions were *kumi*, literally meaning "group." If the province of Kaga is typical, and it probably is, there were no more than a dozen kumi in each county. Since there were several hundred villages in a county, the average kumi would have embraced about two dozen villages.* By contrast, the Maeda's *fuchibyakushō*

---

*Davis, "Kaga Ikkō Ikki," p. 119, estimates that in 1531 there were nine or ten kumi in Ishikawa county, eight in Kahoku, and four in Nomi. *Ishikawa ken Torigoe son shi*, pp. 210–

generally presided over only 10 or 12 villages.* Commensurate with their smaller size, they could—and did—keep a closer eye on local conditions than supra-district officials under the Ikkō structure.

The fuchibyakushō in Noto and their counterparts elsewhere performed a variety of services for the domain and the villagers. For the villagers, they were the first line of defense against the landed retainers' tax agents. If these lower samurai were arbitrary or unreasonable, the fuchibyakushō filed a complaint with senior officials. Fuchibyakushō were also expected to administer the natural resources of the mountain areas for the local residents and the daimyo.[9]

For domain authorities, however, this side of administration was secondary. The most important duty of the fuchibyakushō was overseeing the collection of all local taxes. The principal tax was the annual land tax, which was usually collected in kind. The fuchibyakushō coordinated the actual collection and delivery of these goods. Their responsibility in this department extended to the management of the granaries where the tax rice was stored and to its transport to and from the granaries.

Their other chief duty was to try to expand the land tax base. Fuchibyakushō identified usable but currently uncultivated land. They were expected to encourage reclamation. At this stage in the domain's development, incentives to villagers who undertook the opening of new lands to cultivation or the conversion of dry field to paddy were not well developed. The district chiefs had little with which to perform this part of their jobs except their own persuasive powers and personal leverage.

In some cases farmers could not cultivate land after it was flooded or damaged by some other natural disaster. The fuchibyakushō assessed the unused land's potential for recultivation, and then took steps to ensure that it once again produced grain, and hence taxes, for the domain. To this end he might organize a village or district work force to clear the land of debris

---

11, likewise indicates that there were four kumi in Nomi county in 1547. These kumi could be quite large. Yamanouchi-gumi encompassed about half the territory of Nomi county and was further semiofficially divided into three groups, one of which consisted of only 16 villages. Yamanouchi-gumi is clearly exceptional. It received orders directly from the Ikkō sect headquarters, the Honganji. Orders were usually not addressed to individual kumi but rather to all kumi in a county. In the Tenshō era (1573–91) each of Hakui county's kumi contained 230 villages (Kaneda, *Minami Ōmi son shi*, pp. 43–44).

*See, for example, KHNK, 1: 87–94; *Ishikawa ken Shio chō shi*, pp. 134–35; and Kawa, *Hatta no rekishi*, p. 53. The groups varied in size. KHNK presents one example of 19 villages, but none approached the size of the Hakui county kumi during the Ikkō ikki, and others may have been smaller than 19. Though the size and details of the administrative structure of these groups are often unclear, the Maeda unquestionably saw them as administrative divisions. Documents were frequently addressed to "the peasants [hyakushō] of X group." (See, for example, NSS, 1: 50; and Araki Sumiko, "Kaga-han," pp. 493–96.)

and repair damaged irrigation facilities. Alternatively, he might only need to grant permission for a family to cultivate the land in place of a fellow villager who had given up on it.

In other cases the land was not planted because its cultivator ran away from the village in protest or as the result of a dispute with other residents, so a logical corollary of the duty to preserve the land tax base was the obligation to prevent cultivators from leaving the village. Failing that, the fuchibyakushō was to locate the runaways and encourage them to return quickly before their fellow villagers were forced to assume their tax and corvée obligations.

Rural migration concerned domain policy-makers from the start of Maeda rule. Migration occurred in response to two different stimuli: administrative/political and economic. Early on, some villagers fled simply because they were unsure of what their new lords would do. In other instances they migrated to escape what they perceived as unduly high taxes or harsh treatment by landed retainers and the daimyo's agents. The desertion of individual families or even of whole villages was one form of opposition to samurai rulers.[10] But villagers also migrated to take advantage of economic opportunities elsewhere. Domain attempts to prevent them from going to Sado and other provinces to work gold mines reflect the lure of an early-seventeenth-century gold fever.[11] The rapidly growing city of Kanazawa, the daimyo's administrative headquarters, also offered attractive opportunities for those trying to improve their lot.[12]

The authorities worried that absconding and migration would lead to declining tax revenues. In 1591 they issued a pledge to the residents of Hongo, Urakami, Naiho, and Wada village groups that explicitly expressed this concern. In response to an apparently substantial problem, they promised not to collect back taxes, offered loan rice from the domain storehouse, and promised to deal with irregularities on the part of landed retainers and the daimyo's tax agents. Since they were making these pledges to meet the villagers' complaints, runaways should now "return to your villages and devote yourselves assiduously to the cultivation of your crops."[13]

From the autumn of his Noto enfeoffment, Toshiie repeatedly ordered fuchibyakushō to call back absconding villagers. The first such order was directed to the residents of Toge area in the fall of 1581.[14] Though han authorities occasionally made concessions, as in 1591, or rebuked abusive officials, their orders usually took the form of prohibitive legislation. In addition to bans on going to work in gold mines, domain authorities issued ordinances requiring the reporting of runaways, restricting the contracts of those hired as servants, and prohibiting the hiding of absconders.[15] Enforcing these ordinances was the responsibility of the district chiefs.

The fuchibyakushō were also responsible for the collection of miscellaneous cash taxes on fishermen, charcoal kilns, and other small-scale businesses. Though significant, these taxes represented a relatively minor part of the villagers' tax burden.* Much more important, the fuchibyakushō organized work crews for the fulfillment of corvée obligations. Village labor was used not only to maintain roads and other public works, but also to construct and repair coastal defenses, castles, and other fortifications. Villagers transported military supplies throughout the domain, and they were even called on to work in support of military campaigns outside the domain.[16]

The men who served as district administrators also probably acted as headmen for the villages in which they resided. This is suggested by a series of documents from the Ogino family collection in the vicinity of modern Himi City. Two sets of documents (1593 and 1595; 1596 and 1597) deal with both village and group matters. The Unami village headman and the Unami district official were one and the same: Sukeuemon.†

Finally, the fuchibyakushō served in various miscellaneous capacities. In the military sphere they acted as a coastal guard, reported on potential invasions or disturbances, and occasionally acted as spies in other domains. They also supervised aspects of coastal shipping. At a more personal level, their children often worked in samurai households as servants.[17]

Village Leadership

Through the early seventeenth century, domain appointments in local government and ordinances were directed at districts. From the perspective of the domain, the village was an ill-defined administrative level. To be sure, it was a unit of taxation, and survey magistrates demarcated villages as such. They clarified those boundaries between villages that bore directly

---

*The one possible exception is the tax on salt produced in the domain. The major salt-producing regions were located in the coastal villages of Noto. Salt production accounted for a major part of the total income of several of these coastal villages.

†The first document, ordering the transport of charcoal from a village in Noto to Moriyama castle in Etchu in 1593, is addressed to "Unami mura kimoiri sho." This could mean either "office of the Unami village kimoiri" (village official) or, since this traffic involved a rather large volume and a long distance, more likely, "the Kimoiri's Office in Unami village" (district official). A second document, ordering the shipment of salted fish in 1595, is addressed to "Unami mura kimoiri hyakushō chū"—to "the kimoiri and peasants of Unami village"—and appears to concern only the residents of the village. The following year, 1596, another document encouraging full tax payment and dealing with other tax-related matters for Unami was addressed simply to "Unami village Sukeemon." Finally, a 1597 document was addressed to "Unami-gumi Sukeemon"—"Sukeemon of Unami district"—and two other district administrators. (*Himi shi shi*, pp. 1176–79.)

on taxation—all residents understood which unit was responsible for land tax payments on each plot of arable land. But beyond this, the domain authorities prescribed no offices or duties for village officials.

Despite claims that the early modern daimyo froze villages into unnatural administrative divisions, there is little evidence that this was so in Kaga. The borders set by the land surveys were incomplete. Domain officials did not survey lands exempt from land taxes or uncultivated lands between villages that were not in dispute. The domain was simply not prepared to do this systematically. That level of intervention did not come until such time as it became the focus of an intervillage dispute, a common phenomenon throughout Japan. The many intervillage disputes over lands that later came under the plow or became sources of green manure, kindling, and other resources attest to the lack of firm, clear borders in these previously little used sections between villages.*

Cultivators were generally free to extend their activities into new lands, develop new irrigation and riparian works, and undertake any related endeavors until they came into conflict with a neighboring village's activities. As residents reclaimed land in more remote areas of a village, the domain often created a new village. The formal establishment of new villages (*shinmura*) permitted the authorities to recognize the distinctiveness of these newly cultivated areas—their lower land quality and their separate irrigation systems—minimizing the strain on the cooperative relationships in the old, main village.†

At the village level, the local gentry (kokujin) almost certainly continued to play the dominant role in local affairs. Though there is no clear documentation of this in the form of domain appointments, we have indirect evidence of their continued prominence as resident landholders. The handful of early 1580's records linking individual names to land show that

---

* With the passing of time and the growth of the rural population, competition between villages for access to these lands increased. It became particularly intense as villages expanded arable land into areas that had previously been unclaimed (formally) or utilized cooperatively. Richard Moore, Department of Anthropology, Ohio State University, has maps of a reclamation project cooperatively developed by Sakuraba, Ishin no Mori, Uwanuma, and Nagai villages in modern Miyagi prefecture. Though every map shows a complete division of the land, the boundaries shift substantially from year to year. Villagers did not see the boundaries as immutable.

†There are hundreds of cases of the spinning-off of villages. Instances appear in almost every local history, and documents prepared in the process of compiling the "Shōhō yon nen gochō" reflect boundary changes in several hundred villages. Given the limitations outlined in Brown, "Mismeasure of Land," and the lack of any consistent use of maps in the late-16th- and early-17th-century surveys throughout Japan, I believe that this same flexibility prevailed in other domains as well. (See, for example, Kikuchi, *Shinden kaihatsu*.) Furthermore, Hideyoshi's instructions on surveys did not effectively encourage more than the clear demarcation of boundaries between two villages' arable lands.

a few people in each village were associated with large proportions of village land. The names of the largest can be linked to the Ikkō military organization and the development of other large-scale economic projects in the years before the Maeda arrival. These past leadership experiences, in combination with continued large landholdings, placed the kokujin in a good position to influence village affairs.[18]

Village headmen (*mura kimoiri*) may have played an important role in local life as well, but the han authorities did not define or officially recognize that position until many years after the Maeda's entry into Noto. Domain ordinances do not explicitly mention the office of village headman until 1631.[19] We know enough from other kinds of documents that villagers engaged in a variety of collaborative activities essential to their livelihood and village harmony. Allocating tax payments, conducting warichi, determining land tenure, and the like all required a degree of coordination that must have emerged from local ranks, but what is noteworthy is the lack of direct domain interest in regulating these activities.

Villagers thus had considerable autonomy vis-à-vis the domain in the management of their internal affairs and the way they structured their own administrations. Only when intervillage disputes could not be resolved at the district level or involved taxation did the domain authorities intervene.

Landed Retainers (*Kyūnin*), the Daimyo's Intendants (*Daikan*), and the Villagers

At the same time that the daimyo established new administrative structures at the local level, he appointed samurai intendants (*daikan*) to oversee the lands administered directly by the domain. Daikan were the daimyo's principal administrative agents in the field. Most came from low-ranking samurai families. They were sufficiently low-ranking to be familiar with agriculture and to return to farmer status in several instances (another reminder of the fluidity of class lines at this time).

In addition, of course, Toshiie and his successors gave fiefs to their chief retainers. Through the mid-seventeenth century these landed retainers (kyūnin) held important private administrative responsibilities akin to those of daikan apart from their posts in the domain's military and bureaucratic structures. Their income came from taxes they assessed and collected from the villages in their fiefs.

The daimyo's policy on the appointment and control of daikan reflected concerns similar to those he addressed in granting fiefs to retainers, and although both daikan and kyūnin initially possessed considerable autonomy, conflicts between them and the villages induced the domain authorities to restrict their activities. Eventually this pressure had important transforming effects, but at this stage in domain development, the daimyo simply sought to limit the potential for the official abuse of villagers.

The daikan assessed and collected taxes. As with the fuchibyakushō, a closely related part of their primary charge was to encourage the expansion of the land tax base. In the very early stages of Maeda rule, the daikan also served as land surveyors.[20]

The earliest daikan had a somewhat impermanent air about them. They did not have a standing local office and may have resided in major castles throughout the domain.[21] All of the early daikan worked in somewhat unusual circumstances. Toshiie directly oversaw their work. Before 1589 his personal seal appeared on both the interim and the final tax receipts issued to the villagers. Tax receipts from 1589 on indicate a shift to permanent daikan offices and an official rural residence for at least some of the men. In that year Toshiie chose to withdraw from this activity and leave his agents in full charge of village tax matters.* How many daikan were active at any given time early in the domain's history is unknown. Shortly after the initial stages of a later district reform (ca. 1627), there was at least one per district.[22]

But even with the establishment of permanent offices, there was little stability in the jurisdictions of daikan. In the period 1585–90, nine of the 15 Noto villages for which we have tax data for more than one year experienced at least one change in *daikan*. Three of those experienced at least three changes.[23] (The situation did not improve with the passage of time. In Nafune-gumi, 16 of 37 daikan positions changed in the years 1631–34; four changed twice.[24] These are very high rates of turnover for such a short interval.)

Frequent transfers prevented daikan from establishing close ties with the local population. Such close relations could form a power base from which a daikan might oppose the daimyo or subvert his administrative goals. No document clearly establishes the daimyo's intent, but the tenor of the times certainly encouraged such thinking. In addition, frequent rotation may have been designed to prevent villagers and district officials from gaining sufficient confidence to attempt to bribe the incumbent.†

---

*Kigoshi, "Maeda," p. 31. The establishment of the office of daikan may have been accompanied by the establishment of a compound (*yashiki*) where the officeholder maintained a rural residence. *Noto Wajima Kamikaji-ke monjo*, p. 97, notes one case several decades after 1589.

†Bribery was a very real possibility. As we will see, this was the root of the Urano incident that brought Chō autonomy in Kaga to an end.

At first Toshiie gave both his lower officials and his landed retainers substantial latitude in the exercise of their principal functions—the assessment and collection of taxes. Provided that the tax base was maintained and expanded and the tax system served the domain reasonably well, domain authorities had little interest in the affairs of either daikan or kyūnin. Furthermore, in a period when the daimyo was heavily engaged in military activities in other parts of Japan, it was to his advantage to minimize the han's direct involvement. As long as monetary and military supplies were adequate and the lack of attention did not lead to serious disruptions of public order, attention to national activities took priority.

But the need for institutional safeguards was soon impressed on han officials by village protests of daikan or kyūnin abuse and the persistent absconding of peasants. In response, the Maeda imposed certain limited administrative restraints. (These developments were the first hints of a gradual shift toward greater central control at the expense of daikan and kyūnin.)

In fact, from the start Toshiie had foreseen the possibility of daikan and kyūnin exceeding their authority. In connection with the first harvest after his entry into Noto, he proclaimed: "In addition to the annual tax rice from the assessed fields, the *kyūnin* must not collect any other mountain, river, boat, or ocean tax, etc. If there is anyone who attempts to order other taxes, notification [to the *han* lord] must be made."[25] Again, in a 1583 order, we find the charge: "There is not to be the smallest additional tax. Regardless of what the *daikan* or anyone else says, if there is no official seal to the document, it is not to be recognized."[26] By these orders Toshiie showed that he was particularly concerned that the daikan and kyūnin not take advantage of the confusion inherent in establishing the new Maeda rule. He was certainly well aware that mistreatment could lead to cultivator flight, with crops left unharvested and therefore uncollectable as taxes.

Although there are only a few examples of official sanctions taken against those who violated these orders, they are sufficient to indicate that Toshiie's proclamations defining the duties of the daikan and kyūnin could not be ignored with impunity. In the spring of 1587, he ordered that the dry fields he had granted to a kyūnin be returned. Who the retainer was and what village or villages were involved are unclear, but the sequence of events leading to Toshiie's sanctions was recounted in the order itself. The land had been granted as part of a fief in 1586. The retainer promptly imposed excessive taxes, provoking the inhabitants to flee the village or to refuse to cultivate the land. The wheat crop, probably planted the previous fall, was completely abandoned. As a result of this mismanagement, the land reverted to the daimyo, and new lands were to be granted to the retainer.* Similar actions must have also been taken against errant daikan.

At the time of the Korean expeditions, daikan misconduct was an explicit matter of concern. Early in 1591 Maeda Yasukatsu, the castellan at Nanao and supervisor of Noto provincial administration, ordered villagers to report any misconduct on the part of their daikan. In addition, he instructed the daikan not to collect unpaid taxes.[27] Though this order was clearly part of an attempt to dampen rural discontent and to coax villagers back to their agricultural labors, Toshiie's concern in the late summer of the following year (1592) focused specifically on preventing daikan abuses. His orders reflected the financial strains caused by recent military campaigns and the Korean expeditions. Heavy manpower demands had forced him to send many samurai out of the domain who would normally have served as daikan. This left only a few to oversee tax collection. To ensure necessary military supplies and monies for his activities, Toshiie exhorted the remaining daikan: "Quickly complete the interim tax calculations and present them to Gorobei [Maeda Yasukatsu]. When I return to Kanazawa, there will be a general audit of taxes, and those *daikan* who caused villagers to fall into arrears in their payments . . . certainly will be punished."† In addition to guarding against negligence in tax collection, Toshiie wanted to restrain unscrupulous daikan from capitalizing on the lack of supervision to extort money from the villagers and threaten the domain's interests.

Toshiie followed through on his threat to punish daikan who violated his orders. When he returned from his activities in support of the Korean campaign in 1593, he conducted an investigation of the daikan's accounts as promised. The inquiry revealed that at least one, Hirose Sanai, had both embezzled funds and caused villagers great hardship. Sanai paid with his life for his abuse of power.[28]

Although Yasukatsu's order to report daikan misconduct included an

---

TKSS, 3:66. Toshiie clearly saw this transfer as an incentive for the villagers to return to cultivating the land. One of the final clauses states: "However, since this land is the daimyo's, it must quickly be recultivated."

† *KK*, p. 857. The phrase "mishin o sase" is ambiguous and can be interpreted as either "permit the peasants to fall into arrears" or "cause the peasants to fall into arrears." In light of the earlier warnings against the abuse of taxation powers, the notification that tax records would be checked on Toshiie's return, and the subsequent events noted below, I have interpreted the phrase as indicating causation rather than leniency or neglect of duty. The latter meaning, however, should not be excluded. Indeed, Toshiie could well have intended both meanings. Daikan could "cause" tax arrears in several ways: by making taxes so high that the villagers could not pay the full amount; by collecting personal loans and interest just before taxes were due; by pocketing tax monies before the villagers had paid all their taxes; and so forth.

injunction to report abuses by landed retainers as well, there is no evidence of a kyūnin being treated so harshly during the Korean campaign. Any punishment was most likely limited to a transfer or the reduction of a fief, or both. Since these men were so important to the smooth functioning of the domain's military machine, Toshiie may have been reluctant to take stronger measures against them. As noted previously, before 1600 the kyūnin had wide-ranging authority in their own fiefs. They were generally free to manage their lands as they saw fit, provided that they did not provoke strong protest from the villagers. Within these broad limits, the daimyo could tolerate some abuse of individual cultivators, since it did not directly affect domain tax revenues, only the kyūnin's.*

Throughout this early period, there were very few officials who stood between the daikan or kyūnin and the daimyo. When Toshiie was in the domain, complaints against daikan and kyūnin were to be presented directly to him; when he was absent, complaints were to be reported to his assistant, Maeda Yasukatsu.

Conclusion

The transition to Maeda rule in Kaga did not bring radical transformations in village structures, and the shifts in domain administrative organs at somewhat higher levels were gradual, not wrenching. Rather than approaching the tasks of establishing a new domain administration with the uncompromising zeal of revolutionary ideologues, the Maeda displayed a pragmatic bent. They balanced the needs of the villagers against those of the domain and its landed retainers. In the course of maintaining this balance, they bore in mind their own need to rely on the retainers who supplied the domain with much of its military manpower.

The changes were most marked in rural political structures; yet even here they were selective and gradual. The daimyo built on local resources, and in the process, created a district administrative unit under the fuchibyakushō without disturbing hamlet social and political structures. Village officers were not appointed by the daimyo or his subordinates. Nor were the hamlet leaders or the villages the object of detailed regulations from central administrative officials. Many functions typically thought to have

---

*Kyūnin as well as daikan had the power to approve or disapprove a villager's migration or adoption of a son or daughter (*KHS*, 1: 851). Most important, however, was the latitude kyūnin had in collecting taxes, including the ability to press villagers into personal servitude and to use torture to force payment. On this point, see Iwai, "Shoki Kaga-han," pp. 41–42; Araya, "Kaga-han," pp. 69–75; and *KHNK*, 1: 52.

been the responsibility of villages (e.g., ensuring tax payments, allocating corvée labor duties) were assigned to district officials.

Local talent was used at the district level as an intermediary in the domain's dealings with villages. Fuchibyakushō were an economical way to tap the talent of local men who knew the region well. Since they provided a regular channel for villager complaints, they were valuable in limiting the potential for local revolts against the new domain lords.

Landed retainers and daikan initially were left largely to their own devices in tax matters. The domain leaders were concerned that the villagers not be greatly abused, but in the case of kyūnin especially, they were content to respond to complaints rather than to impose specific restrictions. That Toshiie did not impose universal restrictions on the kyūnin in short order helps to explain why there was no broad opposition to his policies. The daimyo moved slowly, cognizant of the importance of the landed retainers to his military organization. Restrictions evolved over several decades, and they did not mean a wholesale loss of retainer rights. They were designed to correct the abuses of individual retainers (and daikan) that caused cultivators to flee their lands.

The specific steps the Maeda took in establishing their new administration do not necessarily typify developments in other domains, but their experience does teach us something about the early process of domain formation. Though the problems of setting up initial administrative structures were common to any new domain lord, the answers to those problems were not predetermined. Kaga's experience indicates that in some regions of Japan, domain lords were content to avoid the details of village government. Their key concerns were to maintain adequate revenues and a generally tranquil domestic order. As long as those criteria were met, the other demands on their time were too important to divert attention to the minutiae of village affairs. Only as the need to meet these criteria demanded or as domain administration stabilized and expanded beyond the early, spartan administrative staff would daimyo increase their efforts to regulate village affairs.

Village actions had a significant influence on domain policy, at least in the Kaga case. As we have seen, the motor driving increased restrictions on daikan and kyūnin—as least as far as we can tell from available documents—was absconding and village appeals. Ultimately, these protests from below did not simply result in a short-term gain, say, a one-year reduction in land taxes, but produced structural changes in domain administration.

Chapter **7**

Early Land Taxation

Was the late sixteenth and early seventeenth century a period of increased samurai control over the rural population, as is generally contended? In this chapter, though we will touch on the center's role in the matter of taxation, we will concentrate on the whole on what went on at the domain and village level. In this respect Kaga's land tax system is a significant indicator of the relative balance of political capabilities at both levels, of how much the ruling classes could impose their will on commoners, and how much villagers in turn could influence domain policies.

Land Taxation in Kaga: Some Preliminary Observations

It is obvious from the preceding discussion of Kaga land surveys that we need to rethink the role of the domain in land taxation. But before turning to that issue, let us assess the land survey itself as an implement of land taxation. Although there were no actual measures, we can still make a qualitative assessment of what the "surveyors" were doing as they traveled through villages and how effectively they conducted their work.

It is likely that surveyors first went to a central village, perhaps the one where the district chief resided, to review earlier assessment and tax records. At least after the initial investigations, any new data collected were compared against the figures in previous survey documents and other official records. These reviews were probably then supplemented by discussions with village headmen and others about irregularities, reports of unregistered fields, and boundary disputes. Representatives from neighboring villages were questioned to determine the tax responsibility for fields athwart village borders.[1] If the surveyors did any fieldwork, it consisted of little more than making a spot check of the villagers' reports, an inspection of a disputed border, or a sample cutting of rice (bugari) to reevaluate the tax rate. The resolution of such questions may have entailed some actual measurement by the *kenchi bugyō*, but this was an extraordinary rather than routine practice during the general surveys.

One cannot, of course, make a certain judgment about the comprehensiveness of these investigations. But an examination of the documents available to surveyors and of the circumstances surrounding the investigations suggests that the cumulative result was a moderately comprehensive and accurate picture of the villages' taxable land.[2]

Records became progressively more comprehensive, increasingly incorporating new kinds of land into the village land tax totals. Notably, the landed retainers lost the right to keep domain authorities out of their fief (funyūken). Furthermore, mountain dry fields (*yamabatake* or *yama no hatake*) previously taxed under a separate program, if at all, came to be counted in the land tax.[3] Although the Genna survey instructions had not excluded mountain lands as such, these typically slash-and-burn fields continued to be tax exempt as late as 1616 in Yokoji village.[4] The same was true in Etchu after the Keichō survey: the 1613 survey document for Hinata village notes the exclusion of mountain dry fields from the assessed value.[5] By mid-century these fields had come to be treated as part of the land subject to the annual land tax.[6]

Villagers prepared their own documents identifying each family's lands for the purpose of dividing the taxes among themselves and for warichi reallocation, and these records were a logical source of additional information for domain officials. Any substantial measurement of land was done by the villagers as they compiled these documents. Though not completely accurate, the records must have been reasonably close to the mark; anything else would have brought stout protests, if not desertion, by villagers who came out on the short end.

Thus, when surveyors investigated taxable land, they based their estimates on a combination of past survey documents (those from regular investigations, wasteland surveys, and surveys to register hidden fields), the results of han determinations in boundary disputes, and the records that villagers kept for their own use. Some documents specifically indicate that records from a previous survey were transcribed during the investigation—clear evidence that the review process was an important component of land investigations.[7] Domain officials collected other village documents on these occasions (notably the original documents granting tax-exempt stipends to fuchibyakushō), reinforcing the impression that the domain relied heavily on village-held documents.[8]

The effects of repeated investigations were cumulative, and multiple efforts were essential to ensure the maximum registration of taxable land. By 1620 the degree of accuracy and comprehensiveness for most villages was reasonably high. Though some arable land certainly escaped the tax net, the time and expense involved in finding it would no doubt have outweighed any tax benefit.

Other methods to encourage the full registration of arable land were available and widely employed. Most important, the domain enlisted the help of villagers. The domain's policy on unregistered fields (called *onden* or *kakushida*; *onkai* if it was secretly reclaimed land) played simultaneously on the villagers' sense of equity and their desire for personal gain. Authorities counted on villagers to report unregistered fields in their own self-interest: cheaters derived a tax benefit not shared by those whose fields were registered. Aware that villagers might keep some fields off the registers by mutual agreement, authorities offered substantial rewards for people who reported unregistered land.

A clear policy to combat onden is discernible from the time the Maeda troops were no longer tied down in Korea or elsewhere, and the authorities could afford to invest more effort in discovering unregistered land. Once begun, that effort never stopped. By the turn of the seventeenth century, the domain had started encouraging commoners to report onden on the promise of a large reward. In 1600 one Kakugen, ancestor of one of the most prominent district chief families, the Kikuchi, reported onden in Take village; in return Maeda Toshinaga gave him those fields to farm.[9] Four years later, just at the beginning of the Keichō surveys, Toshinaga granted part of the taxes (an increase of one kan gold in the field tax, *nozeni*) recovered with the registering of onden to the villager who reported it.[10]

When onden was reported, domain officials surveyed it (presumably a task small enough to permit actual measurements) to determine its size and the taxes payable on it. In 1604, for example, Toshinaga ordered Kamio Zushō and Obata Uemon to survey onden in Ōta village, assess the amount of tax due, and formally assign added cultivation rights to two villagers, Sōemon and Magōemon.[11]

The domain's efforts in this realm sometimes resulted in a substantial increase in the amount of a village's officially registered land. In Tonami county onden was reported in nine villages in 1604. A huge amount of land was involved—1,900 bales, or about 950 koku, the equivalent of two medium-sized villages—so much in fact that a new village was created from it. The villager-informant was generously rewarded with the tax it yielded for the year.[12] Well-documented examples of this sort are not common before the major land investigations of Keichō-Genna, so it is difficult to determine how representative this case is, but the reward policy appears to have been successful, for it was continued with only minor elaborations thereafter. The 1616 survey regulations codified the measures for dealing with onden for the first time: "Peasants [hyakushō] who obscure or hide the boundaries of fields must be punished. If at this time there is *onden*, it must be revealed. As a reward, the land tax from the *onden* for one year will be bestowed upon the informant [*soshōnin*]. In addition, the permanent allotment of the residence and premises of the peasant who concealed his lands or obscured boundaries must be determined by the headman [*kimoiri*]."[13]

Indeed the very success of the policy created a different problem, as a clause in a major ordinance almost 16 years later attests. It prohibited the reporting of onden in a village for five years after a claim had proved out.[14] Apparently, once a valid claim of onden had been made, counterclaims quickly followed in retribution. These had become such a bother that the domain instituted a cooling-off period during which no further actions could be filed. Another clause in the same document detailed the conditions under which there would be a resurvey to verify that there was, in fact, onden. Reports of *onden* had clearly become widespread enough to stir considerable dissension among the villagers, as well as between them and the domain authorities.[15]

The authorities themselves could discover onden when they stepped in to resolve disputes between villages. At issue in such disputes were rights of access to irrigation water, firewood, natural fertilizers, and reclaimable land. They frequently involved the domain in the determination of village boundaries. Once in the villages for investigative purposes, domain officials could look at almost anything they chose; there were no limits to the kinds of shady or questionable practices they could look into.

By the second decade of the seventeenth century at the latest, all but a small percentage of taxable land was on the domain's books. As new lands were secretly reclaimed, the accuracy of tax rolls was reduced, but these occurrences represented a small fraction of the total. After the Keichō-Genna surveys, increases in the assessed value of villages generally came through the incorporation of legally reclaimed land into the village total, not through the reporting of unregistered land.[16]

To be sure, the extent to which the figures in tax registers conformed to domain principles of valuation is open to question. For example, village assessments do not appear to have changed at all when standards of measure

Early Land Taxation   151

changed, as from 360 bu per *tan* to 300 bu per *tan* in the Genna surveys of Kaga and Noto.¹⁷ The surveys alone determined the value of a village's lands. Even when actual measurements were made, the possibilities for a deliberate manipulation or inadvertent miscalculation were substantial. In compensating for special circumstances, such as heavily shaded fields, as well as for "excessively strict" measurement and different fertility levels (*hatake ori* in the case of Kaga), surveyors had an immense amount of discretion. There was no systematic attempt to place checks on their interpretation of the survey rules and procedures.¹⁸ But for all this, there is sufficient longitudinal consistency in the figures for each village to accept them as a standard against which to measure trends in land taxation. Inequities from village to village and the gain or loss to domain treasuries resulting from inappropriate measurements and valuations generally remained unchallenged and unchanged over the course of the Tokugawa era.*

The Sixteenth-Century Maeda Tax Systems

The daimyo who entered Kaga, Noto, and Etchu in the waning years of the Ikkō ikki made no attempt to impose a new, uniform system of taxa-

---

*Although assessed valuations tended to be stable, there were temporary or one-of-a-kind changes. But while it is easy to see why reductions were made for fields damaged by flooding, landslides, changes in the course of rivers, and the like, the motives for increases in assessed valuation are sometimes unclear. In one respect the general surveys of villages were less comprehensive than the late-16th-century investigations. Domain bureaucrats ultimately excluded wastelands (*arachi*)—arable land that had been taken out of production—from a village's assessed value. Special surveys measured these losses of arable land, and their authors usually listed only the amount of "waste" without citing the cause. Kigoshi, "Maeda," p. 36, sees the proportion of such land as an indicator of runaway peasants. But in fact when the late-16th- and 17th-century wasteland documents do mention causes at all, they mostly impute the losses to natural calamities (see *NSS*, 3: 186, 306; *Tonami shi shi*, pp. 300–301; and *Oku Noto Tokikuni-ke monjo*, pp. 3–5).

Tenshō-era documents recorded wastelands under a special subheading, a reminder to villagers and officials alike that land was available for reclamation. As early as 1585 Toshiie sent orders to Sugawara, Nakagawa, Sugiya, Onomi, and Kumagi village, Fuchū-gumi, and the hyakushō of Fugeshi *kōri* (all in Noto) to cultivate such lands wherever possible and indicated that even if they were not cultivated, taxes would be assessed on them (*KK*, pp. 787, 1143; *KHS*, 1: 303–5). Such measures pressured villagers to find someone to work abandoned fields.

The Keichō surveys made general a practice seen earlier in documents for Iisakano shin (1595, 1598) and Ishibarai villages (1598; *Kamiichi chō shi*, pp. 264–66), namely, excluding waste from the total assessed value without indicating the amount omitted. Many conclude with the statement, "The above lands are conveyed as stated with additional wastelands, streams, ditches, roads, and paddy ridges subtracted from the total" (*Himi shi shi*, pp. 1181–82). Previously cultivated lands that were considered extremely difficult to restore were marked as permanent waste in Genna surveys of Kaga and Noto. By this time the domain had given up hope of recultivating many wastelands.

tion in their domains. Sassa Narimasa, for example, assessed taxes in both cash (in Noto in 1577) and rice (in Etchu in 1585).[19] Even in the same village there was no consistency from year to year. Taxes for Yatabe village were expressed in both rice and cash in 1533, in cash only in 1550, and in rice in 1575.[20] In neither case was the amount explicitly based on an estimate of the productive value of the village's land or on regular inspections of its crops. Nor did it matter, in the end, whether the tax was assessed in rice or cash. Payments could be made in either, or in silk, soybeans, or other products useful to the lord or marketable by him.

The very first taxes collected by the Maeda were based on these old forms of taxation.* The 1583 receipts for Jisha village provide an illustration.[21] The amount of tax due in 1582 was stated in cash. For the purposes of payment, however, this was converted to rice at the rate of about 3.33 bales per kan. All of the payments made and the remainder owed were stated in rice.[22] The tax due was not based on a land survey designed to assess the village's potential to pay taxes. The only survey was one narrowly restricted to investigating crop damage from an unspecified cause.†

Though the Maeda did not immediately follow up with an annual inspection system, they did revise the existing method of assessment shortly after they entered Noto in 1851. Since the tax system they employed, called the *sonmen* (literally, "loss exemption") system, differed from most of the systems discussed in survey literature, we must look at it in some detail.

The revision is reflected in two consecutive tax documents for the Nishiumi district.[23] Taxes for the entire district in 1582 were 406 kan, 851 mon. As in the previous example, this was converted to rice at the rate of 3.33 bales per kan. But by the next tax year the domain had estimated the area of arable and residential land subject to the land tax (99 chō, 110 bu), and it now used the villages' assessed value to calculate their tax obligation. The format in which taxes were stated presumed that all of the produce of the land was the lord's to do with as he pleased.

In practice that obligation was much less than the assessed value. Allowances were made for certain expenditures and compensations. The largest exemption, called the *men* (30 percent in this case), reduced the total tax by whatever amount the lord deigned to grant the villagers for their suste-

---

*Tagawa, "Kaga-han," p. 54; Kigoshi, "Maeda," p. 20. Since documents relating to kyūnin taxation for this period are not available, this discussion is necessarily limited to the structure of taxation under the daimyo.

†The term "kenchi" was used in this document, but *not* as a designation for a full land survey of an actual measurement of arable land. One official was dispatched to estimate how much land was unharvested. This usage is another indication that the term did not carry any implications of a specific method.

nance.* Officials also subtracted enough to compensate the fuchibyakushō; the tax exemption represented their salary rather than a cash grant from the domain treasury. Also exempted were lands lost to cultivation from natural causes (wastelands). The remainder was the tax due.

If the Nishiumi district is typical, the new tax system resulted in a substantial increase in taxes for the residents of the domain. The amount owed in 1583 was just over 1,619 bales of rice; this compares with roughly 1,272 the year before, a jump of better than 28 percent.

It is noteworthy that in these early years, tax payments were sometimes calculated for a district. For example, Toshiie's 1589 tax receipt for the Awagura district does not identify individual villages but simply acknowledges that taxes for the group had been paid.[24] Here we have another indication of the primacy of district administration over the village. The early land surveys did not uniformly transfer to the villages primary responsibility for tax payment.

The district may even have been the basic unit of tax assessment, with the fuchibyakushō allocating the burden to be borne by each community. For example, when crops were extensively damaged in the Tata district in 1583, Toshiie ordered a district-wide exemption (*men*) of 30 percent.[25] A 1587 tax bill for Kumagi district (*sō*) simply declared that a total of 4,000 bales of rice was owed.[26] Like the tax receipts cited above, these documents strongly suggest that it was the district, headed by a fuchibyakushō, that was primarily responsible for tax payments, not villages.

As in the Nishiumi documents, authorities valued land at just over three bales of rice per *tan* (or at a rate of a little more than three *to* to the bale, about one koku per *tan*). This figure is uniform throughout almost all the Kaga documents. The Maeda did not follow the common practice of assigning different values to different grades of fields. In general tax valuations did not consider soil fertility.

Domain ordinances do not explain the basis for determining either the regular or the extraordinary exemptions. Nominal tax rates appear high, perhaps even arbitrarily so, but they were also quite consistent from village to village. A 1585 summary of the exemptions for Noto Island (Table 7) suggests that regular exemptions were partly based on an estimate of each village's overall agricultural productivity relative to the others. The villages were ranked in three grades, superior, average, and inferior, each with a corresponding exemption (of 30 percent, 35 percent, and 40 percent, respectively). Although variations within these categories were recognized (e.g.,

---

*Later in the Tokugawa era the word "men" referred to the official village tax rate, that is, the amount to be collected as taxes, and not, as here, to the amount the villages were permitted to retain.

TABLE 7
Exemption Rates in Notojima Villages, 1585

Village	Surveyor's categorization of land	Rate (percent)	Village	Surveyor's categorization of land	Rate (percent)
Tōri Tanoshiri	Average	35%	Hachiasaki	Inferior	40%
Basshō	Average	35	Enome	Average	35
Musaki	Average	35	Neya	Average	35
Kuki	High ave.	35	Makari	Superior	30
Hon'noura	Superior	30	Minami	Superior	30
Ōura	Superior	30	Kōda	Superior	30
Ubakaura	Average	35			

SOURCE: Tagawa, "Kaga-han," p. 55.

"high average" for Kuki village), this apparently had no bearing on the exemption rate. Instead of varying assessed values for many different grades of paddy and dry field, authorities set different exemption rates (*men*) for villages. But the range of variation was only 10 percentage points.

As can be seen in Table 8, the assessed values also showed much stability under this system. In a sample of 17 Noto villages, seven seemingly experienced no changes at all in the years 1583–91, and nine had just one change. In only one village (Ōzawa) did the value change more than once.

Still, a village's total burden could fluctuate measurably from year to year. In the 1583–92 period changes in the amount of land temporarily lost from cultivation and then later recultivated (Table 9), coupled with an unusual increase in valuation in 1588 (*shittai*; uniformly 24 percent), caused swings of as much as a third in some villages' assessed value, changes that, in the final analysis, were reflected in taxes due.* The frequency of such adjustments in the Etchu and Noto villages sampled suggests that their land was often inspected by some means or another, but only for the purpose

---

*The reasons for sudden jumps of this sort are not clear. They may have been due to land reclamations (Tagawa, "Kaga-han," pp. 58–60) or simply represent attempts by the domain to arbitrarily increase its revenues (Takazawa, "Tenshō-ki nengu san'yōjo"). In all but one of the known cases, the tax hike (usually designated simply as *shittai bun*, "increase") occurred in 1588. None was based on measurements by the daikan or other domain authorities; nominally, they arose in the villagers' own reports of increases in their holdings. A partially damaged ("onawauchi ni oyobazu [worm-eaten]") document describing the increase in taxable land for Tani and Korosa villages in 1588 clearly states that the villagers estimated the increase without a formal measurement (*NSS*, 3: 185). There is evidence throughout the 16th-century surveys and tax receipts that villagers occasionally did report increases in cultivated land to the authorities. For example, Ogishima village reported that it had three more chō of land in 1589 than it had in 1586 (*Ishikawa ken Shio chō shi*, p. 158). Such disclosures were probably made under pressure from domain officials. The standards used to determine the increases are unclear. For a more detailed discussion, see Brown, "Domain Formation," pp. 175–79.

TABLE 8
Changes in Exemption Rates for 17 Noto Villages, 1583–91

Village	1583	1584	1585	1586	1587	1588	1589	1590	1591
Nishiumi-Shimoura	100	117	117	117	117				
Enome		100	100	86	86	86			
Saihōji	100		100	100					
Yawata Shimo-mura Harada			100		83				
Awagura-suzuya			100	100	100	100			
Jike			100	100					
Orido	100		100	88	88				
Ōzawa	100	83	83		100	186			
Shibuta			100	100					
Kokuga				100	100				
Shitsura				100	120				
Takai	100				88				
Takojima			100		88				
Innai					100	100	86		
Morohashi			100	100		100			
Kizumi				100	100	100	88		
Yawata Shimo-mura								100	100

SOURCES: See Appendix A.
NOTE: Figures are index numbers, with the first year of data for each village taken as the base.

TABLE 9
Wasteland as a Percentage of Assessed Value
in Noto and Etchu Villages, 1583–92

		Wasteland (Percent of total value)	Village sample	
Year	Villages		Range (percent)	Median (percent)
1583	7	15.4%	0.4%–27.1%	14.7%
1584	4	43.7	13.4–75.6	43.1
1585	16	28.6	0.0–78.6	32.1
1586	16	15.4	0.0–35.8	13.2
1587	13	13.5	0.0–51.5	11.6
1588	10	0.4	0.0–4.9	0.0
1589	6	12.1	0.0–34.7	9.0
1590–92	3	4.4	0.0–10.3	2.9

SOURCES: See Appendix A.

of detecting major changes in the amount of arable, not variations in crop yields. In effect the sonmen system assumed that villages produced stable yields.[27]

Nevertheless, as Table 10 shows, even though temporary compensations for land lost from cultivation substantially lowered these villages' effective tax rates during the 1580's and early 1590's, as much as 50–60 percent

TABLE 10
Land Taxes as a Percentage of Assessed Value in Noto and Etchu Villages, 1583–92

Year	Villages	Collected taxes (percent of value)	Change in percent (index)	Village sample Range (percent)	Village sample Median (percent)
1583	7	52.6	100	36.6–63.1	54.4
1584	4	36.8	70	14.6–56.3	38.1
1585	16	45.1	86	12.8–65.2	43.3
1586	16	55.1	105	37.8–75.3	54.3
1587	13	56.1	107	23.3–73.7	55.8
1588	10	60.2	114	44.2–77.3	66.0
1589	6	61.9	118	44.2–75.1	63.2
1590–92	3	60.4	115	44.2–69.0	67.9

SOURCES: See Appendix A.

of their assessed value was collected in taxes. In fact the proportion was even higher, for these data are computed from tax receipts that in many instances were written before the taxes were fully paid. (Cases in which the receipts either did not clearly distinguish the amount paid from the amount assessed or showed payment to only one of several overlords were not included in the calculations.) Other sources indicate that villages eventually paid much of the balance due.[28] Consequently, the data in Table 10 and below understate the effective tax rate.

Across the whole period, an average of 45.95 percent of assessed value was collected as taxes from these villages. Significantly, the percentage increased over time, rising from the 20–30 percent range to the 50–60 percent range, close to the two-thirds level suggested by Hideyoshi's "Osaka Wall Writings."*

For tax purposes, reclaimed land (*shinden*) was treated separately from long-standing fields (*honden*) until such time as its productivity had stabilized. Since newly opened lands required substantial investment, and their yields were below average for the first several years, the domain used the tool of tax incentives to encourage villagers to expand arable lands. Most new fields were taxed at reduced rates, and some were not taxed at all early in their development. Eventually, of course, these lands became "old fields" and were taxed at the standard village rate.[29]

Despite annual fluctuations, the domain's tax revenues increased during the first years of the Maeda takeover. The percentage of assessed value taken as taxes dipped briefly in 1584–85, but rose thereafter as the amount

---

*Note, however, that these rates developed before Hideyoshi's orders were issued. The similarity may simply result from his adoption of an already widely accepted standard.

TABLE 11
Changes in Effective Tax Rates for 17 Noto Villages, 1583–91

Village	1583	1584	1585	1586	1587	1588	1589	1590	1591
Nishiumi-Shimoura	100	75	84	86	88				
Enome	100	61	100	107	107	129			
Saihōji	100		121	126					
Yawata Shimo-mura Harada			100		111				
Awagura-suzuya			100	102	113	144			
Jike			100	102					
Orido	100		68	76	87				
Ōzawa	100	54	68		77	104			
Shibuta			100	102					
Kokuga				100	103				
Shitsura				100	103				
Takai	100			113					
Takojima			100		120				
Innai					100	124	138		
Morohashi			100	102		125			
Kizumi				100	105	137	141		
Yawata Shimo-mura								100	132

SOURCES: See Appendix A.
NOTE: Figures are index numbers, with the first year for each village taken as the base.

of wasteland decreased. Wasteland ratios increased the year after a domain-mandated increase in the assessed values of some villages (1588), suggesting villager opposition to the increase, an inability to pay the increased taxes, or crop failure. But domain coffers still profited from the increment in assessed value. Only two villages registered an absolute decline in land taxes over the time span for which there are data, Nishiumi-shimoura and Orido (see Table 11). This upward trend in effective (as opposed to assessed) tax rates attests to an increased effectiveness in the domain's land tax system and political control. The rise in tax revenues may not have been all that dramatic, but the domain frequently managed to up its income by 10 percent or more.*

---

*See Brown, "Domain Formation," pp. 216–20. The data discussed to this point may well not tell the entire story of trends in the effectiveness of the land tax system. The size of a bale of rice changed from three to five *to* with the tax receipts for 1588, but local scholars disagree on the impact of the change. Kigoshi Ryūzō argues that the measuring box (*masu*) remained constant, and the size of a bale rose 67%, subjecting villagers to a very large jump in land taxes ("Maeda," p. 25). Takazawa Yūichi feels that so large an increase is implausible, and sees the new size as simply a shift to a more common measuring unit ("Tenshō-ki nengu san'yōjo," p. 723). Given the relatively gradual changes in tax exemption rates, assessed value, and the like, I am inclined to accept Takazawa's explanation. All the same, the change from the three–*to dobari masu* bale (99.1874 cubic *sun*, about 119.02488 cubic inches) to the five–*to kikuchi masu* bale (62.5 cubic *sun*, about 79.8 cubic inches) postulated by Takazawa still represented a tax increase of over 5%. This would mean that the Maeda land tax system was even more effective than the present analysis has shown.

Tax Billing

There are very few extant tax bills with which to determine the timing and nature of the assessment process. But what we have in hand clearly does not support the argument for a very stringent, even confiscatory land tax system. In fact the available bills reveal a surprising degree of flexibility in tax collection, a system in which the domain was willing to make considerable concessions to villages hard pressed to meet their tax obligation.

Generally, tax bills were issued in either the summer or the fall of the tax year, before the harvest had begun or was completed.[30] These first bills were merely preliminary, subject to adjustment for any crop damage before full payment was made in the late spring and summer of the following year. Once the tax bills were presented and the villagers had a chance to make the first payment, Toshiie himself issued a tax receipt. These receipts, as we have seen in earlier examples, detailed the taxes due, the exempt lands, the payments received to date, and the balance due. The receipt for 1583 for Takai village is typical:[31]

Tenshō 11 Taxes
Shōin District, Takai Village Computation

Assessed value [taka]: 243 bales, 2 to, 2 gō, 5 shaku
   Of this:
   15 bales   Tone's stipend
     Of this: 1 bale, 2 to, 1 shō, 2 gō, 5 shaku   wastelands
   31 bales   wastelands
Remainder: 198 bales, 2 to, 1 shō, 2 gō, 5 shaku
   Of this: 79 bales, 1 to, 4 shō, 4 gō   40% exemption
Tax due [jōnō]: 119 bales, 6 shō, 8 gō, 5 shaku
   Of this:
   65 bales, 1 to, 5 shō, 1 gō received
   25 bales in local warehouse
   15 bales received as 150 bales of salt
     Total: 105 bales, 1 to, 5 shō, 1 gō
Remainder: 13 bales, 2 to, 1 shō, 7 gō, 5 shaku   unpaid [mishin]
   Of this:
   5 bales payable as 2 momme, 9 bun gold,
     due in the 8th month
   5 bales payable as 2 momme, 9 bun gold,
     due by the 10th day of the 7th month
   3 bales, 2 to, 7 shō, 7 gō, 5 shaku forgiven

(Calculated) as above
Tenshō 12.6.15

                                                               Seal [Maeda Toshiie]

Where, as here, a balance was owed, another receipt would be issued the following year and every year thereafter until the account was settled. The final receipt might be in the same form as the original or might be nothing more than a note appended to earlier receipts.[32]

The period for revising the initial tax calculations extended into the spring of the next year. Five or six wasteland survey reports written before 1594 clearly stated that the deduction for wasteland was to apply to the previous year's taxes.[33] In only one instance did the report seem to apply to the tax year in which it was written. The results of these supplementary surveys were reflected in the receipts for tax payments issued thereafter.

The timing of these investigations suggests that the fundamental purpose was to gauge the extent of the damage to the land, not reduced yields.[34] In general wasteland surveys did not specifically define the cause of damage; however, if officials were to inspect anything at that time of year, the damage would have had to be visible to them. This was most likely if the problem was wind-whipped or frost-damaged crops or the havoc wreaked by landslides or floods.* It is possible, however, that some wasteland investigations were directed at evaluating the quality of the harvest of winter crops such as wheat. In an order of escheat for certain kyūnin lands in Etchu, issued in the spring of 1587, Toshiie expressed his concern that the willful acts of landed retainers had led cultivators to abandon that year's wheat crop.[35] Such concern, as well as the timing of the wasteland surveys, suggests that the condition of winter crops was considered in setting land taxes.

The absconding of cultivators apparently did not directly result in wasteland. Though this was a major concern of domain authorities, only one tax receipt, for Ozawa village, in 1584, links the two. Even then, the uncultivated land imputed to absconding was listed separately rather than under the "wastelands" heading in the tax receipt, suggesting that we cannot simply read "desertion" wherever we find the heading "wasteland."[36]

On the other hand, though the available documentation does not establish a clear relationship between absconding and wasteland, it was surely a contributing factor. Supposing that the runaway's fellow villagers did manage to bring in his crop, total output could well have been affected. The loss of labor of even a few men doubtless led to poorly weeded fields, put a strain on the maintenance of irrigation facilities, and prevented the

---

*Crops ruined by high winds, heavy rains, cold snaps, and the like would probably have been left standing until the inspection was over. Villagers would not have wanted to destroy evidence of the damage by plowing these fields under before officials could see the problem for themselves.

villagers from harvesting all their fields before the onset of bad weather.

As in the case of wasteland surveys, authorities used general surveys to check the ability of villagers to pay the previous year's taxes. Most of the initial tax receipts for 1585, 1587, and 1588 are dated after the major land surveys of 1586, 1588, and 1589. They were issued by Toshiie himself and summarized payments made by the summer following the tax year.[37] For example, Innai village was recorded as having 19 chō, 8 tan, 7 se, and 27.7 bu of taxable land in 1589. Multiplying that total by the standard three bales per *tan* yields exactly the assessed valuation shown in the village's receipt for the previous year's (1588) taxes, just over 596 bales.[38] This represents an increase of about 116 bales over the village's 1587 taxes.[39] Clearly, the 1588 taxes were adjusted on the basis of the 1589 land survey.

There are no similar sequences of documents with which to examine the correlation between areas reported in land surveys in 1587 and the previous year's assessed value. Nonetheless, the timing of tax receipts and land survey documents is consistent with the conclusion that the past year's taxes were uniformly checked against the survey results and adjusted appropriately.

In sum, villages were often inspected twice (perhaps three times during years of major land surveys) for the purpose of assessing the land tax. The first inspection was to determine the initial assessment and occurred before the end of the harvest. A second inspection in the spring verified the extent of any damage to fields between the tax billing and the completion of the harvest. Whether such inspections were made routinely or only in response to villagers' demands is unclear. In any case, final bills were prepared and tax payments completed only after the period for making adjustments had elapsed.

One striking illustration of the flexibility of the early Maeda system was the authorities' tolerance of tardy payments and even default. Not only do the first tax receipts of the year show a hefty balance due; even in the final accountings we find that a relatively high proportion of taxes were never paid. Table 12 presents data on the completion of tax payment for the years 1582–92. As can be seen, of the 73 instances for which there are at least interim receipts, only eight show no unpaid tax at all.*

The average initial default of known cases was just under 20 percent, the median about 17.5 percent, the high 68 percent. If these data are di-

---

*In some of these cases the term "mishin," unpaid taxes, does not appear. However, statements that a gold payment was made at the time the receipt was prepared suggest that after the first tax collection but before Toshiie reviewed the payment, some of the tax was still to be paid. See, for example, the 1587 tax receipts for Enome village (*Notojima no kinsei monjo*, p. 22) and Kawanishi village (*WSS*, 2: 284).

TABLE 12
Patterns of Forgiveness of Late and Unpaid Taxes, 1582–92

	Unpaid taxes		
Tax year and village/district	Initially	Percent ultimately forgiven	Date payment completed
1582			
Nishiumi	37%	21%	1583.7.30
Ōzawa	20	34	1583.7.21
Jisha	36	?	1583.7.7
1583			
Orido	30	22	1584.6.15
Nishiumi Shimoura	52	19	1584.6.15
Enome	51	19	1584.6.11
Takai	10	23	1584.6.15
Umawatari-Ushijima	66	18	1584.6.15
Saihōji	62	14	1584.6.15
1584			
Ōzawa	25	0	1585.7.27
Shimoura	38	50	1585.11.16
Iwasaka	68	?	1585.11.26
Enome	10	63	1585.11.26
1585			
Enome	0+	100	1586.6.22
Morohashi	39	0	1586.7.5
Konpōji	6	100	1586.7.8
Ōzawa	22	45	1586.7.11
Nishiumi Shimoura	46	19	1586.7.11
Saihōji	63	12	1587.5.30
Yawata-Shimo	13	6	1587.6.2
Awagura-Suzuya	26	9	1587.6.2
Jike	20	11	1587.6.2
Ushio	7	34	1587.6.2
Shibuta	18	7	1587.6.2
Orido	19	0	1587.6.2
Takojima	18	0	1587.6.2
Mori-Shirakawa	0	0	1587.6.?
Ōta	23	0	1588.9.14
Kamishiro	1	0	?
1586			
Kizumi	5	100	1587.5.20
Sora	0+	100	1587.5.28
Morohashi	29	—[a]	1587.5.30
Saihōji	35	21	1587.5.30
Takai	13	0+	1587.6.2
Orido	18	0	1587.6.2
Nakai	15	33	1587.6.3
Shitsura	38	8	1587.7.4
Nishiumi Shimoura	39	12	1587.7.10
Kokuga	18	15	1588.8.25
Awagura-Suzuya	21	12	1588.9.29
Jike	33	11	1588.10.?
Shibuta	30	15	1588.10.?

TABLE 12
Continued

	Unpaid taxes		Date payment completed
Tax year and village/district	Initially	Percent ultimately forgiven	
1587			
Enome	0	0	1588.8.27
Takojima	0	0	1588.9.7
Kawanishi	13	0	1588.9.8
Kizumi	5	0	1588.9.19
Kokuga	8	?	1588.9.20
Nishiumi Shimoura	14	0	1588.9.26
Wakayama	9	0	1588.9.26
Orido	20	0	1588.9.26
Yawata-Shimo[b]	1	100	1588.9.29
Ōzawa	28	36	1588.9.30
Shitsura	36	0+	1588.9.30
Awagura-Suzuya	2	100	1588.?.?
1588			
Hitani	8	?	1589.8.8
Nozaki-Ōura	8	38	1589.9.13
Enome	3	100	1589.9.13
Morohashi	20	15	1589.9.13
Iwaya	3	100	1589.9.13
Ōzawa	45	0	1589.9.13
Kizumi	18	19	1589.9.13
Innai	16	20	1589.9.14
Sano	18	17	1589.9.15
Awagura-Suzuya	17	14	1589.9.15
1589			
Kizumi	0	0	1591.7.20
Ōzawa	0	0	1591.7.20
Morohashi	8	0	1591.7.20
Yawata-Shimo	7	0	1591.7.20
Ikawa	0	0	?
Tane-Korosa	8	0	?
1590, Innai	0	0	1591.7.20
1591, Yawata-Shimo	?	?	1594.1.28
1592, Ōzawa	0	0	1593.12.27

SOURCES: See Appendix A.
[a] Tax forgiven but to an unknown amount.
[b] Harada bun, part of a village only.

vided into five-percent ranges (1–5%, 6–10%, etc.), the modal range is 16–20 percent. Though there were only eight instances of an arrears of more than 40 percent, between 6 percent and 40 percent of the land taxes were commonly unpaid when Toshiie first reviewed village tax payments.

But as can be seen in Table 13, there was a steep decline in tax shortfalls over time. Through the 1584 tax year, the average amount of initially unpaid

TABLE 13
Average Unpaid Taxes and Tax Forgiveness, 1582–92

Year	Unpaid tax		Unpaid tax forgiven	
	Percent	Occurrences	Percent	Occurrences
1582	31%	3	28%	2
1583	45	6	19	6
1584	35	4	38	3
1585	20	16	21	16
1586	23	13	27	12
1587	11	12	22	11
1588	16	10	35	9
1589	4	6	0	6
1590–92	0	3	0	3

SOURCES: See Appendix A.

tax was over 30 percent. The figure fell to about 21 percent in 1585–86 and declined further in 1587–88. From 1589, unpaid taxes became much less of a problem, reaching no higher than 4 percent of the taxes owed. Here again it is evident that the 24 percent increase (shittai) in assessed value the domain established by fiat in 1588 had no significant adverse effect on taxes paid. Tax arrears never returned to the high levels of the early Maeda years.

Furthermore, substantial portions of the unpaid taxes were never paid. In only 24 of the cases for which we have detailed data did villages pay their taxes completely. Most of these were for 1587 and 1589–92. In 45 other cases forgiveness (although not always the exact amount) can be documented, and these villages never paid the full tax due. In 27 of these, 8 percent to 23 percent of the balance was forgiven; in eight instances the full amount was forgiven.* The median unpaid balance for the 67 cases on which we have complete data was about 11–12 percent. Expressed in five-percent ranges (1–5%, 6–10%, etc.), the modal range of partial forgiveness was 11–15 percent.

Based on this sample, the average rate of default in the early Maeda years was probably around 4–5 percent of all land tax owed. Before 1589 there was no clear declining trend in the proportion of unpaid taxes or the rate of forgiveness. But in the subsequent years, land tax collection clearly became stricter.

The tax payment schedule provides another sign of concession to vil-

---

*Tables 12 and 13 perhaps exaggerate the effect of this forgiveness. In several instances the amount involved was small, though it constituted a sizable proportion of the arrears. In each case of total forgiveness the proportion of unpaid taxes was low, no higher than 6%, and we might suspect that forgiveness was a reward for the prompt payment of the bulk of the amount owed. But in other instances where the amount of unpaid tax was equally low there was no forgiveness at all, so this was clearly not, or at least not uniformly, the case.

lages: a relatively long period in which to complete their tax payments. Most completed receipts (Table 12) were dated in the summer or fall of the next tax year, many months and even as much as a year after the harvest. An additional year was allowed in 17 cases, and in two instances the village got three years. Across the group, final payment was deferred for more than a year in about a quarter of the cases. There is no indication that the domain penalized even the very late payers. Conceivably a penalty was built into the conversion rates when a village paid in cash, salt, or something other than rice, but there is no evidence to document this.

In some instances extended payment and partial tax forgiveness were clearly linked. Many receipts included a heading designated "mitsu-wari," "yotsu-wari," or something similar. The heading "mitsu-wari" indicated that two-thirds of the amount listed there was to be paid later by the villagers, and the other third was to be forgiven completely.[40] Multiple forms of tax forgiveness appear even in a single case, as in the receipt for Kokuga village's 1586 taxes, where eight bales, four shō was forgiven along with 13 bales "mitsu-wari."[41] Why a distinction was made is unclear. In any event, as Table 12 indicates, the practice of tax forgiveness stopped with the taxes assessed in 1589.[42]

Several receipts document still another form of flexibility in the Maeda system by way of an entry marked "ukekoi."[43] The amount shown there was considered paid, although it had not yet been received by the daikan or other domain official. Ukekoi, essentially a pledge by the villages to pay the amount due, represents another form of extended payment.[44] That this pledge was considered adequate guarantee of payment is indicated by the inclusion of the phrase "payment completed as above" at the conclusion of most final tax receipts. It designates Toshiie's acknowledgment that all tax obligations had been fulfilled. The amounts of tax involved were sometimes quite large. The amount of ukekoi for Nishiumi-Shimoura's 1583 taxes was 122 bales of rice.[45]

Historians disagree on which individuals or corporate bodies acted as guarantors of the ukekoi debts. The fuchibyakushō, both as wealthy, locally prominent men and as leaders of multivillage groups, were ultimately responsible. While a case can be made that individual communities were sometimes held responsible by domain authorities, the preponderance of evidence indicates that this was rare. Even where the domain held a collection of villages responsible, the dynamics of local administration would have first led to an effort by the fuchibyakushō to collect payment rather than direct domain contact with the village.[46]

Despite a gradual tightening of han controls on unpaid taxes, the

Maeda's early land tax system can be characterized as flexible overall, and perhaps even as lenient. Although taxes from the second year of their arrival may have been higher than before, the increases were at least partly ameliorated by the domain's apparent willingness to allow villagers to defer their payments for an extended period without penalty. In many cases there was at least some forgiveness of the amount owed.

Forms of Payment

Though the form of tax assessments changed under the Maeda, in other respects the new system was not a radical departure from earlier times. In particular, as noted, the tendency to assess and accept taxes in rice was already well established in the region. The Maeda's use of these practices was no great innovation.[47] What is more, given the widespread scholarly insistence that Hideyoshi converted the country's tax medium to rice, it is especially interesting to find the continued frequent use of gold and local products for tax payments in Kaga han throughout the late sixteenth century. The switch to *assessing* taxes in rice did not mean an immediate shift to *collecting* them in rice. In 27 tax receipts partial payment was made in nine different items, most often salt, charcoal, or soybeans. In addition villagers paid partly in gold in the overwhelming majority of tax receipts.[48] Gold was the medium of choice especially for the final payments, but it was often used as part of the first installment as well.*

As with tax forgiveness, the proportion of tax payments made in alternate crops, handicraft products, and gold declined throughout the period.[49] But this general trend conceals sharp annual variations.[50] In some villages the proportion of taxes paid in gold jumped by as much as 30–60 percent from one year to the next. Such sharp variations suggest a lack of systematic principles governing tax collection. Indeed, there are no extant ordinances or administrative instructions limiting land tax payment entirely to rice or to a fixed ratio of rice to non-rice payments. During this period movement toward the increased use of rice apparently reflected social and economic considerations in the villages, not administrative initiative from the domain.[51] Certainly, the principle of rice collection of taxes was not completely implemented by the early 1590's.

Fluctuations in the value of rice relative to gold and other crops may have influenced the form of tax payment. When the harvests were good, taxes were somewhat more likely to be paid in rice.[52] The exchange rates

---

*Appendix A. Substantial nonrice payments were still widely accepted throughout Japan at this time.

for gold and rice showed marked variation from 1582 to 1592, with rice losing half its value relative to gold.[53] To the extent that this change reflected market conditions, rice may have become the cheapest means of paying taxes. At other times villagers would have found it profitable to sell products that brought a higher price than rice and to pay their taxes in cash. Domain authorities may also have been swayed to accept alternative crops or special local products by shifting markets.

Conclusion

As in the case of surveys and the organization of local administration, the evolution of the domain's land tax system reflects an independent course of development. There is no evidence of any direct central influence or of changes in response to administrative orders from Oda Nobunaga or Toyotomi Hideyoshi. The early system employed in Kaga, the sonmen system, deviated significantly from the kokudaka system that Hideyoshi is said to have introduced nationwide.

Though Kaga did not establish the land tax base through actual measurements conducted under close domain supervision, the methods employed were reasonably effective. Repeated investigations succeeded in registering the vast majority of taxable land by the early seventeenth century. Whether the value of each village listed in the tax rosters was strictly calculated based on domain principles is open to question, but once established, assessed values remained constant.[54]

The sonmen system built on pre-Maeda practices. The change from assessing a flat amount of taxes, stated in either rice or cash, to pinning taxes to an assessed valuation of a village's agricultural potential, though noteworthy, did not bring immediate major changes in the amount of tax owed or the means of payment. At most, one document hints, taxes may have increased some 28 percent. The sonmen system was more rigid in some ways than standard models suggest. It presumed a fixed tax obligation regardless of the harvest, an amount that would be altered only when land was lost from cultivation or converted to arable.

Yet in many ways the system was flexible, again, more so than standard models would have it, and hardly confiscatory. Tax increases were partially offset by the frequent use of significant tax forgiveness. Payments were not due until well after the harvest and might be deferred for a few years. Furthermore, taxes were reduced by allowances for wasteland. The form of payment, too, was flexible. In addition to rice and gold, the authorities accepted a wide variety of local products.

It is true that, like many other domains, Kaga assessed land taxes in rice. But the practice of accepting payment in rice was well established before the Maeda arrival and Hideyoshi's rise to power. There was no rapid, dramatic shift from cash (kandaka) to rice (kokudaka).

This flexibility represents domain concessions to villagers, and perhaps directly to the threat of village opposition. Domain ordinances to fuchibyakushō and others clearly show the authorities' cognizance of this potential and desire to minimize disruptive outbreaks. They may have been successful in this effort, for there are relatively few documented instances of serious village protests in the late sixteenth century when effective land tax rates were at their highest. The threat of opposition combined with limited protest was a potent force against domain and retainer willfulness.

Flexibility also allowed the domain to establish a new tax assessment mechanism and (ultimately) a higher effective tax burden. Over the years the authorities worked to bring the realities of tax collection into line with the amounts of tax they had established in principle. Although they were only partially successful, the tax system did yield increased revenues for the domain. All of this suggests a flexible yet firm political control of the countryside.

That these practices were limited to the first years of their rule suggests that the Maeda were especially concerned that high taxes and strict collection not precipitate widespread disturbances. Once they gained confidence in their ability to control the local population, they did not hesitate to tighten the tax system. By 1595 taxes had been increased in all but three of the villages for which we have serial data.

The added domain control over tax assessment and collection evident in 1589 was due to the establishment of the daikan as a permanent office that year.[55] This change was probably associated with the erection of official domain granaries.[56] Positioning daikan in the districts for which they collected taxes provided a greater opportunity for them to become familiar with local conditions. More important, there was now a domain official in the field who could persistently encourage each district to pay its full share of taxes and press for the return of runaways.

In sum, the Maeda and their retainers appear to have had reasonably effective control over their villages. The system was not without faults—there was desertion and appeals to the daimyo of mistreatment—but on the whole the tax system operated effectively for a ruling class still entwined in heavy military obligations to the hegemon.

PART THREE

Tightening Control

Chapter **8**

Villager-Samurai Tensions

With the advent of peace, first within the domain and then at the national level, the Maeda, like other daimyo, focused more attention on resolving conflicts and inefficiencies in local administration. Ieyasu became Shogun in 1603, and Tokugawa hegemony was secure for the immediate future. Though the tensions between the Tokugawa and Toyotomi families had not been resolved completely, they had reached a modus vivendi. Freed from imminent national conflict, the Maeda could tidy up domain administration.

In any case, they needed to create administrative mechanisms to carry the family through a change in leadership. In 1605 Toshinaga retired in favor of Toshitsune. But Toshitsune, who was still quite young and needed to rely on Toshinaga for guidance, did not have the benefit of the retired daimyo's advice for long. Toshinaga died in 1614, and in his last years he was incapacitated by illness.

At the top of domain administration, the most significant change was the emergence of senior councillors, *toshiyori*, as policy-makers. The daimyo no longer signed domain ordinances. Senior councillors jointly authored most domain ordinances (*ofuregaki*) issued from this time.

As tensions arose between villages and agents of the domain and retainers, the domain increasingly specified duties for district administration. In the process the fuchibyakushō were reorganized into a new class of district chiefs called *tomura*. In addition, the domain added new offices, staffed by samurai, who regulated tax agents and served as boards of appeal for villages. During this second period, details of village administration continued to be a secondary concern for the domain.

The Tomura System

The concept underlying the fuchibyakushō system of local administration—using groups of villages as the principal point of contact between domain authorities and the villages—was elaborated and systematized early in the seventeenth century. Beginning in 1604, village groups throughout the domain were reorganized into new districts known as *tomura-gumi* (literally, "ten-village-groups"), each comprising about a dozen villages.[1] This reform of district administration was part of widespread administrative revisions that began that year and attempted to solidify the Maeda's control over their subjects. The senior councillors initiated and oversaw the reforms, and documents issued under their seals provide the first indications of a systematization or reorganization of the old districts.

The first evidence we have of people being named to head the new village groups comes in a 1606 document sent to Jirōemon of Kurabone village, appointing him *kimoiri* and granting him tax-free status for his lands, valued at 93 bales of rice.[2] Similarly, a later document (1608) granted Kahei of Tsuchiya village a stipend of five bales of rice as "kimoiri bun" (headman's portion).[3] The use of the term "headman" (kimoiri) is not clear, and might mean that these men were village headmen. But in that case, we would not expect the letter of appointment to include compensation (stipend or tax exemption) from the domain. There is no record of domain compensation for any village headman at this time, so it is probable that Jirōemon and Kahei administered a group of villages.[4] The fact that Jirōemon's descendants, at least, held the office of tomura supports this interpretation.[5]

The absence of letters of appointment at the start of district reform (1604) indicates that the first stages were mild, largely involving a change in terminology, not a wholesale change in personnel, village groupings, and administrative functions. This suggestion is supported by other considerations. Continuity in district heads was common. A large number of the new districts were headed by fuchibyakushō. Their survival under the new system implies that it was merely a mild reorganization of the old one. Moreover, the new headmen were drawn from the same strata of influential villagers and samurai-like families as the fuchibyakushō. The Kawai of Tonami county, referred to by the medieval-sounding title of *jito-kata* ("honorable land steward"), appear to have been locally influential since some time in the middle ages.[6] The Fujii of Arie village were Ikkō sect priests.[7]

In some instances appointment as a village group head resulted from downward samurai mobility (again indicating fluid class boundaries). One genealogy relates the following story. Kameda Osumi was a division commander for the Ikkō forces. The Kameda forces later made peace with Shibata Katsuie, and one of them, Kameda Toshitsuna, eventually joined Maeda Toshitsune's retainer band. Though Toshitsuna died without heir, and his 2,000-koku fief was forfeited, his wife bore a son eight months after his death, and this son, Fujirō, was made a tomura headman.[8] The Gotō, too, were descended from a sixteenth-century warrior family that had reportedly held a fief of 300 koku not long before the Maeda's arrival.[9]

In 1616 the domain, as part of its reorganization of local administration in Kaga province, introduced a systematic means of providing a salary for district headmen, allowing them to collect a "plow tax" (*kuwayaku*) of two shō of rice per plow (later per male aged fifteen to sixty) in the villages under their jurisdiction. This practice was extended throughout the domain a decade later. Apart from its significance for district administration, the creation of this salary system marks the first domain attempts to define legally the status of full village members (*honbyakushō*): villagers subject to the tax fell into that category; those not subject to it were treated as second-class residents of the village.[10] Here, not in Hideyoshi's class separation edicts, we have the first efforts to create an identifiable, legally distinct rural class.*

There was also considerable continuity of functions under the new system. The 1606 document appointing Jirōemon kimoiri specifically states that he "must perform the duties he has performed heretofore."[11] Orders concerning local governance distributed throughout the domain in 1607 placed responsibility for the investigation of boundary disputes, water disputes, and similar matters in the hands of the *tomura kimoiri*. The *tomura kimoiri* were responsible for preventing villagers from abandoning their land and for pursuing those who did so.[12] Other functions of the fuchi-byakushō also continued under the tomura system.[13]

Of all these functions, the one to which the domain gave greatest weight was the obligation to prevent villagers from deserting their land. That was the subject of the greatest number of ordinances directed to the tomura. To meet this problem the domain authorities had first relied chiefly on a policy of making a runaway's families and neighbors collectively responsible for his action. In 1601 the domain carried this policy further, fining villages in which runaways were allowed to hide. In 1604, the year of the

---

*Dependent villagers did not pay this tax, though they were subject to corvée service. But their corvée obligations were always lower than those of full village members.

village group reorganization, that responsibility was extended to the guilty village's tomura group.[14]

Later, in 1608, the domain authorities charged the tomura headman with responsibility for dealing with the runaway's possessions and land. This responsibility included the duty to see that the man's fields were properly cultivated and that his tax obligations were met.[15] Though the headman may have turned first to the runaway's fellow villagers for labor, the domain clearly saw this as a shared responsibility of the entire district and expected the tomura to draw on cultivators throughout his jurisdiction to ensure that the land was farmed and land taxes paid.

Like the fuchibyakushō, the early tomura headmen appear to have served simultaneously as the headmen of their home villages. That, at least, is the implication of the explanation of how the Kikuchi family came to be village headmen of Toide village in the mid-seventeenth century. The family's "Ancient Records" states, "The *kimoiri* of Toide village in previous years was [Kawai] Matauemon. Later, when Kawai was appointed to oversee other tomura (*gofuchinin tomura*), [Kikuchi] Jirōzaemon was ordered to replace him as *kimoiri*."[16] Since *gofuchinin* (receiving a stipend from the domain) *tomura* were appointed from within the ranks of the tomura, we may infer that before his promotion, Kawai was both the head of the local tomura group and the village headman.[17]

Only in the matter of runaways did the domain show much concern for what went on in the villages. As under the old system, it was content to leave the details of village administration to the district and village leaders.

The Restricting of Kyūnin and Daikan Autonomy

Coincident with district administrative reform, pressures built to restrict the activities of the daikan and kyūnin. But the domain authorities were unwilling to take any drastic steps that might offend powerful retainers. Under the new system, as under the old, samurai daikan continued to represent the daimyo, and landed retainers maintained their own independent mechanisms for taxing land.

But this apparent lack of change masked important new developments. The domain placed more responsibility in the hands of the tomura and mid-level officials. The actions of the daikan and kyūnin came under greater scrutiny, and the domain increasingly emphasized the role of the tomura where their duties overlapped those of the daikan (e.g., dealing with runaways and encouraging cultivation).

The transformation began in 1601, when Toshinaga inserted the posi-

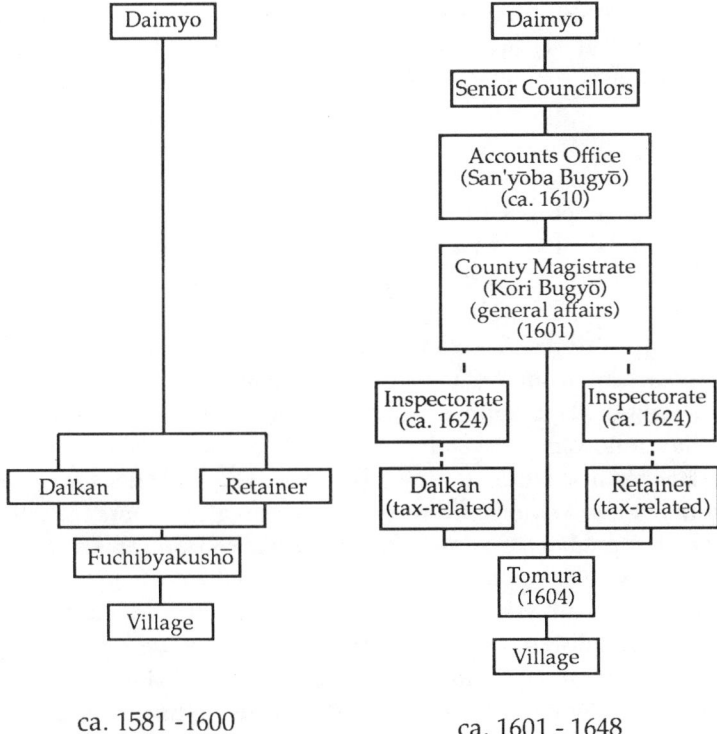

Fig. 4. The structure of rural administration, 1581–1648. The relationship of the Inspectorate to other offices is unclear.

tion of magistrate (bugyō) between himself and the daikan and kyūnin, thereby extending his father's tendency to transfer more responsibility for local administration to intermediate officials. At the same time that power devolved from the daimyo down to the magistrates, powers were transferred upward to them from the kyūnin and daikan. From the daimyo, the bugyō received authority to supervise both the daikan and kyūnin more closely and to deal with any villager complaints against them. Simultaneously, the magistrates absorbed from the daikan and kyūnin whatever judicial powers they had possessed (see Fig. 4).

The 19-clause order in which Toshinaga created this new office dealt with a wide variety of issues.[18] Most of the clauses covered things that were totally unrelated to taxation and rural administration: quarrels among samurai and various matters associated with their residence in towns, such as riots, gambling, and criminal activities. The breadth of responsibilities encompassed in this 1601 order suggests that the position of magistrate was an outgrowth and expansion of the position of castellan at major towns like Nanao and Isurugi. He was not a rural administration specialist as his eventual successor the county magistrate (*kōri bugyō*) would be.*

Of the seven clauses that do have a bearing on rural administration, the most important restricted the authority of daikan and kyūnin to prosecute runaways, impress villagers as servants, and settle on their own any disputes with the villagers under their jurisdiction. One specified that the magistrate was to make a determination concerning the justification for any villager complaints. The others set uniform penalties for hiding runaways and detailed the procedures for establishing legitimate, enforceable servant contracts. Toshinaga issued a supplement to these regulations early in 1602; additional regulations for the control of daikan and other domain tax officials followed at the end of the year.[19]

As reflected in these documents, the villagers' complaints about daikan and kyūnin were concentrated in two major problem areas: the extreme measures they used in the course of assessing and collecting taxes, and their arbitrary impressment of people into their personal service. In the first area of concern, both daikan and kyūnin were prohibited from handing out private decisions in disputes with villagers. Such disputes were to be reported to the magistrate for resolution. This was not simply a matter of ensuring impartiality. Since officials sometimes resorted to torture and corporal forms of punishment, it was also designed to protect the physical safety of villagers.

In response to the other problem, Toshinaga decreed that no villager could be contracted into the service of a retainer for more than one year and forbade daikan and storehouse managers (*kura bugyō*) from commandeering the labor of villagers or the use of their draft animals for their own personal use.† The principal concern here was the direct link between these demands on villagers and their inability to meet their tax obligations. Impressment was apparently a common means by which the daikan and storehouse managers collected private loans from villagers. They insisted on being repaid before any taxes were paid, and if a man could not repay

---

*As we have seen, Maeda Yasukatsu, the castellan of Nanao, supervised the daikan and kyūnin, but whether or not he received an additional title (like "*kōri bugyō*," a title then apparently borne by the Isurugi castellan) is unclear (see *Himi shi shi*, p. 742). The holding of several offices, both civil and military (or the combining of functions if not officially differentiated), indicates the relatively undeveloped and transitional nature of han civil administration at this time.

†*KHS*, 1: 851–52, 869–70. The Bakufu's order prohibiting the sale of persons, the functional equivalent of the servant contract order, was not issued until 1626.

in full, his children, his wife, or he himself was forced to work for the lender until the account was settled. In some cases the service was hereditary. These practices threatened tax revenues by reducing the agricultural labor supply and siphoning off tax revenues before they could be collected. Toshinaga therefore sought to ensure that obligations to the domain took precedence over private interests.[20]

The magistrate's authority over the daikan and kyūnin was reinforced in 1607 and 1608.[21] Both were now wholly prohibited from dealing with runaways on their own; other domain officials were given exclusive authority in this matter. More important, these ordinances covered a quite different area of dispute between the daikan or kyūnin and villagers, the levying of corvée labor, *buyaku*. To this point a prerogative of daikan and kyūnin, the allocating of village labor was now placed in the hands of the magistrate. Daikan and kyūnin were to present statements of their labor needs to him for final determination. This change was prompted not only by the misuse of village labor for private purposes, but also by the need to coordinate and balance the legitimate but potentially conflicting needs of the domain administration and the landed retainers. Hitherto, villagers could be subjected to corvée demands by both the han and the kyūnin simultaneously; and even if the demands did not conflict, they often came at inopportune times and interrupted farming activities. Magistrates could now eliminate such scheduling conflicts.*

In 1614–15, during the Osaka campaigns against Hideyoshi's heirs, domain officials issued regulations that summarized the duties of the bugyō in relationship to the daikan and landed retainers[22]—or more precisely, the *kōri bugyō* (county magistrates), for by this time the office had evolved into one specializing in the administration of rural areas. The county magistrate was given the authority to investigate complaints against the daikan and kyūnin, adjust excessive taxes, investigate the unequal taxation of villages, adjust the interest on daikan's private loans to villagers, oversee public (domain) loans, and deal with runaways.

This new set of regulations did more than define the duties of the county magistrate. We may also view them as a summation of the prerogatives that the kyūnin and daikan had lost. Most of their activities were now scrutinized by a higher office. There were restrictions on their latitude to set taxes. They could no longer deal freely with runaways. Once they lost the free use of conscript labor, their authority had been compromised in

---

*Araya, "Kaga-han," pp. 83–84. In 1610 the han further attempted to resolve such problems by switching to a cash tax, *bugin*, to pay for hired labor instead of conscripting corvée.

each of its fundamental aspects, including the most central of them all—the assessing and collecting of taxes. Although a landed retainer's authority was somewhat less circumscribed by the new county magistrates than the daikan's, he was increasingly treated as a domain official and not as an autonomous fiefholder. All of these changes were introduced to counter abuses of the villagers, to keep them working their lands, and to eliminate conflicting demands on them. The changes were aimed at maintaining a stable, smoothly functioning domain administration, relatively free from open conflicts with its subjects. The ultimate objective was to keep labor on the land and productive, preserving and expanding the financial base of the domain and its retainers.

Over the course of the next decade, the authorities mostly restated or elaborated earlier laws.[23] A few additional, relatively minor restrictions were imposed, however. The kyūnin's right to harvest the fields of absconded villagers was brought under the supervision of the county magistrate. Except in extraordinary circumstances, no kyūnin or daikan could punish a villager without the magistrate's sanction. If a daikan or kyūnin took independent action, he was to file a full report with the Inspectorate (*meyasuba*) for review.

In 1624 the domain's policy-makers decreed that daikan and kyūnin could use only measuring tools specifically approved by the han authorities.[24] This marked the first time that kyūnin were subject to the same unequivocal standard in tax collection as daikan (years after Hideyoshi purportedly established a national standard). Up to now retainers had not only been using their own measures. Some had even used two sets: larger measures when they collected grain and smaller ones when they loaned or sold it to villagers.

The same ordinance required that all kyūnin file reports on the average rate of taxation in their domains with the county magistrate's office. The Inspectorate was to review these reports. For the very first time, the domain expressed an interest in the taxes assessed by landed retainers. Domain authorities had begun to question the kyūnin's effectiveness, and that presaged more serious concerns soon to come.

Early-Seventeenth-Century Tax Assessment

Just as the years spanning the turn of the century witnessed administrative reforms, so they saw important changes in the domain's tax assessment practices and capabilities. The biggest change was to tie tax assessments to annual yield inspections. A change in the form of stating taxes came as a corollary. In the context of samurai urbanization, the reliance on crop inspections, far from increasing the harshness of the land tax system, precipitated a decline in effective tax rates. The high rates of the early Maeda years were not maintained in the early seventeenth century.

Along with these changes came a change of language. The term *"men,"* used earlier to indicate the portion of assessed value *exempt* from taxation, came to signify the exact opposite. For a time, in fact, the term was dropped altogether; taxes due were stated simply as "X bales out of 100" ("hyaku hyō ni tsuki X hyō"). But once it was reinstated, the sense had entirely turned around: the phrase "men mitsu san bu," for example, meant "tax rate, 33 percent." This meaning persisted throughout the early modern era.[25]

The first of the domain's annual inspections took place in 1595. At least one major landed retainer, Yokoyama Nagachika, adopted the inspection system about this time. Not long after, in 1598, Toshinaga spelled out for his daikan how the inspections were to be carried out.[26] Other regulations, in 1615, set out the terms for village appeals of inspection results.[27] It appears, from documents on the 1595 Etchu survey, that the survey crews routinely set tax rates on the daimyo's holdings as they assessed the value of villages.[28] Several reports list both figures.[29] If that was the case, the surveyors would have been supplementing the daikan's tax assessment functions.*

Changes in Land Tax Rates

The new system did not function at all well. As Figure 5 indicates, soon after the system was inaugurated, tax rates fell 10–35 percentage points.† Assessed tax rates for 1595–1604 were generally about 50 percent or less of assessed value, substantially below the common assessed rates of 70

---

*There is some evidence that surveyors similarly supplemented daikan at this time in Kaga and Noto. (See *Hakui shi shi*, p. 129; Oda Kichinojō, *Ishikawa ken*, pp. 355–56.) But since later documents from Kaga and Noto suggest that they only set rates in the villages or parts of villages directly administered by the daimyo, they would not have been involved in the case of retainers' agents.

†The 1593 data in the figure are from a roster transferring villages from Kaga domain to a Bakufu retainer, Hijikata Kawachi no kami, but the actual date of the data is uncertain. Though the document is dated 1605, a comparison with earlier records suggests that the figures are from about 1588 or somewhat later, and not from 1605. In 1604, for example, one of the villages, Tokikuni, had tax rates of 28% and 45%, as opposed to the 65% recorded in the transfer document, and another, Yawata-shimo, had a rate of 35%, as opposed to 70%. The data in the transfer document for Yawata-shimo comes much closer to its 1589 rate of 80%, and the reported rate for Innai of 60% is much closer to its rates of 65%, 62.1%, and 60% in 1587, 1588, and 1590, respectively. The form for stating taxes assessed is also consonant with that of the sonmen, not kemi, assessments. Since there were no data actually ascribable to 1593, I have used these "1605" figures for that year.

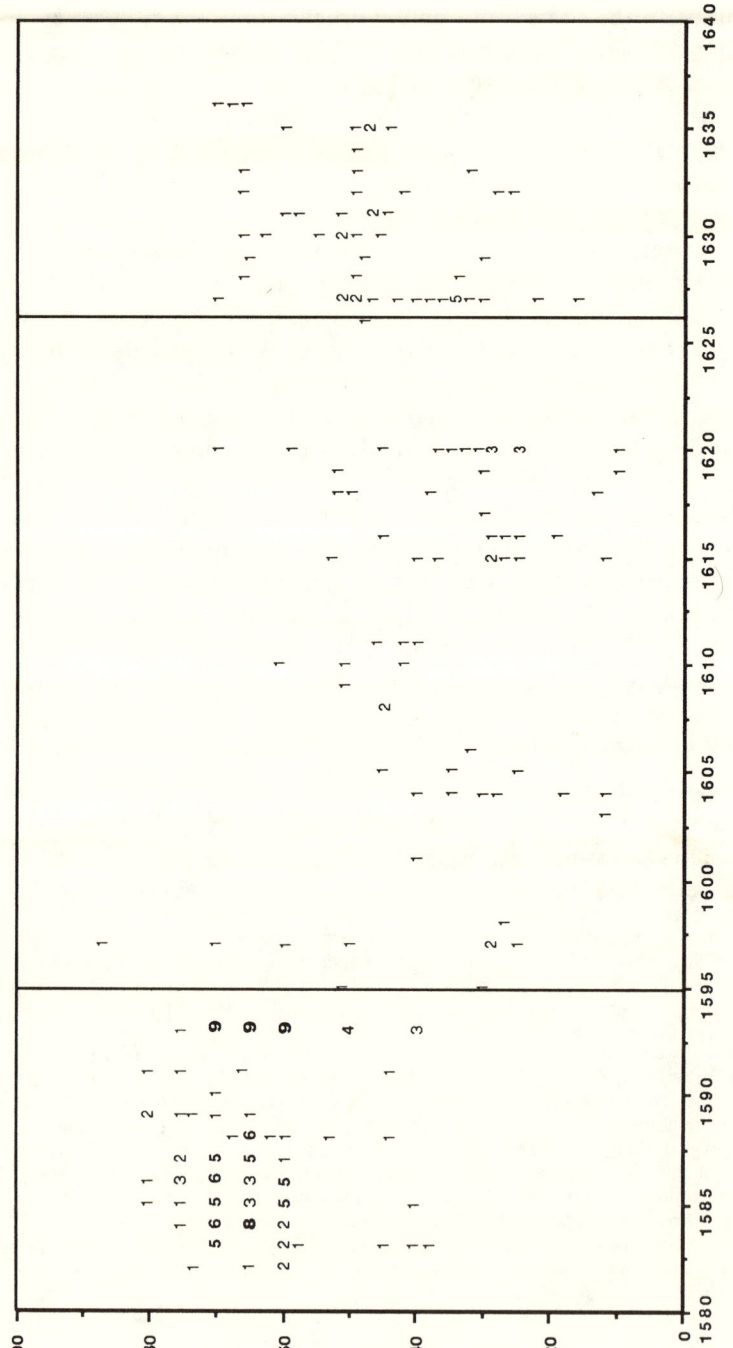

Fig. 5. Assessed tax rates, 1582–1636. Each numeral represents the number of cases at that tax level for a given year. Data are drawn from Appendix A.

percent or more under the sonmen system. For several decades after the switch, tax rates commonly ranged between 10 percent and 40 percent.

The three exceptions to this trend occurred in 1597, in closely proximate villages: Satoyama, with an assessed rate of 60 percent; Tochiage, with just over 70 percent; and Fujibashi, with almost 88 percent. They were extreme cases, even within their own district.[30] As Figure 5 indicates, only three later tax rates fell in this range. Table 14 shows what happened in the eight villages where "pre" and "post" data permit a comparison (both sets of figures represent taxes assessed as a proportion of assessed value).[31] These data also indicate a sharp decline in rates. Although the sample is small, statistical tests indicate that the trend it shows is probably representative.[32]

The conclusion that tax rates fell after Toshinaga installed the inspection system is further borne out when we compare the mean assessed rates for the years 1582–94 and 1595–1626 (Table 14). The mean rate for the pre-inspection period was quite high, 64.7 percent, as against 36.7 percent in the first three decades of the inspections. Though one might wish for a larger sample than is currently available, there is very little chance that this decline is a sampling artifact.[33] Furthermore, when changes in tax rates can be traced in individual villages, there is no indication that falling rates were offset by increases in assessed values. The declines were real.

A similar trend emerges when we examine the percentage of assessed value actually collected as taxes. Though seventeenth-century tax bills do not provide information on tax collections, 1634 domain-wide and provincial data can be compared with earlier rates. Both comparisons confirm a fall in taxes collected.

TABLE 14
Tax Rates for Eight Villages in the Pre-Inspection and Post-Inspection Eras

	Pre-inspection		Post-inspection	
Village	Year	Rate (percent)	Year	Rate (percent)
Konpōji	1588	70%	1620	45%
Saihōji	1586	70	1620	33
Shibuta	1586	60	1627	37[a]
Noda	1586	60	1627	36
Tokikuni	1586	75	1604	28
Yawata-shimo	1587	80	1604	35
Wakayamagumi	1587	65	1620	31
Kawanishi	1587	70	1620[b]	30

SOURCES: See Appendix A.
[a] Rounded up from 36.8.
[b] Daimyo's part only.

Looking first at Noto province, we find that the average rate fell by approximately one-third over the period 1583–1634. The average rate of collection in Noto villages in 1634 was fractionally more than 30 percent of assessed value, as compared with an average of 46 percent for the 73 tax receipts of 1583–92.[34]

Since the pre-inspection data include some villages outside Noto, it is reasonable to compare them with the 1634 domain-wide collected tax rate. This comparison reveals a significant decline of just over 13 points. The mean collected rate fell from 46 percent to only some 33 percent of the domain's assessed value of 1,192,670 koku.[35]

In sum, four different comparisons (of the assessed tax rates of the Noto villages for which there are data for both the late sixteenth and the early seventeenth century; of the average assessed tax rates before and after the inspections began; of the tax collection rates of the sonmen sample and the Noto data of 1634; and of the tax collection rates of the sonmen sample and the domain-wide data of 1634) all support the same conclusion: tax rates, both assessed and collected, declined substantially with the introduction of the inspection system.

Three considerations increase confidence in the validity of this trend. First, although the sonmen-era Noto sample is not large, it is large enough to provide a reasonable basis for a statistical comparison with later data. Further, in reaching the above conclusions the standard applied in statistical tests (the 1 percent level of confidence) is very rigorous. Second, the geographic distribution of the early data creates no apparent bias in the results. The average rates for Noto (30.4 percent) and the domain (32.5 percent) in 1634 suggests that the Noto rates were consonant with the domain average. Noto's assessment and collection rates can be taken as representative of those of other parts of the domain. Finally, the estimated collection rates for the Noto sample are based on data that underreport the total amount of land tax ultimately paid, giving a slight downward bias to tax rates in the late-sixteenth-century sample.

Not only did land tax rates decline; they also became less uniform under the annual inspection system. Comparing the standard deviation for the two periods (that is, measuring the extent to which cases deviate from the mean) shows far less deviation before 1595 than after. The pre-inspection figure of 7.8 is under half the figure for the period of annual inspections, 16.2.[36]

The greater deviation of later tax rates indicates a loss of control over tax resources. Daikan implemented tax assessment standards much less consistently under the inspection system than under the earlier sonmen system. No explanation for this change is to be found in the principles of annual crop inspection. Officials computed the tax at a flat 40 percent of the sample yield and converted the result to a percentage of the village's assessed value. Since the tax rate on the crop samples was constant, the only variable should have been the size of the yield. Under these circumstances, one would expect the variation in tax rates in each period to be fairly small. But it was in fact very large, too large to be the result of natural variation in crop yields. The discrepancy hints of difficulties in the inspection process itself. It suggests that tax rates bore a very imperfect relationship to yields, and that the theoretical advantages and rationality of annual inspections were outweighed by other factors. It underscores the impression that frequent inspections were associated with a loss of the rulers' (daimyo and landed retainers) grip on land tax resources, a loss of effective administrative control. From the standpoint of villagers, the new system of tax assessment must have appeared arbitrary and unfair.

Practical Constraints on the Inspection System

Clearly, Kaga's policy-makers did not anticipate this severe and pervasive decline in tax rates.[37] The domain's financial burdens remained substantial throughout the period when the inspection system was used; a relaxation of demands on the treasury was unlikely. Though the Pax Tokugawa no doubt eased some of the financial pressure, the inspection system was implemented a half dozen years before the penultimate battle between the Toyotomi and Tokugawa forces at Sekigahara. Furthermore, beginning in 1591, Hideyoshi required all daimyo to contribute toward two massive attempts to conquer Korea and China. This was on top of demands for contributions to various large-scale construction projects.

Ieyasu continued these demands. Like Hideyoshi, he called on daimyo to contribute to major public works and castle-building projects. In addition, many daimyo felt obligated to prove their loyalty by spending much time in residence in Edo or keeping family members there (in high style) well before alternate attendance (*sankin kōtai*) became the rule in 1635.[38]

Like other daimyo, the Maeda labored under each of these substantial financial demands. Although the pacification of Japan meant that they no longer constantly defended their borders and did not have to replace destroyed fortifications, their financial commitments to Hideyoshi and the Tokugawa took up much of the slack in the domain's military budget. The Maeda were the first to volunteer a hostage in 1599, when Toshinaga sent his mother to Edo as proof of his loyalty to the Tokugawa.

They also not only contributed to a variety of public works projects in conjunction with other daimyo, but funded some major projects on their own.* So though peace may have brought the daimyo and their retainers some relief, it is highly unlikely that the domain's expenditures shrank sufficiently to account for the nearly 45 percent reduction in assessed tax rates or the one-third decrease in collected taxes noted above. It is also worth reiterating that this downturn began before the commencement of the Tokugawa peace.

Villagers occasionally rose in protest throughout the late sixteenth and early seventeenth centuries, but a fear of widespread eruptions does not appear to have been the cause of the decline in tax rates. Protests did have some impact. As we have already seen, entire villages sometimes deserted their fields in the first decade of Maeda rule, and domain officials offered a variety of inducements to entice them back to their villages. Nevertheless, the level of assessed and collected taxes in the first 15 years of Maeda rule was much higher than after the introduction of the inspection system. The limited documentation of early-seventeenth-century protests suggests that they were infrequent.

Furthermore, though the goal was to adjust tax rates more sensitively to crop shortfalls and thereby relieve the extremes of village distress, there is no evidence that policy-makers intended to reduce tax rates in order to staunch a hemorrhage of protests. After the introduction of the annual inspection system, desertion appears to have been limited largely to individuals, not entire villages.[39] This was no doubt due to lower land tax rates, but failing any other documentation, the change cannot be mustered as proof that increased protests forced lower tax rates from the domain.

To what, then, are we to impute the decline? Since the design was to make taxation more sensitive to the impact of inclement weather and pestilence, the authorities certainly anticipated some occasional, temporary falls in revenues. What they did not see was that the system was doomed by four structural constraints to result in a long-term decline in revenue-raising capabilities.

First of all, effective inspections required knowledgeable inspectors. Perhaps the system would have worked under rusticated samurai, but by the dawn of the seventeenth century, most of Kaga's samurai made their main residence in the castle town of Kanazawa.[40] Charged with carrying

---

*When Toshitsune's daughter was married into the imperial household in mid-century, for example, the domain treasury financed the extension of the Katsura Imperial Villa. In addition, fires destroyed the domain castle and much of Kanazawa in the 1630's, resulting in extensive rebuilding expenses.

out the crop inspections but now bereft of any real knowledge of agricultural processes and village conditions, these urbanized samurai were often unable even to identify appropriate fields for sample cuttings. And because of the policy of rotating both retainer and daikan jurisdictions, few were likely to gain any working knowledge of their assigned territories.[41]

The deploying of inspectors to investigate low and widely varying tax rates reinforces the impression that assessors were often unable to do their job effectively. Indeed, inspectors were specifically encouraged to compare the fields of neighboring villages and evaluate general economic conditions in considering changes in taxes. These policies aimed to raise average tax rates and reveal the domain leaders' lack of confidence in the ability of tax officials to set uniformly appropriate rates. They felt that inspections were manipulated to deprive the domain and its retainers of the income a properly implemented system would have yielded.

Second, effective inspections required adequate time for implementation. In Kaga domain the ordinary pressures of time were greatly increased by the dispersion of retainer fiefs, the domain's large size, and the urbanization of the samurai. These pressures were exacerbated by the duplication of efforts required to tax villages under the jurisdiction of more than one overlord.

Daimyo and retainer fiefs were scattered throughout the three provinces, increasing the time and effort required to complete inspections. Even travel between villages in the same province could be difficult and time-consuming, and it often took as long as a day or even two days when an official had to cross into another province. The task of crop inspection and sampling was arduous by itself. Selecting three or four fields of each grade of paddy to be sampled, measuring the areas to be cut, taking samples, and transporting them to a central location for threshing and measurement required at least half a day for each village.[42] Extended travel time between sites forced inspectors to choose fields quickly so that they could rapidly move on to other villages in their jurisdiction. All assessments had to be finished before harvests were completed. Officials simply did not have adequate time in which to work. They sampled yields more hurriedly than they would have had to do had they been assigned to contiguous villages.

Traveling from the castle town, Kanazawa, to remote villages in Noto and Etchu provinces alone took as much as two days, further aggravating the problem of widely dispersed jurisdictions. Because of the additional time involved, less attention was given to outlying areas than to villages close to Kanazawa. The relatively greater demands made on villagers living close to Kanazawa is suggested by an ordinance issued in 1615. Domain authorities, seeking to clamp down on official abuses, directed their orders solely to the retainers and daikan in Ishikawa and Kahoku counties, those closest to Kanazawa.* The villages in such areas were subjected to greater samurai oversight or interference than their more far removed counterparts. Distance reduced control.

Third, when a village or district was divided among the tax agents of several overlords, there was substantial duplication of inspection efforts and waste of manpower. Each village appeal initiated still another inspection. It is understandable that in 1627 administrators tried to limit this duplication by ordering daikan to rely on rates already set by landed retainers.[43]

Finally, county magistrates and other supervisory officials had no way to check for inaccurate or falsified reports. There was no historical or comparative standard by which superiors could gauge the effectiveness or honesty of individual assessors. Under a pure inspection system, each village, every year, was treated as unique. In general, claims of malfeasance had to come from villagers, and obviously they would report only instances in which they felt cheated, not those from which they benefited. Only when other officials took cuttings in the same village was there any opportunity to check for too-low assessments.

To sum up, it was the shift to this flawed system that produced the declining tax rates. As constructed, the system contained no presumption of an appropriate year-to-year tax level. It forced officials to assess each year's taxes *de novo*, and they were often unable to justify high taxes. The early decline in assessed and collected tax rates was the result of inherent difficulties in carrying out inspections. Little or no knowledge of agriculture, time pressures aggravated by the need to traverse substantial distances, duplication of effort, and the inability of supervisory officials to identify inept or dishonest assessors all contributed to the poor revenue-raising characteristics of the inspection system. As a result, the domain and landed retainers could not make the system function effectively, and they lost a measure of control over villagers.

Curiously, considering how steep the fall in revenues was, the domain was very slow to respond. Some official patience with the new system was perhaps to be expected, and certainly the momentous national events at the turn of the century were an important distraction. But the granting of much more land to retainers (from 235,000 koku in 1612 to 900,000 koku

---

KHS, 2: 288–89. In addition to the misuse of villagers' labor, the abuses included charging excessive interest on loans and the maltreatment of runaways.

in 1616) and the increase in the number of fiefholders (from fewer than 600 in 1612 to more than 1,300 by 1627) may have obscured the dimensions of the problem as well. Much of the responsibility for taxation moved out of the hands of the daimyo and into those of inexperienced tax collectors who worked for retainers, not the domain administration. Toshitsune may even have hoped to improve land tax collections by enlarging the corps of enfeoffed retainers. By granting more land as fief, he not only would have rid the domain officials of some of the responsibility for tax assessment but would have transferred responsibility to people who had a greater personal interest in effective taxation than daikan. Whatever the expectations, in the long run this policy failed to improve the effectiveness of the land tax system.

Early-Seventeenth-Century Land Tax Payment

Since most of the tax-related documents for the early seventeenth century record only tax rates or the amounts of tax rice due, analyzing the means of payment is difficult at best. Cash apparently continued to be a common form of payment. But other than rice, payment in kind was now confined to a few places like the very mountainous Gokayama region in Etchu where it was difficult to grow rice or to areas where special products were produced.[44]

In 1616 domain authorities ordered villagers not to sell their rice before they paid their taxes.[45] This order suggests that cash payments were sufficiently common to be considered problematic. Perhaps the authorities were cognizant of villagers taking advantage of the annual price cycle to sell at the market highs generally available in the spring and then pay their taxes late, in cash. The same document indicated that wood, soybeans, and other products would not be accepted for the late payment of taxes. Another order, issued later the same year, suggests that at least some villagers used poor quality rice to pay their land taxes (saving the best to market themselves); daikan were instructed not to accept inferior rice as payment.[46]

These concerns were expressed just as the domain began to export large amounts of tax rice and were probably tied to efforts to maximize the profitability of that enterprise.[47] From at least 1589, the domain had established a relationship with the Takashimaya merchant house in Tsuruga. The following year, Toshiie sent military supplies and rice there. Takashimaya handled the sale of the rice the next year (1591), and also forwarded the material to the armies engaged in the Korean campaign. But as the domain expanded its export activities, it sought additional outlets. In 1615 it established a magistrate in Otsu to oversee the transport of tax rice.

By 1616 the domain was selling two-thirds of its tax rice outside its borders. One-third was exported to Otsu, and one-third to Tsuruga.[48] The opening of the new outlet at Otsu and the attendant increase in the export of tax rice coincided with orders restricting nonrice tax payment and encouraging the collection of high-quality rice.

At some later point the domain established additional connections with trade centers at Wakasa and Obama.[49] Throughout the Kan'ei and Shōhō periods (1624–47), as the limitations of the local markets in Kaga, Noto, and Etchu became more evident to the domain's financial administrators, these two centers gained in importance. Later, the domain began sending rice boats to Osaka via the western coastal (Nishimawari) route.[50] Reflecting this increasingly outward orientation, the domain issued orders in 1631 that rice must be used for all past-due land taxes.[51]

This marked Kaga's first formal effort to establish rice as the sole medium for the payment of land taxes. It came with the domain's heavy involvement in the national economy. The new policy was associated with sustained, well-organized attempts to export tax rice, not as a response to central ordinances.

The official period for the payment of taxes without penalty was also shortened. In 1603 Yasukawa village was warned that the tax "must be completely paid within the 11th month" of that year.[52] The 1610 tax records for six villages in Fugeshi county also indicate domain impatience at the taxes still owed from the previous fall. Villagers were ordered to provide servants to work as day laborers, to construct new salt farms, or to sell their daughters to make good the debt. Annual interest of 50 percent would be charged on unpaid taxes for which there was no official forgiveness or extension.[53]

In 1628 the domain authorities set the interest on unpaid taxes at 20 percent annually.[54] Later, in 1631, they attempted to make interest charges applicable even in kyūnin lands. Late payments could be made in silver, but the conversion rate from rice was to be based on the early-summer highs. On top of this, the delinquents had to pay 2.5 interest for each month's delay.[55] The change to an official deadline reinforced the daikan's efforts to collect all taxes due promptly and fully. As villagers sought to comply, and as the loopholes in the tax payment procedures were closed off to them, they increasingly resorted to borrowing, contract servant labor, and other devices to meet their obligations. The domain administrators issued instructions restricting the use of contract labor (1601) at about the same time that official policy first emphasized the prompt payment of taxes. The domain's increasing concern with private loans, interest rates, and contract labor paralleled and reflected problems created by putting greater restrictions on tax payments. This policy evolved, along with the office of bugyō, from 1607 and 1608 on.

Conclusion

Maeda Toshinaga and Maeda Toshitsune continued to pursue a pragmatic administrative policy after their father's death, attempting to balance the needs of the villagers against those of the domain and the landed retainers. As it became evident that the Tokugawa order was relatively stable, and that with a decline in military demands they were now somewhat less dependent on the kyūnin and daikan, they took steps to restrict the discretionary authority of these men. The domain supervised them more aggressively at the turn of the century. They were subject to the oversight of first a magistrate and later a county magistrate, by now an office specializing in rural administration. At the same time specific restrictions were placed on daikan and kyūnin: their judicial rights were limited, their authority to conscript labor was curtailed, and their decisions on taxation were routinely subject to higher review.

All the same, the Maeda moved cautiously, cognizant of the importance of the landed retainers to their military organization. The restrictions were enacted over several decades, and in the end they did not result in a wholesale loss of the retainers' prerogatives, but simply provided for a supplemental review. They were designed only to correct the abuses of individual retainers and daikan that caused villagers to flee their lands.

With the passage of time the domain systematized its fuchibyakushō intermediaries into a new office, the tomura. But many of the same families filled these new posts, and though their powers were strengthened in some respects (notably in dealing with runaways) the duties of the tomura built on those of the fuchibyakushō.

Early-seventeenth-century reforms did not bring transformations in village structures. However, the provision for the remuneration of tomura gave rise to the first legal definition of "villager." Kaga's experience suggests that in some regions of Japan, domain lords continued to avoid heavy involvement with village government even in the seventeenth century. Likewise, Kaga's land tax system continued to reflect an independent but gradual course of development. The role of the political center there, if present at all, was indirect.

Although the specific elements of the domain's land tax system were not necessarily typical, there is evidence that the generally experimental and gradual nature of change was typical of the process in other parts of Japan. Rather than stray too far afield, let me note just one example. In some areas of central Japan, the early tax system was soon confounded by changing yields per *tan*. This created a substantial gap between the official tax assessments and actual yields. Some revisions were needed if any equity in taxation was to be maintained. A new system of assessments, called *domen*, was introduced. In general this new system lasted only a few years before being supplanted by the fixed rate (*jōmen*) system.[56] Here, too, we see a process of trial, error, and reform in operation.

Like other domains, Kaga assessed land taxes in rice. However, the shift to rice was still incomplete as late as the first decades of the seventeenth century. Thereafter, the forms of payment were increasingly limited (rice and gold). The emphasis on rice payments and the shortening of payment schedules did not come until the domain became heavily involved in exporting its tax rice to central markets.

With the switch to annual inspections, inefficiencies resulted in a sharp decrease in the effectiveness of land taxation. Tax rates, both assessed and collected, declined dramatically, and they remained low for decades. Indeed, the decline in tax rates was sufficiently precipitous to be characterized as a crisis. In the absence of domain receipts and expenditures for these years, we cannot directly assess the impact on the domain's budget. It is certain, however, that domain leaders were aware of the problem, and they ultimately, if belatedly, attempted to remedy it.

Why the authorities did not act earlier is not clear. They may have been slow to recognize the difficulties created by the interaction of their plans to supervise landed retainers and the demands of inspection-based land taxation. Possibly they saw the difficulties as temporary or, in light of a more stable domestic order, anticipated a peace dividend. They may even have attempted to avoid the problem by transferring more responsibility for taxation to an enlarged corps of landed retainers. In any event they were ultimately forced to seek more drastic remedies as the expenses of maintaining Edo residences, *sankin-kōtai*, and public works absorbed an increasing share of the domain's resources. A recognition of systemic weaknesses spurred the domain to alter the inspection process after 1627.[57]

Throughout this era we see evidence that villagers had a significant influence on domain policy. They were the motor driving increased restrictions on daikan and kyūnin through their absconding and appeals. Though the fall in tax rates was not linked to an outbreak of widespread violent or disruptive protest, village appeals and the threat of opposition were potent forces in setting broad limits to domain and retainer willfulness. The result was not a mere short-term gain (e.g., a one-year reduction in land taxes) but structural changes in domain administration.

Chapter **9**

Reform, Innovation, and Centralization

A new daimyo did not establish his authority over a domain merely by imposing new men and a new superstructure over the existing local administration. Tensions and conflicts between villagers and their overlords were common. So, too, were frictions within retainer bands and between retainers and daimyo (*ie sōdō*). Resolving these problems required that domains ultimately create administrative structures substantially different from those of the earliest years of domain formation.

One principal difference between late-sixteenth- and late-seventeenth-century domains was the strengthening of their central administrative authority. The landed retainers' complete or partial loss of control over their fiefs provides the most striking evidence of increased domain authority. Greater daimyo control over the retainer band was already evident in the late sixteenth century, and the trend continued incrementally in the early seventeenth.[1]

At first, as studies of domain formation in Tosa and Satsuma emphasize, the daimyo sought to ensure their retainers' loyalty by indirect means, cementing family ties through intermarriage and adoption.[2] But by the mid-seventeenth century there had been a radical change in approach. Many daimyo stripped their retainers of their fiefs and put them on a stipend from the han granary. Most retainers in the other domains had lost not only their judicial rights but also the right to set tax rates within their lands. By the end of the century landed retainers in all but 17 percent of the domains had lost discretionary control over private fiefs.[3]

There is evidence of greater centralized control even in the areas directly administered by the daimyo. Domains created new offices, and their instructions to county magistrates, intendants, and village officials became more detailed. New ordinances circumscribed the powers of local officials and subjected their administrative decisions to higher review.*

Increased control, to whatever degree, would clearly have been impossible without an effective, direct link between domain officials in the castle town and the villages. Someone had to replace rusticated samurai administrators and fiefholders. Though many scholars see the development of village autonomy as the foundation for pulling samurai out of the countryside, village self-government, however essential to local administration, was not, in itself, a foundation for domain centralization. By the late sixteenth century villages already exercised as much autonomy as they ever would, yet the fiefholding retainers and the daikan still frequently resided in the countryside. For a domain to pull them off the land entirely and to centralize control of the countryside, it had to create some conduit for ordinances, some office responsible for carrying out domain policy. To do so most effectively, the people who occupied this position not only had to be honest and reliable, but also had to be familiar with agricultural processes and local conditions.

In short, the critical development was the creation of a corps of disciplined, competent district administrators. These administrators were called by a variety of names and took on a variety of duties in different domains. Western readers are most familiar with the title *ōjōya*, but other titles were very common: *warimoto, tomura kimoiri, ōkimoiri, sōdai*.[4] Each domain determined the degree to which it vested powers in these commoner administrators. In rare instances, such as Satsuma, very low-level samurai were left resident on the land as a check on rural administration. In some areas nonsamurai district administrators were relatively weak, sharing respon-

---

*At the heart of standard explanations for this development are assumptions about the land tax burden on the village. Some argue that by confiscating fiefs and reducing the retainers' stipends, daimyo were able to expand their financial base at a time when the land tax rates were as high as possible. Increasing the rates was out of the question, so financially strapped daimyo were forced to cut their retainers' income. Others argue that the retainers' excessive taxation of villagers caused them to abscond, to the point that agriculture, the rulers' major tax base, was threatened. To protect the villages and stabilize their income, daimyo removed retainers and took over the direct administration of their lands. (These opinions are expressed in whole or in part in Hall, "Ikeda House," p. 85; Hall, *Government and Power*, pp. 405–6; Sansom, *History, 1615–1868*, p. 51; Kanai, *Hansei*, pp. 40–43; Kitajima, *Nihonshi gaisetsu*, pp. 114, 117–18; Kitajima, *Edo jidai*, pp. 44–45; Sasaki, *Daimyō*, pp. 96–103, 111–12, 320; and Araki Moriaki, *Bakuhan*, p. 77. For Kaga, see Araya, "Kaga-han," pp. 67–106.) Both interpretations imply that the villagers were so heavily taxed that their ability to continue farming was jeopardized.

sibility with village heads and samurai daikan. In others, such as Kaga, very strong district administration arose, staffed by villagers who wielded the powers of earlier samurai officials. There was nothing predetermined about the policy a given daimyo followed in laying the foundations for fully centralized administration.

As we have seen, to centralize authority and stabilize domain administrations, daimyo commonly pursued a policy of further isolating samurai from villagers. The very fact that they did so indicates that the process of separation continued long after Hideyoshi's time. It was an extended procedure requiring at least a half-dozen decades. The long duration and the great variation in the tempo and degree of change accentuate the role of local conditions and choice on the process rather than the conscious implementation of centrally conceived initiatives by Hideyoshi and his successors.

Class separation in the Japanese case had two basic elements. The first was the isolation of samurai from the general population. The second was the active definition of other classes. In Kaga the first was well under way shortly after the initial Maeda occupation. The mid-seventeenth-century reforms, the Kaisaku hō, completed that process by effectively fictionalizing all fiefs and leaving only a small handful of samurai officials who had administrative contacts with villages.

But this process defined only two classes at best, the samurai and the rest of the population. A distinguishing feature of early modern Japanese society was the clear identification, reflected in a body of laws, of seven distinct classes. The four major classes followed the Confucian social model: samurai, peasants (hyakushō), artisans, and merchants. To these we can add the small classes of imperial aristocrats, religious personnel, and outcastes. Some of these laws attempted to give visible evidence of major class distinctions by governing clothing and housing materials, but the more fundamental and enduring ones ultimately gave each class a well-defined set of obligations and privileges.[5]

Kaga domain's stability permits a long-range view of both the process of centralization (with its implications for class separation) and the pressures that encouraged it. Developments there reveal that though Kaga was typical in the direction of its policies—centralization, class separation, strengthening land taxation—domain planners adopted some unique or pioneering solutions to their administrative problems. In some respects, such as the implementation of the jōmen, or fixed tax rate system, Kaga's policies foretold developments in other regions of Japan. In others, such as the degree to which samurai were shut out of rural administration, domain policies were undoubtedly less typical.

The distinctive aspects of Kaga's institutional growth underscore the sense of experimentation and fluidity that characterized early-seventeenth-century Japan. From Maeda Toshiie's entry into Noto, domain authorities pursued piecemeal reforms that slowly drew the domain into more details of local administration. This general process was evident throughout the country—in the Bakufu territories, as well as the domains.[6] Only when these efforts failed to resolve important conflicts and problems did Maeda Toshitsune institute radical reforms.* The achievements of these reforms were long-lasting, and the administrative structure that grew out of them formed the basis for rural administration until the Meiji Restoration.[7]

Daikan and Kyūnin Effectiveness, 1627–1647

I have noted that 1624 marked the beginning of a retreat from the principles of annual inspections as a basis for tax assessment. The concern in these matters extended to the imposts of landed retainers as well as the daikan's. It was not a sudden new interest, to be sure; Toshinaga had first expressed concern with the kyūnin's problems and excessive consumption 25 years earlier. But the 1624 ordinances extended domain oversight into new spheres,[8] venturing into the issue of how landed retainers assessed land taxes and ordering them to submit reports on their efforts. Yet active intervention and policy shifts were still three years off.

In 1627 the domain retreated still further, requiring tax officials to compare each village's tax rates with those of neighboring villages after they had completed their inspection. If the village's rates were lower than its neighbors' rates, the officials were to disregard the inspection results and raise taxes to the highest local level.[9]

The "Fifty-eight Clause Ordinance" (1631) even more clearly expressed the domain's intention to raise low tax rates.[10] Its provisions suggest that this was also the purpose of the kyūnin tax rate reports ordered seven years earlier. Clause 16 states: "In villages where there are differences in *kyūnin* tax rates, the higher rate is to be collected. The lower rates are to be investigated by the county magistrate's office, and if villagers' explanations for the lower rates are unfounded, the low rates should be raised in accordance

---

*Toshitsune's son Mitsutaka succeeded him but died suddenly in 1645, leaving the title of daimyo to his very young son Tsunanori. Until Toshitsune died, he served as Tsunanori's guardian.

with the high rates."[11] The higher tax rate was also to be used as the standard for the tax rates on the daimyo's lands. Where there were no kyūnin in a village, the county magistrate and the survey magistrate (*kenchi bugyō*) were to investigate and adjust the tax rates.[12]

Significantly, though other clauses indicate the domain was also intent on standardizing tax rates within the villages and minimizing the differences between rates charged by the various fiefholders in a village, that uniformity was to be achieved only by increasing taxes. There is no indication that the authorities ever considered that some village rates might be excessively high. The ordinances provided only for increased tax levels to achieve parity between villages. Clearly, the administration felt many inspection-based tax rates were too low.

Domain authorities, through the county magistrates, were now actively involved in setting the landed retainers' tax rates based on domain standards. They were no longer content with just what a kyūnin could achieve for himself. Policy-makers had moved beyond simply responding to village complaints of high tax rates; the magistrates undertook the task of identifying low rates and insistently sought to raise them.

The 1631 regulations questioned not only the fairness of the daikan and kyūnin, but their effectiveness as well. The unmistakable implication throughout the ordinance: the existing procedures were unable to provide the tax revenues authorities felt were appropriate. This impression is borne out by later complaints that kyūnin were unable to maintain the tax increases that the domain awarded them after its investigations.[13]

The county magistrates, previously empowered to intervene in cases of kyūnin and daikan abuse, now took leadership in establishing tax rates. The kyūnin's authority was substantially compromised. They were bounded by most of the same restrictions as the daikan and exhibited little of the autonomy they had possessed 50 years earlier.

But even these programs proved inadequate, and in the mid-1630's the domain embarked on further reforms. A variety of new circumstances forced the senior councillors to take more interest in problems that they had been able to discount for several decades. Even if we impute the early-seventeenth-century tolerance of low tax assessments and collections to a "peace dividend" that lowered expenditures for a time, there is good reason to believe that by the 1620's that dividend had begun to run out.

By then, routine expenditures for both the domain and its samurai had risen. The expenses demanded by the shogunate, the Maeda ties to the imperial household, and other obligations noted in the last chapter all continued. And in 1631 Kanazawa castle burned, forcing extensive repairs. The losses extended beyond the domain itself to the many samurai and landed retainers now concentrated there, forcing broad concern to raise adequate funds to rebuild.

Furthermore, samurai, now resident in the castle town, found their incomes inadequate to their increasingly luxurious life-style. Removed from the spartan existence of battle-ready soldiers, they aggressively indulged in all the entertainments and social competitions their new urban existence offered.[14] But at the same time the buying power of their rice-based incomes plunged. Even ordinary samurai who might serve as daikan or the kyūnin's tax agents had significant motivation to bolster their income through private initiatives.

One favored recourse, for daikan, kyūnin, and subordinates alike, was to engage in usurious lending. The resort to this practice suggests that usury was an easier way to increase income than raising land taxes, perhaps because pressure could be applied directly to an identifiable individual.[15] For much of the early seventeenth century, this was an unregulated area of private enterprise. The domain, however, had no such neat device to fall back on to raise its income. Indeed, to a large extent the authorities came to see these activities as interfering with the collection of land taxes.

Usury and other signs of corruption did not appear on any notable scale until the 1620's and later, two decades after the great decline in land tax rates. The first evidence of widespread problems appears almost four decades after the change to assessments based on annual inspections, in 1625. In that year all the male members of the family of Oshio Denzaemon (an employee of the domain courts, *kujiba yōnin*) and one of his confederates, Kobayashi Shōhei, were executed for illicit loan activities that robbed the domain of its due.[16] Another major case of corruption was uncovered in 1636 and punished with equal severity.[17]

Particularly noteworthy in the domain's efforts to resolve irregularities between villagers and tax collectors was just this: that the focus was on restricting private lending, not on complaints that villagers bribed officials to obtain lower tax assessments. Though domain ordinances first reveal concern with the issue in 1615, it was only in 1635 that authorities felt the problem common enough to insist that land taxes be fully paid before private debts were repaid. The implication of this order was that loans interfered with the *payment* of taxes due, not with *setting* tax rates.*

---

*KHS, 2: 767; Sasaki, *Daimyō*, pp. 271–72; Mise, "Inaba Sakon," pp. 39–40. The domain restricted the rates on the public storehouses' loans to villagers in 1628, but the decrees did not apply to private loans (KHS, 2: 565). Other than the standard prohibitions against requesting special favors from villagers under inspection, the 1627 and 1631 ordinances offer no hint of serious official corruption in the setting of tax rates.

In the fall of 1636 a substantial underpayment of land taxes in both retainer and domain lands caught the full attention of officials throughout the domain. Toshitsune sent two officials, Okumura Inaba and Tsuda Kanbei, to investigate the daikan accounts.[18] Based on the evidence uncovered, he authorized steps to relieve economic hardship in the villages and to tighten the local administrative structure. These efforts are known as the Kan'ei reforms, after the period in which they were enacted.

To the first end, he ordered a partial forgiveness of loans. The degree of forgiveness was staggered, based on the age of the loans: those contracted before 1635 were completely forgiven, principal and interest; on those contracted in 1635 and 1636, only the interest was forgiven. In addition, a lid of 20 percent annual interest was put on future loans.* At the same time the authorities reiterated their prohibition against any repayment of loans before land taxes were paid.[19] (Lest readers assume that this measure represented an admission by the domain that its land tax rates were too high, note that a domain-wide 3 percent rate increase followed in 1637. What the fate of this effort was is unknown, but even if it was largely successful, the increase proved inadequate over the long run to meet domain goals.[20])

On the administrative front, Toshitsune made several changes. To minimize contacts between officials and villagers that facilitated corruption and graft, the tenure of county magistrates was shortened to one year. To provide checks on the daikan's activities, the territories they managed were intermingled, and the size of each administrative unit was reduced.[21] Relations between these officials and kyūnin agents were restructured so that all came under the supervision of the *san'yōba bugyō*, the magistrate in charge of the Accounts Office and his subordinate officials, the county magistrates. Finally, the *meyasuba* (inspectorate), who had been given authority to oversee some activities of daikan and kyūnin in 1624, now took over the county magistrates' responsibility for hearing village complaints against tax assessors and collectors.[22]

Experimentation

Alongside these changes, senior domain officials now began experimenting with new arrangements for land taxation. There were three thrusts to these experiments: imposing uniform tax rates on villages (*heikin men*), setting fixed tax rates (*jōmen*), and giving official encouragement

---

*Because these measures resembled certain medieval laws (*tokusei rei*) restricting loans, historians refer to them as *han tokusei rei* or "semi–virtuous government ordinances."

to warichi. Precedents also were set for domain assistance to distressed villagers and to tomura reorganization.

These experiments help identify the source of the Kaisaku hō reforms. At about the time that the Kaisaku hō was enacted (intensively from 1651 to 1656), several other domains, notably Owari, Kishū, and Hikone (1644–47), Yonezawa (1652–57), Tsu (intensively, 1649–51), and Okayama and Chōshū (1648–57), made major reforms. The chronological closeness of these efforts seems to argue that Kaga simply modeled its policies on the programs of other domains. But there is no direct evidence at all of imitation, and the domain's clear experimentation with similar policies long before the Kaisaku hō suggests that the primary impulse for the reforms was internal, not external. The actions of the other domains may have affected the timing of Kaga's reforms, but their content came from the domain's own history.

First attempts at uniform tax rates (*heikin men*) for kyūnin may have begun as early as 1620.[23] The phrase "heikin men" also appears in documents describing kyūnin (but not domain) taxation in 1641, a year in which fixed tax rates were implemented in villages with averaged tax rates.* These changes were undertaken in connection with the instituting of branch domains in 1639. That reorganization worked many changes among the landed retainers. Those who went to the branch domains had to receive new grants within the boundaries of the new units. This created a degree of mobility that threatened unusual confusion in both the villages that the retainers took over and the old ones that they left. Averaging village tax rates and setting an explicit standard limited confusion and helped ensure that new tax burdens would not fall disproportionately on a fraction of a village's residents. Nevertheless, as Table 15 well illustrates, neither fixed nor averaged tax rates were effectively maintained on retainer lands. The range of variation in retainer assessments was wide within each year and also from year to year.

Two things doomed this experiment in fixed uniform tax rates. First, these measures may have been intended only to ease the transition to branch domains and not as a permanent structural change. In any case, there is no evidence of aggressive follow-up efforts to maintain them. Second, even if these new approaches were intended as permanent, the effort was not

---

*Sakai Seiichi, *Kaga-han kaisakuhō*, pp. 184–88. Fixed rates were also imposed on the lands of religious institutions. The original purpose may have been different from the kyūnin case: because the amounts of land involved were relatively small, fixed rates may have been easier to maintain. But this was probably later seen as a way to deal with the unpredictability of domain and retainer revenues. Since the domain granted lands to religious institutions to support their activities, the use of fixed rates ensured them a steady flow of income.

TABLE 15
Range of Variation in Land Tax Rates in Kamiyasuhara Village, 1643–53

Year	Number of retainers	Range (percent)
1643	17	5.7–33.0
1644	13	16.6–38.0
1645	11	23.0–38.0
1646	25	23.0–46.0
1647	24	22.8–46.0
1648	12	0.0–40.0
1649	14	19.6–40.0
1650	29	5.3–40.0
1651	30	13.8–40.9
1652	11	25.5–39.1
1653	12	25.5–39.1

SOURCE: *KHNK*, 1: 190–91.

accompanied by structural changes designed to ensure consistent implementation. Consequently, all of the same impediments to the effective use of annual inspections remained to confound the new system.

Regardless of the reasons for the failure of these efforts, the domain was clearly experimenting in the same spirit that underlay its earlier efforts to increase tax revenues: to raise low rates to acceptable levels and achieve uniformity. In this sense the program was consistent with past policies. It was also consistent in principle with another experiment, spearheaded in Noto province by Inaba Sakon, a principal in the Accounts Office (San'yōba) and a county magistrate.

In Noto all landed retainers in Suzu and Fugeshi counties had been removed and their properties put under the direct control of the daimyo's agents in 1627. From this time the land in each village was taxed at a single rate (*heikin men*). At the time tax receipts for the area had been anemic. A good collection of land tax receipts for the 15 villages from Nafune district reveals that 1626 taxes, the year before the removal of the landed retainers, averaged just over 38 percent and ranged from a high of 70 percent for Nafune village, a unique outlier, to a low of 17 percent (also unique). Through 1634 tax rates remained constant at close to the same levels. From 1635, however, the average rates began to rise, just a percentage point for 1635 to 1637, then up four points, to 43 percent, in 1638–39, and up again, to 45 percent, in 1640, a rate that was maintained until 1656. Within each of these periods, annual fluctuations in collected taxes were generally within 0.5 percent of assessments.[24] In other words, the domain administrators who took over the area moved in several stages to reevaluate land tax rates, raising them to new highs; and once appropriate (from the domain perspective) levels had been reached, they successfully kept them there.

This success was made possible in part by a 1633 directive from Inaba that clearly identified tax responsibilities for reclaimed land as falling on the shoulders of three men who were specialists, not the daikan who supervised tax collections from village groups (*kumi*). These men appear to have staffed a new special accounting office called the Gosan'yōba. Although the name is similar to the domain office (the San'yōba), it did not carry the status of "magistrate" (*bugyō*). The three officials served under the county magistrate's jurisdiction (see Fig. 6), and later this responsibility was transferred to him. The same directive also clearly placed tomura completely under the supervision of the county magistrate and prevented daikan from intervening in affairs unrelated to taxation. This created greater specialization in their work, too. In these instances specialization appears to have brought rich rewards.[25]

The Noto experiment provided a model for the domain-wide conversion to a permanent system of fixed land tax assessments.[26] It suggested that a properly ordered administrative apparatus under direct domain control could raise and maintain tax rates. It ultimately provided a context in which the domain could confidently promise its retainers a guaranteed income in return for the loss of their traditional rights in fief. The principles of the Kaisaku hō had begun to emerge through this experiment.

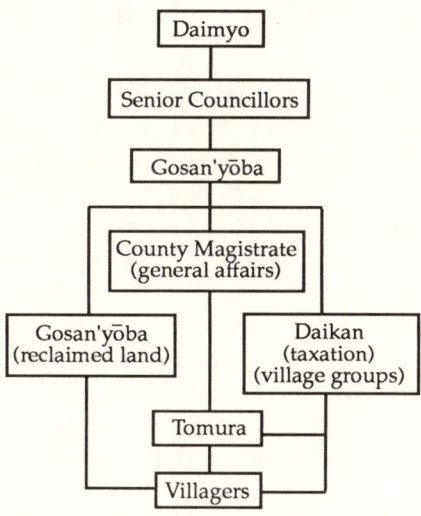

Fig. 6. The structure of rural administration in Noto, ca. 1633–51.

The Noto policies were not quickly exported to other parts of the domain. The new arrangements took several years to prove their efficacy, and during that time the domain was reluctant to reclaim more administrative responsibility for taxation from landed retainers. Earlier measures may have subjected their administration to oversight, but their basic tax perquisites remained intact. Removing them from one part of the domain to another was one thing; eliminating their traditional rights altogether was quite another. Questions remained, for example, about who would specialize in land tax administration, and until such time as they could be answered, the reforms could not be extended to Kaga and Etchu. That meant continued administrative instability and problems in tax assessment and collection outside Noto.

The third thrust of the Kan'ei reforms, redistribution was viewed as a device for forcing a reassessment of the land tax base as well as equalizing the tax burden among shareholders and increasing the likelihood of full land tax payment. It, too, represented an experimental precursor of the Kaisaku hō reforms. But even more significant, it was the domain's first attempt to employ a village innovation to further its own policy objectives.

The immediate stimulus to the adoption of this practice was the reallocating of retainer lands with the creation of branch domains. Concerned to keep the disruption in both the new and the old locations to a minimum, domain authorities encouraged redistribution as a way to ensure that any resulting gain or loss to taxpaying villagers would be spread evenly rather than affecting just the land designated by the headman.[27]

Administrators subsequently continued to encourage land redistribution for other reasons. Domain officials were acutely aware that many villagers were thrown into debt by their land tax burden.[28] Warichi helped alleviate that broader problem. But redistribution also served the equally if not more important purpose of forcing a reevaluation of the land subject to taxation. The land surveys preceding a reallocation helped to reveal lands illegally kept off the tax registers and changes in the quality of fields. Though it might be possible to hide unregistered land from domain officials for a while, repartition generated pressures within the villages against those cultivating unregistered fields, for this was one time when all villagers were particularly conscious of tax inequities.*

Even as the domain began to intrude into and to promote redistributions, it simply built on village institutions. All operational decisions

---

*This observation would carry less force (no force?) when one household was substantially dependent on another. Then coercion could be applied to the dependent household.

remained in the hands of villagers.* Domain planners were clearly using warichi as they found it in the villages, but for their own purposes.

Land Tax Rates

To explore the impact of the domain's modified procedures, let us divide the 1600–1636 period into two subperiods, using 1627, the year the domain first required tax reports from all daikan and kyūnin, as a boundary. Though rates were not raised to sixteenth-century levels at any point across the period, there was a clear increase in mean tax assessment in 1628–36. Assessed tax rates averaged 46.2 percent, against 36.7 for 1600–1627 (see Fig. 5, p. 180).[29]

Thanks at least in part to the officials' use of village-by-village comparisons, the rates continued to climb over the next decade. By 1646 assessed land taxes represented an average of 40 percent of an assessed valuation of 1,340,000 koku, well over the 1634 domain average of 32.5 percent.† But even after this rebound, the rates still fell far short of the 65 percent average in Noto for 1583–92. Moreover, among the villages in the sample, it was exceptional for the assessed rates to match those of the sonmen era. They were commonly well below 50 percent of assessed value. Consequently, the collected rates could not have matched the sixteenth-century level of 46 percent, either.

In addition, rates still varied widely (Fig. 5). There was less dispersion of tax rates in the second period, to be sure, suggesting that the domain had some success in its attempts to standardize land tax rates as well as raising them.[30] But the difference is not statistically significant, and it is not possible to conclude that the reforms substantially improved the consistency of assessments. Even under the modified inspection system, officials still struggled to impose uniform tax standards.

---

*With the compilation of tax figures in the mid-1640's, the domain appears to have reconstructed several hundred villages for its own purposes and this, too, encouraged redistribution. In most cases two or three villages were combined. In some cases villages were split. Superficially, this appears to be a violation of the village as a "natural" community. But in many instances the combining rejoined branch villages formed in connection with reclamation projects with their parent village. The reverse may be true in the case of splits. A reclamation project in some very remote area may have so isolated one part of a village that it deserved to stand alone because of separately managed irrigation systems and other resources. Either case encouraged a repartition ("Shōhō san nen taka mononari chō genkō," manuscript in the Ka-Etsu-Nō Bunko, Kanazawa City Library). For additional discussion, see Kigoshi, "Kaga-han gochō shindendaka."

†KHS, 3: 208–13. This was despite the fact that the villagers of Kaga, Etchu, and Noto had suffered their worst crop shortfall to date in 1641–42. The shortfall had only a temporary impact. (Ishikawa ken saii shi, pp. 90–93.)

Table 15, presented earlier, well illustrates the disparity that could exist in a single village. Three points are noteworthy. First, there was substantial annual variation in rates assessed by individual retainers as well as between retainers. The period covered, 1643–53, was not marked by major famines or natural disasters that might account for this phenomenon. The variations were the result of administrative decisions (misjudgments?), not the whims of nature.[31] Second, the taxes were not specifically allocated by the domain to individual kyūnin. Each retainer inspected the village and then set a rate for his portion of the village's total assessed value (*kokudaka*). Variation in rates does not say anything about the individual targets of taxation. Only if a village was not able to pay the full amount of tax due would a family in default be singled out (probably by villagers) for its failure to pay its share. Corporate tax liability isolated agents from assessments on sections of a village. Finally, some of the variation can be ascribed to the instability of the village's overlords. A different set of retainers taxed Kamiyasuhara village each and every year. Under such circumstances, their agents could hardly have become familiar enough with the village's agricultural conditions and crop yields to know what rate was realizable.

Land Tax Reform and Centralization Under the Kaisaku Hō

The authorities' doubts about the effectiveness of kyūnin and daikan were not assuaged by the slow progress under the Kan'ei reforms. Administrative experiments in Noto promised even greater tax revenues and more stable relations between the domain's officials and the villagers. Ultimately, the policies developed there provided the foundation for Kaga's most famous reforms, the Kaisaku hō.

The Kaisaku hō combined into a coherent program a variety of old domain policies and several significant new ones. Officials began by evaluating earlier attempts to deal with a host of problems—demands on villagers' labor, the villagers' heavy reliance on high-interest loans, lazy cultivators, ineffective land taxation, miscellaneous commercial taxation, the storage and marketing of tax rice, village-samurai tensions, and other related issues—and then selected the programs that promised to promote peace within the domain, adequate revenue flows for the treasury, and effective daimyo control over the landed retainers. Where old programs seemed unworkable, the policy-makers turned to new solutions.

The discussion that follows does not attempt a comprehensive treatment of the Kaisaku hō,[32] but is confined to those elements that complete the processes at the center of earlier chapters: the evolution of land tax practices; class separation; and village contributions to domain institutions. The centralization of domain authority and the fictionalization of fiefs were inextricably tied to these developments as both a tool of reform and an outcome of it. Increasing and stabilizing domain revenues was prerequisite to shifting the retainers away from the taxation of villages to a system of domain stipends. Conversely, removing samurai ignorant of agriculture led to more effective taxation and smoothed village-domain relations. These processes were extended beyond landed retainers. The new administrative and tax measures completely eliminated samurai daikan and replaced them with commoner officials drawn from the ranks of tomura.

In 1648 policy-makers embarked on a systematic reevaluation of the land tax base, tax rates, and the administrative apparatus for assessing and collecting taxes. Unfortunately, hardly any survey registers survive for whole villages from these and succeeding efforts, commonly referred to as the "Keian surveys" (*kenchi*). We have some documents covering reclaimed land, but that is all. Since this poor evidence for widespread actual measurements is an exception to an otherwise well-documented process, we should again interpret the meaning of the word "kenchi" very broadly as "investigations of the land," not as actual, detailed measurements.

These investigations were simultaneously aimed at eliminating the villagers' chief dissatisfactions and the domain's revenue problems. The policy-makers' first solution was to increase the number of county magistrates.[33] How far the domain intended to go with reforms at this time is uncertain, but during the process, it must have found substantial obstacles, for it soon embarked on an extraordinary administrative reorganization.

To pave the way for that effort, investigators circulated among the villages to inspect fields, yields, and general economic conditions to get a better sense of the tax base and evaluate the appropriateness of current levels of taxation. Where necessary, they conducted full or partial surveys of villages. These efforts alone would have proved contentious, but another thrust of these investigations sometimes had momentous consequences for individual families and provoked several acts of violence. As the officials moved through each village, they identified and dispossessed "lazy" cultivators, those who persistently failed to meet their tax obligations. This procedure was little more than an intensive application of existing ordinances that had been enforced in varying degrees since 1616, when the "plow tax" (*kuwayaku*) system for raising tomura salaries began the process of defining the adult males who cultivated lands as a legal class. (Recall that the mere ownership of land or shares was not a criterion; those who did not cultivate the land and certain other people were excluded from the tax and full village membership.) It was these men who bore responsibility for the village's land taxes. If they failed to pay their share consistently, they could be removed from the land.

Under the provisions of these ordinances, the defaulter was expelled from full membership in the community. This meant more than a superficial loss of status. His lands were turned over to a more capable person, and he was now forced to shift for himself; usually his wife and children were forced to work for the new cultivator. Not only was the man economically vulnerable; he had lost all the rights and the privileges of full membership in the village community. During the Kaisaku hō, these regulations were diligently enforced. Moreover, these provisions were now commonly included in the instructions that were annually read to villagers.[34]

The effort to replace those identified as lazy farmers sparked absconding, opposition to some domain actions, and various criminal acts, some of which we might now classify as terrorism. The entire process of identifying the men who habitually failed to pay their share of taxes not only created conflict but had the effect of directing much of the villagers' criticisms, frustrations, and anger at other villagers and commoner officials, not at the domain, its samurai officials, or specific policies. As a result, though there were a few instances of protest, usually carried on through normal channels of appeal, the domain's actions did not provoke a widespread or violent anti-domain protest movement in the countryside. That continued to be the case throughout the enactment of the reforms.[35]

The actual implementation of the reform program is typically dated from 1651, with the first efforts in Ishikawa and Kahoku counties. But experiments in fact began in 1648, with 14 Ishikawa villages as the test areas. Here the lack of actual surveys may have contributed to disputes between domain officials and villagers. The investigation led to a large increase in assessed value and the villages' tax burden. In the subsequent tax year (1649), the villagers paid only half the amount owed. Domain officials entered the villages, completed the harvest under their own direction, and took 60 percent as tax. The combination of tax underpayment and the villagers' complaints that excessive taxation was impoverishing them resulted in a new investigation in 1651 and a reduction in the villages' assessed value.*

In the same year (1651) magistrates, accompanied by armed samurai, entered 31 villages in the Mount Haku region. There they implemented a combination of policies that typified the overall thrust of the reforms: to

---

* *KHNK*, 1: 161. Similar accounts of concerted protest are rare. In 1656 and again in 1658, Ota villagers opposed investigations, and eight families were expelled (Hara, *Kaga-han*, p. 140).

forgive uncollected taxes; to investigate loans, calling lenders to the castle in Kanazawa for interviews, and demanding careful documentation of legitimate loans; to dispense assistance as needed, including for the maintenance of draft animals; to replace lazy cultivators; and to establish storehouses for grain to be lent in emergencies and under carefully controlled conditions. The domain invested 90 gold *kanme* in this effort, but the investment quickly proved its worth: an arrangement that took care of villagers' needs for loans at reasonable rates and secured the regular payments of the land tax at levels acceptable to the domain. With the successful completion of this operation, authorities had a model that could be extended to the other parts of the domain.[36]

Also in 1651, in the midst of the Keian reevaluations, Maeda Toshitsune, guardian of the child-daimyo Tsunanori, appointed Itō Naizen and Kikuchi Daigaku to a new office, that of reform magistrate (*kaisaku bugyō*). The office was created as a special, temporary post to oversee the administrative and tax reforms. Although only middle-rank samurai, both men had extensive experience in agricultural affairs, having worked as survey magistrates and in similar posts.[37] Because of that experience, they proved to be especially valuable in effecting the Kaisaku hō.

This turn to specialists, borrowed from the Noto experiment, had one distinct advantage: it took tax matters out of the hands of officials who were a fundamental part of the problems that created the need for reform. Toshitsune now assigned that responsibility to capable people with whom he had a long and trusting relationship. Their close association with the daimyo, the special nature of their appointments, and the specific focus of their task further isolated them from the pressures of fiefholders and daikan. Their independence enabled them to act resolutely.

But the success of the Kaisaku hō did not, indeed could not, rest solely with a handful of samurai. With rare exceptions, even those most familiar with agriculture were too isolated in the castle town, too removed from the daily routines of agriculture, and too unfamiliar with local conditions throughout the domain to have a firm foundation for reassessing the land tax base or land tax rates in each village. Some direct link with each district (*tomura-gumi*) was essential.

Central administrators found that link among the tomura. As prominent landholders, these men were very knowledgeable about agriculture and village conditions in their districts. It was only because the domain administrators succeeded in earning the cooperation of these villagers that they were able to replace the daikan and kyūnin as the chief local tax agents. The tomura's assistance was critical to the success of rural reforms.

The tomura who assisted the reform magistrates were a newly restructured and highly motivated corps of men. A number of tomura, like daikan and kyūnin, had been charged with usury, robbery, and other forms of misconduct, but by this time domain authorities had taken steps to eliminate the men who were suspect and to ensure the full cooperation of the rest: in 1635 they had combined the original village groupings of a dozen or so villages into substantially larger administrative units—of up to 50 or more villages. By reducing the number of village groups, they at once got rid of the tomura who were ineffective or corrupt and enhanced the status and responsibilities of the rest.

But the domain was still not ready to rely on the tomura until it purged their ranks again, in 1652. Only then was it satisfied that they would make an effective link between lord and village, capable of taking a major role in land tax and local administration. Most districts were now reorganized into units of 50 or more villages; several consisted of more than 100. In addition, tomura were transferred from one province to another with some frequency. This removed some of the opportunity for favoritism but still made use of administrators with a detailed knowledge of agriculture.[38]

In a manner reminiscent of the initial appointment of the *fuchibyakushō*, domain authorities also restructured the tomura system itself. In 1654 the ablest men were elevated to the position of *tomura gashira*, or "head tomura," with authority to coordinate and supervise the activities of the several tomura under their jurisdiction. In return for their services, they received a stipend by specific domain appointment, the only commoner officials to do so since the fuchibyakushō. Eventually, they came to be known as *gofuchinin tomura*, or "stipended tomura."

Through a number of devices domain authorities manipulated status symbols to encourage the full cooperation of the tomura. All of them were called to Komatsu, Toshitsune's residence, for intensive discussions with the reform magistrates.[39] The magistrates quizzed them extensively on conditions in each of the villages under their control and aggressively probed their opinions on matters of domain policy. Through these meetings domain authorities carefully signaled to all that tomura were important officials whose knowledge was respected and valued. More concrete forms of flattery were used as well. Indeed, the tomura were treated almost as though they were samurai. In 1653 Toshitsune bestowed spears on 14 of them and gave horses to four others. Again, in 1654 and 1655, he presented the tomura with gifts—this time of rice and miscellaneous items. And in 1656 all tomura were permitted to wear short swords, an honor usually reserved for samurai.[40] These actions provided visible signs of the daimyo's trust in his new administrators and clearly distinguished them from other commoner officials.*

Such incentives were not confined to the tomura. Toshitsune increased the fiefs of many samurai with close involvement in the Kaisaku hō, especially the three reform magistrates. He also spent a good deal of time with both the reform magistrates and the tomura. Part of that time was spent in business consultations with them, but he also made a point of dining with them. Since senior councillors, men who were often involved in drafting the reform legislation and made many of the decisions on their own, were not, apparently, treated to such extraordinary consideration, these acts convey the impression that the daimyo deliberately employed his prestige to manipulate those most closely involved in the field.[41]

In 1661 the tomura system was reorganized again. To this point the *gofuchinin tomura* had continued to administer the village groups they had headed before assuming their higher posts. Now the domain selected from among them one man from each county to serve solely in a supervisory capacity.[42] These so-called "groupless" (*mukumi*) tomura no longer directly supervised a village.

At about the same time the domain decided to make the office of reform magistrate a permanent part of the domain's administrative structure. The office had been abolished earlier, in 1656, when the work of implementing the reform measures, reevaluating the land tax base, and raising taxes was largely completed. But events in succeeding years demonstrated a continuing need for a specialist in land tax administration. After Toshitsune's death in 1658, and after the disruptions caused by a serious crop failure in 1660, the office was permanently reestablished.[43]

Throughout these changes in administrative organization and policy, villages continued to play a very small role. Instructions to villages did become more common in the 1630's, and in the course of implementing the Kaisaku hō, a number of detailed instructions were directed specifically at villagers. One typical set, issued in 1655, exhorted them to farm their land diligently, pay their taxes dutifully, and dress and behave in an appropriate way. But it did not place any added emphasis on village administration as an arm of domain government.[44]

The one aspect of village self-rule in which the domain did take considerable interest was warichi.[45] The reform magistrates and tomura took every opportunity during their repeated consultations with village leaders

---

*But close as the tomura were to samurai in their trappings, they were still commoners. They and their families were not called on to serve in combat, were not banned from farming, and were not allowed to change their residence.

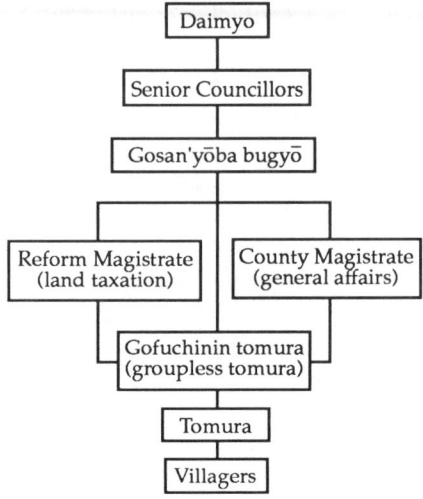

Fig. 7. The structure of rural administration, ca. 1670.

and in the course of their land investigations to encourage repartition as a means of flushing out hidden fields and providing local records in support of their revised assessments. At the same time the domain refused to become enmeshed in regulating warichi. It only slightly modified its earlier restrictions. Now the process could not be initiated unless all of the shareholding villagers jointly requested permission from the district administrators (tomura) and the reform magistrates.[46] So though the authorities did specifically provide for the continuance of the system, and indeed promoted it, they were concerned to see that the system functioned in such a way as to maintain some measure of harmony within the villages. From the domain's perspective, encouraging warichi had one overriding function: to increase tax revenues.

After the Kaisaku hō, domain administrators seldom devoted much attention to the matter. Once the reforms were fully in place, domain authorities stopped insisting on regular repartitions for more than a century. The reason for this loss of interest is not hard to find. The intent all along had been to change the land tax system to a fixed rate system (jōmen). When the authorities succeeded in determining the amount for each village, the whole issue of spreading the tax burden across the community was greatly simplified. The only major challenge to the existing pattern of distribution would come from climatic changes and natural disasters that removed land from production. Convinced that all arable land was now on the land tax registers, and that there was only a limited possibility of villagers secretly reclaiming new land, the authorities saw little need to encourage what for them had merely been a device for assuring the domain's tax revenues. In sum, the domain no longer had clear reason to press ahead with its involvement in redistribution.

The shift to the fixed tax rate system brought with it an innovation in local administrative responsibilities and the full fictionalization of retainer fiefs. In 1653 the domain began to replace samurai daikan with tomura. Within five years the changeover was complete. By 1658 commoners served as the domain's tax agents everywhere.[47] Their duties, however, were considerably lighter than the daikan's, for the new tax system eliminated much of the routine work required under the old one. With a standard rate set for each village, there was no need to make annual inspections of crop yields in each and every village. If crops were particularly poor, a village could petition for a reduction in land taxes, but the general expectation was that villages would deal with ordinary declines on their own. Furthermore, in the event of above-average yields, villagers would keep the surpluses. Ideally, these would be stored against future shortfalls. In principle long-term yield increases could result in increases in the fixed tax rate (as had happened in Noto), but in practice upward reevaluations seldom occurred.

The elimination of annual inspections saved tax administrators a great deal of effort. There were approximately 3,500 villages in the domain. To inspect each one annually had required a formidable expenditure of energy. Furthermore, since some villages had been inspected by several kyūnin and a daikan, a significantly greater amount of manpower had been required than the village total suggests. Under the jōmen system, the domain could rely on far fewer agents, men who were more trustworthy and energetic than the samurai they replaced, and still accomplish more than under the annual inspection system (see below).

The tax administration responsibilities that remained were still substantial. Tomura incorporated reclaimed land into the tax system. They also assessed taxes on reclamation projects still under development. If there was a flood or other damage to crop lands, they evaluated the seriousness and extent of the damage. On their recommendation a samurai-led survey team would be sent out to confirm their findings and remove land from the tax rolls. If there was a serious crop shortfall, they were the first officials to appraise yields and recommend lower tax rates. Under the new system the tomura's chief concern was maintaining the land tax base and collecting taxes, not tax assessments. Though their work would be reviewed by higher-ups and sometimes even by the reform magistrates, front-line responsibility for land taxation clearly lay with these commoner officials.

When the reevaluations of the reform magistrates and tomura were finally completed in 1656, the domain distributed tax bills, called *mura goin*, to all villages except those in the Chō lands. These specified the villages' assessed value, their land tax rates, and their other miscellaneous taxes (*komononari*). Several years later, in 1670, officials reviewed these bills and issued new ones with only minor adjustments.[48] The data in these bills formed the foundation for land taxation until the mid-nineteenth century. Never again did domain officials repeat the exhaustive reevaluations of 1651–56 or base village tax assessments on regular inspections. All later adjustments in tax rates and assessed values were made on a case-by-case basis. Exceptionally dutiful reform magistrates or tomura occasionally increased tax rates on established fields (honden). In response to village claims of hardship, tax officials would temporarily lower rates, too. With the exception of newly reclaimed lands, authorities calculated all later adjustments by adding to or subtracting from the assessed values and tax rates listed in the 1670 *mura goin*.*

Once again, and not surprisingly, when the domain shifted to the jōmen system, it took great pains to set a high base tax rate. This served both domain and kyūnin interests. It paid handsome dividends to the domain coffers. The rates now reached the levels collected in the late 1580's, before the adoption of the inspection system. By 1656 the domain was collecting taxes at about 48 percent of the total assessed value. This represented a 48 percent increase over the rate in 1634, and a 20 percent increase over 1646. The jōmen system capped the rising trends in assessed and collected tax rates that had begun in 1627.

These rates were applied to the highest-ever assessed values (kokudaka)—14 percent above the 1646 level for the domain as a whole, and 9 percent, 13 percent, and 21 percent for Kaga, Noto, and Etchu, respectively.[49] Most of this jump in value came from the incorporating of land reclaimed over the past several decades into the total value of old fields (hondaka). This land had already been listed on the tax rosters, but it had generally been taxed at a reduced rate. The remainder of the increase was listed in the *mura goin* as *teagedaka*, or increases reported by the villagers to the domain.†

---

*Shinden (reclaimed land) and honden were not handled in the same way. In theory reclaimed land was inspected annually by a class of tomura with specific responsibility for that kind of land, the *shinden saikyō*.

† Teagedaka were nominally gifts to the daimyo, offered in gratitude for his assistance to a village's impoverished members.

Available evidence indicates that these rates were collected with only modest adjustments in the years following the Kaisaku hō.[50] The 1670 tax bills show few substantial changes from the ones issued 14 years before. Had most villages been unable to pay these rates, there would have been more and larger adjustments in both assessed values and rates in these documents.[51] Moreover, widespread successful petitions for tax relief do not appear until the late seventeenth century, and there is no evidence of widespread desertion, protest, or hardship to indicate that the villagers found the rates excessive.[52] Consequently, it seems fair to assume that collected rates were roughly the same as the assessed rates.

In any event it is clear that the jōmen system corrected a serious long-term lapse in the domain's revenue-raising capabilities.[53] Fixed assessments halted the erosion of tax revenues that accompanied the introduction of the inspection system and brought rates back to a level domain officials considered acceptable. It also provided the foundation for the removal of almost all routine samurai contact with the domain's villages, permitting the full centralization of authority in the daimyo's hands.

The domain's success in raising the land taxes suggests a need to reconsider frequent claims that the villages suffered from excessive taxation at the hands of the retainers. In the matter of taxes, the Kaisaku hō was clearly a turn to stringency, not leniency. Landed retainers and daikan may have behaved in an extreme fashion toward villagers, but that behavior was not part and parcel of regular attempts to collect more than the villagers could pay. Considered in the light of the success of the Kaisaku hō tax increases, the maltreatment of villagers by retainers and daikan appears more as a sign of frustration over their own ineptitude than anything else. To the extent that increased domain authority was designed to protect the villagers, the goal was to insulate them from the willful use of force by landed retainers and daikan, not to reduce their tax burden. By creating greater consistency in tax rates, the reforms also reduced the grounds for villagers to perceive their community as having been singled out for unfairly high taxes.

Side by side with these administrative and tax reforms, Toshitsune terminated what independent control the retainers still had in their fiefs. One objective of this policy was to eliminate a threat to the peace of the domain. The tensions between villagers and kyūnin, long the object of domain ordinances and piecemeal reforms, ruptured into violence from time to time. Usually villagers (often officials) were on the receiving end, beset by frustrated representatives of the retainers. Riots had not broken out with any frequency, but the potential was there. The wide variation in retainer tax rates also suggested to villagers that some retainers were treating them unfairly.

The retainers were becoming restive, too. Despite their best efforts, many were unable to collect taxes on their own effectively. The variation in rates assessed by retainers within a given village was a painful reminder to some that they were not accomplishing what others had achieved and they might reasonably expect. Furthermore, their cost of living rose as their consumption patterns changed to more sophisticated and urbane tastes. Declining rice prices aggravated these problems.[54]

Finally, although the strategy of rotating retainer fiefs and daikan jurisdictions had succeeded in preventing kyūnin from establishing a base of power independent of the daimyo, it had done so only at the high cost of administrative disruptions and ineffective taxation. Furthermore, the Chō remained an exception to the policy. By effectively eliminating all fiefs the domain could at once simplify administration and increase its internal security.

Toshitsune came down on the kyūnin in two quick strokes. In the summer of 1653 he forbade them to deal directly with the villages in their "fiefs." Then, in the following year, he prohibited them from sending their agents to the villages.[55] Except for the Chō, all kyūnin had now lost any pretense of control over their fiefs.

Some kyūnin opposed the effective abolition of fiefs. The factional splits among retainers that had surfaced earlier in the debates over how to respond to Bakufu threats had already exposed the potential for resistance by even semiautonomous retainers. In one instance a vocal critic was punished and had to return his fief. Yet on the whole the transition to the new system proceeded quite smoothly.[56]

Retainers tolerated these transformations for one simple reason: the domain's assurance that it would collect their full taxes for them. (Nominally, retainers continued to hold fiefs, and their income was still based on the villages' tax yields.) In 1654 the authorities guaranteed each landed retainer a certain fixed income. If tax collections fell below the officially promised level, the domain would make up the difference. Of course if collections went above that level, the domain got the surplus.

Though the guaranteed tax rates did not match the new (1656 and 1670) domain average of 48 percent of assessed value, they represented substantial improvements for many retainers. Initially, the guaranteed amounts were 33 percent for land in Kaga province, 36.5 percent for Etchu and Noto, and 35 percent for Nomi county. In 1656 the figures were revised upward, to 36 percent for Kaga and 41 percent for Etchu and Noto. These rates were well above the domain average of 32.5 percent for 1634, and close to the 40 percent of 1646. Compared with what had been collected from Kamiyasuhara village in 1649–53, these retainers, at least, clearly profited from the new system. But even where individual kyūnin had received more earlier, the difference was probably not sufficient to offset the two key advantages of the new system: a reasonable, guaranteed income and no expenditure of effort or money. These advantages made it easier for the kyūnin to accept the loss of their fiefs and to swallow any injured pride. At the very least their discontent was not so great as to cause major disturbances.

Through all this, though not explicitly exempted from the prohibitions applied to other retainers, the Chō continued to administer their lands. Despite the passage of decades since Nobunaga's investiture, the unique heritage of the Chō lands made it difficult to treat them the same way as other retainers. But ultimately they too were brought under domain control. That conversion was precipitated by an event known as the Urano incident.[57] One Chō retainer, Urano Magoemon, accomplished what many domain lords feared: he successfully built a substantial local power base. He secretly used his position to reclaim a significant amount of land. When an anti-Urano faction planned a survey of all newly reclaimed land in 1665, he organized local tomura to oppose it. As the Chō forces showed themselves incapable of dealing with the situation, domain forces moved in. Urano was captured and forced to commit ritual suicide, and the tomura who cooperated with him were executed (some by crucifixion).[58]

Though this incident did not immediately lead to the confiscation of the Chō lands, the domain did carry out the planned land survey under its own guidelines, and when the family head died in 1671, the Maeda used the issue of succession to force the Chō to administer their fief according to domain law. The process of instituting the Kaisaku hō began the following year. Final tax bills, equivalent to those issued at the conclusion of the Kaisaku hō in other parts of the domain, were finally compiled for the Chō lands in 1679.

Conclusion

The Kaisaku hō marked an irreversible extension of domain control. At the outset of Maeda rule, domain leaders had shown no great interest in the villages other than to assess and collect taxes, fix labor dues, and obtain raw materials for military use. The domain's more active role in local affairs came only gradually, almost reluctantly, after a variety of piecemeal measures had failed to reduce tensions between samurai tax officials and villagers and solve problems in land tax assessment. Even during these reforms, the domain never focused intensively on the village as a key administrative unit, only the district.

In the third period of domain development, 1627–47, domain leaders reinforced the authority of the kyūnin and daikan by putting the prestige of the domain behind their efforts at tax assessment and collection. With the demand for statements of the kyūnin's average taxes in 1624, domain leaders first indicated their doubts about their samurai's effectiveness as tax agents. Over the next two decades the difficulties in land taxation and the abuse of villagers remained intractable. Neither the Kan'ei reforms nor other experiments solved these problems. Nonetheless, these experiments revealed promising avenues of action, if only the problem of retainer fiefs could be worked out. By 1648 domain leaders were prepared to confront that final obstacle.

The fourth period, 1648–72, encompassed the domain's greatest political reform. The Kaisaku hō created specialists in tax administration, the *kaisaku bugyō*. Taxes were raised substantially. The samurai daikan and kyūnin were removed from direct access to the villages. Many of their duties were eliminated under the system of fixed tax assessments; those that remained were transferred to commoners. All lands were brought under direct domain control.

The domain's policies in the last two periods increasingly reflected an awareness that samurai who were no longer resident in the countryside could not, by themselves, adequately understand the productive capabilities of the villages under their charge. Domain perceptions had finally caught up with the reality of the drastically reduced income of the past half-century. For the domain the principal challenge had rested in developing a cadre of officials who were knowledgeable about local conditions and agriculture and who would be faithful servants of the daimyo.

To create such a cadre, Toshitsune resorted to the tactics that had worked so well when the domain was first organized. He promoted a small group of able commoner officials who had proved their willingness to serve the domain. He rewarded them with samurai-like privileges, and drew them into his confidence. He accorded the reform magistrates similar treatment. These efforts were well rewarded. The tomura and reform magistrates demonstrated that land tax rates and the tax base could be increased. Daimyo and landed retainer need not inevitably compete for limited financial resources. There were other options.

One outcome of the reforms was the completion of the process of class separation. With a few, generally short-lived local exceptions, Maeda retainers had never been close to the land. Now landed retainers were removed completely from any private administrative control over their fiefs. Even samurai daikan were abolished.

Not only had warrior (*hei*) been removed from villagers (*nō*), the cultivator class was given clear, positive definition. Regulations detailing villagers' obligations were widely circulated and routinely proclaimed in each community. By virtue of their opportunity to participate in agriculture, villagers were clearly distinct from other classes. If they failed to live up to their obligations, they lost the opportunity to continue as members in good standing of the village community.

One element of the reform grew out of village institutions, notably, land redistribution. This was the first time since the domain prohibited the sale of shares that policy-makers addressed some aspect of land tenure. Domain authorities took the initiative only when there was a pressing need to step in—the need for greater land tax revenues. It also employed the minimum amount of intervention necessary to get accurate tax rolls and ensure an equitable distribution of land taxes so that capable cultivators would not be forced off the land. In so doing, domain policy built on redistribution, a village institution, accepting it as it was rather than transforming or abolishing it.

In some measure the reforms benefited all the major parties—the shareholding villagers, the domain, and the retainers. True, small numbers of villagers were literally put out by the reforms, and some reacted violently. But tax protests were rare and generally restricted in scope or confined to proper channels. Where they did occur, they sometimes resulted in adjustments of land tax levels.

For the villagers, the allocation of the tax burden was more equitable, and relief, in the form of domain loans, was now available at interest rates that were much more reasonable than heretofore. Intense conflicts with samurai officials were virtually eliminated. The cause of many disputes, annual assessments of tax levies, were eliminated, replaced by a predictable standard that could be, and frequently was, lowered when natural conditions warranted. The new standard may have been high, but villagers could learn to live with it, confident that it would not arbitrarily be set higher as under the annual inspection system.

Landed retainers, on their side, now had a guaranteed income that was probably in most cases greater than what they had garnered for themselves. They no longer had to conduct their own assessments and collect tax rice on their own. The domain administration took full responsibility for these duties.

The big winner, however, was the domain itself. Its tax revenues increased; two threats to internal security had been removed—samurai-village tensions and autonomous fiefholders. At the successful completion of the first tax collections in 1656, Toshitsune boasted to the Bakufu of his success, and Kaga had laid the foundation for its reputation as the best-administered domain in the land.*

A primary motivation for centralization lay in ineffective taxation, rather than the alleviating of overtaxation. Evidence from Kaga contradicts the assertion that daimyo sought to increase revenues primarily by reducing support for retainers through the confiscation of fiefs. Domain revenues probably did increase, but so did the retainers' income, and apparently without any reduction in the number the domain supported. A more efficient land tax system was behind the domain's success, not the absorption of retainers' incomes. A second stimulus to reform was the need to curb the samurai's abuse of villagers and to reduce the chronic (although seldom spectacular) tensions between them.

With the loss of Chō autonomy, Maeda Tsunanori had brought the entire domain under his direct administrative control.† Kaga was now a unified small state, fully conscious of itself as a public authority (kōgi) acting largely on its own. To be sure, the domain was not in a position to deny, at least openly, the Bakufu's claims to act as a larger public authority. Indeed, to do so would have risked the destruction of political relationships throughout Japan that protected the Maeda from attack by other daimyo. Like other domains, Kaga acknowledged the supremacy of the Bakufu in a combination of ritual and policy matters related to a limited national order (e.g., alternate attendance, gift exchanges and marriage, military service). Nonetheless, its sense of autonomy in matters of local administration remained intact. Although it had arrived at social and political configurations that had much in common with those of other domains, the orders of hegemons and shoguns had played no direct role. It had come to these results in its own way, at its own pace, and in response to its own needs.

---

*Sasaki, Daimyō, pp. 269–70. Sasaki believes that, since this report was made, the domain's reforms must have had Bakufu permission. I am more inclined, in the absence of confirming evidence, to see in the report support for Gilbert Rozman's contention that Edo was a collection point for ideas from all over Japan, ideas that the shogun and daimyo alike then considered in light of their own needs (see Rozman, "Edo's Importance").

†I refer here to the main han. Its relationship with the branch domains of Toyama and Daishōji is a subject for another investigation, but since they were treated as separate domains, they do not constitute an exception to this general observation.

Chapter **10**

Conclusion

The Autonomous Domain

With the extension of the Kaisaku hō reforms into Chō family lands in 1672, the Maeda completed the basic task of shaping a stable domain. Territorial boundaries were secure within an enduring national order: the Maeda were bound by multiple ties of marriage to the Bakufu, the imperial court, and other important daimyo; they dutifully participated in the Bakufu's military campaigns and contributed without opposition when extraordinary levies were assessed. The Maeda samurai were firmly under control, concentrated in the castle town and financially dependent on domain authorities. And the rural population had been brought in hand. The structure of rural administration and taxation would not materially change until the early nineteenth century, and even that was a short-lived deviation from the pattern established under the Kaisaku hō. Corporate village responsibility for tax assessments and payment was the rule. Lands were valued in rice (kokudaka), and land taxes were collected exclusively in rice, too. Social classes were now quite distinct.

So simply stated, nothing suggests a departure from the standard descriptions of this period of Japanese history. But this superficial view conceals the historical energies that achieved many of these results. Some important developments in the domain's institutional and social history were the unplanned by-product of a confrontation between domain policies and the practical constraints of local circumstances, but for the most part they were shaped by a combination of external and internal political choices. In general external influences were strongest in the very first decades of the domain's formation and confined largely to matters affecting its existence—transfers, war, and the threat of shogunal punishment. Internally, policies shared four interrelated characteristics: gradualism, experimentation, pragmatism, and local initiative.

External Influences

Despite the overbearing tone of central ordinances, the pomp with which Hideyoshi and the others surrounded themselves, and a semblance of effective administration, there was a great disparity between the early hegemons' nominal authority and their capacity to effect change in Kaga. The aura created by central ordinances was not matched by the reality of effective power.[1] To be sure, the hegemons were able to make the Maeda bow to the many demands they made on the domain lords' person. Daimyo had to provide hostages; to live within the confines of the sections of the Laws of the Military Houses that regulated marriage, adoption, succession, collusion with other daimyo, and lèse majesté; and to provide military service on demand. There also were times when they had to submit to transfer at the behest of a liege lord. Toshiie and Toshinaga's entry into Kaga, Noto, and Etchu was a direct result of that process. But for all this, the role of external forces in shaping Kaga's institutions and policies was quite limited and never direct.*

Indeed, on the one occasion when Tokugawa Ieyasu tried to move the Maeda from the region, his efforts ended in failure. The success that Toshinaga and later Toshitsune had in negotiating with the shogunate to avoid punitive expeditions and the loss of their domain suggests that the hegemons' authority to transfer daimyo or confiscate their lands was sometimes subject to successful opposition, at least in the case of a large domain. The Maeda accepted transfers only when the inducements were great.

The Maeda's transfer into the region opened an important opportunity to increase control over retainers and weaken their independent base

---

*Although beyond the scope of this study, the fate in Kaga of two prominent Bakufu laws should at least be touched on, the "one castle per province" ordinance and the anti-Christian ordinances. The first does not appear to have had any impact. It is true that construction stopped on Takaoka castle soon after Toshinaga died, but this was a year before the "one castle" ordinance. It is also true that some of the castle's internal facilities were later destroyed. *TKSS*, pp. 805–6, ascribes that destruction to the law, but presents no documentary evidence to this effect in a volume that goes to great lengths to cite written support. In fact, even then Takaoka did not completely lose its military function. It is odd that the destruction of a castle planned to rival Kanazawa and so newly and well begun has left little documentary residue. According to one local history (*Oyabe shi shi*, 1: 258), Kaga domain maintained at least six castles through 1638. The Bakufu's anti-Christian ordinances, by contrast, do seem to have had some impact. But domain authorities clearly used them selectively for their own internal purposes, making members of the retainer band the principal targets. None of these men were permitted to recant (a standard practice), and all were condemned to death, suggesting an ulterior political motive (Hara, *Kaga-han*, pp. 109–14).

of support. It gave them a chance to reduce the potential threat from autonomous landed retainers. After the transfer, Toshiie and Toshinaga never let their retainers settle on the land, greatly limiting their association with the villages in their fiefs. That outcome could not be claimed as Oda Nobunaga's primary intent in moving Toshiie and then Toshinaga into the Hokuriku, but it was a significant development that would not have been possible at this time without the transfer.

Regional factors also affected the domain's development. The most obvious was the existence of hostile forces nearby. Dealing successfully with this threat (in league with the emergent hegemons) guaranteed the continuation of the domain. But the successful pacification of the Hokuriku, to which the Maeda contributed, had other significant consequences. It was a step on the way to clarifying the boundaries between samurai and commoner. Many of the members of the local warrior gentry who joined the Maeda retainers were killed in battle, and their family lines extinguished; the ties of their nonsamurai relatives to the world of the warrior were broken. Many of the others, who had confined their efforts to local self-defense, were, with pacification, no longer useful to the domain as warriors. They had lost their opportunity to demonstrate the skills and valor that might earn them a place in the retainer band.

In Kaga the hegemons' influence in transforming local administration and society was generally indirect, not direct. When the shogunate set standard weights and measures for the central markets it controlled, the domain compradors adjusted to that system of measurements, an adjustment they carried home. But Kaga leaders clearly did not respond to direct central initiatives and change its system of weights and measures until it suited their purposes to do so. Still, as these examples show, even though indirect, central authority's influence was sometimes consequential.

Internal Dimensions

Even as models, the institutional arrangements encouraged by central authorities were unused in Kaga's rural administration. Local problem-solving was the driving force in domain policy. In approaching these challenges, Kaga took a gradual, tentative, pragmatic approach based on independent judgments by both domain and village authorities. These characteristics shaped the growth of domain institutions and societal changes.

Gradualism. Change, especially at the lowest levels of society, came gradually. The slow pace is implicit in the four stages through which I have analyzed the domain's early history.

The first period, 1581–1600, represented an initial settling in. Administrative arrangements, policies, and land investigations were down and dirty, and the Maeda made only minimal changes in local operations, those necessary to achieve stability and a reasonable income while they were heavily engaged in combat locally and elsewhere. These included the creation of district administration under the fuchibyakushō; preliminary assessments of the land tax base; and the flexible implementation of a modified land tax system. Daikan and kyūnin possessed a high degree of autonomy within their responsibilities as tax assessors and collectors. The separation of warrior from villager was not forced: it grew out of fief grants that permitted little retainer involvement in village affairs and the decline of warfare in the region. Local talent was willingly employed by the Maeda, not removed to be replaced by outsiders.

The following two decades, 1601–26, witnessed the Maeda's first attempts to organize a more fully bureaucratic administration, one free of the first period's martial character. They placed tentative restraints on the daikan's and kyūnin's activities in the villages but still accepted the need to rely on them and trusted in their basic competence as administrators. Toshinaga and Toshitsune replaced the existing system of land taxation with a more rational, less arbitrary (in principle) system based on annual inspections, made a start on the systematic evaluation of villages' taxpaying potential, elaborated rural administrative structures, and provided for appeals from villagers in order to resolve tensions between samurai and commoners—over runaways, labor conscription, taxation, and physical abuse—problems that, untended, threatened substantial rural unrest. Class separation moved a notch forward as samurai were brought into the castle town, and the responsibilities of full-fledged villagers began to be defined in domain law with the imposing of the plow tax.

Between 1627 and 1647, though Toshitsune simply tinkered with the existing system in some parts of the domain, intruding into the work of daikan and kyūnin, implementing ordinances to protect villagers, and so forth, he experimented boldly with new, more radical approaches to taxation and administration in Noto. The domain reinforced the daikan and kyūnin in their tax collection and assessment efforts, but in so doing took steps that expressed official doubt about their competence as land tax administrators.

Change in village administration came as gradually as social change. The domain relied on the district, not the village, as the basic unit of rural administration. It oversaw at least some aspects of the warichi system of land allocation, but not until the 1640's did administrators address themselves to legally defining some of the duties of village officials. In terms of direct domain administration, they remained far less important than the district officials. Especially throughout the late sixteenth and early seventeenth centuries, village self-government was largely free of domain interference, continuing a late-medieval tradition of communal administration. Villages chose their own leaders and administrative structures during this time. Villages were not frozen as administrative units by kenchi; boundaries were routinely adjusted by splitting and joining villages.

Only the last period in the domain's formation, 1648–72, saw intense, sometimes radical reforms. The most dramatic changes focused on efforts to remedy the problem of ineffective taxation and to centralize daimyo authority. Daikan and kyūnin lost their administrative roles; land tax specialists, the *kaisaku bugyō*, were appointed within the intermediate ranks of domain administration; and commoner offices (the tomura) were elaborated and strengthened. The system of fixed tax rates facilitated all of this by simplifying and raising assessments. The formal obligations of village taxpayers were spelled out in some detail, and those obligations were actively enforced.

The incremental nature of change was especially evident at lower levels of society. Rural society exhibited more elements of continuity with early-sixteenth-century Kaga, Noto, and Etchu than sharp breaks. Local samurai who made their peace with the Maeda did quite well. Those who remained on the land had opportunities to benefit from the Maeda arrival. Their new status as fuchibyakushō, and later tomura, may have been an important change, but it was not a wrenching one. Most local samurai remained in villages as members of the rural elite, uninhibited by the daimyo's retainers. Except for a few short-lived examples of indigenous local warriors, most Maeda retainers never lived on private fiefs. Immigrant Maeda retainers did not settle in the villages, and likewise did not disturb the existing order. Consequently, in the typical village, the control of land and the social structure changed slowly.

The divide between samurai and commoner also developed gradually. Class separation was not an early Maeda preoccupation, nor, in the rural areas, did it take the form of an explicit policy orientation. Even such legal strictures as Hideyoshi's Sword Hunt and Class Separation edicts appear ancillary to the process of class separation, not central. Domain survey procedures were incapable of identifying villagers as a class distinct from samurai. Castles did not belong to landed retainers, but to the daimyo. Peace allowed the Maeda to vacate small, relatively vulnerable fortresses and gradually consolidate samurai in a few large ones. The kyūnin's already limited administrative rights were further limited by their absentee status and the frequent changes in and scattered locations of their jurisdictions. Their administrative rights did not involve tasks that threatened the position of locally powerful and wealthy families.*

In granting fiefs, the Maeda took care from the start to insulate immigrant retainers from the indigenous population, coopting prominent local residents to serve as intermediate conduits to the villages. These local farmer-warriors were not arbitrarily de-classed. Their military duties were eliminated gradually as battles moved away from the domain and their civilian administrative obligations took precedence. Although a sword hunt was carried out in southern Kaga in 1587,† there is no evidence of any effort to disarm commoners in the parts of Kaga province then under Maeda control. The continued semi-samurai status of the fuchibyakushō and tomura was also revealed by the domain's requirement immediately before Sekigahara that they present themselves as hostages during the crises, just as landed retainers had to provide hostages.

The Maeda took more than three decades to evince any interest at all in the villagers' land use rights. The domain's simple survey procedures were useless as tools for defining tenure or redistributing local wealth. Villagers alone defined tenurial rights at this time. The domain finally took one small step in this direction in 1615, when it prohibited the sale of land use rights. (The shift from assessing corvée to a cash labor tax based on land rights was likely the stimulus for this change.) But otherwise it left these issues entirely in the hands of villagers until the 1630's. Even when it did become involved, it did so only minimally, confining its influence to systematizing potentially disruptive aspects of warichi and encouraging its use.

Experimentation. Throughout Kaga's first century the daimyo and his advisers tested diverse mechanisms for accomplishing typical daimyo goals —securing control of retainers, subjects, and the economic resources of the domain. Whether in local administration, land taxation, or retainer control, Maeda Toshitsune ultimately incorporated the most successful experiments in the Kaisaku hō reforms.

Land investigations represent a case in point. Early Kaga documents reveal unsettled principles for valuing land. Variations in land registration were evident between Toshiie and Toshinaga, and even within each

---

*Within the existing local order, however, as representatives of the villages and districts, the village elites might be the object of tax officials' wrath and physical abuse.

†The place where this sword hunt was said to have occurred, Enuma kōri, was then under the control of Yamaguchi Munenaga and Niwa Nagashige. Furthermore, as often as this document (reproduced in Kodama et al., *Shiryō ni yoru Nihon*, pp. 38–39) is cited as evidence that the policy of disarming commoners succeeded, most references fail to mention that it concludes with a note that townsmen were still permitted to carry swords.

domain. Experimentation was evident until the Keichō-Genna surveys. The demands of defense and related pressures prompted a conservative use of land investigations, in which the Maeda accepted a less rigorous estimate of taxable land and patiently relied on other devices to provide a reasonably complete picture of the tax base: the encouragement of warichi, enticements to villagers to inform authorities of unregistered land, repeated reviews of documents, and interviews with village and district officials.

In the 1630's Toshitsune tested the policy of encouraging the warichi system. In addition to revealing unregistered land, the aim was to provide some measure of fairness in the allocation of land taxes, and thereby maximize the chances for each shareholding family to avoid bankruptcy and to continue as active taxpayers. Based on the results, he relied much more heavily on that policy during the Kaisaku hō reforms.

As land taxation passed through three distinct forms of assessment, sonmen, kemi, and jōmen, the domain experienced wide fluctuations in its tax revenues. Even within one system, there was experimentation. Throughout the first decades there was considerable experimentation and flexibility in the grace period allowed villagers in paying taxes, the forms of acceptable tax payment, and the practices of forgiveness. Not until national stability was within sight could the daimyo devote attention to more systematic efforts at standardization.

Local administrative arrangements passed through several different configurations. While villages were allowed to go pretty much their own way, Toshinaga and Toshiie progressively enlarged, elaborated, and strengthened the authority of district administrators, first exploring their use as replacements for the landed retainers' and the daimyo's own samurai tax agents in Noto, and then extending the policy throughout the domain. At a somewhat higher level of administration, the domain's temporary appointment of a small, energetic coterie of samurai specialists (the *kaisaku bugyō*) in agricultural administration ultimately provided the foundation for a permanent transformation of rural administration.

Pragmatism. In all these matters the Maeda struck a balance between the benefit and the costs of each action, be it further involvement in local affairs or potential conflict with the Shogun. This pragmatism showed in their decisions to negotiate and explain the domain's position when its loyalty was questioned and to cement their ties to the hegemons with marriages and hostages. While some retainers' arguments for directly challenging Bakufu authority to protect the daimyo's traditional prerogatives may have appealed to the Maeda's pride, they wisely resisted them.

Kaga's land investigations and land tax system are filled with pragmatic trade-offs. A certain laxness in the early surveys was the price the daimyo paid to maintain the cooperation of his new subjects while his samurai were still heavily engaged in military activities. Even during later actual measurements, procedures were kept as simple as possible, procedures in which the marginal increase in accuracy was considered insufficient to merit additional efforts at precision.

Similarly, the early flexibility in the tax system was clearly an expedient. Although some tax revenues were lost, leeway in the timing and form of payment minimized the risk of seriously alienating taxpaying villagers. It may also have made it possible to manage tax assessments and collections with less manpower at a time when samurai were needed at the battlefront as much as or more than they were needed as administrators.

Landed retainers also had to be tolerated until the daimyo's military dependence on them lessened. Under these circumstances the domain pursued a policy of reviewing their activities in civil administration and providing for appeals and minimal restrictions on them. Only when peace made them less essential and when they could be provided with attractive alternatives to fiefholding did Toshitsune move to abolish their effective control of fiefs.

Local Initiative. The importance of local initiative represents the final characteristic of Kaga's development. Local initiative has dual dimensions. First, of course, it involves the steps the domain administration introduced on its own. But local initiative was also manifested in the positive contributions of important individual villagers and village taxpayers acting as corporate units. In addition, there were instances in which the simple overlapping of domain and village interests furthered a policy or set of policies.

Even as late as the seventeenth century, the domain's concessions and skillful negotiating with the Bakufu did not quell the sense that the daimyo shared with the shogun a legitimate claim to represent public authority (*kōgi*). Certainly many of the domain's policy initiatives were taken independent of the Bakufu, and several, like the establishing of fixed land tax rates (*jōmen*), the restricting of the sale of land use rights, and the prohibiting of the sale of people, predated similar Bakufu ordinances. Kaga's methods and use of land surveys were distinctive. Despite the imperious ring to Hideyoshi's land survey orders, they had no impact in the Maeda domains on the methods by which land value was calculated and expressed or on land tenure. The use of rice as the sole proper form of land tax payments was correlated with changes in the ways in which the domain disposed of its tax goods: the increased reliance on national markets to get the best price for its rice. Likewise, the domain's willingness to rid its administrative ranks of samurai daikan and transfer their responsibilities to commoner officials reflects an independent bent unencumbered by a strict sense of what work was proper only for samurai. The domain's emphasis on districts and its decision to place more and more responsibility in the hands of commoner leaders suggest an openness to creative approaches to administration. The tactics of change employed throughout the decades of domain formation reflect a general tendency to promote or strengthen the position of able men regardless of social origin, gradually reducing the number of rural administrative officials to achieve greater reliability and control.

Villagers, at least collectively, initiated their own administrative policies, upon some of which the domain built. They did not just react in protest to domain initiatives. Village political structures and the methods of choosing officers were determined without reference to any explicit domain policy throughout the period we have analyzed. Land tenure was first and foremost a matter for villagers to determine, and the warichi system they developed became a significant element in domain policy. Commoner officials even took a leading role in shaping and carrying out the Kaisaku hō reforms.

Interestingly, in those areas where historians do not insist on the efficacy of hegemonic directives, there is a tendency to emphasize the ability of daimyo to impose their own agenda on commoners and retainers.[2] It is a truism that law gains the greatest compliance when the population it affects subscribes to its content. In a world without mechanized transportation and mass communication, this is particularly so. In seventeenth-century Kaga, at least, successful policies affecting villagers were those that represented a confluence of domain, retainer, and village interests. From one perspective, land taxation is an excellent case in point.

Since land measurements were inexact and crop sampling did not yield consistent results, villagers and retainers alike grew increasingly discontented. In the villagers' case, the discontent expressed itself in desertion and complaints filed through the domain's administrative hierarchy. To many of them land tax assessments appeared arbitrary. Opposition (such as it was) to surveys and inspections in no small part came because the results were demonstrably unreliable, not because they were harsh in themselves. The fact that nearby villages of comparable agricultural yields were taxed at substantially lower rates or had lower assessed values gave rise to resentment. In this sense the capricious nature of land taxation at least as much as its absolute weight contributed to tensions within the domain. The lack of consistency and verifiability also increased the potential for extortion by survey officials.

Many of these problems frustrated the tax agents and their superiors, too. Inconsistency in results suggested to them that they were being cheated of their rightful share of crops. As the expenses of urban living rose and income remained unpredictable, these anxieties grew. One result was the physical abuse of villagers.

Despite the superficial rationality of annual inspections, they conflicted with the domain's policies for controlling its subordinate officials and landed retainers. The distance between the castle town and the villages to be taxed made inspections difficult, and the dispersal of fiefs and daikan jurisdictions and frequent changes of jurisdiction prevented tax assessors from learning the productive capabilities of the land in their charge. Samurai urbanization compounded the problem by denying assessors any real understanding of agriculture. The system was a spectacular failure.

If the failure had been less impressive, one wonders if the impetus to remove samurai from all contact with the land (as retainer or daikan) would have been as strong or resulted in as forceful a policy as the Kaisaku hō. All participants in the land tax system, administrators and subjects alike, desired improvements. The question was how to break the cycle of frustration. After much consideration, a new policy was developed that was successful precisely because it contained significant advantages for all major players. Taxpayers benefited from more predictable, more stable, and perhaps even more equitable taxes. They gained security from the domain program to provide regular relief in the event of significant crop shortfalls. The elimination of annual assessments and a sharp reduction in samurai-villager contacts cleared away major bones of contention between the two groups. Landed retainers got more stable income with less effort. The domain gained higher, more predictable revenues and greater internal security. Regardless of the "fairness" of taxes under the Kaisaku hō (as measured by any standard; there were always unhappy individuals), taxpaying villagers could learn to live with them—and live with them they did, for two centuries.

Other successful policies for the rural sector also embodied the desire of villagers (or at least influential villagers) to protect their own interests.[3] Indeed, the stimulus for these policies came from the villagers themselves—through desertion or formal complaints about disruptions to their livelihood. Warichi is the most long-lasting example, but many villagers' interests also overlapped with those of the domain, a fact that encouraged administrators to take steps to prevent tax assessors' abuses. Such an overlap in interests was not simply incidental or ancillary. Whether in the context of domain or national policies, it was an essential condition for the success of policies that would affect villagers' lives.

As these examples all illustrate, the relationship between daimyo administration and domain subjects was more important than that between daimyo and hegemon in shaping the development of Kaga domain. Nor was the influence of local forces a matter of active protests, as descriptions of the anti-survey activities in Tohoku, Higo, Yamashiro, and Omi tend to portray the matter.[4] In our review of developments in Kaga, violent opposition (and even nonviolent varieties such as absconding) appear to have been infrequent and were most notable during the Kaisaku hō reforms, not the early decades of the domain. The variant systems and distinctive pace of change in Kaga resulted from the fact that more subtle interactions of the domain, its retainers, and villages were the primary foci of policy.

The Broader Context

At the outset of this study, I noted a tendency to analyze state-society relations in an either-or framework: a given state is either strong or weak. But that dichotomy leads to some confusion. The problem created by the lack of a middle ground is nicely illustrated in Immanuel Wallerstein's description of sixteenth-century Europe. He sees the emergence of strong states then as "an essential component of the development of modern capitalism." To build their position, these states employed "bureaucratization, monopolization of force, creation of legitimacy, and homogenization of the subject population." They also employed "absolutism" as one device for reinforcing their authority. But Wallerstein goes on to assert that "the powers of the monarch were in fact quite limited, not only in theory but in reality. [Even] the strongest states in the sixteenth century were hard pressed to demonstrate clear predominance within their frontiers of the means of force, or command over the sources of wealth, not to speak of primacy of the loyalty of their subjects."[5] These "absolutist" states were "strong" only relative to their predecessors. Even as Wallerstein makes the limitations of the state clear, he is still confined to describing it as "strong."

Two specific examples bear out the vulnerability of this characterization.

Contemporaneous with the object of our study, the tsar of Russia managed a military middle service class. This class was the creation of the tsars and continued to perform regular military duties for them through the seventeenth century. They were routinely called to annual reviews, frontier patrol, and defensive siege service. They were remunerated with income from specifically designated service lands, but initially they did not directly manage those lands or collect the income from them. The service lands were small, supporting several dozen households at most, and widely scattered. There were approximately 25,000 of these military servitors. They may not have been fully professional in the modern sense, but they were career and lifetime soldiers, dependent on the tsar.

Over the years a combination of the crown's political and military needs and their own economic circumstances gave the members of this class leverage to turn the lands from which they gained income into personal estates, with the central government gradually (and at its own expense) increasing the group's control over the local villagers to the point of ultimately tying them to the land as serfs. In effect the state bargained for the continued support of the members of the middle service class by strengthening their economic and political position. The process took more than two centuries, but in the end firm pressure from one segment of society allowed it to overcome its institutional limitations and decisively influence policy. In so doing, it not only furthered its own position within the state, but also altered the state's policy toward a very large proportion of its subjects. Furthermore (and in a direct parallel to Japan's early hegemons), it is noteworthy that in the process of this change, a number of laws were issued that were never enforced.*

John Rule describes a similar, if less grand, confounding of bureaucratic professionalism in France, one that had a more beneficial outcome to the state. The late-seventeenth-century secretary of state had two distinctively different duties. Under the authority of his own office, he issued written opinions. But in addition, he "modified, supplemented, tempered, and explained the will of the [sovereign]." Two sources of authority, one bureaucratic and the other based on personal ties to the king, were combined in the duties of a single office. One of the secretary's specific responsibilities was to rule on pleas associated with feudal privileges. Instead of using this power to investigate claims impartially, the incumbents employed it as a device to reward government functionaries (*commis*). Most of those whose privileges were denied were *les grandes* and ministers' families, which is to

---

*There are several Russian parallels to the tactics employed by daimyo and hegemons to shore up the state's authority: dispersal of the lands from which the service classes derived income, the use of land surveys, and the legal separation and identification of social classes, for example. More explicit and detailed comparisons would be interesting. See Hellie, *Enserfment*.

say, those who might challenge the king. Judicial authority in these matters was not independent of the king or objectively rendered. It was marshaled to strengthen the position of the people who assisted the king in the exercise of his authority, and it was dependent on his personalistic feudal role as dominant seigneur.[6]

These two examples are by no means unique. In many other instances a bureaucracy of sorts was in place, but had yet to become first and foremost a loyal, effective servant of the emerging state. Venality of office, tax-farming, and other practices remind us that competent bureaucratic structures and instruments of control were *in the process* of development. To build their power, state leaders struck compromises with various elements of society, playing one against another, and often buying cooperation outright. Kings touted absolutism and argued that they should not be confined by law. They created as much of an atmosphere of supreme authority as they could, but as in Japan, the reality fell substantially short of the claim.

Despite some important institutional differences, both Japan and the "absolutist" states of Europe were engaged in very similar processes—establishing domestic peace, increasing the viability of the emergent state, bolstering its effectiveness through the manipulation of other political actors, creating new institutional controls, and proclaiming ideologies of absolute authority. In both cases the state did not possess the power to back up its claim to absolute and undivided sovereignty.

Absolutist states and Japan appear to share a configuration of nominal authority and capability that is intermediate between "strong" and "weak" states. Both were stronger than the political organizations that preceded them, but they still depended heavily on other political actors who were not formally part of the government. It is in just this kind of configuration that making a distinction between nominal authority and state capability is most useful. Arranging the potential interactions of these concepts in a grid defines four basic forms of state-society interaction (Fig. 8). This arrangement incorporates the need for some assessment of the breadth of authority in both categories while focusing attention on the quality of state-society relations through the interaction of the two.[*] It is not bound by an *a priori* definition of certain structures, such as a bureaucracy or central taxation, as indicative of strength.

---

[*]Some element of relativity is unavoidable in comparing states. Joel Migdal notes at the outset of his work *Strong Societies and Weak States* that political scientists have had difficulty creating a measure of state strength. Until such time (if ever) one is successfully developed, comparisons may have to be between well-defined areas of state activity (e.g., police and military matters, land reform or tenure, education). A state may be strong in one area and weak in another. In each area, however, the standard of comparison must be clearly specified.

		Capability	
		high	low
Nominal Authority	high	strong	"flamboyant"
	low	"minimalist"	weak

Fig. 8. Interaction of the nominal authority and capability of a state.

The basic characteristics of "strong" and "weak" states were introduced earlier and require no further discussion. Here I wish to concentrate on the two other configurations to suggest the potential range of intermediate options.

One configuration, possessing a relatively narrow range of legitimate activities, may be able to carry out the state's objectives effectively within that scope. These I consider "minimalist" states. This description does not necessarily suggest a state in decline. The state may capitalize on its strengths to expand its generally accepted range of authority. For example, a state whose primary function is limited to defense might effectively protect itself from invaders, but it may also employ the pressure of defense needs to expand its legitimate scope of domestic activity. It demands concessions from other political actors and greater control of economic and other resources on the pretext of protecting all. Minimalist configurations are an apt description of the successful late-fifteenth- and early-sixteenth-century daimyo. Initially their authority was limited to the lands under their direct control except in the areas of defense and diversity disputes between different jurisdictions, retainers, villages, or towns. Many of the larger among them (like counterparts in Europe) employed pressures of defense and the fruits of war to expand their control of their retainers.[7] Where they did not reduce the proportion of domain land granted as fiefs, they dismantled traditional retainer autonomy (funyūken) and expanded their control of financial resources in retainer fiefs, enabling them to support larger, more dependable salaried armies.

In the remaining configuration, the state has a relatively wide generally recognized, legitimate scope of action, but little capacity to impose its policies or to carry out the functions society nominally expects it to fulfill. It is this configuration that I believe best fits early modern Japan (and perhaps sixteenth-century European states as well).[8] Since the state's reach exceeds its grasp in this configuration, I think of these as "flamboyant" states. Because the divergence between nominal authority and capability is substantial, it is tempting to think of the flamboyant configuration as representing a weak, failed effort at state formation. The state is unable to fill some roles established for it. But this is not necessarily the only possibility. In building a configuration in which nominal authority is well developed before capabilities, state leaders potentially lay a foundation for the expansion of those capabilities or employ displays of the state's nominal authority to serve important symbolic functions—for example, reinforcing an image of common nationhood or destiny, a role cultivated by the Tokugawa shoguns and a traditional function of the emperor throughout much of Japanese history.

Some may have reservations about the use of the term "flamboyant" as connoting a general lack of substance behind an ostentatious facade. I think the discussion so far makes it clear that I do not wish to suggest this. In addition, the term implies a showiness that may not always be present, but in the case of early modern Japan, all the pomp that the term implies was present—and fully marshaled on behalf of the hegemons in the political use of Noh drama, monumental castle architecture, and tea ceremonies, among many examples.[9] Furthermore, there is a highly bombastic tone to many ordinances. Hideyoshi, for example, threatened to pursue daimyo into their castles and kill them if they did not survey each field according to his wishes—a threat he never followed through on in even the most egregious cases.[10] Many early modern European courts employed the same kind of ostentation to similar political effect.

Japan

With this tension between nominal authority and state capability in mind, the preceding chapters used Kaga domain's history to examine some of the common interpretations of the relationship between the villages, domains, and hegemons who created the early modern political order. As indicated along the way, Kaga was not an isolated example of the failure of central authorities to effect their will. Even where developments in Kaga seem unusual or unfamiliar, they have exact counterparts or analogues in other parts of Japan.

Neither the case of Kaga nor these other examples, alone or together, can provide a definitive reinterpretation of the birth of early modern Japan. Broadly stated, our journey through Kaga domain's history raises questions about the effectiveness of central political authority as the self-conscious architect of the political, social, and economic transformations that marked the transition to early modern Japan. It suggests possible patterns that bear further investigation. At the local level, the following propositions might be tested fruitfully:

1. Political and social changes were gradual; domain authorities took an interest in village affairs only as expanding regional and national stability freed them from defense concerns and afforded them a secure place in the early modern order.

2. Domain administrators experimented a great deal with local administrative institutions and policies, making their own choices about which problems to tackle first and how to resolve them. Through this process, the interaction between existing community powers and the domain led to different patterns of rural administration throughout Japan.* More than policies conceived by Hideyoshi and his successors, local factors and late-medieval village institutions continued to shape domain and communal development well into the seventeenth century. In Kaga this meant building on the legacy of the Ikkō ikki, but other parts of Japan gave rise to widespread analogues through which commoners contributed to the Tokugawa settlement.[11] When a daimyo moved into a new territory, continuity in village elites was common, if not universal.[12]

3. Through much of the early period, villages and commoners retained a substantial degree of local administrative autonomy and therefore had the opportunity to contribute to the institutional foundations and policies of domains. This was reflected especially in village administrative organization and the definition of land use rights.

4. The administrative roles assigned to samurai, the final degree and form of domain centralization, and the balance among the mechanisms through which centralization was accomplished (e.g., samurai urbanization, the confiscation of fiefs, increased domain oversight) depended on the specific pressures a daimyo faced in the sixteenth and seventeenth centuries, most commonly, military incursions, inadequate revenues, discontent among his subjects, or a fractious retainer band. These varied with time as well as region. Nationwide peace itself changed the dynamic between landed retainer and daimyo, lessening the retainers' opportunities to

---

*As partial explanation for local institutional diversity throughout early modern Japan this study has examined the *formal* institutional contributions of pre-Maeda local organizations to the new order. Hitomi Tonomura, *Community and Commerce*, pp. 151–187, shows that it is also important to consider continuities in the *informal* inter-village relationships, even where transformation of the formal structures suggest such ties disappeared. Tonomura demonstrates the power of old inter-village shrine ties even in a region in which hegemonic edicts had more impact than they did in Kaga.

betray their overlord for personal gain and thereby decreasing his need for even tighter controls to maintain their loyalty. Even where the fictionalization of fiefs was complete, the triumph of the daimyo's authority may have brought benefits to landed retainers, too.* The final settlement often was the result of several decades of experimentation and adjustment in which the tensions in samurai-villager relations were reduced to some tolerable level.

5. The legal establishment of a distinct village status system was a long-term process, one already under way before the 1580's in some regions and one that continued long after Hideyoshi's death. Hardened class divisions resulted from the gradual intrusion of domain authority into the details of village life, as well as the establishment of peace within a region. In different parts of the country, the crystallizing of social divisions proceeded at very different paces and through a variety of mechanisms. Surveys (whether the daimyo's own or Hideyoshi's) and centrally proclaimed ordinances on social classes could not effectively define members of a "peasant" (hyakushō) class at the time they were issued. Many rural warriors who aspired to samurai status lost that opportunity simply because battle sites moved away from their home territories. The removal of samurai to castle towns was one part of this process, but the elimination of many or all retainer rights in land, as well as the clear legal definition of a cultivator class, took longer.

6. Substantial practical constraints restricted the effectiveness of taxation, especially the widespread use of crop inspections. These constraints were the result of common strategies employed to control landed retainers, notably, dispersed fiefs and daikan jurisdictions, frequent rotation, and samurai urbanization, which between them made inspections impossibly time-consuming and robbed samurai of sufficient knowledge of agriculture to select fields appropriate for sampling.

7. Heavy taxation was only one and perhaps not even the main source of villager discontent over surveys and assessments. For villagers, the arbitrariness of the system was at least as objectionable, if not more so. The lack of consistency and verifiability also invited official abuses.

*Kaga and other domains where the samurai were completely removed from routine contact with or presence in villages have been considered the norm, and those cases in which samurai remained on the land, notably Satsuma and Tosa, seen as exceptional. But as John Morris's work on Sendai shows, there were also cases in between (Morris, *Kinsei Nihon chigyōsei*). Indeed, compared with Kaga, those regions in which samurai daikan continued to function seem to be part of a mid-range experience. As the case of Tosa nicely illustrates, domains did not create a permanent balance between samurai and village administrators at the start of the new administration. Samurai were first removed from the land and then, under the policies of Nonaka Kenzan, encouraged to return, retaining their formal military status.

At the risk of some repetition, the following correlates may apply at the national level:

1. Late-sixteenth- and early-seventeenth-century social and political change was usually generated locally. In general the policies of emerging central political authorities only indirectly and sporadically influenced this process. Their greatest contribution was establishing a peaceful environment in which domain, district, and local leaders could work out stable administrative arrangements. Despite the emerging sense of kōgi (public authority) at the national level, it was a perception that coexisted and still competed with the "small kōgi" of the domains. Their own use of the term reflected a strong sense of autonomous identity (reflected in independent decisions) that did not quickly disappear.

2. The contrast between pre- and post-Taikō kenchi society was less dramatic than is often portrayed. The processes of transformation did not complete their courses until the mid-seventeenth century or later. As a corollary of Hideyoshi's inability to establish nationally standardized surveys, the kokudaka system cannot be treated as a nationally revolutionary innovation in land tenure, local taxation and administration, or social class relations.[13] Surveys were technically incapable of defining field or village boundaries well enough to set land rights or restrict village growth. Though assessment procedures made the village the taxpaying unit, they did not freeze the physical and economic evolution of these communities. Villages continued to expand and control their resources, either alone or in collaboration (and often in contest) with neighboring communities.[14] Villages were also the primary site for the defining of land tenure.

3. The establishment of final assessed values for domains provided an explicit standard for valuing daimyo fiefs, but the figure was developed through a tacitly negotiated convention between daimyo and hegemon. This process left much room for daimyo to influence the size of the commitment they wished to make to a hegemon. In the context of the times, the creation of an explicit statement of domain value, acknowledged by both hegemon and daimyo, was a major innovation. Hideyoshi and his successors secured a fixed basis on which to assess extraordinary military levies. The lack of a rigid national standard facilitated the integration of hegemon and domain lord by providing a zone in which compromise was possible. In this sense the kokudaka system was, to use the historian Wakita Osamu's phrase, "a device for unification." Within the domains the establishment of explicit land values was frequently linked to the weakening of retainer autonomy (the decline of funyūken).

4. Despite each domain's distinctive path of development, daimyo pursued policies that moved Japan in a common direction. Trends like the separation of social classes, the turn to land surveys, and the rise of small-scale family farming had their genesis in broad-based, common problems faced by all domains and their residents: the pressures of war, the adjustment to peace, the growth of national markets, and so on. As the daimyo experimented with different means to cope with these problems, they developed policies from a limited range of potential solutions. Much of the social, political, and economic transformation of late-sixteenth- and early-seventeenth-century Japan must be measured through the cumulative impact of diverse local histories, and explained by reference to forces that transcended the reach of any one political actor or class of actors.* Hideyoshi's edicts nicely symbolize the trends of the time, but in many parts of Japan, these processes were well under way before his rise, and they continued without his direction or that of the Bakufu because they were stimulated and conditioned by local needs and circumstances.

5. Policies directed at the personal behavior of daimyo could affect domain social structure and administration, although that was not the primary motive underlying the hegemon's orders. Most importantly, fief transfers created opportunities for daimyo to reduce their retainers' involvement in the villages and to increase their dependence on their liege lord.

6. Some daimyo used central ordinances to reinforce domain policies that were already moving in the same direction.[15] Many also used central ordinances as models. Such influence was real, but it was subtle and indirect. Where central influence of any sort appears clear, the circumstances that permitted it to operate—a domain's recent defeat by hegemons, proximity to agents of central power, or lack of resources (human and natural) and power; the strength of the central authority's motivation to act; and so forth—require careful delineation. This kind of analysis permits an assessment of the degree of compliance with central orders. It also sheds light on the substantial institutional variation evident in early modern Japan, even in cases like Kaga, where there were no serious popular disturbances such as occurred in Higo and Tohoku.

These hypotheses assume, of course, that the degree of central influence at local levels is problematic. The case for making this relationship the

---

*Identical solutions, however, do not imply identical motivations. For example, in some instances the abolition of landed retainer status (or its fictionalization) was the direct result of a need to secure tighter control of landed retainers and in others, like Kaga and Bizen, was more immediately linked to difficulties landed retainers had in dealing with rural taxpayers.

object of explicit investigation does not rest alone on the evidence I have presented on the implementation of the Taikō kenchi. The time required for Kaga to standardize its own survey procedures within a small section of Japan and its inability (despite its reputation for very effective administration) to tax effectively early in the seventeenth century also stimulate this doubt. If domain authorities, possessing relatively greater knowledge of local conditions and easier access to villages, could not make these and other programs work, the central authorities certainly could not compel clear class separation, the redistribution of wealth, and a uniform system of land tenure by sending their own agents on a quick tour of a province.

Some might argue that the daimyo were granted license to interpret central ordinances on their own, but this begs the central question of who had the ultimate capacity to set local policy on critical administrative and social issues like setting domain values, determining land tenure, and defining class status. The case for discretionary latitude would be plausible if there was evidence of a dialogue between central and domain authorities over whether and how to implement laws that affected internal domain affairs. Yet one searches in vain for some systematic, broad-based analogue to the sixteenth-century Spanish colonial administrators' practice of notifying the crown, "I obey but do not comply," when centrally conceived policies struck them as inappropriate.

We also might conclude that latitude was granted if deviations were only minor. Many, however, were major. Kaga was hardly the only or even the worst offender. Satsuma declined to make actual measurements despite Hideyoshi's direct, written orders, and even with one of his agents on site; that was clearly not just a matter of operating within a limited degree of latitude. The failure of some domains to employ kokudaka measures even at the nominal domain level is another example.

Even if such breaks with policy could be documented as explicitly granted, the very ceding of so broad a latitude calls into question the resolve behind at least some central ordinances. The frequent, and sometimes gross, manipulation of the entire process of valuing land often went unchastised. These cases severely compromised any real effort to create a nationally uniform system of land values and registers.

With so much latitude in practice, it is hard to agree that the daimyo were, in a meaningful administrative sense, "accountable to the overlord's laws, to the expectation of . . . good administration."[16] To argue that domain lords were held to some standard of good administration would require a redefinition of the key terms: "accountability" and "good administration." At most they must be interpreted in the very broadest of contexts—perhaps the daimyo's maintenance of public order within their domains and adherence to laws that governed their personal behavior and preserved a peaceful national order. (Fief transfers and attainders were useful in strengthening the central control of major markets, eliminating a threatening daimyo, and surrounding others with shogunal allies, but our exploration of the subject does not support the view that shoguns consistently employed them to enforce administrative ordinances or a clearly defined standard of good administration.) Even in this light the local impact of central directives remains problematic. In reshaping the standard of "good administration" in this fashion, we lose the expectation that central directives on many administrative, economic, and social matters were executed or even that there was a conscious intent to implement them.

Even if there were no constitutional limits on the hegemons, they faced very practical constraints. Unlike central authorities in Western Europe, they lacked an overriding incentive to enforce nationally uniform social policies, survey methods, tax systems, and standards even though, in principle, they may have possessed the means. They had reason to encourage agricultural productivity, secure resources for defense, and so forth, but they had no compelling international or domestic crisis pushing them to risk inflaming the daimyo by meddling directly in domain administration. The marginal gains they might have achieved were not worth the heavy costs of enforcement. Perhaps Hideyoshi thought it well that his daimyo follow the procedures enunciated in the survey orders, class separation edicts, and related measures, but to get the job done, he in effect relied on what a later age would call jawboning. He and his successors were unwilling to pursue a policy of systematic enforcement. To the extent that they sought change at the local level, they wanted to obtain it with minimal risks to their own position.

In suggesting the need to take the efficacy of the state as problematic, I do not deny that there were new, significant, widely recognized, and legitimate areas of central authority in Japan. Nor do I dispute the contention that the state's authority to act—its capability—grew during this era. A strong case has been made for both.[17] The effective power of central authorities was real within certain spheres: the ability to order most daimyo into new domains, the right to command them in battle and demand various forms of military service from them, and the authority to manage key aspects of their personal lives, to name the most obvious.

In fact, while central ordinances often fell short of effective state action, they contributed to the development of nominal authority. Daimyo did not explicitly challenge the central ordinances even when they failed to act on them. They (and the new ideological constructs that undergirded the hegemon's actions) became an established part of seventeenth-century political discourse.[18] By helping to build nominal authority, by reinvigorating the principle of a central political authority, the first hegemons laid a foundation for the expansion of state capabilities. That potential was partly realized in realms beyond the personal or martial control of daimyo. The Bakufu effectively adjudicated diversity disputes and, over time, also expanded its legitimate use of force to keep domestic peace. It conscripted daimyo resources for an increasing array of projects, including flood control in areas that did not affect its own lands. A consciousness of Japan as a single entity was strengthened and extended even among commoners. Regardless of the mixture of personalistic, bureaucratic, or simply Machiavellian measures, the new political order that Hideyoshi and the Tokugawa crafted was remarkably successful in that regard. The peaceful environment that resulted, with its social stability and economic growth, and the consequent national economic and cultural integration added substance to the image of one nation projected by the Great Heroes and their successors.

Yet simply because their authority was real in some arenas of political activity does not mean that it was so in others. Nor does their effective authority in one sphere (e.g., the ability to transfer daimyo) necessarily imply that such power was actively employed to extend their authority in another. Studies of the Taikō kenchi have provided the strongest, most commonly cited evidence of an effective central influence on internal domain policy, but the evidence from Kaga and a number of other domains, as well as data on the reasons for fief attainders, suggests that sanctions were not applied with a view to achieving consistent national implementation.

The disjunction between image and reality encourages a characterization of the early modern Japanese state as flamboyant. The central authority created by the Great Pacifiers and managed by their heirs may have been comparable to many of the absolutist states of Europe, but that still left the Meiji government with the daunting task of building a truly capable central administration.

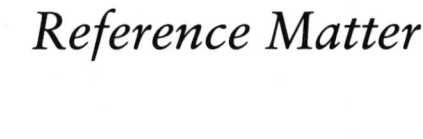

Appendix **A**

Sources of Village Tax Data, 1582-1636

Where data were cited in bales of rice rather than koku, I have converted to koku at the rate of two bales per koku. Copies of the manuscripts noted by asterisk were kindly provided by Kigoshi Ryūzō. Convenient tabular reference for much of the Tenshō era data may be found in Takazawa Yūichi, "Tenshō-ki nengu san'yōjo no kōsatsu: Noto kuni Maeda ryō ni okeru," in Suzu Shi Shi Hensan Iinkai, ed., *Suzu shi shi* (Kanazawa: Suzu-Shi Yakusho, 1978), *Tsūshi hen*: 712–17. For complete authors' names, titles, and publication data on the sources cited, see the Bibliography.

1582
    Ōzawa   Kigoshi, "Kaga-han seiritsu ki," p. 13
    Tadago   *Suzu shi shi*, 3: 104

1583
    Nishiumi   *Suzu shi shi*, 3: 627
    Orido   *Suzu shi shi*, 3: 604–5
    Ōzawa   Kigoshi, "Maeda," p. 22
    Saihōji   *KK*, pp. 766–67
    Tadago   *Suzu shi shi*, 3: 14
    Takai   *Suzu shi shi*, 3: 735–36
    Umawatari-Ushijima   *Suzu shi shi*, 3: 14

1584
    Bessho   Tagawa, "Kaga-han," p. 55
    Enome   Tagawa, "Kaga-han," p. 54
    Hachikazaki   Tagawa, "Kaga-han," p. 55
    Han'noura   Tagawa, "Kaga-han," p. 55
    Iwasaka   *Suzu shi shi*, 3: 742–43

Kōda	Tagawa, "Kaga-han," p. 54
Kuki	Tagawa, "Kaga-han," p. 55
Makari	Tagawa, "Kaga-han," p. 54
Minami	Tagawa, "Kaga-han," p. 54
Musaki	Tagawa, "Kaga-han," p. 55
Neya	Tagawa, "Kaga-han," p. 54
Nishiumi-Shimoura	*KHNK*, p. 554
Nozaki	Tagawa, "Kaga-han," p. 55
Ōura	Tagawa, "Kaga-han," p. 55
Ōzawa	Kigoshi, "Kaga-han seiritsu ki," p. 13
Tori-Tanoshiri	Tagawa, "Kaga-han," p. 55
Ubakaura	Tagawa, "Kaga-han," p. 55

1585

Awagura-Suzuya	*Oku Noto Tokikuni ke monjo*, 1: 4
Enome	*Notojima no kinsei monjo* 1: 22
Jike	*WSS*, 2: 443–44
Kamishiro	Oda Kichinojō, *Kaga-han*, pp. 258–59
Konpōji	*Suzu shi shi*, 3: 739–40
Mori-Shirakawa	Sakai Seiichi, "Kaga-han shoki," p. 16
Morohashi	*KK*, pp. 804–5
Orido	Kigoshi, "Kaga-han seiritsu ki," p. 13
Ōta	Tagawa, "Kaga-han," pp. 24, 56, 58
Ōzawa	Kigoshi, "Kaga-han seiritsu ki," p. 13
Saihōji	*Suzu shi shi*, 3: 105
Shibuta	*WSS*, 1: 451
Takojima	Kigoshi, "Kaga-han seiritsu ki," p. 13
Yawata	Wakabayashi Kisaburō, *Kinsei komonjo saihō no shiori*, p. 62
Ushio	*WSS*, 1: 221

1586

Awagura-Suzuya	*Oku Noto Tokikuni ke monjo*, 1: 5–6
Enome	*Notojima no kinsei monjo*, 1: 22
Jike	*WSS*, 1: 222; 2: 450
Kizumi	Kigoshi, "Kaga-han seiritsu ki," p. 13
Kokuga	*NSS*, 3: 145
Nakai	*KK*, pp. 821–23
Nishiumi-Shimoura	*Suzu shi shi*, 3: 628–29
Morohashi	Kigoshi, "Kaga-han seiristu ki," pp. 9–11
Noda	*WSS*, 1: 452
Orido	*Suzu shi shi*, 3: 605
Saihōji	*Suzu shi shi*, 3: 105–6
Shibuta	*WSS*, 1: 451–52
Shitsura	*KK*, pp. 813–14
Sora	"Anamizu-machi Hosoki-ke monjo"*

Sources of Village Tax Data, 1582–1636

Takai — *Suzu shi shi*, 3: 736
Teraji — *WSS*, 2: 211–12
Tokikuni — *Oku Noto Tokikuni ke monjo*, 1: 4

1587
Awagura-Suzuya — *Oku Noto Tokikuni ke monjo*, 1: 6
Enome — *Notojima no kinsei monjo*, 1: 22
In'nai — Kigoshi, "Kaga-han seiritsu ki," p. 13
Nishiumi-Shimoura — *Suzu shi shi*, 3: 628–29
Kawanishi — *WSS*, 2: 284
Kizumi — Kigoshi, "Kaga-han seiritsu ki," p. 13
Kokuga — *NSS*, 3: 146
Orido — *Suzu shi shi*, 3: 605–6
Ōzawa — *KHNK*, 1: 547
Shitsura — *KHNK*, 1: 562
Takojima — Kigoshi, "Kaga-han seiritsu ki," p. 13
Wakayama — *KHNK*, pp. 555–56
Yawata-shimo — *NSS*, 2: 439–40

1588
Awagura-Eijiri — *Oku Noto Tokikuni ke monjo*, 1: 7
Awaya-Suzuya — *Oku Noto Tokikuni ke monjo*, 1: 7–8
Enome — *Notojima no kinsei monjo*, 1: 24
Hitani — Sakai Seiichi, "Kaga-han shoki," p. 17
In'nai — Kigoshi, "Kaga-han seiritsu ki," p. 13
Iwaya — *KK*, p. 826
Kizumi — Kigoshi, "Kaga-han seiritsu ki," p. 13
Morohashi — *Morohashi son shi*, pp. 343–44
Nozaki-Ōura — *Notojima no kinsei monjo*, 1: 22–23
Ōzawa — *KK*, pp. 825
Sano — *WSS*, 2: 297–98

1589–90
Igawa — *NSS*, 3: 275
Kizumi — Kigoshi, "Kaga-han seiritsu ki," p. 13
Morohashi — *Morohashi son shi*, p. 346
Ōzawa — Kigoshi, "Kaga-han seiritsu ki," p. 13
Tane-Korosa — *NSS*, 3: 169–70
Yawata-shimo — *NSS*, 2: 440
1590, In'nai — "Noto-kuni monjo"*

1591–93
Nanao — *Ishikawa ken Kashima gun shi*, p. 362
Yawata-shimo — *NSS*, 2: 440–41
1592, Ōzawa — "Noto komonjo"*
"1593" (actual date uncertain), *NSS*, 2: 122–30, for:

Abuyamachi, Abuyamura, Azumi, Bungōmyō, Etomari, Fujimaki, Fukumizu, Fushido, Hanazono, Hara, Haragi, Hariyama, Higashihama, In'nai, Inomo, Iori, Ishizaki, Iwanori, Kaji, Kamidana, Kamikaragawa, Kamishitsumi, Kashima, Kawachi, Kawada, Kawashima, Kumabuchi, Kurojima, Kurokawa, Matsunoki, Mawaki, Mikohara, Nakatani, Nishinomiya, Oda, Ogawa, Ōmachi, Ōno, Onogi, Sasanami, Senro, Shikanami, Shikinami, Shimokarakawa, Shiraishi, Sohama, Sōra, Tenjindani, Tokikuni, Ujima, Yamazaki, Yawatashimo, Yotsumachi

1595–1601

Fujibashi	*Tonami shi shi*, p. 301
Higashi Ebisaka	Kigura, "Kamisaka-ke monjo," p. 54
Minojima	Sakai Seiichi, "Kaga-han shoki," p. 18
Satoyama	*Tonami shi shi*, p. 301
Shinmura	*Tonami shi shi*, p. 301
Tochiage	*Tonami shi shi*, p. 301
Ure	*TKSS*, 3: 394
1598, Ishibarai	*Kamiichi chō shi*, pp. 266–67
1600, Himimachi	*Himi shi shi*, p. 1180
1601, Tokikuni	*Oku Noto Tokikuni ke monjo*, 1: 9

1603

Higashi	*KHS*, 1: 895 (combined with Nishi Hirokami)
Nishi Hirokami	*KHS*, 1: 895

1604

Higashi	*KHS*, 1: 895 (combined with Nishi Hirokami)
Nishi Hirokami	*KHS*, 1: 895
Iori	*NSS*, 2: 121
Tokikuni	*Oku Noto Tokikuni ke monjo*, 1: 12
Yawata-shimo	*NSS*, 2: 441

1605–6

Chiyomachi	*Hakui shi shi, Kinsei*: 129
Tokikuni	*Oku Noto Tokikuni ke monjo*, 1: 12
Yanase	*Tonami shi shi*, pp. 304–5
1606, Kanaya-Hongo	Sakai Seiichi, "Kaga-han shoki," p. 20

1608–9

Saishōji	*Fukumitsu chō shi*, 1: 688
Tokikuni	*Oku Noto Tokikuni ke monjo*, 1: 18
1609, Yōrōji	Sakai Seiichi, "Kaga-han shoki," p. 21

1610

Hamakeiden	Sakai Seiichi, "Kaga-han shoki," p. 21
Yōrōji	Sakai Seiichi, "Kaga-han shoki," p. 21

1611

Iori	*Kashima gun shi*, pp. 355–56
Mawaki	*Oku Noto Tokikuni ke monjo*, 1: 14–15

1615

Higashi Hongo	Sakai Seiichi, "Kaga-han shotō," pp. 9–10
Himimachi	*Himi shi shi*, p. 1186
Inamimachi	*Inami chō shi*, 2: 40 (two separately recorded village segments combined into a single tax rate)
Jin'e	*Suzu shi shi*, 3: 631
Minojima	*Fukuoka chō shi*, pp. 295, 1209
Nishi Inami	*Inami chō shi*, 2: 40

1616–17

Himimachi	*Himi shi shi*, p. 1186
Jin'e	*Suzu shi shi*, 3: 631
Minojima	*Fukuoka chō shi*, pp. 1209–10
Onaga	*Hakui shi shi*, Kinsei: 853
Tokikuni	*Oku Noto Tokikuni ke monjo*, 1: 25
1617, Yokota	*TKSS*, 1: 410

1618

Han'yano	*NSS*, 3: 426
Roshunji	*TKSS*, 3: 410
Yokota	*TKSS*, 3: 410

1619

Han'yano	*NSS*, 3: 426
Sōyama	*TKSS*, 3: 410–11

1620–26

Fugeshimachi	*WSS*, 4: 23
Hikari	*WSS*, 2: 25
Ikari	*Yanagida son shi*, p. 259
Jin'e	*Suzu shi shi*, 3: 632
Kawaimachi	*Wajima chō shi*, pp. 59–60
Kawanishi	*WSS*, 2: 284
Konpōji	*Ishikawa ken shi*, 3: 784–85
Kōtokuji	*WSS*, 2: 515
Mochida	*Monzen chō shi*, p. 73
Obako	*Yanagida son shi*, p. 1270
Saihōji	*Suzu shi shi*, 3: 106
Shinobu	*WSS*, 2: 462
Tokikuni	*Oku Noto Tokikuni ke monjo*, 1: 30
Wakayamagumi	*Suzu shi shi*, 3: 205–6
Yokota	Sakai Seiichi, "Kaga han shoki," p. 22
1626, Tokikuni	*Oku Noto Tokikuni ke monjo*, 1: 42

1627
- Fukamidani — *WSS*, 2: 111–12
- Hakumai — *WSS*, 1: 3
- Higashi Innai — *WSS*, 1: 5
- Higashiyama — *WSS*, 1: 4–5
- Ikari — *WSS*, 1: 7
- Kanegura — *WSS*, 1: 7–8
- Nafune — *WSS*, 1: 3
- Nishi Innai — *WSS*, 1: 5
- Nishiyama — *WSS*, 1: 7
- Noda — *WSS*, 1: 3–4
- Obako — *WSS*, 1: 7
- Odaya — *WSS*, 1: 6
- Sato — *WSS*, 1: 6
- Shibuta — *WSS*, 1: 5–6
- Shinobu — *WSS*, 1: 4
- Soriji — *WSS*, 1: 4

1628
- Tokikuni — *Oku Noto Tokikuni ke monjo*, 1: 46
- Wakayamagumi — *Suzu shi shi*, 3: 207

1629
- Sosogi — *Oku Noto Tokikuni ke monjo*, 1: 50–51
- Wakayama-Nobutake and Nakada — *Suzu shi shi*, 3: 389 (*shinden* excluded)

1630
- Ebisaka — Sakai Seiichi, "Kaga-han shoki," p. 23
- Kosakai — Sakai Seiichi, "Kaga-han shoki," p. 23
- Soyama — *TKSS*, 3: 411
- Tokikuni — *Oku Noto Tokikuni ke monjo*, 1: 56
- Unami — Sakai Seiichi, "Kaga-han shoki," p. 23

1631
- Ebisaka — Sakai Seiichi, "Kaga-han shoki," p. 23
- Kosakai — Sakai Seiichi, "Kaga-han shoki," p. 23
- Tokikuni — *Oku Noto Tokikuni ke monjo*, 1: 59
- Unami — Sakai Seiichi, "Kaga-han shoki," p. 23

1632
- Nishiyama — *WSS*, 2: 469
- Minamiyama — *Suzu shi shi*, 3: 334–36
- Shirataki — *Suzu shi shi*, 3: 391–92
- Tokikuni — *Oku Noto Tokikuni ke monjo*, 1: 60–61

1633
- Shimoseki — Sakai Seiichi, "Kaga-han shoki," pp. 22–23
- Tokikuni — *Oku Noto Tokikuni ke monjo*, 1: 64, 69–70

1634
 Kashima gun   *Kashima gun shi*, p. 357
 Noto   *Kashima gun shi*, p. 357
 Shimoseki   Sakai Seiichi, "Kaga-han shoki," pp. 22–23

1635
 Kawakubo   *Yatsuo chō shi*, 1: 316–17
 Kiriyama   *Yatsuo chō shi*, 1: 316–17
 Shimoseki   Sakai Seiichi, "Kaga-han shoki," pp. 22–23
 Yatsuo   *Yatsuo chō shi*, 1: 316–17

1636
 Nafune   *WSS*, 2: 646
 Shirataki   *Suzu shi shi*, 3: 392
 Tokikuni   *WSS*, 1: 349
 Yatsuomachi   *Yatsuo chō shi*, 1: 316–17

Appendix **B**

Glossary

Bakufu. "Tent government," the Shogun's house administration
bugari. "*Bu*-cutting," harvest sampling for the purpose of determining land taxes
bugyō. Magistrate
buyaku. Corvée labor dues; often converted to cash payments in the seventeenth century
chigyō. Early modern fief from which landed retainers derived tax income but over which they generally exercised little administrative or judicial power
Chō family. Long-standing resident gentry of Noto who allied themselves with Oda Nobunaga and the Maeda in the early modern era
Chōsokabe family. Sengoku (q.v.) daimyo who ruled the part of Shikoku that became Tosa domain
daikan. In Kaga domain, one of the daimyo's samurai tax agents
daimyo. "Great Name," baronial lords of the early modern era
fuchi. Stipend from the daimyo given to some rural administrators in Kaga domain
fuchibyakushō. "Stipended peasants," local farmer-warrior gentry who received a stipend from the Maeda in return for their assistance during the early years of domain formation
funyūken. "Principle of non-entry," a landed retainer's right to refuse his lord entry into his fief
gedai. In Kaga, the subretainer in charge of assessing and collecting land taxes for his fief-holding lord
genin. Servant
gō. District; an affiliated group of villages, smaller than a county (*kōri*)
gofuchinin tomura. "Stipended tomura," a *tomura* (q.v.) who supervised other tomura in a county and received a salary from the domain
gosanke. The three branch families of the Tokugawa house who were to provide heirs if the direct shogunal line did not provide a suitable candidate for shogun
gun'yaku. Formally, an extraordinary military levy; commonly employed in three

senses: (1) the obligation of a daimyo to provide men, money, and supplies for the military operations under the command of Oda Nobunaga, Toyotomi Hideyoshi, and the Tokugawa shoguns; (2) the similar obligation of landed retainers to their daimyo; (3) a tax on villages to provide corvée and supplies for military operations. In practice, this category of extraordinary levies on daimyo extended to contributions to the imperial household and the maintenance of key public works

han. An early modern domain ruled by a daimyo

hatake ori. "Dry field break," Kaga domain's unusual way of recognizing in land surveys the inferior fertility of dry fields by reducing the area measured before calculating the land's putative yield for tax purposes

hatamoto. Direct retainers of the shogun; smaller than daimyo but ruled their own fiefs

Hei-nō bunri. "Warrior-peasant separation," the legal differentiation of samurai from commoners

heikin men. In early-seventeenth-century Kaga, averaging the tax rates of all landed retainers and the daimyo into a single rate for a village

hikichi. Land not included in a *warichi* (q.v.) redistribution in Kaga domain

honbyakushō, see *Takamochi hyakushō*

honden. "Basic fields," commonly used for fields long in production (paddy or dry) in contrast to reclaimed lands not yet fully incorporated into the tax registers

hyakushō ikki. Often translated as peasant revolts, but the phrase carries a much broader range of meanings in the early modern era, encompassing peaceful as well as violent protests and demonstrations by commoners

hyakushō uke. "Peasant contracts," for villages to pay a fixed tax to the proprietor in the medieval era; responsibility for allocating the obligations within the village and delivering the tax monies and goods lay with the villagers, not the proprietor's agents

Ie sōdō. "House disturbance," disruptive factional disputes within a domain's samurai ranks, often between the daimyo and his landed retainers

Ikkō ikki. A league of local forces in Kaga, organized around the Ikkō Buddhist sect to oppose or limit the influence of outside lords

jōmen. "Fixed" tax rate; established for an entire village. In principle the rate was set for a number of years, but in practice it often became a permanent ceiling; taxes could be reduced in bad times, but not raised.

kaisaku bugyō. Reform magistrate; initially a temporary position established to help carry out Kaga domain's major reform, the Kaisaku hō, and later made into a permanent office specializing in land tax assessment and collection

Kaisaku hō. Kaga domain's mid-seventeenth-century reforms, which eliminated retainer fiefs, strengthened mechanisms for land taxation, and increased domain revenues from land taxes

Kanazawa. The principal castle town of Kaga domain

kandaka. Late medieval practice of assessing land value as a putative cash tax yield; measured in gold coins, *kanme, kan,* or *kanmon.*

kemi. Crop inspections, usually based on *bugari* (q.v.) and conducted annually

kenchi. Investigations of the area and value of land; several methods were commonly employed, not all of which involved the actual measurement of area; usually translated as "land survey"

kenchi buchō, see *kenchichō*

kenchi bugyō. Land survey magistrate

kenchichō. Land survey register. Often thought to detail field-by-field measurements of paddy, dry fields, and residential land, along with indications of land quality, assessed value, and owner. In fact, a variety of names are used for land investigations, some of which bear a resemblance to this image, others of which simply summarize the data for either large parts of a village or for an entire village: *kenchi buchō, mizuchō, nawauchichō,* and *uchiwatashijo.*

kimoiri. Village headman

Kinsei. Early modern era, ca. 1600–1868

kōgi. "Public authority"; daimyo and shogun used this concept to legitimate their rule by claiming to act for the public good, not for their private benefit

kokudaka. The value of a village, domain, or fief expressed in the putative rice yield of its lands

kokujin. Late medieval provincial warrior.

kokumori. The assessed value of one *tan* of land, expressed in its putative rice yield

kōri. A county

Kōri bugyō. County magistrate; before the Kaisaku hō (q.v.) in Kaga, in charge of all civil affairs; thereafter, his responsibilities no longer included land taxation

kuji. A share to be redistributed under the *warichi* (q.v.) system of corporate village land tenure

kujichi. Land subject to redistribution under *warichi* (q.v.)

kuwayaku. Plow tax; assessed on certain categories of males aged 15 to 60 (Japanese count); a major factor determining legal peasant status in Kaga domain

kyūnin. A landed retainer

mawari kenchi. Circumferential survey; used to measure large sections or an entire village without measuring individual fields

mizuchō, see *kenchichō*

murakiri. The process of clarifying boundaries between two villages

nawauchichō, see *kenchichō*

sankin-kōtai. The system of alternate attendance in which the Tokugawa required daimyo to spend (usually) alternate years in Edo; when not there, important members of the daimyo's family were left behind as hostages

sashidashi. Land investigations in which villagers or retainers made estimates of the area and value of their own lands and submitted them to daimyo

Sengoku era. Ca. 1470–1575

shinden. Reclaimed land

sonmen. System of land tax assessments in which taxes based on fixed exemptions for peasants were reduced by the amount of damaged land and officials' salaries; the Maeda employed this system only in the sixteenth century

Taikō kenchi. Land investigations conducted under the auspices of Toyotomi Hideyoshi

taka. The assessed value of land and/or land use rights.

takamochi hyakushō. A villager holding superior rights to cultivate land in a village; such a villager usually participated in paying taxes (to the domain and village) and in managing the corporate village affairs. Village officers generally came from this class of villager. Also called *honbyakushō*.

tomura. Head of a group of villages, initially about a dozen; successors to *fuchibyakushō* (q.v.)

tozama. An "outer" or autonomous daimyo, one not closely allied to the Tokugawa family before the Battle of Sekigahara (1600)

uchiwatashijō, see *kenchichō*

warichi (also *denchiwari*; *chiwari*; etc.). System of corporate land tenure in which villagers periodically reallocated cultivation rights among themselves

Notes

For complete authors' names, titles, and publication data on the works cited in short form in these Notes, see the Bibliography following. The following abbreviations are used in the citations:

> ES   *Etchū shiryō*
> IKS   Heki Ken, *Ishikawa ken shi*
> KHNK Wakabayashi Kisaburō, *Kaga-han nōsei shi no kenkyū*
> KHS   Heki Ken, *Kaga-han shiryō*
> KK   Heki Ken, *Kano komonjo*
> NSS   *Nanao shi shi* (*Shiryō hen* unless otherwise noted)
> TKSS *Toyama ken shi* (*Shiryō hen* unless otherwise noted)
> WSS   *Wajima shi shi* (*Shiryō hen* unless otherwise noted)

BOOK EPIGRAPHS: Emmanuel Le Roy Ladurie, *The Peasants of Languedoc*, tr. John Day (Urbana: University of Illinois Press, 1974), p. 4; Vivienne Shue, *The Reach of the State: Sketches of the Chinese Body Politic* (Stanford Calif.: Stanford University Press, 1988), p. 28.

Chapter 1

1. I refer here to the *shugo*. For brief but more detailed studies of the political organization of this era, see Varley, "Ashikaga Yoshimitsu"; the related articles in part 2 of the same volume by Cornelius J. Kiley, Nagahara Keiji, and John W. Hall; Harrington, "Regional Outposts"; and Arnesen, "Provincial Vassals."

2. Some had a purely secular orientation, such as the *do ikki*, or "leagues of the land" of Omi and Yamashiro. Others were religiously based, such as the Ikkō *ikki*, organized around the Buddhist Ikkō sect. On the latter, see Davis, "Kaga Ikkō Ikki." For a broader treatment of these activities, see Davis's "Ikki in Late Medieval Japan."

3. Hall, "Foundations of the Modern Japanese Daimyo," provides a standard typology of daimyo development in the 15th, 16th, and 17th centuries.

4. On this subject, see Katsumata (with Collcutt), "Development of Sengoku Law."

5. On this point and others below, see Birt, "Samurai in Passage."

6. On this and other political influences of 16th-century Buddhism, see McMullin, *Buddhism and State*.

7. For a full account of Hideyoshi's career, see Berry, *Hideyoshi*.

8. For a recent biography of Ieyasu, see Totman, *Tokugawa Ieyasu*.

9. See Fujiki (with Elison), "Political Posture"; Asao (with Jansen), "Shogun and Tennō"; Elison, "Cross and Sword"; and Elison, "Hideyoshi."

10. For a complete translation of the 1615 version, see Tsunoda et al., *Sources of Japanese Tradition*, 1: 326–29.

11. The *sankin-kōtai* system is often called the "alternate attendance system." For an analysis of the significant long-term effects of this policy, see Tsukahira, *Feudal Control*.

12. The principle of a two-tenths difference between land grades is referred to as *ni to sagari*.

13. On late-16th- and early-17th-century economic developments, see Yamamura, "Returns on Unification"; Yamamura, "Pre-Industrial Landholding Patterns"; and Smith, *Agrarian Origins*.

14. Araki Moriaki, "Taikō kenchi no rekishiteki zentei."

15. Yamada Moritarō, *Nihon shihonshugi bunseki*. Suzuki Ryōichi has been considered a postwar proponent of this point of view (see his *Oda Nobunaga*).

16. Fujita, *Kinsei nōsei*, in his own, unique use of the terminology, refers to this as the establishment of "pure feudalism."

17. Hayakawa, *Nihon rekishi dokuhon*; Nakamura Kichiji, *Kinsei shoki*; Kitajima, *Nihon kinsei shi*; Wakita, *Oda Seiken*; Wakita, *Kinsei hōkensei*.

18. Hall, "Japan's Sixteenth-Century Revolution"; Berry, *Hideyoshi*, especially chap. 6, "Federation and Its Motives," pp. 147–67.

19. Ishii Ryōsuke, *History*, especially pp. 59–79.

20. Sansom, *History, 1615–1867*, p. 48.

21. White, "State Growth." See also Fujiki, *Toyotomi heiwarei*, on the hegemonic monopoly of force, the prohibition of private settlement of disputes, etc.

22. Initially, comparison with Europe was one device that helped make Japanese history comprehensible in the West. John Henry Wigmore, a legal historian, was clearly interested in comparative perspectives as he compiled his multivolume study on early modern Japanese law. Professor Kan'ichi Asakawa of Yale employed a comparative approach from the beginning of his academic career in the late 19th century. Edwin Reischauer's essay in Rushton Coulborn's classic comparative effort, *Feudalism in History*, built on Asakawa's rather positive evaluation of feudalism's contributions to modern Japan. Joseph Strayer's introductory essay to *Studies in the Institutional History of Early Modern Japan* continued this focus; and John Whitney Hall, in the following essay, attempted to bring some methodological rigor to the comparative analysis and questioned the applicability of the term "feudalism" to early modern Japan. In this essay and a review of Japanese

perspectives on the Tokugawa, Hall noted the gradual disappearance of feudal elements in the new state. See Wigmore, "Introduction," in part 1 of *Law and Justice*, pp. xii–xiii; Coulborn, *Feudalism in History*, pp. 26–48; Strayer, "Tokugawa Period"; and Hall, "Feudalism in Japan." Hall's "The New Look of Tokugawa History" demonstrates some of the increasing sensitivity of Japanese scholars to the limitations of past applications of the concept of feudalism to their country.

An influential stream in 20th-century Japanese historical writing also compared medieval and early modern Japanese institutions with those of Europe. Studies of landholding, manors, and other arrangements linked to feudalism often focused explicitly on such matters. See, for example, the opening sections of Fujita, *Kinsei nōsei*. Ishii Shirō, *Nihon kokusei*, chap. 1, reviews common Japanese interpretations and discusses their European counterparts. Mid-20th-century Japanese scholars emphasized the unique characteristics of Japan's early modern state in reaction to a perceived overreliance on the Western pattern of institutional development. They sought a more distinctly Asian or Japanese context. Nonetheless, they often remain implicitly bound by the more general predisposition established in European models of state development—the emergence of powerful central administrations. Several prominent examples are discussed below. See also Kobayashi, "Sengoku sōran," p. 361.

23. Berry, "Public Peace."

24. White, "State Growth." White also evaluates others whose work does not explicitly employ the term "absolutism."

25. Sansom, *History, 1615–1867*, p. 48; White, "State Growth," p. 10.

26. Ishii Ryōsuke, *History*, pp. 61–65, 74–75.

27. Hall, "Hideyoshi's Domestic Policies," p. 206, relies heavily on the work of Ishii Ryōsuke. Ishii has summarized his interpretation of Japanese history in an article translated into English as "Japanese Feudalism." See especially p. 26.

28. Hall, "Hideyoshi's Domestic Policies," p. 206. Hall, in his most recent statement, argues: "In the final analysis it was the shogunate's capacity to govern the daimyo that gave stability to the *bakuhan* state. . . . By keeping the relationship between daimyo and shogun a precarious one and by making the daimyo accountable to bakufu *regulations and codes of conduct* [my emphasis], the shogun was given numerous opportunities to transfer, reduce in size, or disinherit any daimyo. . . . Reductions and seizures were the result of disciplinary action by the shogun. Using the provisions of the Buke sho hattō [1615], the shogun could penalize a daimyo for . . . many . . . seemingly minor acts that violated the code." In a later passage, he states: "The commonly given description of the power structure that supported the Edo bakufu inevitably leaves the impression that the Tokugawa shogunate was all-powerful. . . . The truth is that many of the elements of power in the seventeenth century failed to retain their meaning in the nineteenth." ("Bakuhan System," pp. 150, 161.) Harold Bolitho argues: "The Buke sho hattō also seemed to foreshadow something new. Its thirteenth and final clause urged the daimyo to appoint none but capable men as *han* administrators, thereby sounding a note to which the granting of formal certificates of enfeoffment two years later was to add resonance. The Tokugawa bakufu was claiming for itself ultimate responsibility in *han* internal affairs." ("The Han," p. 194.)

29. Ishii Ryōsuke, "Japanese Feudalism," pp. 19–20.
30. Sansom, *History, 1334–1615*, pp. 316, 318.
31. Hall, *Government and Local Power*, p. 290.
32. Kanai, *Hansei*, p. 21.
33. See, for example, Hall's summary of Hideyoshi's major policies in "Hideyoshi's Domestic Policies," p. 194. For a recent Japanese appraisal, see Mizubayashi, *Hōkensei*, pp. 114, 119–21. Hall states: "The land survey became the foundation on which rested both the mura and the legal structure by which the samurai class related to the peasantry and the peasantry related to the land" ("Introduction," p. 16, but see also pp. 7, 11, 34). Asao, "Sixteenth-Century Unification," pp. 51–53, and Susser, "Toyotomi Regime," pp. 139–40, 150, both note some exceptions but still emphasize the effectiveness of Hideyoshi's efforts. See also Wakita, "Social and Economic Consequences of Unification," pp. 103, 107–8, 115; and Furushima, "Village and Agriculture," p. 480 and passim.
34. For example, Hall, in the quote above, makes the argument that the basic units of measurement of area and volume were standardized. See also Kodama, *Kinsei nōmin seikatsu shi*, pp. 16–17; Kanai, *Hansei*, p. 21; Sasaki, "Tōitsu kenryoku," pp. 58, 80; Oishi, "Kinsei," pp. 46–48; Mihashi, "Kinsei zenki," p. 18; Sansom, *History, 1334–1615*, p. 318; Andō Seiichi, *Edo jidai*, p. 2; Wakita, "Kokudaka System"; and Berry, *Hideyoshi*, pp. 117, 120. See also Susser, "Toyotomi Regime." Susser notes that "the cadastral survey was not uniformly carried out throughout the realm" (p. 139) but never clarifies the extent to which this was true. He then goes on to say that "Hideyoshi . . . tried to make his hold over his vassals as secure as possible by basing grants on an actual cadastral survey" (p. 139), and that "in effect, the *Taikō kenchi* established nationwide the system of assessing land value in terms of productivity" (p. 140). Readers are left with the distinct impression that variations were minor. Yamamura, "From Coins to Rice," p. 359, also stresses the minor nature of the variations.
35. Sansom, *History, 1334–1615*, p. 318.
36. Araki Moriaki, *Bakuhan taisei shakai*; Sasaki, *Bakuhan kenryoku*.
37. Yamamura, "Returns on Unification," pp. 328, 339–49; Yamamura, "Pre-Industrial Landholding Patterns," pp. 283, 285; Wakita, "Kokudaka System," p. 301. Yamamura sees the surveys as having some redistributive effects.
38. Jansen, "Tosa in the Sixteenth Century," p. 96. Susser, "Toyotomi Regime," p. 148, represents a more common perspective.
39. Nagahara (with Yamamura), "Sengoku Daimyo," p. 41, stresses that the kandaka system in the Gohōjō lands included all arable land and not just paddy. Residential lands were included in calculating the yield based on the assumption that any land not used for housing would have been cultivated.
40. Yamamura, "Returns on Unification," is the principal exception.
41. Why a greater emphasis was placed on collecting taxes in rice is a subject of scholarly controversy. See Wakita, "Kokudaka System," pp. 312–13, for the major interpretations of the significance of the switch to payment in rice. For a more recent view, see Yamamura, "From Coins to Rice." Although this development is frequently stressed in studies of the late 16th century, we shall see (chapters 7 and 8)

that the increased emphasis on tax payment in rice was imposed gradually and not by any means completely.

42. See, for example, Hall, "Hideyoshi's Domestic Policies," p. 220. Before the Taikō kenchi and the implementing of the kokudaka system, taxes could be reduced by fixed amounts for specific purposes, such as repairing shrines or irrigation systems, but the exemption did not fluctuate with actual crop yields. See Nagahara (with Yamamura), "Sengoku Daimyo," pp. 44–46; and Wakita, "Kokudaka System," pp. 313–14.

43. Berry, *Hideyoshi*, p. 118.

44. Both documents are translated in Tsunoda et al., 1: 321–22, 319–20, respectively.

45. Susser, "Toyotomi Regime," pp. 148–49, discusses two examples. See also Asao, "Sixteenth-century Unification," pp. 52–53; and Wakita, "Social and Economic Consequences," pp. 107, 115.

46. On the link between survey registers and restrictions on the possession of swords, see Berry, *Hideyoshi*, pp. 119–20. The Sword Collection Edict (reprinted in ibid., pp. 102–3) does not make survey registration as such a basis for prohibition, simply using the vague, undefined category "farmers." Since the few lists of weapons collected do not mention from whom they were collected, drawing a direct connection between the two is unwarranted. On the use of survey registers to determine who could transfer to a new domain with a daimyo, see Susser, "Toyotomi Regime," p. 148; and Miyakawa, *Taikō kenchi ron*, 3: 396, doc. 138. In this and similar documents, Hideyoshi ordered the Mizoguchi and Uesugi families to leave behind all peasants listed in the survey registers. Miyakawa (1: 357) refers to this "principle of domain transfer" as the "complete separation of warrior and peasant." Retainers were thereby "placed under the complete control of the daimyo." The earliest examples cited, however, come only from 1598, at the very end of Hideyoshi's life. It would be a mistake to take them as documenting similar uses for earlier survey registers.

47. Elison, "Cross and Sword," p. 68. Elison also traces other policies generally associated with Hideyoshi back to Oda, namely, the destruction of rural fortifications, land surveys, and daimyo transfers.

48. For one excellent study, see Birt, "Samurai in Passage."

49. Hara, *Kaga-han*, pp. i–iii, 2–8. Berry, *Hideyoshi*, p. 108, notes that the process of removing samurai from the land continued long after Hideyoshi's edicts and cites an example. She points out that the full implications of this policy were not drawn out until the Tokugawa's order restricting daimyo to one castle per province. But like many others, she assumes rather than demonstrates a causal connection between Hideyoshi's orders and this social transformation. She does not discuss any case in which Hideyoshi's orders were the clear source of separation or provide evidence showing to what extent this transformation had already taken place. On p. 109, she speaks of incentives for daimyo to implement the policy on their own, but fails to discuss cases in which Hideyoshi's orders were demonstrably the inspiration of daimyo action rather than, e.g., daimyo self-interest.

50. Berry, *Hideyoshi*, pp. 102–11; Susser, "Toyotomi Regime," pp. 140–45;

Hall, "Japan's Sixteenth-Century Revolution," pp. 19–20; Hall, "Hideyoshi's Domestic Policies," pp. 217–20; Mizubayashi, *Hōkensei*, p. 124; Hall, "Introduction," p. 16.

51. Takeyasu, *Kinsei tochi seisaku*, contends that from the very beginning of the Tokugawa era, deficiencies in the land survey process permitted peasants to accumulate a surplus. Hayami, "Nihon keizai shi," argues that Japan's economic and demographic growth in the 17th century would not have been possible if there had been a "complete confiscation" of the peasants' labor surplus. Of the members of the Quantitative Economic History Group, only Nishikawa Shunsaku's research bears directly on the impact of land taxation, and he focuses on a much later period ("Seisan, shōhi to shotoku katoku," in Shinbō et al., *Sūryō keizaishi nyūmon*, pp. 151–54, 165–66). Most of his colleagues ascribe 18th- and 19th-century economic transformations to other factors. See, for example, the essays in Nishikawa et al., *Nihon keizai*; Shinbō et al., *Sūryō keizaishi nyūmon*; and Shinbō and Yasuba, *Kindai ikōki*. Nishikawa Shunsaku found that without the financial contribution of nonagricultural activities, Chōshū villages would have been unable to pay the land tax. That conclusion and Thomas C. Smith's study of farm family by-employments indicate a need for caution in assessing the economic impact of land tax rates. These studies remind us that agriculture was not the sole source of income for Tokugawa villagers.

52. Miyakawa, *Taikō kenchi ron*, 1: 370–71, suggests that this phenomenon raises the possibility of an early Kinsei peasant-based surplus in at least parts of Japan.

53. Standard descriptions of this process for the Bakufu lands are found in Andō Hiroshi, *Tokugawa*, pp. 212–13; and Ōishi Tsunetaka, *Jikata hanrei roku*, 1: 143–66. On Kaga domain, see Oda Kichinojō, *Kaga-han*, pp. 358–66. Sasaki, *Daimyō*, p. 22, and Sasaki, *Bakuhan kenryoku*, pp. 101–10, present data from 17th-century Kaga domain budgets.

54. Though Western scholars generally accept this picture of the system's increased revenue-raising capability, they do not necessarily see it as confiscatory. In addition to Berry, *Hideyoshi*, p. 121, see Hall, "Hideyoshi's Domestic Policies," p. 220. Yamamura, "Returns on Unification," pp. 354–55, is skeptical that tax reform at this time effectively increased land tax rates. Yamamura is fighting the general tendency to emphasize the weight of the late-16th-century tax burden. Berry and Hall are more representative.

55. On Hideyoshi's two-thirds dictum, which is generally considered to mark the beginning of the kemi system, see Berry, *Hideyoshi*, p. 121. An English translation of this document appears in ibid., pp. 144–45; see especially item 3. It is unclear from Berry's account whether the daimyo were free to set their own tax policy (p. 116) and to take the standard expressed in this document as merely advisory (p. 150), or whether Hideyoshi in fact mandated equalized tax rates (p. 146).

56. The phrase "near money" comes from Yamamura, "From Coins to Rice," p. 361. Yamamura sees Japan's early modern hegemons as deliberately promoting this use of rice as a way to promote trade and commerce. While this evaluation

of intent may be debatable, the effect—the widespread use of rice and rice-based notes as currency—is not.

57. Jansen, "Tosa in the Seventeenth Century," pp. 115–29, 131–39; Hall, *Government and Local Power*, chaps. 10–13; Hall, "Ikeda Mitsumasa."

58. Hall, *Government and Local Power*, pp. 291, 318–23. See also Jansen, "Tosa in the Sixteenth Century," pp. 96–98; and R. Sakai, "Consolidation of Power," p. 136.

59. Hara, *Kaga-han*, pp. i–iii, 2–8.

60. Fujino, *(Shintei) Bakuhan*, apps. 1, 2. Much of the land gained by transferred daimyo appears to have come from discontinued fiefs, not from fiefs reduced as punishments. The majority of affected domains had less than 70,000 koku.

61. Ibid., app. 1. Bolitho, "The Han," p. 196, stresses the insecurity of daimyo tenure—citing as evidence the 95 confiscations and 250 transfers that took place between 1615 and 1650—but then notes (p. 205) that "the death of Tokugawa Iemitsu . . . in 1651 virtually marked the end of any consistent assault on *han* prerogatives and responsibilities. Thereafter, Tokugawa authority began to deteriorate and . . . never regained its original impetus." (Similarly, see Hall, "Bakuhan System," p. 150.) Bolitho, *Treasures*, pp. 7–10, also disagrees with the position I have outlined. For all the stress he lays on the effectiveness of Bakufu controls on domain administration (transfers, two different kinds of Bakufu inspectors, etc.), other than presenting anecdotal evidence, he does not analyze the extent to which these were effectively employed to enforce administrative ordinances. The purposes they served almost exclusively were to eliminate potential competitors and consolidate Bakufu control of strategic territories (commercial as well as military). Even James White's discussion of the Bakufu's increased exercise of force in "State Growth" focuses largely on what legal scholars call diversity cases, conflicts that transcend the boundaries of a single domain. The cases White examines are also relatively close to Edo and because of their size can be seen as serious threats to the stability of the existing order; they were not cases involving only one domain. Still, many states like Tokugawa Japan have used the device of adjudicating diversity disputes to increase their power.

62. On Hideyoshi and the relationship of transfers to the management of internal domain policies, see Berry, *Hideyoshi*, p. 129. On the lack of enforcement mechanisms, see ibid., p. 137; Bolitho, *Treasures*, pp. 9–10; and Bolitho, "The Han," p. 194.

63. See, for example, the treatments of Befu, "Village Autonomy"; Vlastos, *Peasant Protests*; and Bix, *Peasant Protest*.

64. White, "State Growth"; Migdal, *Strong Societies*.

65. Hall, *Government and Local Power*, pp. 9–10, cites patrimonial bureaucracy as a common element in Japanese history and sees the early modern era as one that effectively relied on this means to rule. The increasingly bureaucratic nature of government shaped the attempts to legitimate shogunal rule (pp. 350–51). At a practical level the Laws of the Military Houses forced daimyo to accept shogunal meddling in the operations of domains (p. 368). In characterizing the early modern

state as I do, I agree with Berry who, in "Public Peace," moves away from conceiving of the early modern state as a Weberian "rationalized" order. See also White, "State Growth," p. 7. This may also be the kind of phenomenon Conrad Totman has in mind when he refers to the early modern order as an "integral bureaucracy" (*Japan Before Perry*, p. 137).

66. Hall, *Government and Local Power*, p. 15. Both Jansen, "Tosa in the Sixteenth Century," and R. Sakai, "Consolidation of Power," show a measure of sensitivity to the problem of variation. However, the two domains are generally treated as exceptional in the extent to which they permitted the continuance of rusticated samurai.

67. A widely known example is the way in which scholars deal with the practice of recording the names of two "owners" next to each measured plot of land (*buntsuke*) in a survey document. In Hideyoshi's view only one person had rights to a given field.

68. This effort resulted in several essays on land-surveying practices and tenure systems. The findings of the most pertinent are noted in the following chapters.

69. In approaching my subject in this fashion, I am following one of the uses the *Annales* historians have made of local historical materials. This is also part of the approach of others sympathetic to the use of social science concepts and methodologies in historical studies. See, for example, Skocpol, "Emerging Agendas"; and Berkhofer, *Behavioral Approach*.

70. Hara, *Kaga-han*; Matsushita, *Bakuhansei shakai*.

71. Hanley and Yamamura, *Economic and Demographic Change*, pp. 53, 56, 61; Smith, "Premodern Economic Growth," p. 132; McClain, *Kanazawa*, p. 2. From the early 18th century, the overall rate of population growth in Kaga domain was approximately the same as for the nation as a whole (1621–1872), 0.16% a year (Hanley and Yamamura, pp. 56, 61). In the absence of any unique natural conditions, disasters, or plagues, this suggests that growth patterns in the preceding century or so were also close to the national average.

72. Calculated from area estimates in Nakamura Satoru, *Meiji ishin*, app. chart 2; and population estimates in Hanley and Yamamura, *Economic and Demographic Change*, p. 40.

73. Shimode, *Ishikawa ken*, p. 134.

74. Yamaguchi Keiji, "Han taisei," pp. 101–21, outlines the different ways of categorizing domains and discusses several daimyo whose rise predated that of Oda Nobunaga but who ultimately went through transfers, including Tokugawa Ieyasu.

Chapter 2

1. Fujino, *(Shintei) Bakuhan*, apps. 1, 2.

2. For a discussion of the significance of Nobunaga's struggle against this sect, see McMullin, *Buddhism*. The period of the Ikkō sect's control in the Hokuriku is commonly referred to as the Ikkō *ikki*. For a history of the movement, see Davis, "Kaga Ikkō Ikki."

3. Shimode, *Ishikawa ken*, pp. 117–19; Wakabayashi, "Kaga-han," in Kodama, *Monogatari Hanshi*, p. 108. For an extended treatment of Toshiie, see Iwasawa, *Maeda Toshiie*. Most of Iwasawa's work is devoted to Toshiie's life outside the domain. His youth and rise to prominence within Nobunaga's forces are treated in chaps. 2 and 3.

4. Quoted in Elison, "Cross and Sword," p. 74.

5. Shimode, *Ishikawa ken*, p. 113; Sakai Seiichi, *Toyama-han*, p. 32.

6. Sakai Seiichi, *Toyama-han*, p. 33.

7. Shimode, *Ishikawa ken*, p. 120.

8. *NSS, Tsūshi-hen*: 299.

9. Iwasawa, *Maeda Toshiie*, pp. 86–87.

10. *NSS, Tsūshi-hen*: 300. For a more complete history, see McClain, *Kanazawa*.

11. Sakai Seiichi, *Toyama-han*, pp. 36–37.

12. Shimode, *Ishikawa ken*, p. 119; Davis, "Kaga Ikkō Ikki," p. 129.

13. Sakai Seiichi, *Toyama-han*, p. 37.

14. Davis, "Kaga Ikkō Ikki," p. 129; Iwasawa, *Maeda Toshiie*, pp. 110–15.

15. Sakai Seiichi, *Toyama-han*, p. 38.

16. Iwasawa, *Maeda Toshiie*, pp. 70–71.

17. Quoted in Berry, *Hideyoshi*, p. 218.

18. Elison, "Hideyoshi," pp. 236–37.

19. Tanaka Yoshio, *Jōkamachi Kanazawa*, p. 5.

20. Ibid.

21. Bolitho, *Treasures*, p. 4.

22. Quoted in Totman, *Tokugawa Ieyasu*, p. 59.

23. Hara, *Kaga-han*, pp. 52–57, describes these events. As a reward, Honda's fief was increased substantially.

24. This pattern of marital interrelationships between the Maeda and the Tokugawa was a typical means through which major daimyo were tied to the shogunate. The shogun reinforced the pattern by arranging marriages between daimyo houses, too. For a full discussion of Maeda involvement in marital politics, see Taitō, "Kaga-han."

25. Tanaka Yoshio, *Jōkamachi Kanazawa*, pp. 5–6; Shimode, *Ishikawa ken*, pp. 127–28; *IKS*, 2: 275–78.

26. Hara, *Kaga-han*, pp. 51–63, 79, explores the use of kōgi at this time. On pp. 74–78 he also explores daimyo-Bakufu relations, especially in the context of the employment and policies of Honda Masashige. Takazawa, "Maeda Toshinaga," and Kigoshi, "Keichō-ki Kaga-han," analyze retainer control and the development of factions threatening enough to prompt Toshinaga to have some retainers assassinated.

27. Sakai Seiichi, *Toyama-han*, p. 65.

28. Wakabayashi, *Maeda Tsunanori*, pp. 6–7.

29. Though there is no direct evidence on what motivated Toshitsune in this matter, local historians tend to emphasize to one degree or another his desire to protect Kaga domain from possible reduction or confiscation. For a discussion of

the most prominent explanations, see Brown, "Domain Formation," pp. 61–63.

30. Fujino, *(Shintei) Bakuhan*, app. 1, parts 2 and 3.

31. See, for example, Hall, *Government and Local Power*, p. 389; DiCenzo, "Daimyo," pp. 53–55; and F. Oda, "Saga Han," pp. 218ff.

32. *Oyabe shi shi*, 1: 258.

Chapter 3

1. Sakai Seiichi, "Kaga-han shotō"; Kigoshi, "Kaga-han seiritsu ki."

2. See, for example, *Toide chō shi*, pp. 243–44; *Ishikawa ken shi shiryō*, p. 159; and Nakamura Kichiji, "Shoki Kaga-han," p. 426.

3. *IKS*, 3: 770, discusses several documents claiming that Oda sent officials to survey the provinces of Kaga, Noto, and Etchu. In the most intriguing of these, the *Etsu-Nō-Ka san shū shi*, we find the assertion that Sugaya Nagayori and Fukutomi Yukikiyo were sent out to conduct a survey in 1581. But though the two were in fact ordered into Noto with Toshiie, there is no evidence that they conducted any surveys. Authors of local histories in the Toyama prefecture area are perhaps more inclined to stress Oda's role to account for Etchu's having a *tan* of 360 bu, rather than 300 bu as in Kaga and Noto. As they would have it, Oda's death interrupted the survey process before it reached Etchu. See *Toide chō shi*, pp. 246–47.

4. See, for example, *Kosugi chō shi*, p. 85; and *Kurobe shi shi*, 1: 90. Wajima, "Kinsei sonraku," p. 43, goes further and argues, in a similar vein to Araki Moriaki and Sasaki Junnosuke, that in this recording of field and holder, the kenchi was designed to develop small independent landholders.

5. McClain, *Kanazawa*, p. 28. See also p. 21 for the national pattern of surveys in which McClain places Kaga developments.

6. I have found references to a total of 10 *nawauchichō* and *mizuchō* that bear a resemblance to the land survey documents of Hideyoshi. For one of these, Sen-kōji village (Ishikawa county), a survey is reported for 1583, but no survey document has been located, only a fief grant that includes this village. Oda Kichinojō, *Kaga-han*, pp. 221, 223, reports a survey for Okinami village (Fugeshi county) dated 1583.9.22. Although I have not seen the survey document myself, Kigoshi, "Maeda," p. 21, fn. 1, verifies its existence.

7. See, for example, Kigoshi, "Kan'ei-ki Chōke ryō ni okeru kenchi."

8. Oda Kichinojō, *Kaga-han*, pp. 219–21, presents an excerpt from this survey. See *NSS*, 3: 327–33, for a full copy.

9. Miyakawa, *Taikō kenchi ron*, 3: 170–270, presents some typical survey documents that are thought to be actual measurements.

10. *KHNK*, 1: 62. This same kind of contrast between vague and precise expressions of area size can be seen in early sashidashi Taikō kenchi documents and later, more standardized documents from actual measurements. See the *mizuchō* for Kano village and the Amakawa village *kenchichō* in Miyakawa, *Taikō kenchi ron*, 3: 156–69, 170–218, respectively.

11. *KHNK*, 1: 62, and Kigoshi, "Maeda," p. 23, concur with this evaluation.

12. *KK*, p. 1174.

13. Kigoshi, "Maeda," pp. 23, 25. Evidence for these surveys is found not only in copies of survey documents but also in tax receipts. They were conducted after relations between the Uesugi and Toyotomi forces had stabilized in 1585, and the Maeda domains were less threatened by strong neighboring military forces.

14. Ibid., p. 20.

15. *KK*, p. 743.

16. *KHNK*, 1: 64; Kigoshi, "Maeda," p. 26. See the discussion in Brown, "Domain Formation," pp. 141–42.

17. *Himi shi shi*, pp. 1172–73, 1232–33.

18. Ibid., pp. 1172–73.

19. Sakai Seiichi, "Kaga-han shoki," p. 19, considers all Tenshō survey documents to be of the sashidashi type and therefore has no quarrel with Wakabayashi's and Kigoshi's evaluations of the earliest Kaga and Noto survey documents.

20. *Himi shi shi*, p. 1174.

21. Ibid., p. 1176.

22. *ES*, 2: 50.

23. See the survey documents for Akigashima, Kosuganuma, and Inamochi villages in *TKSS*, pp. 392–94; and the survey document for Iisakano shin village in *Kamiichi chō shi*, pp. 264–65.

24. *Kosugi chō shi*, p. 86; Oda Kichinojō, *Kaga-han*, pp. 226–27; *ES*, 2: 115.

25. *Tonami shi shi*, pp. 306–7.

26. Data from these documents are presented in Sakai Seiichi, "Kaga-han shotō," p. 8. Printed copies of a number of documents may be found in *Himi shi shi*, pp. 1179, 1181–82; and *Fukuoka chō shi*, pp. 1050, 1143, 1231, 1232.

27. *Tonami shi shi*, pp. 301–2; *Kamiichi chō shi*, pp. 265–66.

28. See *Kamiichi chō shi*, pp. 265–66, on Isakano shin and Ishibari villages; and *Tonami shi shi*, pp. 301–2, on Yasukawa village.

29. Oda Kichinojō, *Kaga-han*, p. 92.

30. This is a generous estimate of the growth in the number of villages. Given that villages were combined or disestablished as well as established during this period, the actual number of villages at the time of the surveys may have been even larger. If so, that would only reinforce my claim.

31. *IKS*, 3: 782; *Ishikawa ken Takamatsu chō shi*, p. 201.

32. *IKS*, 3: 782–83; *KHS*, 2: 376.

33. See *Hakui shi shi*, p. 130, for one clear example of a village partly administered by the daimyo. Without exception, the survey documents I examined for this period (15 from 1616, 33 from 1620) do not give the tax rate for villages or parts of villages administered by landed retainers.

34. *Kashima chō shi*, pp. 430, 433; *NSS*, 3: 96, 113.

35. *NSS*, 3: 53, 94–95, 111, 113, 146, 188, 334, 426; *KHNK*, 1: 129; *Kashima chō shi*, pp. 434, 453.

36. The manuscript is in the Toyama University Library, Toyama City. It is part of the Kawai Monjo Collection, section Ume no Yon.

37. A more detailed outline of these procedures, as well as standard methods, appears in Brown, "Mismeasure of Land," pp. 115–55.

38. According to the area figures and kokudaka estimates in "Shōhō san nen taka mononari chō genkō," a manuscript in the Ka-Etsu-Nō Bunko, Kanazawa City Library, the kokumori for Enuma and Nomi counties was 1.7 and 1.2 koku per *tan* for paddy and dry fields, respectively, until the mid-17th century, when they were given the same value—1.7 per *tan*.

39. *ES*, 2: 419.

40. See Brown, "Domain Formation," pp. 167–73, on the origins of this practice. *WSS*, 2: 212, 276, presents the first documentation of its use.

41. Iwasawa, *Maeda Toshiie*, p. 162.

42. Berry, *Hideyoshi*, pp. 117, 120. Similarly, see Susser, "Toyotomi Regime," pp. 139–40.

43. Measuring rods of varying length were in use during the Taikō kenchi era in Awa, Settsu, Chikuzen, Satsuma, Osumi, Hyuga, Hizen, Hitachi, and Shinshu provinces; Sendai, Akita, Nanbu, and Shinjō domains. After 1600, variations were evident in Satsuma, Ise (in part), Matsushiro, Owari, Kaga, Iwashiro, Iwaki, Rikuzen, Akita, Nanbu, and Shijō. See Iinuma, *Kokudakasei*, pp. 128, 160–62; and Oda Kichinojō, *Kaga-han*, pp. 217ff, for Kaga. Kanzaki, *Kenchi*, pp. 63, 68, discusses the Taikō kenchi and Tokugawa standards. On the final example of the short rod, see Iinuma, *Kokudakasei*, p. 180. This list is very conservative. More variant regions and domains could probably be discovered by culling the recent work of local historians. Although most examples of variant standards discussed here and below come from the late 16th and early 17th centuries, Iinuma's data indicate that variations persisted throughout the early modern era.

44. Hegemons may have encouraged but did not force this transformation. For other viewpoints, see Nagahara (with Yamamura), "Sengoku Daimyo," pp. 28–30. Wakita, "Kokudaka System," p. 304, argues that the kandaka system was not typical. Yamamura extends the kandaka region into Shikoku, northern Kyushu, and the Chugoku. I believe that the differences between Wakita and Yamamura over which areas to count as kandaka reflect the difficulty of characterizing politically diverse regions. Yamamura poses a top-down paradigm for the transformation ("From Coins to Rice," pp. 353–54, 364). My inclusion of part of Hokuriku in the category of rice-based assessments relies on my analysis of pre-Maeda land taxation below.

45. See, for example, Wakita, "Kokudaka System," p. 310.

46. Iinuma, *Kokudakasei*, p. 146; Takahashi, *Miyagi ken*, pp. 133–36.

47. Iinuma, *Kokudakasei*, p. 150.

48. Takayanagi and Takeuchi, *Nihon shi jiten*, p. 1130.

49. After the defeat of their allies the Takeda, the Sanada had joined Ieyasu and then Hideyoshi (Hirasawa, *Kinsei sonraku e*, pp. 231, 234, 260).

50. Miyakawa, *Taikō kenchi ron*, 3: 324–25, reproduces the instructions to the Aizu surveyors. See also Miyazaki, *Aomori ken*, pp. 127–28; and Handa Ichitarō, "Ushū Yūri karidaka kō," pp. 14–15.

51. Oda Kichinojō, *Kaga-han*, p. 253 reproduces this report. The same source also gives the domain's assessed value for 1590 in koku, but the data are suspect. They exclude figures from Niikawa, which had been entrusted to the Maeda three years earlier. They also exclude Enuma, which was not yet part of Kaga han. But

neither was Nomi county, yet it was apparently included in the value of Kaga province. These confusions suggest that later data were attributed to 1590 by an author unfamiliar with developments in Kaga han. Under the circumstances, it is difficult to be fully confident that Toshiie used koku in his reports to Hideyoshi.

52. Yasuzawa, *Kinsei sonraku keisei*, p. 72.

53. Handa Ichitarō, "Ushū Yūri karidaka kō," pp. 14–15.

54. Yamamura, "From Coins to Rice," p. 359. Berry, *Hideyoshi*, p. 112, argues, without substantiation, that "most remaining provinces, largely held by *tozama*, were examined by representatives of local daimyo who, in general, employed Hideyoshi's guidelines." Later, on p. 118, she reiterates, again without documentation: "Active surveys were taking place in some of these [tozama] areas, and they tended to conform to Hideyoshi's own guidelines for inspection and measurement."

55. Berry, *Hideyoshi*, pp. 113, 114.

56. Such reports may not have come from "proprietors," but they still originated with people other than a daimyo agent, individuals who had a vested interest in distorting the results. For claims of tozama submission, see, for example, ibid., p. 117; and Araki Moriaki, *Taikō kenchi to kokudaka sei*, pp. 126–28, 132–44. See Iinuma, *Kokudakasei*, p. 150, on Matsumoto domain; Miyazaki, *Aomori ken*, p. 128, on Tohoku; and Iinuma, *Kokudakasei*, p. 146, on the Date, who continued to use their own kandaka system. Handa and Yokoyama, *Yamagata ken*, p. 108, discuss the lack of evidence confirming actual measurement. According to Matsushita, *Bakuhansei shakai*, pp. 209–33, Satsuma did not make any surveys under Hideyoshi. See also his careful and critical studies of the mechanics and uses of surveys in other Kyushu domains in the same volume. Matsushita's subsequent article "Yanagawa-han shoki" reinforces the argument I make for the manipulative techniques and variant procedures used in land investigations.

57. On the ikenchi, see Brown, "Mismeasure of Land," p. 138; and Ōishi Tsunetaka, *Jikata hanrei roku*, 1: 77, 85. As we will see, the villagers who gathered data for the warichi surveyed large sections of the village at one time.

58. Yamamura, "From Coins to Rice," p. 357, says: "These [the Unifiers'] surveys measured the real yields of paddies far more accurately than had surveys by Sengoku daimyo."

59. Oda Kichinojō, *Ishikawa ken*, p. 320.

60. Yasuzawa, *Kinsei sonraku keisei*, pp. 26–33.

61. *Hansei seiritsu*, p. 493.

62. Kashiwakura, "Tokugawa," p. 1017.

63. Ibid., pp. 1018–19.

64. Iinuma, *Kokudakasei*, pp. 107–8, 151. Land was graded, however, and social distinctions among the listed landholders were indicated by writing the family names in different size characters and in different locations, along with a note on the person's status (Jansen, "Tosa in the Sixteenth Century," pp. 96–98).

65. Yamamura, "From Coins to Rice," p. 359.

66. In addition to the evidence on Shinano already presented, see Hirasawa, *Kinsei sonraku e*, pp. 263–64. On Satsuma, see Matsushita, *Bakuhansei shakai*, pp. 209–33.

67. Berry, *Hideyoshi*, p. 118.

68. There were limits to how far hegemons and daimyo were willing to go for the sake of exactness. Although more precise techniques became known during the 17th century, they were never widely introduced. See Brown, "Mismeasure of Land"; and Brown, "Never the Twain Shall Meet."

69. See, for example, the description of the Imagawa surveys cited in Nagahara (with Yamamura), "Sengoku Daimyo," pp. 39–40, especially table 1.1. Differentiation under Oda's surveys is widely recognized.

70. Berry, having noted that Hideyoshi's agents only surveyed 20 to 30 (of more than 70) provinces and having indicated numerous limitations (*Hideyoshi*, pp. 112–18), then asserts, with scant analysis of any data but Hideyoshi's edicts, "Hideyoshi improved upon the most advanced registration techniques of his age to achieve exceptional results. He oversaw the registration of much of the country's land; he demanded that Toyotomi deputies or daimyo officials . . . supervise that registration; he defined universal standards of measurement that were employed widely; he required the direct inspection of land." Substantial evidence of the effectiveness of Hideyoshi's orders and the conscious imitation of his efforts by independent daimyo is needed to validate such assertions. If, with his own agents present in Satsuma, Hideyoshi could not get a well-implemented survey based on actual measurements, it is impossible to assume compliance in areas where daimyo implemented their own.

The synchronous or near-synchronous use of similar standards is not adequate to establish a causal relationship, since Hideyoshi's own standards of measure generally came from those already in use (the size of a *tan* is the exception). For example, contrary to Berry, p. 263, n.35, which cites the use of Hideyoshi's standard measuring rod in Kaga as evidence of his impact on measures, this standard was in use before the Maeda's alliance with him in mid-1583; hence the source of the common standard lay outside their subordinate relationship to him, perhaps in the shared tutelage of Oda Nobunaga (on related concerns, see Iinuma, *Kokudakasei*, pp. 128–29). Furthermore, Berry's argument for Hideyoshi's influence in this instance cannot explain why the Maeda failed to adopt Hideyoshi's other standards simultaneously (e.g., the 300-bu *tan*) or why diverse measuring standards persisted in other areas directly investigated by Hideyoshi's agents (e.g., Awa and Chikugo). To document a causal role of Hideyoshi's edicts calls for a long-term analysis of local data, compiled by administrative units or daimyo rather than provinces, as is common despite the fact that they were not administrative units. (Above, I have counted provinces as an expedient to place Kaga's experience in broader context and to show that even these limited data reveal a more complex process than is widely thought, raising questions about the reach of Hideyoshi's state.) Such local analysis will likely revise evaluations of additional cases like Satsuma and Kaga that are often seen to support claims of Hideyoshi's influence.

71. Hall, *Government and Local Power*, p. 357.

72. Kashiwakura, "Tokugawa," pp. 1026–30.

73. Iinuma, *Kokudakasei*, pp. 178–81.

74. Hall, "Japan's Sixteenth-Century Revolution," p. 18, indicates that the

Gamō were moved because they lied about their survey results. But he does not cite his source, and I have not found any evidence to that effect. The move came in 1598, three years after Gamō Ujisato's death. The survey was conducted during his tenure as daimyo. The land investigations, which were begun in 1591 and completed within the Bunroku era (1592–95), ran into stiff local opposition (Kobayashi and Yamada, *Fukushima Ken*, pp. 96–102). But assuming Hall is correct, this lone example (at most) suggests that there were very broad limits to the process I have described.

75. Matsushita, *Bakuhansei shakai*, pp. 220–28. The survey of the Date domains may also have taken place under these considerations. See Iinuma, *Kokudakasei*, p. 146.

76. Wakita, "Kokudaka System," argues that just the opposite was true: the system was devised for the specific purpose of fostering unification.

77. Berry, *Hideyoshi*, p. 118, argues that survey deviations from Hideyoshi's principles were the result of the "imperfect judgment of his magistrates . . . working . . . with . . . biased informants." She further argues that this imperfect judgment should not "conceal the extent of his reach." However, such variations as the use of kandaka instead of kokudaka, the use of a variety of survey methods (e.g., the continued reliance on sashidashi), some of which were imprecise even for the time, and the use of nonstandard measuring rods cannot be ascribed to imperfect judgment or biased informants. They help define the limits of Hideyoshi's reach.

78. Elison, "Cross and Sword," Elison, "Hideyoshi," and Wheelwright, "A Visualization," all stress the importance of "image" in reinforcing the authority of Oda Nobunaga and Toyotomi Hideyoshi.

Chapter 4

1. See Hayami, "Ryōshu"; Hayami, "Kinsei shoki"; and Hayami, "Kenchi tōrokunin."

2. For a more complete discussion of these and other limitations of survey techniques, see Brown, "Mismeasure of Land."

3. The latter was theoretically possible, for by the late 16th century the compass and astrolabe had been introduced in Japan. For a full discussion of the more precise techniques that the Japanese rejected, see Brown, "Never the Twain Shall Meet." Some readers may feel that paddy ridges should have eliminated the need to mark field boundaries; however, villagers were known to shift ridges surreptitiously so as to encroach on a neighboring field or extend their plots incrementally into uncultivated areas through a process called *kirisoe*. Paddy ridges made very unstable barriers. And of course dry fields would not have had ridges to define them.

4. See Furushima, "Warichi seido"; and the introductory sections of Aono, *Nihon kinsei warichisei shi*.

5. Furushima, "Warichi seido"; Aono, *Nihon kinsei warichisei shi*, pp. 201–3. Much of the early work on warichi focused on the question of how it arose, an issue I hope to deal with in future research.

6. The list of domains is based on the two works cited in n. 5. The assessed

value for all Japan is from Hanley and Yamamura, *Economic and Demographic Change*, p. 71, and the data for domains come from individual domain entries in Takayanagi and Takeuchi, *Nihon shi jiten*. Data were not available for all the domains listed by Furushima and Aono. Furthermore, several classic studies treat entire provinces instead of domains; rather than risk duplication, I have therefore excluded the provincial data. As a result, a number of areas (e.g., most parts of Echigo) are omitted from these calculations.

7. Inoue, *Niigata ken*, pp. 145–46. The warichi system was so widespread in Echigo that the area quickly became the focus of some of the earliest articles on the practice. The most important of these are cited in Furushima, "Warichi seido." See also the section on Echigo in Aono, *Nihon kinsei warichisei shi*. In addition, many local histories from the area devote at least some space to the subject.

8. For example, see Araki Moriaki, *Bakuhan taisei shakai*, pp. 49–54, 182–90.

9. Hara, *Kaga-han*, pp. 32–33.

10. Itō, "Kinsei shoki daimyō ryō," p. 29.

11. Kigoshi, "Kan'ei-ki Chōke ryō Kashima hangun," pp. 19–21, 23.

12. The villagers' exemption from the Chō house and horse tax are recorded in official explanations of their failure to pay the tax (ibid., pp. 24–28).

13. "Kawai roku," p. 913; Tochinai, *Kyū Kaga-han*, pp. 134–36.

14. *TKSS*, p. 912.

15. "Kawai roku," p. 913.

16. The most commonly cited hypothetical case used to illustrate this process has a village of 100 koku divided into 10 shares valued at 10 koku each (ibid.)

17. Tochinai, *Kyū Kaga-han*, pp. 136–42; "Kawai roku," p. 913; *Hakui shi shi*, p. 671.

18. See, for example, the request submitted in 1679 by Omachi village in *Hakui shi shi*, p. 659.

19. This assertion accords with Popkin's argument in *The Rational Peasant*, pp. 22–27, 32–39, 46–58, that villagers will cooperate only in those activities least likely to provoke a dispute over the allocation of insurance benefits.

20. The data for these villages suggest that in mandating a maximum of 20 years between redistributions, the domain gave legal force to a customary interval. The impact of this 1838 regulation biases the intervals in the sample toward the 20-year span, but apparently in only two or three cases. Even in these the impact is generally small.

21. *Tonami shi shi*, p. 371. These two examples were selected because they illustrate the variation that could occur between villages in the same general area. Similar variations can be found in many of the local histories from the Toyama and Ishikawa prefectural areas.

22. Ibid., table 5.3 note.

23. See, for example, Oda Kichinojō, *Kaga-han*, p. 488; and Tochinai, *Kyū Kaga-han*, p. 82.

24. The document, "Go Kaisaku shimatsu kikigaki," is transcribed in *KHNK*, 1: 639–700. The passage on warichi is at p. 642.

25. Quoted in Takazawa, "Warichi," p. 138.

26. *WSS*, 1: 55–57.
27. *Noto Wajima Kamikaji-ke monjo mokuroku*, pp. 100–101.
28. *KHS*, 2: 634.
29. Examples of sales and mortages of land rights in the 17th century are common in printed local histories. See, among others, *WSS*, 1: 111, 117, 134, 136, 364.
30. The following discussion is based on *KHNK*, 1: 68–74.
31. Ibid., p. 71, table 6. Transcriptions of these and similar documents can be found on pp. 387–467 of this volume.
32. *Suzu shi shi*, pp. 359–60.
33. Ibid., pp. 260–61. For other generally similar examples, see *WSS*, 2: 678–86.
34. These data are presented in a table in *Tonami shi shi*, p. 415; the original documents from which they were taken appear in *Kaga-han shoki tomurayaku kaneko monjo*, pp. 136–47, 166–72.
35. *Suzu shi shi*, p. 261.
36. *KHS*, 2: 362–63. The prohibition was repeated in 1631 (ibid., p. 634).

Chapter 5

1. See Hall, *Government and Local Power*, chaps. 12–13; R. Sakai, "Consolidation of Power"; and Jansen, "Tosa in the Seventeenth Century." On Sendai, see Morris, *Kinsei Nihon chigyōsei*. The mechanisms through which officials and villagers interacted also varied from one domain to another.
2. Davis, "Kaga Ikkō Ikki." McMullin, *Buddhism*, presents the conflict between the Ikkō believers and Oda in national historical context.
3. Urata, "Shoki Maeda-ke kashindan," p. 3.
4. Kigoshi, "Keichō-ki Kaga-han," pp. 338–39. Toshiie continued to place ranking retainers in the kashindan of his sons.
5. Urata, "Shoki Maeda-ke kashindan," p. 22, n. 10.
6. Okumura, "Maeda Toshiie," pp. 33–34.
7. *KHNK*, 1: 44–45.
8. Ibid., pp. 45–46.
9. Urata, "Shoki Maeda-ke kashindan," p. 8.
10. Ibid., pp. 3, 9; *WSS, Tsūshi hen*: 193.
11. *Notojima no kinsei monjo*, p. 16.
12. Urata, "Shoki Maeda-ke kashindan," pp. 3, 9; *ES*, 2: 51–52.
13. This is not a particularly surprising conclusion given that the great majority of these men belonged to what is commonly called the kokujin class.
14. Hara, *Kaga-han*, pp. 31–34.
15. *KHNK*, 1: 45. Both McClain, *Kanazawa*, p. 27, and Tsuchiya, *Hōken shakai hōkai katei*, p. 60, present somewhat different estimates. Since Wakabayashi is the doyen of Kaga studies, I have accepted his estimates.
16. For a discussion of some of the earliest means daimyo employed to restrain their retainers, see Hall, "Ikeda House," p. 80; and Hall, "Foundations," pp. 71–72.
17. For relevant documents on the forests, see Okumura, "Maeda Toshiie,"

p. 36. Some district officials (*fuchibyakushō*) did receive grants allowing them to collect duties on these resources. Such user fees were not uncommon (see Totman, *Origins*, app. 2: "*Han* Forests and Fiscal Policy"). On the miscellaneous taxes, see *Yanagida son shi*, pp. 251–52; *KK*, pp. 739, 899–900, 1015–16; and *IKS*, 3: 16–17.

18. *KHS*, 1: 281–82, 359, 532–33, 565–66, presents some examples. At other times a smaller region, still larger than a village, was designated (ibid., pp. 260–61).

19. For discussion and documents on several widely dispersed holdings, see *KHNK*, 1: 51–52; Urata, "Shoki Maeda-ke kashindan," p. 10; and Okumura, "Maeda Toshiie," pp. 35–36.

20. See the fief distribution grants in *KK*, pp. 757–58, 777–78, 852, 916, 1015–16; *WSS*, 1: 265–66; *IKS*, 3: 161–67; *Tonami shi shi*, pp. 305–6; and *Oku Noto Tokikuni-ke monjo*, p. 21; and the retainer holdings listed in "Kan'ei kyū nen hachi gatsu Tonami gun Toide mura Matauemon gumi furudaka shinkai sashiagedaka mononari onchō," in *TKSS*, 3, *Furoku*: 6–14. In all these sources, where a retainer's holdings were obviously large, there were fewer part-village holdings.

21. *KK*, pp. 899–900.

22. *Tonami shi shi*, pp. 305–6.

23. Only seven of the 45 villages in district chief Matauemon's jurisdiction in 1629–31 were under the control of just one master ("Kan'ei kyū nen . . . ," as cited in n. 20, above).

24. *KK*, pp. 1015–16.

25. *Oku Noto Tokikuni-ke monjo*, p. 21.

26. "Kan'ei kyū nen . . ." (see n. 20, above). Twenty-one of 45 villages experienced at least one change during the three years recorded in this document.

27. Urata, "Shoki Maeda-ke kashindan," pp. 3, 7.

28. All data are from ibid., p. 18.

29. Wajima, "Kaga-han," p. 82, imputes the appearance of "fuchibyakushō" only in Noto to the region's susceptibility to invasion from the sea (most of the known fuchibyakushō were from coastal villages). This does not seem to be an adequate explanation, for fuchibyakushō were appointed as late as 1588, well after any major threat of an invasion of the domain was over. Furthermore, both Kaga and Etchu provinces had extensive, vulnerable coastlines.

30. *Suzu shi shi*, p. 667.

31. Ibid., p. 711.

32. *KHNK*, 1: 534, 536, 538.

33. Some number of these grants to temples and shrines are printed in *KK* and *KHS*, passim. Other, similar conveyances can be found in city, town, and village histories of Ishikawa and Toyama prefectures.

34. For a discussion of a famous shrine that had declined during the 16th century, with a resulting loss of local influence, and then made a comeback with Maeda support, see Kigoshi, "Keichō-ki Kaga-han," especially pp. 332–37.

35. Hara, *Kaga-han*, pp. 10–12; *KK*, p. 1708.

36. *KHNK*, 1: 530; *Fukuoka chō shi*, p. 1205.

37. *KHNK*, 1: 539. For other examples of local assistance to Toshiie, see ibid., pp. 530, 536, 546. See also Chap. 8, below.

38. *Ishikawa ken Shio chō shi*, p. 128. Yukinaga was one of the local men who helped Toshiie set up his first headquarters at the Kita Shrine.

39. *Ishikawa ken Unoke chō shi*, p. 155.

40. Evidence for Ikkō links may be found also in the biographies of families that became *tomura*, the fuchibyakushō's successors. Their genealogies are reprinted or summarized in many of the village, town, and city histories of Ishikawa and Toyama prefectures. *KHNK*, 1: 524–93, gives two of the larger genealogical compilations.

41. Hara, *Kaga-han*, pp. 12–13.

42. Hara argues (ibid., pp. 9–15) that the distinction between these grants marks the beginning of the separation of warrior and peasant. For his discussion of distinctions between types of grant, see pp. 10–11.

43. *Ishikawa ken Unoke chō shi*, pp. 170–71.

44. *Oshimizu chō shi*, p. 195.

45. See *KHNK*, 1: 524–93. *Kanō shiwa*, p. 58, and *Himi shi shi*, pp. 738–39, discuss three examples of villagers in Etchu who might be ranked as fuchibyakushō. Genealogies for Kaga *tomura* include men who received land from Toshiie (see *KHNK*, 1: 525, 530). Such cases, I believe, deserve to be considered on a par with fuchibyakushō.

46. On Jirōzaemon, see *Tonami shi shi*, p. 385. The authors claim that Jirōzaemon was a village *kimoiri*, but there is no evidence that his function was so limited. Certainly this is not clear from the document that bestowed the fuchi. On Kambei, see *KHNK*, 1: 525. The genealogy uses the term "tomura." That title did not appear until the mid-17th century, though variants were used earlier in the century (e.g., *tomura kimoiri*). The use of the term for Rokurōzaemon is clearly anachronistic, but the purport of the claim is clear. On the Watanabe, see *Unoke chō shi*, pp. 172–73.

47. McClain, *Kanazawa*, p. 35.

48. See Owada, "Sengoku daimyō Gohōjō-shi," on the Tokugawa's adoption of the Gohōjō system of village administration.

Chapter 6

1. See, for example, Befu, "Village Autonomy."

2. Davis, "Kaga Ikkō Ikki." For the broader context, see Davis, "Ikki in Late Medieval Japan."

3. This and the preceding example are from *Oshimizu chō shi*, p. 153.

4. Ibid., pp. 154–55; *Tōgi chō shi, Tsūshi hen*: 128.

5. *Yanagida son shi*, p. 234.

6. *Tōgi chō shi, Tsūshi hen*: 129.

7. *Ishikawa ken Oshino son shi*, p. 63; *Kokufu son shi*, p. 28.

8. *Ishikawa ken Unoke chō shi*, p. 49.

9. Wakabayashi, "Kaga-han no tomura," pp. 54–55; *KHNK*, 1: 101–2.

10. Kigoshi, "Maeda," pp. 36–37; *KHS*, 1: 424.

11. See, for example, the Keichō 4.2.14 document in *KK*, p. 898.

12. McClain, "Castle Towns," especially pp. 282–83.

13. *KK*, p. 846. Han policies on the recultivation of wasteland also reflect this concern.

14. *KK*, pp. 710–11. For another example, see *KK*, p. 735.

15. *KK*, pp. 819, 898 (documents dated Tenshō 16.12.25 and Keichō 4.2.14); *KHS*, 1: 837–39, 851–52, 870–71, 885–86 (documents dated Keichō 6.5.17, 7.3.26, 7.12.7, and 9.5.26).

16. *KHNK*, 1: 95–96, 100–101.

17. Ibid., pp. 96–98.

18. Hara, *Kaga-han*, pp. 18–23.

19. *KHS*, 2: 638. Clause 2 of a 1607 *ofuregaki* mentions "mura mura kimoiri," but it is unclear whether this means the (tomura) kimoiri who presided over the several villages or the kimoiri of an individual village. Since the commoner officials referred to in the remainder of the document are tomura, it is likely that the reference is to them, not village officials. A document issued in 1611 by Yokoyama Yamashiro no kami to one of the villages in his fief mentions the "headman of the present village [tō mura kimoiri]" (Sakai Seiichi, *Kaga-han kaisakuhō*, pp. 200–201). Though it is clear from examples of the latter sort that formal offices were recognized, the lack of documents specifying their duties suggests that they still played a very limited role in the thinking of domain officials and landed retainers.

20. Kigoshi, "Maeda," p. 29. There is no evidence that daikan were used as land surveyors after the very early period of Maeda rule.

21. Ibid.

22. *Noto Wajima Kamikaji-ke monjo*, pp. 86–87.

23. Kigoshi, "Maeda," pp. 30–31.

24. *Noto Wajima Kamikaji-ke monjo*, p. 86.

25. *KK*, p. 739.

26. *Suzu shi shi*, pp. 13–14.

27. *KHS*, 1: 424; *KK*, p. 846. After promising that loan rice would be provided and demands for unpaid taxes (*mishin*) would cease, Yasukatsu encouraged villagers to return and devote themselves wholeheartedly to farming.

28. *KHS*, 1: 476.

Chapter 7

1. The last is a clear corollary of the clarifying of village boundaries, a matter we will take up shortly. It is also in conformity with later kenchi regulations.

2. In theory one might estimate accuracy by comparing late Edo survey and Meiji land tax reform data. For Kaga that would require detailed records of what the domain surveyors did in adjusting for dry fields or else the full unadjusted data on which they calculated a village's assessed value. I have not located the requisite documents for even one village.

3. The same 1589 documents that first mention *hatake ori* in Tokikuni and Ono villages indicate that the annual tax for mountain dry fields was calculated separately and was not included in calculating the village's assessed value. A survey document for Yamada village includes the same notation. (See *WSS*, 2: 212, 276;

Hamade, *Morohashi son shi*, pp. 344–45.) A 1587 ordinance suggests that some mountain dry fields were reclaimed land and therefore subject to exemption from the main land tax: "Since here and there mountain dry fields have been newly reclaimed and the previously taxed fields have gone to waste, the annual land tax is to be assessed on those mountain dry fields." To further encourage the retention of old fields, villagers were told, "If the previously taxed fields have not become wasteland, they are to be exempted." Though this was presumably a short-term measure, the clear implication is that up to this point no systematic effort had been made to tax reclaimed lands. (*KHS*, 1: 347; *KK*, p. 809.)

4. These fields were called *nagibatake*. Eleven other Noto villages surveyed in 1620 that cultivated mountain fields this way had a comparable exemption. Slash-and-burn agriculture was typical in the mountain areas of Noto (*WSS*, 2: 54). Where this technique was widely used, it must have been difficult to keep tax records, since fields would have been constantly going in and out of production. (See for example, the documents describing nagibatake in *Monzen chō shi*, p. 73; *Ishikawa ken shi shiryō*, pp. 157–59; *IKS*, 3: 484–85; *WSS*, 2: 284, 462, 515; *Yanagida son shi*, pp. 259, 1270; *Suzu shi shi*, pp. 106, 632.)

5. *Himi shi shi*, pp. 1184–85.

6. It is clear from the way the tax on these fields was recorded and later assimilated into the basic land tax that it was not one of the domain's miscellaneous taxes (*komononari*).

7. For example, the copy of the 1586 survey of Tokikuni village was made on 1620.11.3. That was precisely the time of the Genna 6 land survey. The copy was made by three officials, two of whom, Asano Shokan and Uemura Hachizaemon, were *kenchi bugyō* for the Genna investigation. (*WSS*, 2: 211.)

8. See *KHNK*, 1: 542, for one example. If the officials took any documents, they left copies in the village officials' collections.

9. *Toide chō shi*, pp. 1365–66.

10. *Shinminato shi shi*, p. 630.

11. Sakai Seiichi, *Kaga-han kaisakuhō*, p. 140; *Kaga-han shoki tomurayaku Kaneko monjo*, p. 4.

12. *Toide chō shi*, pp. 244–45.

13. *KHS*, 2: 377.

14. Ibid., p. 639; *Oshimizu chō shi*, p. 183.

15. *KHS*, 2: 632.

16. Kigoshi, "Kaga-han no muradaka"; Kigoshi, "Kaga-han gochō shindendaka ni tsuite."

17. Brown, "Domain Formation," pp. 163–64.

18. See Brown, "Mismeasure of Land."

19. Iinuma, *Kokudakasei no kenkyū*, pp. 44–45.

20. *Himi shi shi*, pp. 782–83.

21. *Suzu shi shi*, p. 104; *KK*, p. 1177.

22. Other receipts from the same district for 1582 taxes or earlier further substantiate the use of cash for the first two years of Maeda rule (*Suzu shi shi*, pp. 11–12). Since cash and rice assessments in the pre-Maeda period appear to have

been interchangeable, it is possible that taxes for some villages were based on rice assessments as well.

23. Both documents are from ibid., p. 626. See p. 158 for a typical tax bill/receipt.

24. *WSS*, 1: 224.

25. *Suzu shi shi*, p. 14.

26. *Nakajima chō shi*, p. 413; *KK*, p. 815.

27. For a more detailed comparison of the interrelationship between taxes collected, wasteland, reclamation, and shittai, see Brown, "Domain Formation," pp. 211–12.

28. As we will see, typically only 5–10% of the assessed taxes went unpaid.

29. Domain policies and incentives did not stabilize until the mid-17th century, but the special treatment accorded newly opened land required a separate set of books. By the 1616 regulations, reclaimed land had to be part of the village total in province-wide surveys. Even if it was not incorporated in this sweeping fashion, all reclaimed land was ultimately added to the existing registers and taxed at the standard village rate.

30. For example, the 1582 tax bill for Nishiumi district was dated 7.20, that of 1583, 11.20 (*Suzu shi shi*, pp. 626–27). The 1583 tax bill for Ozawa village was dated in the 11th month, that of 1587 for Kumagi 7.10 (Ōzawa: Kigoshi, "Maeda," p. 22; Kumagi: *Nakajima chō shi*, p. 413).

31. *Suzu shi shi*, pp. 735–36.

32. Konpōji village's Tenshō 13 tax receipt (ibid., pp. 739–40) is one example. Ushio village's interim receipt for its 1585 taxes was issued in 1586.7, and final payment was acknowledged by Toshiie's seal on the same document in 1587.6 (*WSS*, 1: 221).

33. *Oku Noto Tokikuni-ke monjo*, pp. 3, 5; *NSS*, 3: 186, 306; *KK*, p. 1012.

34. In the one report of an investigation of crop damage—due to lack of water (*hiyake*; lit., "scorched")—there is no indication that the previous year's taxes were affected. All internal evidence suggests that the exemption applied only to the year in which the survey was conducted, 1590 (*NSS*, p. 186; *hen* 3: 186).

35. *TKSS*, p. 66.

36. Takazawa, "Tenshō-ki nengu san'yōjo," pp. 713, 717 n. 3. Kigoshi, "Maeda," and Takazawa, "Tenshō-ki nengu san'yōjo," both consider wasteland an indicator of cultivator desertion. But if officials consistently made a distinction between "wasteland" and abandoned land, then there is virtually no evidence supporting that position.

37. The three survey documents for 1586 are exceptions; all are dated 1586.4.10. The earliest tax receipt for 1585 was dated 1586.4.8, but all the others for that year are dated two or more months later (1586.6.22 or after). The one extant 1588 survey document is dated 1588.4.13; the tax receipts for the previous year are all dated 1588.8.27 or later. Kigoshi, "Maeda," p. 25, indicates that a similar phenomenon was evident following the 1589 surveys: receipts for the 1588 tax year were all issued after those surveys.

38. *KK*, p. 824; manuscripts in the Noto kuni monjo collection, Ka-Etsu-Nō Bunko, Kanazawa Shiritsu Tōshokan, Kanazawa.

39. Manuscripts in the Noto kuni monjo Collection (see preceding note).

40. This meaning of "mitsu-wari" and similar expressions is made manifest in the temporary receipt for Yawata-Shimomura's 1585 taxes, where the final entry states: "30 bales are divided in four; 7 bales, 1 *to*, 5 *shō*, is forgiven" (Wakabayashi, *Kinsei komonjo saihō*, p. 62; *NSS*, 2: 439).

41. *NSS*, p. 145.

42. For a quick overview, see Takazawa, "Tenshō-ki nengu san'yōjo," pp. 712–17.

43. For examples, see the receipts for the Tenshō 12 taxes of Nishiumi-shimoura and Enome villages in *KHNK*, 1: 554, and Tagawa, "Kaga-han," p. 54, respectively.

44. Kigoshi, "Maeda," p. 38.

45. *KHNK*, 1: 554.

46. Kigoshi, "Maeda," p. 38; Takazawa, "Tenshō-ki nengu san'yōjo," pp. 736–38. For a more complete discussion of the evidence on this point, see Brown, "Domain Formation," pp. 238–43.

47. Ōzawa, Jisha, and Nishiumi-shimoura paid some 60–73% of their 1582 taxes in rice.

48. Takazawa, "Tenshō-ki nengu san'yōjo," pp. 712–17.

49. Ibid., pp. 738–40.

50. Ibid., chart 4, p. 739.

51. Yamamura, "From Coins to Rice," imputes the switch to rice-based assessments to central policy. Though I do not believe central authority was as effective as he postulates, there is no reason why the economic mechanism he describes as underlying the shift could not operate at the domain level.

52. According to Takazawa, "Tenshō-ki nengu san'yōjo," chart 4, p. 739, the amount of tax paid in gold declined in 1588, the same year as the percentage of unpaid taxes declined. His table on pp. 712–17 shows a rough correspondence between the amount of nonrice payment and the levels of unpaid taxes for all the villages for which there are serial data. It seems reasonable to take the prompt payment of taxes as an indicator of a relatively bountiful harvest.

53. Ibid., chart 8, pp. 740–43.

54. Once this base was established through the provincial surveys, officials made explicit additions for reclaimed land and explicit subtractions, primarily for wasteland, but the basic village value always remained as a distinct entry in the tax registers.

55. Kigoshi, "Maeda," p. 31. Takazawa, "Tenshō-ki nengu san'yōjo," p. 736, presents evidence indicating that the daikan office was not so clearly permanent before 1589 as Kigoshi would have it. Takazawa suggests that the tax collectors Kigoshi calls *uketori daikan* may not have been full-fledged daikan but were merely their subordinates.

56. Takazawa, "Tenshō-ki nengu san'yōjo," p. 736.

Chapter 8

1. Secondary sources lead to this conclusion (e.g., genealogies of tomura), but references to tomura do not appear in domain ordinances until 1606. See Wajima, "Kaga-han," pp. 71–72, for a review of some of the literature on this subject. See also *ES*, 2: 94–95; and Hara, *Kaga-han*, pp. 58–62 (which includes a full citation of a key document). For somewhat different interpretations, see Wajima, "Kaga-han," pp. 72–76; *Ishikawa ken Shio chō shi*, pp. 150–51; Wakabayashi, "Kaga-han no tomura," pp. 59–61; *KHNK*, 1: 111–14, 524–93 (genealogies); and Nojima, "Kaga-han," pp. 36–38.
2. *Himi shi shi*, p. 739.
3. *TKSS*, 3: 897.
4. See ibid., p. 83, for what may be the earliest (1596) letter of appointment of a village headman, Shoji of Fukuda village. This document makes no reference to a tax exemption or stipend. There is some question about Shoji's official position as well. The volume editors' interpretation that this document refers to a village (*mura*) kimoiri rests on a reading of "the village headman of Fukuda" for "Fukuda mura kimoiri no koto." But since most documents make "mura" part of a village's official name, one would expect to find something like "Fukuda-mura mura kimoiri . . ." The phrase in the document might just mean "the headman at Fukuda village," a rather vague expression that could simply refer to a village group head who resided in Fukuda village. Fuchibyakushō were quite commonly identified this way.
5. *Himi shi shi*, p. 740.
6. *Toide chō shi*, pp. 494, 501.
7. *Kashima chō shi*, p. 422.
8. Kawa, *Imaehama to Imaeda*, pp. 313–14. See also *Ishikawa-ken Unoke chō shi*, pp. 157–58, which does not discuss the Kameda family in the early han period at all but does not dispute the position of Osumi in the Ikkō military organization.
9. *Ishikawa ken Oshino son shi*, p. 64; *Gotō-ke monjo mokuroku*, pp. 21, 22, 25.
10. *KHS*, 2: 393; *KHNK*, 1: 116–17; Wajima, "Kaga-han," pp. 73–74; Hara, *Kaga-han*, pp. 93–96.
11. *Himi shi shi*, p. 739.
12. Cited in Sakai Seiichi, *Kaga-han kaisakuhō*, pp. 142–44.
13. *Himi shi shi*, p. 741.
14. In addition to the example of concessions to villagers to encourage the return of runaways cited in an earlier chapter, see the orders issued on Keichō 7.12.6 in *KHS*, 1: 870. For ordinances on the collective responsibility for runaways, see *KK*, pp. 819, 898 (Tenshō 16.12.25, Keichō 4.2.14); and *KHS*, 1: 837–39, 851–52, 870–71, 885–86 (Keichō 6.5.17, 7.3.26, 7.12.7, 9.5.26).
15. *KHS*, 2: 37.
16. *Toide chō shi*, p. 469.
17. See ibid., pp. 494–526, for a detailed description of the Kawai family.
18. *KHS*, 1: 837–39.
19. Ibid., pp. 851–52, 869–70.

20. Ibid., pp. 869–70.
21. Sakai Seiichi, *Kaga-han kaisakuhō*, pp. 142–44; *KHS*, 2: 36–37.
22. *KHS*, 2: 288–89, 359–61.
23. Ibid., pp. 386–88.
24. Ibid., pp. 507–8.
25. For the earliest examples, see Sakai Seiichi, "Kaga-han shotō," p. 12; Sakai Seiichi, "Kaga-han shoki," p. 20; *Oku Noto Tokikuni-ke monjo*, p. 12; and *Nakajima chō shi*, p. 413.
26. *Fukuoka chō shi*, p. 1209; *KK*, p. 890.
27. *KHS*, 2: 288–89.
28. The tax bills for Arimine and Iisakano shin villages (*TKSS*, 3: 394–95) and Ure village (Sakai Seiichi, "Kaga-han shotō," p. 12) were prepared by the same four men who signed the land survey documents.
29. Sakai Seiichi, "Kaga-han shoki," p. 18; Sakai Seiichi, "Kaga-han shotō," p. 6; *Tonami shi shi*, pp. 300–301; *Inami chō shi*, 2: 35; *Kamiichi chō shi*, p. 266.
30. *Tonami shi shi*, p. 301.
31. Exemptions for wasteland and the like were subtracted in computing the tax due, rather than as adjustments to assessed value.
32. To assess the extent to which these figures might be the result of small sample size and fall outside the normal range of representative samples, a standard statistical test, a matched-pairs test, was performed on the data. It indicates that the difference between the tax rates for the two periods are statistically significant at the 1% level of confidence (the smaller the percentage, the greater the likelihood that the result is not simply a sampling artifact). The test statistic of 13.9574 is much larger than the critical value of 3.499: $t_{(n-1)} = 7$.
33. In an analysis of variance test performed on data for a slightly longer period, to 1636 (see Brown, "Practical Constraints"), the average tax rate was 41%, substantially higher than for the 1595–1626 period. The difference between the two periods is statistically significant at better than a 1% level of confidence: $F_{(1, 137)} = 6.63$; the test statistic was 229. Nonparametric tests (the Wilcoxon two-sample test, the t-test approximation, and the Kruskal-Wallis test) all produced similarly significant results for the longer period. Despite the difference in time span, the decline in tax rates is confirmed.
34. *ES*, 2: 257–58. This difference is statistically significant at the 1% level of confidence. In a one-tailed t test at the 1% level of significance, the critical value of T at a conservative 60 degrees of freedom is 2.660; the test statistic was 7.4129.
35. *ES*, 2: 257–58. The same test and critical value were employed as above. The test statistic was 6.5348, far greater than the critical value.
36. Later period $s^2 \div$ early period $s^2 = 4.248$; $F_{(94, 144)} = 1.32$. The difference is statistically significant at better than a 2% level of confidence.
37. The following discussion of the factors behind the decline is selective. For a full discussion, see Brown, "Practical Constraints."
38. On the expenses of the *sankin-kōtai*, see Tsukahira, *Feudal Control*, pp. 81–103. For a detailed description of one major Tokugawa project financed by daimyo—the reconstruction of Osaka castle between 1620 and 1629—see Hauser,

"Osaka Castle." For a brief summary of major domain expenditures, see Mise, "Inaba Sakon," pp. 39–40.

39. The 1631 regulations also included provisions on runaways (*KHS*, 2: 630). Yamamura, "Returns on Unification," p. 348, stresses the peasants' increased capacity to forestall authorities from taking a bigger bite of their income in the 17th century.

40. The Chō, as noted, were the only major retainers to hold a distinct residential fief beyond the early decades of the 17th century. McClain, *Kanazawa*, pp. 35–37, discusses the urbanization of samurai in that town.

41. The late-16th-century daikan rotation rate was discussed in Chap. 6. Of the 37 positions in Nafune-gumi from 1631 to 1634, 16 changed once, and 4 twice (*Noto Wajima Kamikaji-ke monjo mokuroku*, p. 86). The rate of turnover clearly continued to be very high.

42. For a detailed description of this process and examples of the documents assessors prepared, see Andō Hiroshi, *Tokugawa*, pp. 212–62.

43. *KHS*, 2: 151.

44. For examples from Gokayama area villages, see *TKSS*, 3: 410–11; and *KHS*, 2: 304.

45. *KHS*, 2: 380–81.

46. Ibid., p. 387.

47. Sasaki, *Daimyo*, pp. 160–61, takes the position that these exports actually cost the domain money because rice fetched a slightly lower price in Osaka than in Kanazawa. He argues that the intention was to increase the value of rice that landed retainers sold in the local markets by decreasing the supply. The price correlations of local and Osaka prices in Takase, "Zenkoku shijō kakuritsu" and "Bakuhanseika," effectively refute Sasaki's argument.

48. *KHS*, 2: 387.

49. Takase, "Bakuhanseika," p. 35.

50. Ibid.

51. *KHS*, 2: 635.

52. *Tonami shi shi*, p. 341.

53. *Oku Noto Tokikuni-ke monjo*, pp. 22–25.

54. *KHS*, 2: 565.

55. Ibid., p. 625.

56. See Tanaka Seiji, "Kinsei zenki"; and Nakaguchi, "Kinsei shoki sohō." The assessment systems described in such manuals of local administration as Andō Hiroshi, *Tokugawa bakufu kenji yōryaku*, Ōishi, *Jikata hanrei roku*, and Murakami and Arakawa, *Sanpō jikata taisei*, substantiate the experimental nature of early land taxation (e.g., *harumen-sei*, *sebiki kemi hō*, *arige kemi hō*, *tantori hō*).

57. The implications of the trends in taxation outlined here for Kaga domain's economic development are discussed in Brown, "Practical Constraints."

Chapter 9

1. Hall, "Ikeda House," p. 80; Hall, "Foundations," pp. 71–72.
2. R. Sakai, "Consolidation of Power"; Jansen, "Tosa in the Seventeenth Century."
3. According to Kanai, *Hansei*, p. 41, the domains that retained, at least in name, the system of landed retainers accounted for 55% of Japan's assessed land value (kokudaka). Morris, *Kinsei Nihon chigyōsei*, believes that Sendai retainers maintained substantial contacts with their fiefs; he has significant reservations about how much control they really lost. Even if the proportion of domains in which retainers held autonomous rights over fiefs was much larger than Kanai suggests, there was a major trend in the other direction.
4. Andō Seiichi, *Edo jidai*, p. 80, gives other examples.
5. Hall, "Rule by Status."
6. In addition to the case studies of Tosa, Satsuma, and Bizen mentioned previously, see *Hansei seiritsu shi* for Yonezawa; and Totman, *Politics*, pp. 65–77.
7. The one exception to this statement is the brief period after 1821, when the tomura and the *kaisaku bugyō* were abolished in an unsuccessful attempt to revitalize agricultural administration. Both offices were reestablished in 1839.
8. Araya, "Kaga-han," pp. 81–82.
9. *KHS*, 2: 550–52. These regulations governed *mitate kenchi* (lit., "inspection surveys"), wasteland surveys, and tax rates.
10. Ibid., pp. 629–40.
11. Ibid., p. 632.
12. Ibid., p. 634. Land survey documents for Etchu villages at the turn of the century and for Kaga and Noto villages from at least 1616 suggest that the two officers were already performing this function within the daikan's jurisdiction, if only on an extraordinary basis.
13. *Noto Wajima Kamikaji-ke monjo mokuroku*, pp. 101–2.
14. McClain, *Kanazawa*, pp. 63–67.
15. Most Japanese historians believe that taxes could not have been raised further, that they were already as high as they could go. See, for example, Mise, "Inaba Sakon."
16. Ibid., p. 39.
17. Sasaki, *Daimyō*, pp. 271–72.
18. Mise, "Inaba Sakon," p. 39; Yamada Shirōzaemon, *Mitsubo kikigaki*, pp. 230–33.
19. Mise, "Inaba Sakon," p. 40.
20. *TKSS*, 3: 416–17. Follow-up orders in 1640 show that the authorities made at least one attempt to maintain this increase. Clearly some retainers were unwilling or unable to implement it.
21. For more on these changes in unit size, see Mise, "Inaba Sakon," pp. 42–47.
22. Meyasuba were apparently not established in Etchu until 1637 (ibid., p. 47).
23. Sakai Seiichi, *Kaga-han kaisakuhō*, pp. 183–84.

24. *Noto Wajima Kamikaji-ke monjo mokuroku*, p. 102.

25. Ibid., pp. 86–88.

26. Ibid., pp. 84–85, 101–4.

27. A good indication of this logic is found in the *oboegaki* transcribed in *Tonami shi shi*, pp. 370–71. As we have seen, the document granting a retainer a partial claim on a village left unstated exactly where or from whom he could collect taxes (see the charts in KHNK, 1: 189–92; and TKSS, 3: 6–14). Village documents tell a similar story. In the case of Ōta village, for example, we have a 1640 tax assessment that shows how the tax was to be divided among the retainers without tying the amounts to specific fields or villagers, and a 1642 diary that shows how much each villager paid or owed without tying the amounts to any specific retainer. Notices of the tax owed were addressed either to the village headman (kimoiri) or to him, along with one or two other people who appear to be lesser village officers. But receipts for cash payments were addressed to the entire village. In both cases one lump sum was reported even though the document was issued by more than one retainer. (*Kaga-han shoki tomurayaku Kaneko monjo*, pp. 27–30, 54–59 passim.) In fact, since villages in Kaga domain periodically reallocated their land, and the size and arrangement of fields could change at the same time, retainers could hardly have been assigned the right to tax specific well-defined fields.

28. KHNK, 1: 139–41, discusses some of the principal measures taken to counter mid-17th-century taxpayer indebtedness.

29. $F_{(1, 92)} = 7$; the test statistic was 8.8. The difference is significant at the 1% level of confidence. Nonparametric tests yielded comparable results.

30. The standard deviation shrank from 16.4 to 14.4.

31. "Kan'ei kyū-nen hachigatsu Tonami gun Toide mura Matazaemon gumi furudaka, shinkai sashidashidaka mononari chō," in TKSS, 3: *Furoku*, shows similar if less dramatic tendencies.

32. For a full treatment of the Kaisaku hō, consult Sakai Seiichi, *Kaga-han kaisaku hō*; Hara, *Kaga-han*; and KHNK, vol. 1.

33. In the Oku Noto counties of Suzu and Fugeshi the number was increased from one to three (Hara, *Kaga-han*, p. 124).

34. For an example of one early ordinance (1625), see ibid., pp. 94–95; and on this aspect of class separation more generally, pp. 93–105. Village headmen and their children were exempted from the plow tax as compensation for the administrative office. The instructions transcribed in ibid., pp. 94–95, also define the classes of rural residents who were exempted—generally, hereditary servants of both samurai and hyakushō; dependent households (*genin*) that did not cultivate land; and outcastes (*hinin* and *eta*). For a typical example of instructions to be read to villagers, from 1655, see ibid., pp. 132–34.

35. Ibid., pp. 138–49; Sakai Seiichi, *Kaga-han kaisakuhō*, pp. 309–16.

36. KHNK, 1: 161–62; Sakai Seiichi, *Kaga-han kaisakuhō*, pp. 233–34 (and pp. 350–51 on the return on the domain's investment).

37. KHNK, 1: 10, 238.

38. Wakabayashi Kisaburō, "Kaga-han no tomura seido kakuritsu ni tsuite oboegaki," *Nihon Rekishi*, 236 (Jan. 1968): 95–96. For examples of regrouping,

see *Tonami shi shi*, pp. 385–87. On tomura transfers, see Sakai Seiichi, *Kaga-han kaisakuhō*, pp. 254–55.

39. *KHNK*, 1: 163, 645, 648.

40. Ibid., pp. 163–64, 203, 662, 668. Great importance continued to be placed on the tomura throughout the Edo period—for their role in civil and criminal matters, as well as in the realm of taxation. Much of what we know of village conditions comes from the extensive document collections of their descendants.

41. Hara, *Kaga-han*, pp. 126–27, 129. On the role of senior councillors, see Sakai Seiichi, *Kaga-han kaisakuhō*, pp. 244–50.

42. *KHNK*, 1: 243.

43. Ibid., pp. 163–64, 234–36.

44. Hara, *Kaga-han*, pp. 132–34.

45. Documents in *Tonami shi shi*, pp. 372–73, provide illustrations of warichi activity at this time.

46. *KHS*, 2: 634.

47. *KHNK*, 1: 244–45.

48. "Ka-Nō-Etsu san ka koku taka mononari chō," manuscript 7021, in Kanazawa Shiritsu Toshokan, Kanazawa, contains copies of all of the 1670 *mura goin*. Each of these documents notes all the changes made in the assessed values and taxes since the issuance of the 1656 goin.

49. I am indebted to Kigoshi Ryūzō for allowing me to draw on his summary of the data in two manuscripts in the Early Modern Manuscript Collection of the Kanazawa Shiritsu Toshokan—"Shōhō san nen taka mononari chō genkō" and "San ka koku taka mononari chō." Kigoshi presents some of these data in his article "Kaga-han gochō shindendaka," p. 58, chart 9. The provincial figures presented here do not include Enuma and Neii counties, the two branch domains.

50. This does not mean that there were no demands for tax reductions. They clearly occurred in 1660 and 1668, years of fairly severe crop shortfalls (see "Kawai roku," pp. 937, 939–40). In response to these pressures, there were investigations for the purpose of temporarily lowering the rates on paddy only, but few long-term reductions were incorporated in 1670 tax bills.

51. This conclusion is based on my transcriptions of some 3,500 1670 *mura goin*. Many local histories reproduce these bills.

52. Large-scale requests for rate reductions come much later. In 1737, 2,217 villages requested a tax rate reduction, and 1,015 villages received one (*KHS*, 7: 34). See also Tanaka Yoshio, "Kaga-han."

53. The long-term impact of fixed tax rates is still to be investigated. The data in Thomas C. Smith, "The Land Tax in the Tokugawa Period," in Hall and Jansen, *Studies in Institutional History*, pp. 283–99, permit a preliminary estimate of later land tax trends in Kaga domain. Based on his 19th-century figures for Fugeshi, Kahoku, and Hakui counties in Noto (p. 287), the tax rate fell by 4% on average. If research should show that this was the extent of the fall, the jōmen system, despite the sacrifice of the opportunity to keep up with increased yields, would have at least solved the immediate problem of how to restore and maintain revenues better than the kemi system had.

54. Sakai Seiichi, *Kaga-han kaisakuhō*, p. 237.
55. *KHNK*, 1: 163.
56. Hara, *Kaga-han*, p. 128.
57. The incident is commonly treated as either an early form of village revolt or an *ie sōdō*, a dispute among a daimyo's retainer band (*KHNK*, 1: 261; Itō, "Kinsei shoki daimyō ryō").
58. Fukaya et al., "Kanbun nana-nen Kaga-han kenchi," presents a more comprehensive treatment of this incident. For an older view, see Itō, "Kinsei shoki daimyō ryō."

Chapter 10

1. The emphasis on the power of Hideyoshi and the early shogunate owes in good part to the abundance of early modern Japanese document collections. Their volume alone makes a balanced use of central and local data difficult and reinforces the tendency of historians to rely on central directives to develop their interpretations: local materials are read largely as verification of central ordinances. As much as historians know that the absence of evidence may have meaning, a "history with mirrors" may only be practical once the boundaries of known data become clear. (This characterization of the usefulness of lacunae in data is drawn from Jeffrey P. Mass, "Introduction" to Mass and Hauser, *Bakufu in Japanese History*, p. 1.) In the 40 years since Araki Moriaki argued for the revolutionary impact of the Taikō kenchi, sufficient evidence has been unearthed and analyzed for historians to move beyond the perspective generated by examining centrally issued ordinances. We can now ask if documentary voids like the lack of standard survey registers in domains such as Kaga, Satsuma, and Bizen have something to tell us. (The absence of registers in Kaga and Satsuma has already been discussed. Even though Hall, *Government and Local Power*, pp. 318ff, indicates that very little is known about the Taikō kenchi in Bizen, and specifically notes, on p. 300, the lack of registers during Hideyoshi's reign, his discussion of the Ikeda surveys on pp. 390-92 assumes that the earlier standard ones had taken place.) This question could be extended to matters like the sword hunt and class separation edicts and related ordinances.

2. McClain built his analysis in *Kanazawa* as a counterargument to this kind of interpretation.

3. Many scholars treat domain laws restricting the sale of land, the systematization and conversion of labor dues to cash or rice payments, and related policies as designed solely to serve the interests of the han treasury. Hara, *Kaga-han*, p. 92, for example, claims that 17th-century kenchi created a stable tax revenue ("*anteiteki na nengu shūnō o kakuho*") and strengthened the domain's financial base. He also argues that the prohibiting of the sale of land, the demand for tax payments before rice sales, and the lightening of labor dues were all in aid of increasing the villagers' ability to pay land taxes.

4. Wakita, "Social and Economic Consequences of Unification," p. 108, notes the impact of violent opposition more than most, but even he describes compromises in survey practice only in terms of exempting some land from measurement

or the annual tax and making some exemptions from the corvée, not deviation from standard measures or procedures.

5. Wallerstein, *Modern World-System*, 1: 134, 144–45.

6. Rule, "Reading of the Rolle."

7. Charles Tilly makes a similar argument for emerging states in early modern Europe. He stresses the interactions between the demands of defense and the expansion of a state's domestic authority. See "War Making and State Making as Organized Crime," in Evans et al., *Bringing the State Back In*, pp. 169–91. Particularly noteworthy in light of my discussion below are his comments regarding Richelieu's claims for a monopoly of the use of force—claims that came long before the state's effective accomplishment of a monopoly (p. 174).

8. Kasaya, "Nihon Kinsei shakai," takes a similar position in arguing that some elements of daimyo autonomy could not be integrated into the Bakufu control system.

9. See Wheelwright's analysis of Oda Nobunaga's use of monumental art in "A Vizualization"; and Elison's descriptions of Azuchi castle in "Cross and Sword," pp. 62–66, and Hideyoshi's political manipulation of tea, Noh drama, and poetry in "Hideyoshi," pp. 234–36, 239–44. On the use of ritual, era names, titles, and other devices in diplomacy, see Toby, *State and Diplomacy*, especially chaps. 3, 5. The use of religious and philosophical traditions in late-16th- and early-17th-century Japan to legitimate the emerging order is analyzed in Ooms, *Tokugawa Ideology*, chaps. 2–3.

10. See Ōishi Shinzaburō, "Kinsei," p. 52.

11. See Birt, "Samurai in Passage."

12. For evidence beyond Kaga, see Owada, "Sengoku daimyō Gohōjō-shi," on the Tokugawa's adoption of the Gohōjō system of village administration.

13. The Bakufu's mid-17th-century orders of land surveys, taken by some as applying nationwide, were as ineffective in this regard as Hideyoshi's. See, for example, Yamamura, "From Coins to Rice," p. 359, relying on Ōishi Shinzaburō, "Kinsei," p. 52. See also Iinuma, *Kokudakasei no kenkyū*, on varying survey standards in the 17th century. Indeed, one might argue that in some instances the domain tail wagged the hegemon dog. In restricting the sale of land use rights and adopting the jōmen system of tax assessment, the Maeda followed principles that the Bakufu would not put into practice until the early 18th century. Other domains also adopted the jōmen system long before the Bakufu: Matsue, in 1687; Okayama, 1654; Matsuyama, permanently from 1679; and Tōdō, 1652 (Kodama, *Kinsei nōmin seikatsu shi*, p. 40; Kanai, *Hansei*, pp. 58–59; Suga, "Matsuyama han," pp. 53, 55–56; Sasaki, *Daimyō*, pp. 315, 327–29).

14. Often the expansion of arable land produced whole new villages, *shinden mura*. In fact, the names of many villages, wards, and hamlets throughout Japan today include the words *shin* (new), *kaihatsu* (development), or the like, clearly reflecting this heritage.

15. Harafuji, "*Han* Laws."

16. Hall, "Hideyoshi's Domestic Policies," p. 206. Berry, *Hideyoshi*, notes that there is no evidence under Hideyoshi of a "scheme to enforce compliance" (p. 137),

but in earlier references to his surveys, she speaks of his "demanding," "establishing," etc. (pp. 114, 118).

17. See, for example, White, "State Growth," Totman, "Preindustrial River Conservancy."

18. See Ooms, *Tokugawa Ideology*, on the political discourse through which a rationale for the new order was developed. While Ooms examines ideology, Thomas Keirstead (*The Geography of Power*) analyzes institutional transformations of the *shoen* in terms of "discourse" in order to avoid a sense of unidirectional, linear history and to open a sense of possibility as opposed to an image of determinism (Chapters 2 and 3, which deal respectively with conceptions of *hyakushō* and land records, will be of particular interest to readers). Although my approach differs from Keirstead's deconstructionist analysis, my effort has roots in similar objections to writings in Japanese history that impose uniformity on complex developments and which reduce the resulting variety of outcomes to a single form. These concerns are part of diverse scholarly efforts to deal with the limitations of linear analytic models. Although Ooms, Keirstead, Harry D. Harootunian (*Things Seen and Unseen*), and others derive their inspiration from theories of literary criticism and linguistics, other scholars develop alternative approaches from the models provided by non-linear science (of which "chaos" theory is most widely discussed). On the latter see Alan Beyerchen, "Non-linear Science," and "Clausewitz, Nonlinearity, and the Unpredictability of War"; and Randolph Roth, "Is History a Process?"

Bibliography

Andō Hiroshi, ed. *Tokugawa bakufu kenji yōryaku.* Tokyo: Kashiwa Shobō, 1966.
Andō Seiichi. *Edo jidai no nōmin. Nihon Rekishi Shinsho* 49. Tokyo: Shibundō, 1966.
Aono Shunsui. *Nihon kinsei warichisei shi no kenkyū.* Tokyo: Yūzankaku, 1982.
Araki Moriaki. *Bakuhan taisei shakai no seiritsu to kōzō.* Tokyo: Ochanomizu Shobō, 1959.
———. "Ryūkyū ni okeru chiwari seido no kigen to hensen," 2 parts, *Osaka Furitsu Daigaku Kiyō: Jinbun Shakai Kagaku,* 29 (March 1982): 49–58; 30 (March 1983): 41–49.
———. "Taikō kenchi no rekishiteki zentei," 2 parts, *Rekishigaku Kenkyū,* 163 (May 1953): 1–17; 164 (July 1953): 1–22.
———. *Taikō kenchi to kokudaka sei.* Tokyo: Nihon Hōsō Shuppan Kyōkai, 1969.
Araki Sumiko. "Kaga-han shoki no tomura seido ni kansuru ni, san no mondai." In *Ishikawa ken Oshino son shi,* pp. 485–507. Kanazawa: Oshino Son Shi Henshū Iinkai, 1964.
Araya Kurō. "Kaga-han ni okeru shūkenteki hōkensei no kakuritsu," *Shakai-keizai Shigaku,* 6 (May 1936): 67–106.
Arnesen, Peter J. "The Provincial Vassals of the Muromachi Shoguns." In Mass and Hauser, eds., *Bakufu in Japanese History,* pp. 99–128.
Asao Naohiro. "'Bakuhansei dai ichi dankai' ni okeru seisanryoku to kokudaka-sei," *Rekishigaku Kenkyū,* 264 (April–May 1962): 51–55.
———. "Bakuhansei kokkaron no shomondai," *Nagoya Rekishi Kagaku Kenkyū Kai Kikanshi,* 21 (July 1970): 1–10.
———. "The Sixteenth-century Unification." In Hall, ed., *Cambridge History of Japan,* 4, pp. 40–95.
Asao, Naohiro (with Marius B. Jansen). "Shogun and Tennō." In Hall, Nagahara, and Yamamura, eds., *Japan Before Tokugawa,* pp. 224–70.

Befu, Harumi. "Village Autonomy and Articulation with the State." In Hall and Jansen, eds., *Studies in Institutional History*, pp. 301–14.

Berkhofer, Robert F., Jr. *The Behavioral Approach to Historical Analysis*. New York: Free Press, [1969].

Berry, Mary Elizabeth. *Hideyoshi*. Cambridge, Mass.: Harvard University Press, 1982.

———. "Public Peace and Private Attachment: The Goals and Conduct of Power in Early Modern Japan," *Journal of Japanese Studies*, 12.2 (Summer 1986): 237–71.

Beyerchen, Alan. "Nonlinear Science and the Unfolding of a New Intellectual Vision," *Papers in Comparative Studies* 6 (1988–89), 25–49.

———. "Clausewitz, Nonlinearity, and the Unpredictability of War," *International Security* 17: 3 (Winter 1992/93), pp. 59–90.

Birt, Michael. "Samurai in Passage: The Transformation of the Sixteenth-Century Kanto," *Journal of Japanese Studies*, 11 (Summer 1985): 369–99.

Bix, Herbert P. *Peasant Protest in Japan, 1590–1884*. New Haven, Conn.: Yale University Press, 1986.

Bolitho, Harold. "The Han." In Hall, ed., *Cambridge History of Japan*, 4, pp. 183–234.

———. *Treasures Among Men: The Fudai Daimyo in Tokugawa Japan*. New Haven, Conn.: Yale University Press, 1974.

Brown, Philip C. "Domain Formation in Early Modern Japan: The Development of Rural Administration and the Land Tax System in Kaga Han, 1581–1631." Ph.D. dissertation, University of Pennsylvania. 1981.

———. "'Feudal Remnants' and Tenant Power: The Case of Niigata, Japan, in the Nineteenth and Early Twentieth Centuries," *Peasant Studies*, 15 (Fall 1987): 1–26.

———. "The Mismeasure of Land: Land Surveying in the Tokugawa Period," *Monumenta Nipponica*, 42 (Summer 1987): 115–55.

———. "Never the Twain Shall Meet: European and Japanese Land Survey Techniques in Tokugawa Japan," *Chinese Science*, 9 (1989): 53–79.

———. "Practical Constraints on Early Tokugawa Land Taxation: Annual Versus Fixed Assessments in Kaga Domain," *Journal of Japanese Studies*, 14.2 (Summer 1988): 369–401.

Coulborn, Rushton, ed. *Feudalism in History*. Princeton, N.J.: Princeton University Press, 1956.

Crick, Bernard, "Sovereignty." In *International Encyclopedia of the Social Sciences*, 15: 77–82. New York: Crowell, Collier, 1968.

Davis, David L. "Ikki in Late Medieval Japan." In John W. Hall and Jeffrey P. Mass, eds., *Medieval Japan*, pp. 221–47. New Haven, Conn.: Yale University Press, 1974.

———. "The Kaga Ikkō Ikki, 1473–1580." Ph.D. dissertation, University of Chicago, 1978.

DiCenzo, Ronald J. "Daimyo, Domain, and Retainer Band in the Seventeenth Cen-

tury: A Study of Institutional Development in Echizen, Tottori, and Matsue." Ph.D. dissertation, Princeton, N.J., 1978.
Elison, George. "The Cross and the Sword: Patterns of Momoyama History." In Elison and Smith, eds., *Warlords, Artists, and Commoners*, pp. 55–86.
———. "Hideyoshi, the Bountiful Minister." In Elison and Smith, eds., *Warlords, Artists, and Commoners*, pp. 223–44.
Elison, George, and Bardwell L. Smith, eds. *Warlords, Artists, and Commoners: Japan in the Sixteenth Century*. Honolulu: University Press of Hawaii, 1981.
Etchū shiryō. Ed. Toyama Ken. 2 vols. Tokyo: Meicho Shuppan, 1972. Originally published in 1909.
Evans, Peter B., Dietrich Rueschemeyer, and Theda Skocpol, eds., *Bringing the State Back In*. Cambridge: Cambridge University Press, 1985.
Fried, Morton H. "State: The Institution." In *International Encyclopedia of the Social Sciences*, 15: 143–50. New York: Crowell, Collier, 1968.
Fujiki Hisashi. *Toyotomi heiwarei to sengoku shakai*. Tokyo: Tokyo Daigaku Shuppankai, 1985.
Fujiki, Hisashi, with George Elison. "The Political Posture of Oda Nobunaga." In Hall, Nagahara, and Yamamura, eds., *Japan Before Tokugawa*, pp. 149–93.
Fujino Tamotsu. *(Shintei) Bakuhan taisei shi no kenkyū: Kenryoku kōzō no kakuritsu to tenkai*. Tokyo: Yoshikawa Kōbunkan, 1975.
Fujita Gorō. *Kinsei nōsei shi ron: Nihon hōken shakai shi kenkyū josetsu*. Tokyo: Ochanomizu Shobō, 1950.
Fukaya Katsumi, Yoshitake Keiichirō, and Hosaka Satoshi. "Kanbun nana-nen Kaga-han kenchi hantai sōdō no kentō," *Minshūshi Kenkyū*, 9 (1971): 103–33.
Fukumitsu chō shi. 2 vols. Tonami, Toyama: Fukumitsu Machi, 1971.
Fukuoka chō shi. Takaoka: Fukuoka Machi Yakuba, 1969.
Furushima Toshio. *Nihon hōken nōgyōshi/Kazoku keitai to nōgyō no hattatsu. Furushima Toshio chosaku shū*, vol. 2. Tokyo: Tokyo Daigaku Shuppankai, 1974.
———. "Village and Agriculture During the Edo Period," *The Cambridge History of Japan*, 4, pp. 478–518.
———. "Warichi seido ni kansuru bunken," *Nōgyō Keizai Kenkyū*, 16.4 (Dec. 1940): 134–62.
Gotō-ke monjo mokuroku. Kanazawa: Ishikawa Ken Kyōdo Shiryōkan, 1970.
Hakui shi shi, Kinsei hen. Kanazawa: Hakui Shi Yakusho, 1975.
Hall, John Whitney. "The *Bakuhan* System." In Hall, ed., *Cambridge History of Japan*, 4, pp. 128–82.
———. "Feudalism in Japan—A Reassessment." In Hall and Jansen, eds., *Studies in Institutional History*, pp. 15–51.
———. "Foundations of the Modern Japanese Daimyo." In Hall and Jansen, eds., *Studies in Institutional History*, pp. 65–78.
———. *Government and Local Power in Japan, 500–1700*. Princeton, N.J.: Princeton University Press, 1966.
———. "Hideyoshi's Domestic Policies." In Hall, Nagahara, and Yamamura, eds., *Japan Before Tokugawa*, pp. 194–223.

———. "The Ikeda House and Its Retainers in Bizen." In Hall and Jansen, eds., *Studies in Institutional History*, pp. 79–88.

———. "Ikeda Mitsumasa and the Bizen Flood." In Albert M. Craig and Donald Shively, eds., *Personality in Japanese History*. Berkeley: University of California Press, 1970, pp. 57–84.

———. "Introduction." In Hall, ed., *Cambridge History of Japan*, 4, pp. 1–39.

———. "Japan's Sixteenth-century Revolution." In Elison and Smith, eds., *Warlords, Artists, and Commoners*, pp. 7–21.

———. "The New Look of Tokugawa History." In Hall and Jansen, eds., *Studies in Institutional History*, pp. 55–64.

———. "Rule by Status in Tokugawa Japan," *Journal of Japanese Studies*, 1.1 (1974): 39–50.

———, ed. *The Cambridge History of Japan*. 4 (Early Modern Japan). New York: Cambridge University Press, 1991.

Hall, John Whitney, and Marius B. Jansen, eds. *Studies in the Institutional History of Early Modern Japan*. Princeton, N.J.: Princeton University Press, 1968.

Hall, John Whitney, Nagahara Keiji, and Kozo Yamamura, eds. *Japan Before Tokugawa: Political Consolidation and Economic Growth, 1500 to 1650*. Princeton, N.J.: Princeton University Press, 1981.

Handa Ichitarō. "Ushū Yūri karidaka kō," *Chihō shi Kenkyū*, 151 (Feb. 1978): 14–25.

Handa Kyōon and Yokoyama Akio. *Yamagata ken no rekishi*. Kenshi Shiriizu 6. Tokyo: Yamakawa Shuppansha, 1970.

Hanley, Susan B., and Kozo Yamamura. *Economic and Demographic Change in Pre-industrial Japan, 1600–1868*. Princeton, N.J.: Princeton University Press, 1977.

Hansei seiritsu shi no sōgō kenkyū: Yonezawa han. Tokyo: Yoshikawa Kōbunkan, 1963.

Hara Shōgo. *Kaga-han ni miru bakuhansei kokka seiritsu shi ron*. Tokyo: Tokyo Daigaku Shuppankai, 1981.

———. "Nihon hōkensei no kōzōronteki rikai o meguru mondaiten," *Rekishi Hyōron*, 228 (1969): 43–54.

Harafuji Hiroshi. "*Han* Laws in the Edo Period—with Particular Emphasis on Those of the Kanazawa *Han*," *Acta Asiatica*, 35 (1979): 46–71.

Harootunian, H. D. *Things Seen and Unseen: Discourse and Ideology in Tokugawa Nativism*. Chicago: University of Chicago Press, 1988.

Harrington, Lorraine F. "Regional Outposts of Muromachi Bakufu Rule: The Kantō and Kyushu." In Mass and Hauser, eds., *Bakufu in Japanese History*, pp. 66–98.

Hauser, William. "Osaka Castle and Tokugawa Authority in Western Japan." In Mass and Hauser, eds., *Bakufu in Japanese History*, pp. 153–72.

Hayakawa Jirō. *Nihon rekishi dokuhon*. Tokyo: Hakuyōsha, 1937.

Hayami Akira. "Kenchi tōrokunin o megutte," 2 parts, *Mita Gakkai Zasshi*, 54.11 (Nov. 1961): 21–40; 55.7 (July 1962): 44–59.

———. "Kinsei shoki no kenchi to honbyakushō mibun no keisei," *Mita Gakkai Zasshi*, 49.2 (Feb. 1957): 50–81.

———. "Nihon keizai shi ni okeru chūsei kara kinsei e no tenkan," *Shakai-keizai Shigaku Zasshi* 37.1 (1971): 95–105.

———. "Ryōshu no kenchichō to mura no kenchichō," *Shakai-keizai Shigaku* 22.2 (Sep. 1956): 88–93.

Heki [Hioki] Ken. *Ishikawa ken shi*. Kanazawa: Ishikawa Ken, 1974. Originally published in 1927–33.

———. *(Kaitei zōhō) Kanō kyōdo jii*. Kanazawa: Hokkoku Shuppansha, 1973. Originally published in 1956.

———, ed. and comp. *Kaga-han Shiryō*, vols. 1–3, 7. Osaka: Seibundō Shuppan, 1970. Originally published in 1929–36.

———. *Kanō komonjo*. Rev. Matsumoto Mitsumasa. Tokyo: Meicho Shuppan, 1973.

———, comp. *Kanō dokushi nempyō*. Rev. Matsumoto Mitsumasa. Tokyo: Meicho Shuppan, 1972.

Hellie, Richard. *Enserfment and Military Change in Muscovy*. Chicago: University of Chicago Press, 1971.

Himi shi shi. Takaoka: Himi Shi Yakusho, 1963.

Hirasawa Kiyoto. *Kinsei sonraku e no ikō to heinō bunri*. Tokyo: Ogura Shobō, 1973.

Iinuma Jirō. *Kokudakasei no kenkyū: Nihon-gata zettaishugi no kiso kōzō*. Tokyo: Minerubua Shobō, 1974.

Inami chō shi. 2 vols. Toyama: Inami Machi, 1970.

Inoue Toshio. *Niigata ken no rekishi. Kenshi Shiriizu* 15. Tokyo: Yamakawa Shuppansha, 1970.

Ishii, Ryōsuke. *A History of Political Institutions in Japan*. Tokyo: University of Tokyo Press, 1980.

———. "Japanese Feudalism," *Acta Asiatica*, 35 (1978): 1–29.

Ishii Shirō. *Nihon kokusei shi kenkyū: Kenryoku to tochi shoyū*. Tokyo: Tokyo Daigaku Shuppankai, 1966.

Ishikawa ken Oshino son shi. Kanazawa: Oshino Son Shi Henshū Iinkai, 1964.

Ishikawa ken saii shi. Kanazawa: Ishikawa Ken Kanazawa Chihō Kishōdai, 1971.

Ishikawa ken shi shiryō. Ed. Ishikawa Ken Kyōiku Iinkai. Kanazawa: n.p., 1969.

Ishikawa ken Shio chō shi. Kanazawa: Shio Machi Yakuba, 1974.

Ishikawa ken Takamatsu chō shi. Takamatsu: Ishikawa Ken Takamatsu Machi Yakuba, 1974.

Ishikawa ken Torigoe son shi. Kanazawa: Ishikawa Ken Torigoe Mura Yakuba, 1972.

Ishikawa ken Unoke chō shi. Kanazawa: Unoke Machi Yakuba, 1970.

Itō Tasaburō. "Kinsei shoki daimyō ryō no ichi keitai: Noto no Chō no Bawai," *Rekishi Kyōiku*, 2.10 (1955): 21–30.

Iwai Chūyū. "Shoki Kaga-han no nōsei ni tsuite," *Ritsumeikan Bungaku*, 79 (1951): 40–53.

Iwasawa Yoshihiko. *Maeda Toshiie.* Tokyo: Yoshikawa Kōbunkan, 1966.
Jansen, Marius B. "Tosa in the Seventeenth Century: The Establishment of Yamauchi Rule." In Hall and Jansen, eds., *Studies in Institutional History*, pp. 115–29.
———. "Tosa in the Sixteenth Century: The 100 Article Code of Chōsokabe Motochika." In Hall and Jansen, eds., *Studies in Institutional History*, pp. 89–114.
Kaga-han shoki tomurayaku Kaneko monjo, Tonami shi shi shiryō hen. Tonami, Toyama: Tonami Shi Kyōiku Iinkai, 1976.
Kaga shi shi, Tsūshi hen, ge. Kanazawa: Kaga Shi Yakusho, 1978.
Kamiichi chō shi. Toyama: Kamiichi Machi, 1970.
Kanai Madoka. *Hansei. Nihon Rekishi Shinsho* 90. Tokyo: Shibundō, 1966.
Kaneda Takanobu. *Minami Ōmi son shi.* Kanazawa: Ōmi Kōminkan, 1970.
Kanō shiwa. Takaoka: Kanō Shinkō Kan, 1970.
Kanzaki Akitoshi. *Kenchi: Nawa to sao no shihai. Rekishi Shinsho* 202. Tokyo: Kyōikusha, 1983.
Kasaya Kazuhiko. "Nihon Kinsei shakai no atarashii rekishizō o motomete," *Nihonshi Kenkyū*, 333 (May 1990): 35–61.
Kashima chō shi, shiryō hen. Kanazawa: Ishikawa Ken Kashima Machi Yakuba, 1966.
Kashiwakura Ryokichi. "Tokugawa jidai no kokumori no ichi mondai," *Kokushi Ronshū* (Kyōto Daigaku Bungakubu Dokushikai), 1959: 1017–36.
Katsumata, Shizuo, with Martin Collcutt. "The Development of Sengoku Law." In Hall, Nagahara, and Yamamura, *Japan Before Tokugawa*, pp. 101–24.
Kawa Yoshio. *Hatta no rekishi.* Kanazawa: Hatta Kōminkan, 1960.
———. *Imaehama to Imaeda no rekishi.* Komatsu, Ishikawa: Imae Machi Kōminkan, 1969.
"Kawai roku." In Hanpō Kenkyūkai, ed., *Hanpōshū*, vol. 6: *Zoku Kanazawa-han.* Tokyo: Sōbunsha, 1966.
Keirstead, Thomas. *The Geography of Power in Medieval Japan.* Princeton, N.J.: Princeton University Press, 1992.
Kigoshi Ryūzō. "Kaga-han gochō shindendaka ni tsuite," *Nihonkai Bunka*, 7 (March 1980): 39–86.
———. "Kaga-han no muradaka," *Rekishi Chimei Tsūshin*, 11 (July 1988): 6–11.
———. "Kaga-han seiritsu-ki no kokudaka to men," *Nihonkai Bunka*, 5 (March 1978): 1–45.
———. "Kan'ei-ki Chōke ryō Kashima hangun ni okeru kōso," *Kanō Shiryō Kenkyū*, May 1985: 18–35.
———. "Kan'ei-ki Chōke ryō ni okeru kenchi fusei jiken to tomura seido," *Hokuriku Shigaku*, 35 (Nov. 1986): 1–36.
———. "Keichō-ki Kaga-han kashindan no kōsei to dōkō." In Tomoya Tanamachi, Tsurusaki Hiro, and Kigoshi Ryūzō, eds., *Shirayama manku: Shiryō to kenkyū*, pp. 324–54. Ishikawa-ken Ishikawa-gun Tsurugi-machi: Shirayama Honmiya Kaga Ichinomiya Shirayama Hime Jinja: Shirayama Hime Jinja Gozōei Hozonkai, 1985.

———. "Maeda shoki kenchi to sonraku," *Hokuriku Shigaku*, 25 (Nov. 1976): 19–40.
Kigura Toyonobu, ed. "Kamisaka-ke monjo," *Etchū Shidan*, 28 (March 1964): 52–59.
———. "Kamisaka-ke monjo (zoku)," *Toyama Shidan*, 33 (March 1966): 34–38.
Kikuichi Toshio. *Shinden kaihatsu*. Tokyo: Kokin Shoin, 1958.
Kitajima Masamoto. *Edo jidai*. Tokyo: Iwanami Shoten, 1964.
———. *Nihon kinsei shi*. Tokyo: Mikasa Shobō, 1939.
———. *Nihon shi gaisetsu*, vol. 2. Tokyo: Iwanami Shoten, 1976.
Kobayashi Seiji. "Sengoku sōran kara bakuhan taisei no seiritsu e." In Sasaki Junnosuke and Ishii Susumu, eds., *Shinpen Nihonshi kenkyū nyūmon*, pp. 343–51. Tokyo: Tokyo Daigaku Shuppankai, 1982.
Kobayashi Seiji and Yamada Akira. *Fukushima ken no rekishi*. Kenshi Shiriizu 7. Tokyo: Yamakawa Shuppansha, 1970.
Kodama Kōta. *Kinsei nōmin seikatsu shi*. Tokyo: Yoshikawa Kōbunkan, 1977. Originally published in 1958.
Kodama Kōta et al., eds., *Shiryō ni yoru Nihon no ayumi, Kinsei hen*. Tokyo: Yoshikawa Kōbunkan, 1955.
Kokufu son shi. Kokufu, Ishikawa: Kokufu Mura Yakuba, 1956.
Kosugi chō shi. Kosugi, Toyama: Kosugi Machi, 1959.
Kurobe shi shi. 2 vols. Uozu, Toyama: Kurobe Shi Yakusho, 1964.
McClain, James L. "Castle Towns and Daimyo Authority: Kanazawa in the Years 1583–1630," *Journal of Japanese Studies*, 6.2 (Summer 1980): 267–99.
———. *Kanazawa: A Seventeenth-Century Japanese Castle Town*. New Haven, Conn.: Yale University Press, 1982.
McMullin, Neil. *Buddhism and the State in Sixteenth-Century Japan*. Princeton, N.J.: Princeton University Press, 1984.
Mass, Jeffrey P., and William B. Hauser, eds. *The Bakufu in Japanese History*. Stanford, Calif.: Stanford University Press, 1985.
Matsushita Shirō. *Bakuhansei shakai to kokudakasei*. Tokyo: Hanawa Shobō, 1984.
———. "Chikugo no kuni Tanaka-han, Arima-han no kokudaka to nengu: Kinsei shoki o chūshin ni," *Keizaigaku Kenkyū* (Kyūshū Daigaku Keizai Gakkai), 45 (July 1980): 231–58.
———. "Yanagawa-han shoki no kokudaka to nengu," *Keizaigaku Kenkyū* (Kyūshū Daigaku Keizai Gakkai), 49 (July 1984): 213–29.
Migdal, Joel S. *Strong Societies and Weak States: State–Society Relations and State Capabilities in the Third World*. Princeton, N.J.: Princeton University Press, 1988.
Mihashi, Tokio. "Kinsei zenki no nōgyō." In *Taikei Nihonshi sōsho (Sangyōshi 2)*. Tokyo: Yamakawa Shuppansha, 1974.
Mise Kazuo. "Inaba Sakon to Kan'ei-ki no Kaga hansei: Kanjō kikō no kakuritsu o megutte," *Kokugakuin Zasshi*, 86.10 (Oct. 1985): 27–55.
Miyakawa Mitsuru. *Taikō Kenchi Ron*. 3 vols. Tokyo: Ochanomizu Shobō, 1977. Originally published in 1959.

Miyazaki Michio. *Aomori ken no rekishi. Kenshi Shiriizu* 2. Tokyo: Yamakawa Shuppansha, 1970.
Mizubayashi Takashi. *Hōkensei no saihen to Nihonteki shakai no kakuritsu* [Kinsei]. Vol. 2 of *Nihon Tsūshi*. Tokyo: Yamakawa Shuppansha, 1987.
Monzen chō shi. Kanazawa: Monzen Machi, 1970.
Morris, John F. *Kinsei Nihon chigyōsei no kenkyū*. Osaka: Seibundō, 1988.
Murakami Tadasu and Arakawa Hideyoshi, eds. *Sanpō Jikata Taisei. Nihon Shiryō Sensho* 12. Tokyo: Kondō Shuppansha, 1976.
Nagahara, Keiji, with Kozo Yamamura. "The Sengoku Daimyo and the Kandaka System." In Hall, Nagahara, and Yamamura, eds., *Japan Before Tokugawa*, pp. 27–63.
Nakaguchi Hisao. "Kinsei shoki sohō no kenkyū." *Chihō Shi Kenkyū*, 145 (Feb. 1977): 35–52.
Nakajima chō shi, Shiryō hen. Nakajima, Ishikawa: Nakajima Machi Yakuba, 1966.
Nakamura Kichiji. *Kinsei shoki nōsei shi kenkyū*. Tokyo: Iwanami Shoten, 1971. Originally published in 1938.
——— . *Nihon hōkensei saihensei shi*. Tokyo: Mikasa Shobō, 1939.
——— . "Shoki Kaga-han no denso ni tsuite." In Nakamura Kichiji, ed., *Chūsei shakai no kenkyū*, pp. 397–448. Tokyo: Kawade Shobō, 1930.
Nakamura Satoru. *Meiji ishin no kiso kōzō*. Tokyo: Miraisha, 1976.
Nanao shi shi, vols. 1–3; *Tsūshi hen*; *Shiryō hen*, vols. 1–3. Kanazawa: Nanao Shi Yakusho, 1968–74.
Nettl, J. P. "The State as a Conceptual Variable," *World Politics*, 20 (July 1968): 559–92.
Nishikawa Shunsaku et al., eds. *Nihon keizai no hatten*. Tokyo: Nihon Keizai Shinbunsha, 1976.
Nojima Jirō. "Kaga-han no tomura seido no seiritsu ni tsuite," *Nihon Rekishi*, 239 (April 1968): 36–41.
Noto Wajima Kamikaji-ke monjo mokuroku. Kanazawa: Ishikawa Kenritsu Toshokan, 1977.
Notojima no kinsei monjo, vol. 1. Kanazawa: Notojima Kyōiku Iinkai, 1978–79.
Oda, Franklin S. "Saga Han: The Feudal Domain in Tokugawa Japan." Ph.D. dissertation, Princeton University, 1975.
Oda Kichinojō. *Kaga-han nōseishi kō*. Tokyo: Tōe Shoin, 1929.
——— , comp. *Ishikawa ken Kashima gun shi*. Nanao, Ishikawa: Kashima Gun Jichikai, 1928.
Ōishi Shinzaburō. "Kinsei." In Kitajima Masamoto, ed., *Tochi Seido*, 2. *Taikei Nihonshi Sōsho* 7. Tokyo: Yamakawa Shuppansha, 1975, 21–194.
——— . *Kyōhō kaikaku no keizai seisaku*. Tokyo: Ochanomizu Shobō, 1976.
Ōishi Tsunetaka. *Jikata Hanrei Roku*. Rev. Ōishi Nobutaka, ed. Ōishi Shinzaburō. 2 vols. *Nihon Shiryō Sensho*. Tokyo: Kondō Shuppansha, 1976.
Oku Noto Tokikuni-ke monjo, vol. 1. Ed. Nihon Jōmin Bunka Kenkyūjo. Tokyo: n.p., 1954.

Okumura Satoshi. "Maeda Toshiie kashindan no tenkai," *Chihō Shi Kenkyū*, 18. 3 (1968): 30–38.
Ōno Mitsuhiko. "Maeda Toshitsune seiken no seiritsu: Keichō-ki Kaga hansei no dōkō," *Kainan Shigaku* 20 (1982): 1–23.
Ooms, Herman, *Tokugawa Ideology—Early Constructs, 1570–1680*. Princeton, N.J.: Princeton University Press, 1985.
Oshimizu chō shi. Kanazawa: Ishikawa Ken Oshimizu Machi Yakuba, 1974.
Owada Tetsuo. "Sengoku daimyō Gohōjō-shi no hyakushō to samurai," *Kenkyū Hōkoku* (Shizuoka Daigaku Kyōiku Gakubu), 27 (1976): 17–31.
Oyabe shi shi. 2 vols. Kanazawa: Oyabe Shi, 1971.
Popkin, Samuel L. *The Rational Peasant: The Political Economy of Rural Society in Vietnam*. Berkeley: University of California Press, 1979.
Roth, Randolph. "Is History a Process? Nonlinearity, Revitalization Theory, and the Central Metaphor of Social Science History," *Social Science History* 16: 2 (Summer 1992), pp. 197–243.
Rozman, Gilbert. "Edo's Importance in the Changing Tokugawa Society," *Journal of Japanese Studies*, 1.2 (Autumn 1974): 91–112.
Rule, John C. "The Reading of the Rolle: The Secretary of State as *Conseiller* and Advisor," *Proceedings of the Annual Meeting of the Western Society for French History*, 15 (1988): 84–92.
Sakai, Robert. "The Consolidation of Power in Satsuma-han." In Hall and Jansen, eds., *Studies in Institutional History*, pp. 131–39.
Sakai Seiichi. *Kaga-han kaisaku hō no kenkyū*. Osaka: Seibundō, 1978.
———. "Kaga-han shoki ni okeru men ni tsuite." In Sakai, ed., *Kinsei Etchū no shakai-keizai kōzō*, pp. 16–29. Tokyo: Meicho Shuppan, 1975.
———. "Kaga-han shotō ni okeru kenchi ni tsuite." In Sakai, ed., *Kinsei Etchū no shakai-keizai kōzō*, pp. 3–15. Tokyo: Meicho Shuppan, 1975.
———. *Toyama-han*. Toyama: Kōgen Shuppan, 1974.
Sakamoto, Tadahisa. "Kaga-han ni okeru hashiribyakushō kisei no hensen," *Handai Hōgaku*, 39 (Aug. 1989): 65–94.
Sansom, George. *A History of Japan, 1334–1615*. Stanford, Calif.: Stanford University Press, 1961.
———. *A History of Japan, 1615–1867*. Stanford, Calif.: Stanford University Press, 1963.
Sasaki Junnosuke. *Bakuhan kenryoku no kiso kōzō: "Shōnō" jiritsu to gun'yaku*. Tokyo: Ochanomizu Shobō, 1964.
———. "Bakuhansei no kōzōteki tokushitsu," *Rekishigaku Kenkyū*, 245 (Sept. 1960): 8–21.
———. *Daimyō to hyakushō*. Tokyo: Chūō Kōronsha, 1966.
———. "Tōitsu kenryoku no keisei katei." In Kitajima Masamoto, ed., *Seiji shi*, 2. Taikei Nihonshi Sōsho 2: 15–156. Tokyo: Yamakawa Shuppansha, 1974. Originally published in 1965.
Shimo Niikawa gun shiko. 2 vols. Tokyo: Meicho Shuppansha, 1972. Originally published in 1909.

Shimode Sekiyo. *Ishikawa ken no rekishi. Kenshi Shiriizu* 17. Tokyo: Yamakawa Shuppansha, 1972.
Shinbō Hiroshi and Yasuba Yasukichi, eds. *Kindai ikōki no Nihon keizai.* Tokyo: Nihon Keizai Shinbunsha, 1979.
Shinbō Hiroshi, Hayami Akira, and Nishikawa Shunsaku. *Sūryō keizaishi nyūmon.* Tokyo: Nihon Hyōronsha, 1975.
Shinminato shi shi. Shinminato, Toyama: Shinminato Shi Yakusho, 1963.
Skocpol, Theda. "Bringing the State Back In: Strategies of Analysis in Current Research." In Evans et al., eds., *Bringing the State Back In,* pp. 3–37.
———. "Emerging Agendas and Recurrent Strategies in Historical Sociology." In Skocpol, ed., *Vision and Method in Historical Sociology,* pp. 356–91. Cambridge: Cambridge University Press, 1984.
Smith, Thomas C. *The Agrarian Origins of Modern Japan.* Stanford, Calif.: Stanford University Press, 1959.
———. "Farm Family By-Employments in Preindustrial Japan," *Journal of Economic History,* 29.4 (Dec. 1969): 687–715.
———. "Premodern Economic Growth: Japan and the West," *Past and Present,* 60 (1973): 127–60.
Southall, Aidan. "Stateless Society." In *International Encyclopedia of the Social Sciences,* 15: 157–68. New York: Crowell, Collier, 1968.
Sternberger, Dolf. "Legitimacy." In *International Encyclopedia of the Social Sciences,* 9: 244–48. New York: Crowell, Collier, 1968.
Strayer, Joseph R. "The Tokugawa Period and Japanese Feudalism." In Hall and Jansen, eds., *Studies in Institutional History,* pp. 3–14.
Suga Kikutarō. "Matsuyama-han ni okeru jōmensei no kenkyū, [part] 1," *Shakai-keizai Shigaku Zasshi,* 11:8 (Nov. 1941): 51–70.
Susser, Bernard. "The Toyotomi Regime and the Daimyo." In Mass and Hauser, eds., *Bakufu in Japanese History,* pp. 129–52.
Suzu shi shi, Shiryō-hen 3. Kanazawa: Suzu Shi Yakusho, 1978.
Suzuki Ryōichi. *Oda Nobunaga.* Tokyo: Iwanami Shoten, 1967.
Tagawa Shōichi. "Kaga-han shoki zeisei no ikkōsatsu," *Hokuriku Shigaku* 24 (Nov. 1975): 50–61.
Taitō Chiaki. "Kaga-han Maeda-ke no engumi ni kansuru kōsatsu." Tanaka Yoshio, ed., *Nihonkai chiiki shi kenkyū,* 6: 143–81. Tokyo: Bunken Shuppan, 1984.
Takahashi Tomio. *Miyagi ken no rekishi. Kenshi Shiriizu* 4. Tokyo: Yamakawa Shuppansha, 1969.
Takase Tamotsu. "Bakuhanseika no zenkoku shijō no keisei to Kaga-han: Nishi mawari senro no kaitaku," *Nihonshi Kenkyū,* 159 (Nov. 1975): 33–61.
———. "Zenkoku shijō kakuritsu ni tomonau Kaga-han no taiō saku," *Kanjishi Kenkyū,* 25 (Oct. 1975): 15–36.
Takayanagi Mitsutoshi and Takeuchi Rizō, eds. *Nihonshi Jiten.* 2d ed. Tokyo: Kadokawa Shoten, 1976.
Takazawa Yūichi. "Maeda Toshinaga no kachū tōsei (sobyō)." Takazawa, *Hokuriku ni okeru kinseiteki shihai taisei keisei-ki no kiso kenkyū,* Shōwa 58–

nendo Kagaku Kenkyūhi Hojokin (Sōgō Kenkyū A) Kenkyū Seika Hōkokusho (March 1984): 6–14.
———. "Tenshō-ki nengu san'yōjo no kōsatsu: Noto kuni Maeda ryō ni okeru." In *Suzu shi shi, Tsūshi Hen*: 703–50. Kanazawa: Suzu Shi Shiyakusho, 1978.
———. "Warichi seido to kinseiteki sonraku," *Kanazawa Daigaku Keizai Ronshū*, 6 (1967): 125–42.
Takeyasu Shigeji. *Kinsei tochi seisaku no kenkyū*. Osaka: Osaka Furitsu Daigaku Keizai Gakubu, 1962.
Tanaka Seiji. "Kinsei zenki no chōsohō o megutte," *Nihonshi Kenkyū*, 176 (April 1977): 120–40.
Tanaka Yoshio. *Jōkamachi Kanazawa*. Tokyo: Nihon Shoin, 1969.
———. "Kaga-han kaisaku shihō hōkai katei no ichi kōsatsu," *Hokuriku Shigaku*, 6 (Nov. 1957): 33–52.
Tilly, Charles. "War Making and State Making as Organized Crime." In Evans et al., eds., *Bringing the State Back In*, pp. 169–91.
Toby, Ronald P. *State and Diplomacy in Early Modern Japan: Asia in the Development of the Tokugawa Bakufu*. Princeton, N.J.: Princeton University Press, 1984.
Tochinai Reiji. *Kyū Kaga-han denchiwari seido*. Tokyo: Mibu Shoin, 1936.
Tōgi chō shi, Shiryō hen; Tsūshi hen; Zoku shiryō hen. Kanazawa: Tōgi Machi Yakuba, 1974–77.
Toide chō shi. Takaoka, Toyoma: Takaoka Shi Toide Chō Shi Kanko Iinkai, 1972.
Toide shiryō. Toyama: Toyama-ken Nishi Tonami Gun Toide Machi Yakuba, 1923.
Tonami shi shi. Tonami, Toyama: Tonami Shi Yakusho, 1965.
Tonomura, Hitomi. *Community and Commerce in Late Medieval Japan: The Corporate Villages of Tokuchin-ho*. Stanford, Calif.: Stanford University Press, 1992.
Totman, Conrad. *Japan Before Perry*. Berkeley: University of California Press, 1981.
———. *The Origins of Japan's Modern Forests: The Case of Akita*. Honolulu: University of Hawaii Press, 1985.
———. *Politics in the Tokugawa Bakufu, 1600–1853*. Cambridge, Mass.: Harvard University Press, 1967.
———. "Preindustrial River Conservancy: Causes and Consequences," *Monumenta Nipponica*, 47.2 (Spring 1992): 59–76.
———. *Tokugawa Ieyasu: Shogun*. South San Francisco: Heian International, 1983.
Toyama ken shi, Shiryō hen 3, Kinsei jō; Shiryō hen 4, Kinsei chū; Shiryō hen 5; Kinsei ge. Toyama: Toyama Ken Chō, 1974–82.
Tsuchiya Takao. *Hōken shakai hōkai katei no kenkyū*. Tokyo: Kōbundō, 1927.
Tsukahira, Toshio G. *Feudal Control in Tokugawa Japan: The Sankin Kōtai System*. Cambridge, Mass.: Harvard University Press, 1966.
Tsunoda, Ryusaku, William T. DeBary, and Donald H. Keene, eds. and comps., *Sources of Japanese Tradition*, vol. 1. New York: Columbia University Press, 1958.

Urata Shōkichi. "Shoki Maeda-ke kashindan no jikata chigyō ni tsuite no ikkōsatsu," *Hokuriku Shigaku*, 17 (Nov. 1969): 1–25.

Varley, H. Paul. "Ashikaga Yoshimitsu and the World of Kitayama: Social Change and Shogunal Patronage in Early Muromachi Japan." In John W. Hall and Toyoda Takeshi, eds., *Japan in the Muromachi Age*, pp. 183–204. Berkeley: University of California Press, 1977.

Vlastos, Stephen. *Peasant Protests and Uprisings in Tokugawa Japan*. Berkeley: University of California Press, 1986.

Wajima chō shi. Wajima, Ishikawa: Wajima Machi Yakuba, 1954. *Tsūshi-hen*; *Shiryō hen* (6 vols.).

Wajima shi shi. 7 vols.: Kanazawa: Wajima Shi Yakusho, 1971–76.

Wajima Shunji. "Kaga-han no shoki tomura no seiritsu." In Wakabayashi Kisaburō, ed., *Kaga-han shakai keizai shi no kenkyū*, pp. 71–82. Tokyo: Meicho Shuppan, 1980.

———. "Kinsei sonraku no seiritsu: Noto Nishiumi-gō no baai," *Hokuriku Shigaku*, 4 (Sept. 1955): 38–49.

Wakabayashi Kisaburō. "Kaga-han." In Kodama Kōta, ed., *Monogatari Hanshi*, 4: 105–90. Tokyo: Jimbutsu Ōraisha, 1964.

———. *Kaga-han no nōchi sokuryō*. Tokyo: Nōrin Tōkei Kyōkai, 1956.

———. *Kaga-han nōsei shi no kenkyū*. 2 vols. Tokyo: Yoshikawa Kōbunkan, 1970–72.

———. "Kaga-han no tomura, mura kimoiri seido no seiritsu katei," *Shirin*, 42 (Sept. 1959): 40–64.

———. *Maeda Tsunanori*. Tokyo: Yoshikawa Kōbunkan, 1961.

———, comp. *Kinsei komonjo saihō no shiori*. Kanazawa: Hokkoku Shuppansha, 1975.

Wakita Osamu. *Kinsei hōkensei seiritsu shi ron: Shokuhō seiken no bunseki* II. Tokyo: Tokyo Daigaku Shuppankai, 1977.

———. "The Kokudaka System: A Device for Unification," *Journal of Japanese Studies*, 1 (Spring 1975): 297–320.

———. *Oda Seiken no kiso kōzō: Shokuhō seiken no bunseki* I. Tokyo: Tokyo Daigaku Shuppankai, 1975.

———. "The Social and Economic Consequences of Unification," in Hall, ed., *Cambridge History of Japan*, 4, pp. 96–127.

Wallerstein, Immanuel. *The Modern World-System*, vol. 1: *Capitalist Agriculture and the Origins of the European World-Economy in the Sixteenth Century*. New York: Academic Press, 1974.

Watkins, Frederick M. "State: The Concept." In *International Encyclopedia of the Social Sciences*, 15: 150–56. New York: Crowell, Collier, 1968.

Wheelwright, Carolyn, "A Visualization of Eitoku's Lost Paintings at Azuchi Castle." In Elison and Smith, eds., *Warlords, Artists, and Commoners*, pp. 87–112.

White, James W. "State Growth and Popular Protest in Tokugawa Japan," *Journal of Japanese Studies*, 14.1 (Winter 1988): 1–26.

Wigmore, John Henry. *Law and Justice in Tokugawa Japan.* 10 vols. Tokyo: University of Tokyo Press, 1969.
Yabunami son shi. Toyama-ken, Oyabe shi: Yabunami Son Shi Hensan Iinkai, 1968.
Yamada Moritarō. *Nihon shihonshugi bunseki.* Tokyo: Iwanami Shoten, 1939.
Yamada Shirōzaemon, ed. *Mitsubo kikigaki.* Kanazawa: Ishikawa-ken Toshokan Kyōkai, 1931.
Yamaguchi Keiji. "Han taisei no seiritsu." In *Iwanami kōza Nihon rekishi*, 10: 101–64. Tokyo: Iwanami Shoten, 1967.
Yamamura, Kozo. "From Coins to Rice: Hypotheses on the *Kandaka* and *Kokudaka* Systems," *Journal of Japanese Studies*, 14.2 (Summer 1988): 341–67.
———. "Pre-Industrial Landholding Patterns in Japan and England." In Albert M. Craig, ed., *Japan: A Comparative View*, pp. 276–323. Princeton, N.J.: Princeton University Press, 1979.
———. "Returns on Unification: Economic Growth in Japan, 1550 to 1650." In Hall, Nagahara, and Yamamura, eds., *Japan Before Tokugawa*, pp. 327–72.
Yanagida son shi. Kanazawa: Ishikawa Ken Fugeshi Gun Yanagida Mura Yakuba, 1975.
Yasuzawa Shūichi. *Kinsei sonraku keisei no kikō bunseki.* Tokyo: Yoshikawa Kōbunkan, 1972.
Yatsuo chō shi. 2 vols. Toyama: Yatsuo Machi Yakuba, 1967.

Index

In this index an "f" after a number indicates a separate reference on the next page, and an "ff" indicates separate references on the next two pages. A continuous discussion over two or more pages is indicated by a span of page numbers, e.g., "pp. 57–58." *Passim* is used for a cluster of references in close but not consecutive sequence. Page numbers in italics refer the reader to the Glossary.

Abandoned land, 151n, 276n36. *See also* Runaways
Absconding, *see* Runaways
Absolutism, 10–11, 12, 26, 229, 231
Accuracy: of *Taikō kenchi*, 15–16, 65n, 76, 264n10; early Kaga surveys and, 62–63, 148f; rejection of precise techniques and, 268n68, 269n3. *See also* Standardization
Adoption, 7, 23, 50, 145n
Akechi Mitsuhide, 5, 49
Alliances, *see* Adoption; Concubinage; Marriage alliances
Alternate attendance (*sankin-kōtai*) system, 8, 23, 252, 256n11
Annual inspections (*kemi* system), 251; crop sampling (*bugari*) and, 21, 148, 185, 235, 250; varieties of, 21n; villager agricultural surplus and, 21–22, 260n51; early-seventeenth-century change to, 178–83; tax rates and, 179–83, 283n53; practical constraints on, 183–87; failure of, 184–87, 228; land taxation experimentation and, 190, 225;

Kaisaku hō reforms and, 211; beginning of, 222, 260n55
Anti-survey protests, 227–28, 229, 235, 268n74, 284n4
Aono Shunsui, 270n6
Arachi, *see* Wasteland
Araki Moriaki, 10, 13, 16–17, 21n, 77, 264n4
Araya Kurō, 177n
Asakawa Kan'ichi, 256n22
Asao Naohiro, 13n
Ashikaga family, 1–2
Ashikaga Takauji, 1
Attainders, 24
Authority, *see* Central authority; Public authority
Autonomy: city governments and, 2–3; of retainers, 3, 178, 192, 281n3; of *daimyo*, 6–7, 11–12, 13; land rights and, 16–17; of Chō family, 46n, 60, 99–101, 119–20, 212–18 *passim*, 280n40; of rural communities, 133–34, 193; of tax officials, 174–78, 222
Azukeru ("to hold in trust"), 13–14

Bakufu, 7, 250; Laws of the Military Houses, 8, 12, 14, 24, 55, 220, 257n28, 261n65; demonstrated concerns of, 24; Maeda and, 53–56; nominal authority and, 240; impact of land survey orders, 285n13. *See also* Central authority; Central ordinances; Hegemons; Tokugawa family
Bakufu-Domain State theory, 10–11
Bashaku ikki (teamster protests), 3
Berry, Mary Elizabeth, 11ff, 19, 25, 77, 80, 259n46, 259n49, 267n54, 268n70, 269n77
Bizen province, 23, 115–16
Bolitho, Harold, 257n28, 261n61
Branch fiefs, 55–56
Bugari (crop sampling), 21, 148, 185, 235, 250
Bugyō, *see* County magistrate; Land survey magistrate; Magistrate; Reform magistrate
Buke sho hattō, *see* Laws of the Military Houses
Bureaucracy, 261n65
Buyaku (labor dues), 91, 111, 139, 177, 250. *See also* Contract labor

Cash assessment system, *see* Kandaka system
Castellan, position of, 176
Castles: at Azuchi, 5; restriction on, 55, 220n, 259n49; Maeda and, 55–56, 220n; concentration of retainers in, 123–24; *daimyo* control of, 223. *See also* Kanazawa; Samurai urbanization
Central authority: arguments for historical reconstitution of, 11, 14–24; cautionary perspectives on strength of, 11–12; domain administration and, 13–14, 24, 34–35, 220–21, 261n61; switch to rice-based assessments and, 14, 277n51; land survey policies and, 14–19, 236; origins of class separation and, 19–20; land tax system and, 20–22, 76–88; role in local administration, 22–24, 111, 221; strong state-weak state dichotomy and, 25–27, 229–32; influence on Kaga policies, 75–76, 220–21, 237; image and, 87, 232–33, 269n78; time required for policy implementation and, 185, 238; late-sixteenth vs. late-seventeenth century domains and, 192–93; configurations of, 229–33. *See also* Central ordinances; Hegemons; Nominal authority vs. state capability; *Taikō kenchi*
Central ordinances: compliance with, 76–88, 238, 285n16; impact of, 220n; historiographic reliance on, 284n1. *See also Taikō kenchi*
Chigyō, *see* Retainer fiefs
Chiwari system, *see* Warichi system
Chō family, 43f, 250; domains of, 45, 46n, 99; autonomy of, 46n, 60, 99–101, 119–20, 212–18 *passim*, 280n40; land surveys and, 60f; land rights and, 99–101, 117; *Kaisaku hō* and, 214f; Urano incident and, 215. *See also* Noto Peninsula
Chō Tsuratatsu, 44, 46, 99
Chōsokabe family, 81, 85f, 250
Circumferential survey (*mawari kenchi*), 252
Class separation (*hei-nōbunri*), 251; growth of legal barriers and, 8–9; central authority and, 13, 19–20; survey registers and, 15, 16–17, 20, 223, 267n64; establishment vs. implementation of, 19–20; transfer of *daimyo* and, 118; village autonomy and, 134; legal status as *hyakushō* and, 173; *Kaisaku hō* reforms and, 194; samurai urbanization and, 222; gradual development of, 223–24, 235
Commoner district chiefs, *see* Tomura
Concubinage, 7, 46
Contract labor, 188–89. *See also* Sale of people
Corvée labor, *see* Labor dues
County magistrate (*kōri bugyō*), 100, 176, 177–78, 196, 198, 201, 252
Crop damage, 153, 159, 276n34. *See also* Exemptions; Natural disasters
Crop sampling (*bugari*), 21, 148, 185, 235, 250
Crop shortfalls, 259n42, 283n50
Crossed ropes (*jūji nawa*) measurement method, 73, 93

Daikan (*daimyo* tax agent), 250; Chō family and, 100; office of, 133, 167,

277n55; villagers and, 133, 141f; *uketori daikan* and, 133n, 277n55; control over, 142, 198; surveyors and, 179. *See also* Tax officials
Daimyo (baronial lords), 250; centralization of authority of, 3–4, 192–94, 204–15; as "potted plant *daimyo*," 6, 40, 42, 115, 116; autonomy of, 6–7, 11–12, 13; power of hegemons over, 6–7, 13–14, 23–24, 220, 257n28; in Sengoku era, 19; retainer bands and, 20, 117–20; routes to status as, 39–40; heirs to status as, 55; automonous (*tozama*), 77, 85, 253; domain administration issues facing, 88; land tenure rights and, 111–12; accountability of, 238–39. *See also* Domain administration; Maeda family; Transfer of *daimyo*
Daimyo's intendants, *see Daikan*
Date family, 39f, 78, 80, 269n75
Davis, David L., 136n
Denchiwari system, *see Warichi* system
Desertion, *see* Runaways
Dewa domain, 81, 85
District administrators, *see Fuchibyakushō; Tomura*
District (*gō; tomura-gumi*), 250; as administrative unit, 135–37, 153, 171f, 222. *See also Fuchibyakushō; Tomura*
Do ikki (leagues of the land), 255n2
Domain (*han*), 251
Domain administration: experimentation and, 3, 190, 195, 216, 222, 224–25, 234, 237; in Sengoku age, 3–4; influence of hegemons on, 13–14, 24, 34–35, 220–21, 261n61; villager influence on, 25, 35–36, 88, 107–8, 146, 190, 226–27, 228–29; key aspects of domain formation and, 34; internal influences in, 35–36, 221–29; battle of Sekigahara and, 52; challenges for domain residents in, 88; small districts in, 133–34; senior councillors (*toshiyori*) in, 171; early-seventeenth century changes in, 171–78; pragmatism in, 189, 225–26; centralization of domain authority and, 192–94, 204–15; successful policies and, 227–28. *See also* Kaga domain; Maeda family; specific Maeda *daimyo*

Domain allocation, *see* Retainer fiefs; Transfer of *daimyo*
Domen system, 21n, 190
Dry fields: quality grades and, 9, 73; exemption for, 21, 148, 274n3; survey compensation for (*hatake ori*), 74, 251

Echigo province, 97
Echizen province, 47–48, 49
Edo, 6, 8. *See also* Alternate attendance system
Elison, George, 20, 259n47
Emperor, 7
Enfoeffed samurai, *see Kyūnin*
Etchu province: location of, 30f; Maeda and, 47, 49; early surveys in, 65–68, 264n3; *Keichō* survey of, 68–71, 79; land taxation in, 155f
Europe: sixteenth-century contacts with, 2; comparison of Japan with, 12, 229–32, 256n22, 285n7
Exemptions: for dry fields, 21, 148, 274n3; in *warichi* system, 103–5; in *sonmen* system, 152–55; to plow tax, 282n34
Experimentation: domain administration and, 3, 190, 195, 216, 222, 224–25, 234, 237; land tax system and, 190, 198–203, 225, 280n56; land surveys and, 224–25; local administration and, 225, 234

Feudalism, Japanese, 10f, 21n
Fiefs, *see* Branch fiefs; Kaga domain; Retainer fiefs; Transfer of *daimyo*
Fields: hidden (*onden*), 17, 149–50; boundaries of, 94; long-standing (*honden*), 102–3, 251. *See also* Dry fields; Land quality; Paddy; Reclaimed lands; Runaways; *Warichi* system
Five Elders, 5, 50
Fixed tax rate system, *see Jōmen* system
"Flamboyant" states, 232, 240
Flat yield rate (land value), 69–70
France, bureaucratic professionalism in, 230–31
Fuchi (stipend), 46, 125, 128, 148–49, 250
Fuchibyakushō (district administrators), 250; stipend (*fuchi*) for, 125, 128, 148–49, 250; forms of reward and, 125–28, 273n42; purpose in appointment of, 126–27, 129–30; functions of, 127–29,

135–39, 153; class separation and, 128–32 *passim*; pre-Maeda leadership and, 129; village headmen and, 139, 172; relation to *tomura*, 172; user fees and, 272n17; document references to, 278n4. See also Tomura
Fujino Tamotsu, 24
Fujita Gorō, 10
Fukuno village, 62, 108f
Fukutomi Yukikiyo, 43f, 46, 264n3
Funyūken (right of nonentry), 3, 17–18, 100, 148, 250
Furushima Toshio, 270n6

Gedai (subretainer), 250
Genin (servant), 250
Gofuchinin tomura (stipended *tomura*), 174, 208f, 250
Gohōjō family, 5, 40, 83, 86, 258n39
"Good administration," standard for, 238–39
Gosanke (Tokugawa branch houses), 55, 250
Gosan'yōba (special accounting office), 201
Gradualism: in Kaga domain history, 190, 221–24, 234; change in local administration and, 222–23; class separation and, 223–24, 235
Gun'yaku (military levy), 6, 10, 250

Hall, John Whitney, 11, 13, 15, 23, 28, 256n22, 257n28, 261n65, 268n74, 284n1
Han (domain), 251. See also Domain administration; Kaga domain; *Daimyo*
Hanley, Susan, 270n6
Hara Shōgo, 20, 23, 30, 109–10, 273n42, 284n3
Hatake ori procedure, 74, 251
Hatakeyama family, 119, 126
Hatamoto (shogunal retainers), 90, 251
Hayakawa Jirō, 10
Hayami Akira, 21, 91, 260n51
Hegemons: control over *daimyo* and, 6–7, 13–14, 23–24, 41, 238–39, 257n28; alternate attendance system and, 8, 23, 252, 256n11; influence on domain administration, 13–14, 24, 34–35, 220–21, 261n61; foreign policy and, 14n; local administration and, 22–24, 111, 221; Maeda relations with, 40–44, 48–49, 51, 166, 183–84, 225–26; *daimyo* obligations to, 85–86, 183–184, 196, 279n38; image and, 87, 232–33, 269n78; land disposition and, 90–91. See also *Gun'yaku*; Oda Nobunaga; Tokugawa Ieyasu; Toyotomi Hideyoshi
Heikin men (tax rate averaging/uniform tax rates), 198, 199–200, 203, 251
Hei-nōbunri. See Class separation
Heki Ken, 53n, 176n
Hellie, Richard, 230n
Hidden fields (*onden*), 17, 149–50
Hideyoshi, see Toyotomi Hideyoshi
Hikichi (land not in *warichi* redistribution), 103, 251
Hioki Ken, see Heki Ken
Historiographic research: central authority as issue in, 10–14; use of local histories in, 28–30, 284n1; linear analytic models in, 286n18
Honbyakushō (villager status), see Hyakushō
Honda family, 119, 122f
Honda Masashige, 52n, 53, 263n26
Honden (long-standing fields), 102–3, 251
Hostage-holding, 8, 23, 47, 51, 52n, 183–84, 220, 224
Hyakushō (villager status), 15, 16–17, 90, 173, 189, 235, 251
Hyakushō ikki (rural protests), 251
Hyakushō uke (tax contract), 4, 20, 134, 251

Ie sōdō (house disturbance), 251
Ieyasu, see Tokugawa Ieyasu
Iinuma Jirō, 266n43, 267n64
Ikenchi measurement method, 80
Ikki, 3, 20, 134, 255n2. See also Ikkō ikki; Rural protests
Ikkō ikki, 251, 255n2; Maeda and, 42ff, 47, 98–99, 109–10, 116f, 126f, 234; *fuchibyakushō* and, 135; *tomura* and, 273n40
Immigrant retainers, 98, 111, 117f, 223f
Impressment, 176–77
Inaba Sakon, 200f
Inoue Toshio, 270n7
Inspectorate (*meyasuba*), 178, 198
Investiture, see Transfer of *daimyo*

Ishida Mitsunari, 5f
Ishii Ryōsuke, 12, 257n27
Ishii Shirō, 18n, 257n22
Itō Tasaburō, 46n
Iwasawa Yoshihiko, 47n, 263n3

Jansen, Marius, 17
Jōmen (fixed tax rate) system, 190, 251, 283n53; crop sampling and, 21n; experimentation with, 198–201; *Kaisaku hō* reforms and, 210–11, 212f, 223; domain initiative and, 225, 226, 285n13
Jūji nawa (crossed ropes) measurement method, 73, 93

Kaga domain: characteristics of, 30–34; external influences on, 34–35, 220–21; internal influences in development of, 35–36, 221–29, 234; local initiative and, 35–36, 226–27; development of, 40–56, 233–40; early land surveys in, 59–68; *warichi* system in, 97, 101–11; samurai land tenure in, 98–101; early land taxation in, 147–67; land tax system in, 151–67; *sonmen* assessment system and, 152–57, 181; villager-samurai tensions and, 171–91; change to *kemi* system in, 178–83; pragmatism in administration of, 189, 225–26; gradualism in history of, 190, 221–24, 234; "Fifty-eight Clause Ordinance," 195–96; patterns in development of, 233–40; population growth in, 262n71
Kaga land surveys: in late sixteenth century, 59–68, 147–48; procedures in, 60, 62, 66–75, 147–51; evidence for central initiative in, 60–61, 68, 75–76; format of survey documents, 61–72 *passim*; measurement units in, 62, 66–67; in early seventeenth century, 68–75, 148–51; policy regulations and, 71–72; variations from standard survey model, 75–76
Kaga province: early land surveys of, 60–65; Genna surveys of, 71–75, 79
Kaisaku bugyō, see Reform magistrate
Kaisaku hō reforms, 251; Chō family and, 46n, 219; class separation and, 194, 216–17; implementation of, 206–9;

land tax reform and, 213–15, 217–18; retainer autonomy and, 213–15; Kaga domain administration and, 216, 219, 223; role of villagers in, 217, 227; experimentation and, 224f; failure of annual inspection system and, 228f
Kanai Madoka, 15, 281n32
Kanazawa (castle town), 47, 53, 251; samurai in, 184–87
Kandaka (cash assessment) system, 78–79, 251, 266n44, 275n22
Kan'ei reforms, 198–204
Kasaya Kazuhiko, 14n
Katanagari (sword hunts), 13, 19, 223, 259n46
"*Keian* surveys," 205
Keichō survey, 68–71, 151n
Keirstead, Thomas, 286n18
Kemi system. *See* Annual inspections
Kenchi (land surveys), as term, 59n, 80, 152n. *See also* Land surveys
Kenchi buchō, see Land survey register
Kenchi bugyō, see Land survey magistrate
Kenchichō, see Land survey register
"Kenchikata Hisho" (manual), 73–75
Kigoshi Ryūzō, 142n, 151n, 157n, 277n55, 283n49
Kimoiri, see Village headman
Kinsei era, 11n, 21n, 252
Kitajima Masamoto, 10
Kodama Kōta, 16
Kōgi (public authority), 8, 11, 54, 226, 236, 252
Kokubu village survey, 61–62
Kokudaka (rice-based assessment) system, 10, 14, 252; role of land surveys in change to, 15; comprehensiveness of, 17–18, 236; *tantori* method and, 18n; effectiveness of, 18–19; compliance with, 78–79, 165, 190, 238; negotiation of domain value and, 84–87; tax collection and, 165–66; domain initiative and, 226–27; switch to, and central authority, 258n41, 260n56, 277n51
Kokujin (provincial warriors), 116, 134, 140, 252. *See also* Local gentry, pre-Maeda; *Tomura*
Kokumori (official yield estimate), 69, 80–82, 252

Kōri (county), 4, 252
Kōri bugyō, see County magistrate
Kuji (warichi lottery groups), 104, 252
Kujichi (land subject to warichi redistribution), 103, 252
Kumabuchi village, 62f, 108f
Kurosawa Akira, 2
Kuwayaku (plow tax), 173, 205–6, 222, 252, 282n34
Kyūnin (landed retainers), 252; land rights and, 99; administrative rights of, 121, 141, 146, 223–24; concentration in castle towns, 123–24; cessation of family lines and, 124; autonomy of, 178, 281n3; tax collection standard and, 178, 195–96; Kaisaku hō and, 214–15, 217. See also Chō family; Retainer fiefs; Tax officials

Labor dues (buyaku), 91, 111, 139, 177, 250. See also Contract labor
Land desertion, see Runaways
Land quality, 9; early Kaga surveys and, 61–62, 151, 153; Keichō survey and, 69; Genna surveys and, 73–74; hatake ori procedure, 74; procedural variation and, 80–81, 151; daimyo initiatives and, 84; warichi system and, 102–3, 108
Land redistribution system, see Warichi system
Land survey magistrate (kenchi bugyō), 79, 196, 252, 275n7; Kaga surveys and, 62, 70n, 148
Land survey register (kenchichō), 252; class separation and, 15, 16–17, 259n46; determination of use rights and, 16–17, 76, 91–92; listing of villager names in, 91, 108–9; adjustments to data in, 92–93; absence of evidence and, 284n1
Land surveys (kenchi), 252; in Sengoku age, 3; standard procedures for, 9; class separation and, 15, 16–17, 20, 223, 267n64; determination of land tenure and, 16–17, 76, 91, 92–94; impact of, 59, 226, 285n13; kenchi as term and, 59n, 80, 152n; use of actual measurements in, 67f, 70–71, 75f, 82; time required to complete, 70; functions of, 75; daimyo initiatives and, 83–84; Chō family and, 100–101; conducted by villages, 105; survey process and, 147–48; previous year's tax billing and, 160; tax assessment and, 179; "Keian surveys," 205–6; experimentation and, 224–25; pragmatism and, 226; anti-survey protests, 227–28, 229, 235, 268n74, 284n4; circumferential survey (mawari kenchi) and, 252. See also Kaga land surveys; Sashidashi land survey system; Taikō kenchi

Land tax system: conversion to kemi system, 9; role of central authority in, 20–22, 76–88; Kaga survey formats and, 61–70 passim; unpaid taxes (mishin) and, 144, 160–63, 188; early survey process and, 147–51; in sixteenth-century Kaga domain, 151–67; measuring box (masu) in, 157n; tax billing and, 158–65, 212; flexibility of Maeda system and, 160–65, 166–67; pledges (ukekoi) and, 164; forms of payment and, 165–66; pragmatism and, 189, 226; experimentation and, 190, 198–203, 225, 280n56; mura goin and, 212; factors in compliance with, 227–29. See also Annual inspections; Taikō kenchi

Land tenure rights: legal status as villager and, 16–17; surveys in determination of, 16–17, 76, 91, 92–94; usufruct and, 89–90; disposability and, 90–91; samurai and, 90–91, 98f, 111; "revolution" in, 91–92; villager landholding and, 91–92; warichi system and, 94–98, 101–11; of pre-Maeda samurai allied with Maeda competitors, 98–99; corporate land tenure and, 101–11, 112; sale of, under warichi system, 108, 110–11; inequality within villages, 109–11; prohibition of sale of land, 110, 224, 226, 284n3, 285n13; village authority over, 112, 224, 227, 236; involvement of Maeda in, 224; double ownership (buntsuke) and, 262n67. See also Retainer fiefs; Sale of land, prohibition of; Warichi system

Land valuation (taka), 69–70, 253; variations across regions and, 84–88; changes in, 154–55, 212–13; wasteland as percentage of assessed value, 155, 156–57;

taxes as percentage of assessed value, 155–56. *See also Kandaka* system; *Kokudaka* system; Land tax system
Landed retainers. *See Kyūnin*
Laws of the Military Houses (*Buke sho hattō*), 8, 12, 14, 24, 55, 220, 257n28, 261n65
Loans to villagers, 176–77, 197f
Local administration: role of central authority in, 22–24, 221; village leadership and, 139–41; structure of, 175, 201; involvement of *daimyo* in, 193, 265n33; gradual change in, 222–23; experimentation and, 225, 234; manuals of, 280n56. *See also Fuchibyakushō*; Retainer-villager relationships; *Tomura*; Village headman; Villages
Local gentry, pre-Maeda: fate of, 90–91, 118–20; land tenure rights and, 98–99, 109–11. *See also Fuchibyakushō*; *Kyūnin*; *Tomura*

McClain, James, 30, 32, 59
Maeda family: development of Kaga domain, 34, 39–57; retainer fiefs and, 40–44, 52, 120–24; relations with hegemons, 40–51 *passim*, 166, 183–84, 225–26; *Ikkō ikki* and, 42ff, 47, 98–99, 109–10, 116f, 126f, 234; battle of Sekigahara and, 51–52; branch fiefs and, 55–56; samurai land tenure and, 98–101; domain administration and, 116–17, 171; early rural administration and, 133–46; land tax system of, 151–67; administrative initiatives and, 226–27, 285n13
Maeda Mitsutaka, 54f, 195n
Maeda Nagatane, 52, 53n
Maeda Toshiie: development of Kaga domain, 40–44; *Ikkō ikki* and, 42ff; territorial expansion and, 44–50; land surveys and, 65, 75, 225; reporting of domain valuation and, 79, 266n51; Chō family and, 99, 119–20; land tenure and, 109–10; retainers and, 117–20, 141; *fuchibyakushō* and, 126–31; *daikan* and, 142–45; local administration and, 142–45, 225; land tax system and, 151n, 153, 158–64 *passim*, 187; reforms and, 195

Maeda Toshimasa, 51f
Maeda Toshinaga: territorial expansion and, 48–50; Kaga domain and, 50–52, 53; relations with Tokugawa, 51, 183–84; Etchu land surveys and, 60, 66; retainers and, 117–18, 195, 263n26; land tax system and, 149, 222; local administration and, 171, 174–77, 189, 195, 225
Maeda Toshitsune: Kaga domain and, 50f, 52–56; retirement of, 54–56; relations with Tokugawa, 184n; administrative policy and, 189; reforms and, 195, 198, 207, 208–9, 214, 216, 218; policy experimentation and, 222
Maeda Tsunanori, 195n, 207, 218
Maeda Yasukatsu, 144–45, 176n, 274n27
Magistrate (*bugyō*), 174–78, 198, 250. *See also* County magistrate; Land survey magistrate; Reform magistrate
Malfeasance of office: Bakufu administrative enforcement and, 24; tax officials and, 144, 197
Markets, national: rice as medium for tax payment and, 187–88, 190, 226–27; price variations and, 280n47
Marriage alliances, 3, 7, 23; Maeda and, 48–54 *passim*, 219, 263n24
Marxist historians, 21
Mass, Jeffrey P., 284n1
Matsumoto domain, 78, 80
Matsushita Shirō, 30, 267n56
Mawari kenchi (circumferential survey), 252
Measurement procedures: use of actual measurements, 67f, 70–71, 75f, 82; crossed ropes (*jūji nawa*) method, 73, 93; "Kenchikata Hisho" methods, 73–75; variations in, 79–84; *ikenchi* method, 80; determination of land tenure rights and, 92–94; measuring box (*masu*) in, 157n. *See also Sashidashi* land survey system; Standardization
Measurement units: relationships among, xv–xvi; standardization and, 16, 77–78, 85, 178, 258n34, 266n43, 268n70; Kaga surveys and, 62, 66–67, 68. *See also* Standardization
Men: meaning of term, 29, 153n

Meyasuba (Inspectorate), 178, 198
Migdal, Joel, 23n, 231n
Migration, rural, 138, 145n. *See also* Runaways
Military activity: territorial acquisition and, 40–44; village administration and, 65, 144
"Minimalist" states, 232
Mishin (unpaid taxes), 144, 160–63, 188
Miyakawa Mitsuru, 21, 259n46
Mizubayashi Takashi, 14
Mizuchō, *see* Land survey register
Moore, Richard, 14on
Morris, John, 235n, 281n32
Mountain dry fields, *see* Dry fields
Murakiri (boundary clarification), 252

Nakamura Kichiji, 10
Natural disasters, 105–7, 137, 151n
Nawauchichō, *see* Land survey register
Negotiation: Maeda-Tokugawa relationship and, 50–57, 220; of domain value, 84–87, 236
Niikawa county, 69f
Nishikawa Shunsaku, 260n51
Nobunaga, *see* Oda Nobunaga
Nominal authority vs. state capability: state-society relations and, 25–27, 231–33, 239–40; Hideyoshi's land surveys and, 77–84. *See also* Central authority
Nonentry, right of (*funyūken*), 3, 17–18, 100, 148, 250
Noto Peninsula: early land surveys of, 42, 60–65, 151; Maeda expansion and, 42, 44–47; Genna surveys of, 71–75, 79; *fuchibyakushō* in, 125, 128–29, 272n29; land taxation in, 154–57, 182, 200–201; structure of rural administration in, 201. *See also* Chō family

Oda Kichinojō, 179n, 264n6, 266n51
Oda Nobunaga: career of, 4–5, 6; assassination of, 5, 49; class separation and, 19f; Maeda domain and, 40–44, 48–49, 166; strategy of transfer, 42, 49; early Kaga land surveys and, 59, 84, 264n3; Chō family and, 99, 119–20; Ikkō ikki and, 116, 126
Official yield estimate (*kokumori*), 69, 80–82, 252

Ōishi Shinzaburō, 21n
Okajima Kazuyoshi (Maeda retainer), 117
Okinami survey, 61
Onden (hidden fields), 17, 149–50
Ooms, Herman, 286n18
Osaka campaigns, 6, 40, 53
Oshimizu, districts of, 135–36

Paddy, 9, 74, 269n3. *See also* Fields; Land quality
Personalistic ties, 23n, 46f, 230–31
Plow tax (*kuwayaku*), 222, 252, 282n34; status as village member and, 173, 205–6
Policy implementation, time required for, 185, 238
Politics: and variations in land valuation, 84–87
Popkin, Samuel L., 270n19
"Potted plant *daimyo*," 6, 40, 42, 115, 116
Pragmatism: in domain administration, 189, 225–26
Provincial warriors (*kokujin*), 116, 134, 140, 252. *See also* Local gentry, pre-Maeda; *Tomura*
Public authority (*kōgi*), 8, 252; concept of, 11, 54, 226, 236

Reclaimed lands (*shinden*), 137, 150, 156, 252, 275n3, 276n29, 277n54
Reform magistrate (*kaisaku bugyō*), 207–10, 216, 223, 225, 251, 281n7
Reforms, *see* Kaisaku hō reforms; Kan'ei reforms
Reischauer, Edwin, 256n22
Retainer bands, 20, 46, 53, 118–20, 192, 220
Retainer fiefs (*chigyō*), 250; right of nonentry (*fuñyūken*) and, 3, 17–18, 100, 148, 250; domain centralization and, 120–21; retainer-villager relationships and, 120–24, 237; redistribution of fiefs and, 123f, 193n, 202, 237; distinguished from grants to *fuchibyakushō*, 126, 127–28; land tax system and, 186–87, 211; Kaisaku hō reforms and, 211, 213f
Retainer-villager relationships: retainer fief grants and, 120–24; tensions and, 121, 176, 192, 213–14, 222, 234–35; *fuchibyakushō* and, 129–32 *passim*; magistrates and, 176–77, 178
Retainers: early attempts to control, 3,

271n16; right of non-entry (*funyūken*) and, 3, 17–18, 100, 148, 236, 250; Maeda family and, 117–20, 141, 195, 263n26; collection of taxes by, 120–21, 282n27; Maeda control of, 120–24, 220–21, 263n26; assessed land value and, 281n3. *See also* Immigrant retainers; *Kyūnin*; Retainer band; Retainer fiefs; Samurai

Rice-based assessment system, *see Kokudaka* system

Rozman, Gilbert, 218n

Rule, John, 230–31

Runaways: district administration and, 137–38, 173–74, 176; wasteland vs. abandoned land and, 151n, 276n36; wasteland surveys and, 159–60; village responsibility for, 173, 278n14; "lazy farmers" and, 205–6; regulations on, 280n39. *See also* Migration, rural

Rural protests (*hyakushō ikki*), 116, 190–91, 206, 251; resistance to tax demands, 167, 184, 190–91, 280n39; anti-survey protests, 227–28, 229, 235, 268n74, 284n4. *See also* Ikki

Russian military service class, 229–30

Sakai (city), 3

Sakai Seiichi, 199n, 265n19

Sale of land, prohibition of, 110, 224, 226, 284n3, 285n13

Sale of people, 95, 226. *See also* Contract labor

Samurai, 2, 8, 88; land rights and, 90–91, 98f, 111; gradual changes in status of, 172–73, 222ff. *See also* Daikan; Fuchibyakushō; Immigrant retainers; *Kyūnin*; Local gentry, pre-Maeda; Reform magistrate; Retainer-villager relationships; Retainers; *Tomura*

Samurai urbanization, 4, 8, 280n40; *daimyo* initiatives and, 20; failure of annual inspection system and, 184–85, 228; samurai income and, 197; class separation and, 222, 259n49; gradualism and, 222

Sankin-kōtai (alternate attendance) system, 8, 23, 252, 256n11

Sansom, George, 12f, 15f

Sasaki Junnosuke, 16–17, 20, 218n, 264n4, 280n47

Sashidashi land survey system, 15, 80, 252, 264n10, 265n19

Sassa Narimasa, 43–44, 152; Maeda family and, 47–48, 49, 127

Satsuma domain, 23, 79, 86, 94, 115–16, 235n, 238

Scott, James, 94

Sekigahara, battle of, 5, 40, 51–52

Sendai domain, 115–16

Sengoku era, 1–4, 9, 19, 252. *See also* Kandaka system

Senior councillors (*toshiyori*), 171, 196

Shinden (reclaimed land), 137, 150, 156, 252, 275n3, 276n29, 277n54

Shogun, office of, 7. *See also* Hegemons

Shōken Hyōzaemon, 85

Slash-and-burn agriculture, 275n4

Smith, Thomas C., 32, 260n51, 283n53

Sō, *see* Villages

Sonmen assessment system, 152–57, 166, 225, 252

Standardization: Hideyoshi survey procedures and, 15–16, 82–84, 236, 268n70, 285n13; early Kaga survey procedures and, 60, 62, 66–68; domain compliance with, 76–84, 221, 268n74; Tokugawa survey procedures and, 87; land taxation experimentation and, 225; prior to Hideyoshi, 268n70. *See also* Measurement units

State: defined, 11n

State-building, 11–14, 23–24. *See also* Central authority

State-society relations: and nominal authority vs. state capability, 25–27, 231–33, 239–40

Stipend (*fuchi*), 46, 125, 128, 148–49, 250

Stipended peasants, *see* Fuchibyakushō

Strayer, Joseph, 256n22

Strong state-weak state dichotomy, 25–27

Survey procedures: standardization of, under Hideyoshi, 15–16, 82–84, 236, 268n70, 269n77, 285n13; in early Kaga surveys, 60–70 *passim*, 147–51; standardization of, and Tokugawa, 87

Susser, Bernard, 13n, 258n34

Sword hunts (*katanagari*), 13, 19, 223, 259n46

Tagawa Shōichi, 152n, 154
Taikō kenchi (Hideyoshi land surveys), 252; central authority and, 13, 14–19, 58, 236; basic consequences of, 15; precision as characteristic of, 15–16, 65n, 76, 264n10; standardization of survey procedures and, 15–16, 82–84, 86, 236, 268n70, 269n77, 285n13; determination of land rights and, 16–17; principle of non-entry and, 17–18; local administration and, 22–23; format of Kaga survey documents and, 61–65; compliance with, 76–84; factors in variation and, 84–88; time required for implementation of, 238
Taka, see Land valuation
Takamochi hyakushō (class of villager), 102, 253
Takashimaya (merchant), 187f
Takayanagi Mitsutoshi, 270n6
Takazawa Yūichi, 154n, 157n, 277n52, 277n55
Takeda Shingen, 2
Takeuchi Rizō, 270n6
Takeyasu Shigeji, 21, 260n51
Tantori method, 18n
Tax assessment procedures, see *Domen* system; *Jōmen* system; *Kandaka* system; *Kokudaka* system; *Sonmen* assessment system
Tax collection: early procedures for, 4; *fuchibyakushō* and, 137; forms of payment and, 165–66; annual inspection system and, 181–82
Tax contract (*hyakushō uke*), 4, 20, 134, 251
Tax forgiveness, 161–64
Tax officials: abuse of office and, 143–44, 178, 189, 197, 216; restraints on, 174–78, 189, 195, 216, 222f. See also *Daikan*; *Kyūnin*
Tax payment: unpaid taxes (*mishin*), 144, 160–63, 188; timing of, 158, 163–64, 188f, 277n52; Maeda flexibility and, 160–65, 166–67; rice as medium for, 165–66, 187–89; policies designed to optimize, 176–77, 197, 284n3; early-seventeenth-century means of, 187–89
Tax rates: decline in, with annual inspections, 21, 179–83, 190, 279n32f; land valuation and, 85; *kyūnin* and, 178, 265n33; variation in, 182–83, 199f, 203–4, 213–14; factors in decline in, 184–86; standardization of, 196; uniform/averaged (*heikin men*), 198, 199–200, 203, 251; *Kan'ei* reforms and, 203–4; *Kaisaku hō* and, 212–13
Tax reductions, 151n, 259n42, 283n50. See also Exemptions
Taxes, miscellaneous, 138
Three Heroes, 4–10. See also Hegemons; Oda Nobunaga; Tokugawa Ieyasu; Toyotomi Hideyoshi
Tilly, Charles, 285n7
Toby, Ronald P., 14n
Tokugawa family, 19, 24; land tax system and, 20–22, 151; stages of feudalism and, 21n; Maeda and, 50–52, 53–56; hostage-holding and, 51, 183–84; branch houses (*gosanke*), 55, 250; standardization of survey procedures and, 87; landholding policy and, 94; *sankin-kōtai* system and, 252
Tokugawa Hidetada, 8, 53
Tokugawa Ieyasu, 2, 4, 7, 171, 183; career of, 5–6; Maeda family and, 50–52, 53
Tokugawa peace, 10, 183f
Tomura (commoner district chiefs), 172–74, 253; Chō family and, 100; *fuchibyakushō* and, 172, 189; *tomura kimoiri* and, 172ff, 273n46, 274n19; village groups (*tomura-gumi*) and, 172–73; functions of, 173–74; *gofuchinin tomura* and, 174, 208f, 250; tax officials and, 174; reforms and, 205, 223; *Kaisaku hō* and, 207–12 passim; *tomura* as term and, 273n46; document references to, 278n4; abolition of office of, 281n7; plow tax exemption and, 282n34; in Edo period, 283n40
Tomura-gumi (village group), 172–73. See also *Fuchibyakushō*; *Tomura*
Tomura kimoiri, 172ff, 273n46, 274n19
Tonomura, Hitomi, 234
Tosa domain, 23, 33, 81, 97, 116, 235n, 262n66; Chōsokabe family in, 81, 85f, 250
Toshiie, see Maeda Toshiie

Toshinaga, *see* Maeda Toshinaga
Toshitsune, *see* Maeda Toshitsune
Toshiyori (senior councillors), 171, 196
Totman, Conrad, 261n65
Toyotomi Hideyoshi, 2, 4; career of, 5f; Sword Collection Edict, 9, 13, 19, 223, 259n46; land surveys, 13, 14–19, 140n; efforts at standardization and, 15–16, 82–84, 86, 236, 268n70, 285n13; class separation and, 19, 173, 194, 223, 259n46; "Wall Writings of Osaka Castle," 22, 156; land tax system and, 22, 156, 166, 260n55; rice-based assessment system and, 22, 165; two-thirds dictum (tax rate), 22, 260n55; local administration and, 24; central authority and, 25, 58, 87–88, 284n1; Maeda domain and, 46–50; Okinami survey, 61; landholding policy, 91–97 *passim*; financial demands on *daimyo* and, 183; impact of, 233, 237, 239, 268n70; ostentation and, 233. *See also Taikō kenchi*
Toyotomi Toshiie, *see* Maeda Toshiie
Tozama (autonomous *daimyo*), 77, 85, 253
Transfer of *daimyo*, 6–7; central authority and, 24, 220, 239; changes in domain leadership and, 40; Nobunaga's strategy of, 42, 49; land tenure rights and, 90, 110–11; opportunities provided by, 115, 237; class separation and, 118; "principle of domain transfer" and, 259n46; sources of fiefs gained by, 261n60

Uchiwatashijo, see Land survey register
Uesugi Kagakatsu, 44, 48
Uketori daikan (subordinate tax collectors), 133n, 277n55
Unpaid taxes (*mishin*), 144, 160–63, 188
Urano incident, 215
Usufruct, 89–91, 101

Village groups (*tomura-gumi*), 172–73. *See also Fuchibyakushō; Tomura*
Village headman (*kimoiri*), 252, 273n46; Chō family and, 100; village administration and, 141; *onden* and, 150; *tomura kimoiri* and, 172ff, 273n46, 274n19. *See also Tomura*

Village labor, *see* Contract labor; Labor dues
Villagers: status as (*hyakushō*), 15, 16–17, 90, 173, 189, 235, 251; migration and, 20n, 138, 145n; confiscation of agricultural surplus and, 21–22, 260n51; influence on domain policy, 25, 35–36, 88, 107–8, 146, 190, 226–27, 228–29; surveys by, 80, 148; *warichi* system and, 94–96, 97–98, 105–6, 107, 202–3, 209–10, 228–29; corporate land tenure and, 101–11; resistance to tax demands, 167, 184, 190–91, 280n39; loans to, 176–77, 197; sources of income, 260n51. *See also* Retainer-villager relationships; Runaways; Rural protests; Villages
Villages (*sō*): administrative autonomy in, 3f, 134, 222–23, 224, 234, 236; *daimyo* tax collection contracts with, 4; collective taxation of, 9, 15, 95–96; *sashidashi* surveys and, 15, 252; land tenure rights and, 94–96, 97–98, 105–6, 107, 112, 224, 227, 228–29, 236; as basic administrative unit, 134; new, 140, 149–50, 265n30, 285n14; boundaries of, 150, 223, 274n1; variation between, 185–86, 227–28, 270n21; with multiple overlords, 186; sources of tax data for, 243–49

Wajima Shunji, 264n4, 272n29
Wakabayashi Kisaburō, 70n, 108, 206, 264n10, 271n15
Wakita Osamu, 10, 17, 236, 266n44, 284n4
Wallerstein, Immanuel, 229
Wari (redistributed land sections), 105
Warichi (land redistribution) system, 18n, 94–98, 253; domain involvement in, 35, 97, 202–3, 210, 225; villager influence on, 94–96, 97–98, 105–6, 107, 202–3, 209–10, 228–29; variations of, 98n; villager land tenure in Kaga and, 101–11; exemptions, 103–5; procedures in, 103–5; natural disasters and, 105–7; intervals between redistributions, 106–7; origin of, in Kaga, 107–8
Wasteland (*arachi*): taxation and, 151n, 277n54, 279n31; vs. abandoned land, 151n, 159, 276n36; as percentage of assessed value, 155; surveys of, 159–60

Weak states, *see* Strong state-weak state dichotomy
Weber, Max, 26f
White, James, 12f, 25–26, 261n61
Wigmore, John Henry, 256n22

Yamaguchi Keiji, 262n74
Yamamura, Kozo, 17, 79, 260n54, 260n56, 266n44, 270n6, 277n51, 280n39
Yoriki (aide), 46n

Zeniya Gohei, 31

Library of Congress Cataloging-in-Publication Data

Brown, Philip C., 1947–
   Central authority and local autonomy in the formation of early modern Japan : the case of Kaga domain / Philip C. Brown.
     p.   cm.
   Includes bibliographical references and index.
   ISBN 0-8047-2036-3 (Alk. paper) :
   1. Kaga-han (Japan)—Politics and government.   I. Title.
DS894.59.I539K343   1993
952'.154—dc20   93-10240
                                                                         CIP